UNDERSTANDING THE POLITICAL PHILOSOPHERS

'I know of no better text for introducing newcomers to the history of political philosophy.'

Craig Duncan, *Ithaca University, USA*

008

'The author has an engaging style and succeeds in communicating his enthusiasm for the subject matter.'

Andrew Mason, *University of Southampton, UK*

'*Understanding the Political Philosophers* represents an engaging yet challenging introduction to political philosophy ... The author writes in a clear, unpretentious and interesting way about even quite difficult concepts and arguments. As a result, this work offers the teacher of political philosophy an effective text for courses combining discussion of classic and contemporary political ideas.'

David West, *Australian National University*

This absorbing study invites you to climb inside the heads of the major political philosophers, as it were, and to see the world through their eyes. Beginning with Socrates and concluding with post-Rawlsian theory, Alan Haworth presents the key ideas and developments with clarity and depth. Each chapter provides a concentrated study for a given thinker or group of thinkers, and together they constitute a broad account of the main arguments in political philosophy.

There are chapters on **Socrates, Plato, Aristotle, Hobbes, Locke, Rousseau, the Utilitarians, Marx, Rawls, and post-Rawlsian developments**.

This is a fascinating, lively and engaging treatment of the topic, and will appeal to any student of political philosophy or political thought.

Alan Haworth is a philosopher based at London Metropolitan University, where he teaches Political Philosophy, Ethics and the History of Ideas. His previous books are *Anti-Libetarianism: Markets, Philosophy and Myth* (1994) and *Free Speech* (1998).

UNDERSTANDING THE POLITICAL PHILOSOPHERS

From Ancient to Modern Times

Alan Haworth

Routledge
Taylor & Francis Group

LONDON AND NEW YORK

First published 2004
by Routledge
11 New Fetter Lane, London EC4P 4EE

Simultaneously published in the USA and Canada
by Routledge
29 West 35th Street, New York, NY 10001

Routledge is an imprint of the Taylor & Francis Group

© 2004 Alan Haworth

Typeset in Minion by RefineCatch Limited, Bungay, Suffolk
Printed and bound in Great Britain by MPG Books Ltd, Bodmin

British Library Cataloguing in Publication Data
A catalogue record for this book is available from the British Library

Library of Congress Cataloging in Publication Data
A catalogue record for this book has been requested

ISBN 0–415–27590–3 (hbk)
ISBN 0–415–27591–1 (pbk)

To the memory of my father,
James 'Jack' Haworth,
born May 1914; died February 2000

It is evident that the human is a political animal in a way that the bee and the other gregarious animals are not. For nature does nothing without a purpose, as we say, and, out of all the animals, only humans have been endowed by nature with language. Of course, other animals can make vocal sounds, and so express pain and pleasure. They are, by their nature, able to feel pleasure and pain and to communicate such feelings to each other. But there is more to language than mere voice. With language, we are able to distinguish the useful from the harmful and, likewise, the just from the unjust. For the real difference between humans and other animals is that humans alone have a sense of good and evil, of justice and injustice – and it is the association of living beings who share a sense of these things which goes to make a household and a city.

Aristotle

Contents

CONTENTS

Acknowledgements

——·◦◯◦·——

To begin at the beginning, I should thank Adrian Driscoll first. It was Adrian who suggested that I write an introduction to political philosophy. I was initially sceptical, but once I started to think about taking a historical approach, I began to warm to the idea. For their encouragement, I should like to thank Tony Bruce of Routledge's philosophy section and – most especially – Siobhan Pattinson, also of Routledge. Siobhan's approach has been imaginative and constructive throughout. While I am on the subject of beginnings, I should also like to thank Dr Veronica Tatton-Brown of the British Museum's Department of Greek and Roman Antiquities. This is for drawing my attention to the *stylus* in the museum's collection. I expect she has forgotten, but if she ever reads this she will no doubt be reminded of our correspondence. The moment of the *stylus* was important to me. I had been sitting in a field, in Devon, working at my laptop when – quite naturally as it seemed to me – I began to wonder exactly what it was that Plato had written his dialogues *with*. That was why I wrote to Dr Tatton-Brown. The *stylus* brought it home to me that philosophy really is a conversation across time, that there is a direct line of connection running from Plato and his associates to political philosophers working now, including those with whom I have been privileged to work, and that to engage in the collective enterprise of political philosophy means recognising the existence of something far bigger than yourself or any other individual participant.

Rodney Pickering, David Lloyd-Thomas and Jonathan Wolff were kind enough to comment on various sections of an earlier draft. All three responded promptly after having read the material quite closely. I am deeply indebted to them for the comments they made. I am equally indebted to the two anonymous readers who, at Routledge's request, made numerous critical comments on the entire text. These were offered in an extremely positive and constructive spirit. (Thank you, whoever you are.) To all five, could I just say that I took every single critical point you made very seriously indeed, even those I subsequently decided not to take on board. However, I think you will see that I have made quite a few modifications in the light of your remarks, and I am sure the book is much better

ix

as a result. I do hope you like the final result. Also – and of course – I take full responsibility for any mistakes, illogicalities, et cetera, which remain.

I would say that writing this book is probably the most ambitious literary project in which I have ever engaged. It has taken me about two and a half years to write – not a huge amount of time, but longer than it normally takes to walk to the chemist's. It is a period during which I have enjoyed positive encouragement and support from some wonderful colleagues at London Metropolitan University, a terrific network of friends, and a loving family environment. Without the consequent routine, and emotional stability, I doubt that I would ever have managed to write this. To take the university first, it is – of course – the case that I have to thank the Research Committee of the School of Arts and Humanities (as it was when the award was made) for making sure that I had at least some relief from teaching to work on the book. Otherwise I think that, this time round, the people who deserve a special mention are the philosophy students of LondMet. That is because this book has its origins in a course I have been teaching there. It is impossible to estimate just how much I must have learnt from constantly having to explain the ideas I discuss here, and defend them against objections from such lively-minded people. That said, I should add that I must especially thank the particular group of students I have been teaching for the past two years, especially those who took my courses on current issues in moral and political philosophy and recent political philosophy, for the encouragement and forbearance they have shown.

As I would hate to miss anyone out, I shan't mention any friends by name – at least not any living friends. However, I am only too well aware that many of those who were around when I published my last book will be unable to read this one. One such friend, an especially close one, was my late father, to whom this book is dedicated. Another was Mike Kreisky. I well remember that, the last time I saw Mike, I was enthusiastically explaining this project to him. This makes it all the sadder that he will never see its fruition. Yet another was my wonderful mother-in-law, Barbara Dawkins, who always took such an interest in my work. I know she would have enjoyed this book a great deal.

As for family, as ever I have Rowan to thank for making sure that I never take life too seriously, for keeping things on an even keel and for guarding my (metaphorical) space to write. My son Matt has also been something of an inspiration. I don't know how, but he seems to have acquired Aristotle's enthusiasm, not for philosophy especially, but for marine biology. Finally then, as both are scientists, let me just say this. Following Newton, scientists are frequently apt to describe themselves as standing on the shoulders of giants. Maybe so, but philosophers don't work that way. What philosophers do is spend their time talking to ghosts. Thank you for sharing so many supper-time conversations, not just with me, but with Plato, Aristotle, Hobbes and the rest. If you ever get around to reading this book, I hope you will think it was worth it.

Introduction
Why study political philosophy?

This book has two related aims. One is to introduce you to the ideas and the arguments of the major political philosophers. The other is to introduce you to their subject, political philosophy itself. I do not keep these aims separate, by devoting some sections to the first, others to the second. On the contrary, I take it that, in achieving the former, I will *thereby* achieve the latter. This is possible because philosophy has a special relationship with its past – so let me start with that.

Consider the difference between philosophy and – for example – a science. Normally, you would not try to introduce someone to chemistry or physics by recounting the ideas of past scientists. You would treat these as superseded and concentrate on current theory and recent experimental research. Or, as another example, take history. There would be something rather strange about trying to introduce history by concentrating almost exclusively on the work of past historians, for an introduction to history itself is one thing, whereas an introduction to the work of historians is another, – a subject for 'historiography', which is just one specialised branch of history. But, even in the latter case, history must base its account of the past on primary sources and other more or less reliable evidence.[1] If my two aims are simultaneously achievable, as I am claiming they are, then philosophy must be different from these other subjects.

So, how is it different? The answer is that philosophy's relationship with its past results from the way an idea can assume a life of its own. That idea may have been first nurtured in privacy by this or that thinker, but, once it has become public, it gains independence. This happens most strikingly where the idea is challenged by others, who raise objections against it; where it is then defended by yet others, perhaps in a modified form; where further objections are then raised, and so on. The process can go on over generations – millennia even – and the result is that, although Plato, Locke, Marx and the others are physically long gone, their ghosts remain with us, demanding our attention. So, if you want to know what it's like to be a political philosopher, try to imagine yourself seated at a table with the others – the ghosts and the living – and engaged in a lively and long-running discussion with them, one which had been going on well before

1

you entered the room, and which is likely to continue long after you have left it. Think of it like that and you should see why it is so hard to remain a bystander here; why 'introducing you to the great political philosophers' has to involve much more than just 'telling you what they said'. It means finding you a place at the table from which you can follow the discussion, figure out for yourself where you stand in relation to the arguments which are going on, and – should you feel so inclined – contribute.

Who are the 'major' political philosophers on whom I have chosen to concentrate, then? And what did they write? Well, I have already mentioned Plato. After a brief account of Socrates and his times (in the next chapter) I turn to Plato's description of the type of state which – as he thought – would embody the virtue of justice to a perfect degree. You can find his argument in the work which is known, these days, as *The Republic*, and which he wrote almost 2,400 years ago, in Athens. After that, I turn to a contrasting, equally influential, Greek work, Aristotle's *Politics*. Part II is devoted to the work of the great seventeenth and eighteenth century 'social contract' theorists. There are chapters on Thomas Hobbes, whose *Leviathan* was published in 1651; John Locke, author of the *Second Treatise of Government* (1689); and Jean-Jacques Rousseau, author of *The Social Contract* (1762). These are three of the most influential books ever to have been written. In Part III, which moves from the early nineteenth century to the present, I discuss the classical utilitarians, especially Jeremy Bentham and John Stuart Mill. They claimed to found their political standpoint on the principle of 'greatest happiness', according to which 'the greatest good is the greatest happiness of the greatest number'. I also discuss the work of Karl Marx and, after that, present a chapter on the American philosopher John Rawls, whose masterpiece *A Theory of Justice* was published in 1971 (Rawls 1972). There are many political philosophers writing now – most likely the majority of those writing in English – who believe that his book is the most powerful and influential work on the subject to have been produced in recent years. The penultimate chapter, 'After Rawls', contains a brief discussion of some alternatives to his approach and in the final chapter I offer a few comments on future prospects.

Some readers – those to whom the subject of political philosophy is already familiar – will find few surprises in this list (which is just as it should be, given that this is meant as an introduction). But there will be many others, I am sure, who won't recognise quite a few of the names I have listed. In my experience, most people – even intelligent and knowledgeable people – are familiar with only a few. Take a group of such people, ask them who Shakespeare was, or who Newton was, and they will be sure to tell you. You would expect the political philosophers to be just as well known, but ask the same group who Locke was, or J.S. Mill, and you are quite likely to draw a blank, or so I have learnt.

This is more than a pity. It is a cause for great regret. There are at least two reasons why. The first is that every single philosopher listed has played an enormously significant role in the development of Western political thought; quite as significant a role as that played by Shakespeare and Dickens in the development of English literature, or by Newton, Darwin or Einstein in that of science. Just as there is a tradition of English literature, and a tradition of scientific enquiry, so there is a great tradition of political thought; and it seems to me that, if it is right to expect every educated English-speaking person to have some knowledge of the first, and every educated person (English-speaking or not) of the second, then it must be right to expect the same in the case of the third.

But the second reason is the more compelling of the two. It is that our own ways of thinking about the social and the political are the direct descendants of conceptions developed by past political philosophers. I mean that we think the way we do only because they thought the way they did. It is because understanding where we are now must involve knowing how we got here in the first place that we should study their ideas – and in the case of politics it is especially difficult to dodge the requirement to understand where we are. This is the more compelling of the two reasons because, great traditions notwithstanding, you don't have to take any notice of them. Certainly, nobody is forced to become a writer, a literary critic, or a scientist – or even to take an interest in the arts or the sciences. By contrast, *everyone* except Robinson Crusoe is constrained by circumstance to live in political relationships with his or her fellows.

It is on the basis of this consideration – their influence – that I have selected philosophers and their work for discussion. For my purposes, they qualify as 'great' philosophers simply through having done so much to affect our own ways of seeing the world. There may well have been others – some more imaginative or more logically rigorous than those I have chosen – but, as these have remained obscure, I have discounted them. (And, of course, it is this principle of selection which explains why readers already familiar with the subject will find no surprises in my list of names.) I do realise that any list of 'great' philosophers is bound to be contentious. On reading this book, many trained, 'academic' philosophers will find themselves wanting to insist that I should have spent more time on such-and-such an argument, or to object that I have completely ignored so-and-so. It is in the very nature of the subject that this should be the case (and, of course, I can't include everyone).[2] However, I am confident that the majority of philosophers will agree that the selection I have made accurately represents the tradition we have inherited, and, I am sure, even those who are unhappy with the latter will recognise that it represents a consensus.

To these reasons, I would add a third, namely that if you know little or nothing of the great tradition of political thought, you are missing out. The subject is so absorbing and so frequently inspiring. But, rather than labour the point with an explanation, I will leave you to read on and to judge for yourself. With that said, let us now move on – or should I say 'move back' – to the Athens of the fourth century BC. It is where the story opens.

Part I

Athens

1

—o☙o—

Socrates

Our story opens in Athens because it was in that city that the earliest major work of political philosophy – *The Republic*, as it is now called – first encountered the light of day. This was in approximately 375 BC. (The precise year isn't known.) Its author, Plato, would have written it with a *stylus*, a pointed implement with which he inscribed his sentences on rolls of papyrus. The first copies must have been made using the same laborious technique. Since then there have been times when any copy of an ancient Greek work must have led a precarious life: the fall of the Roman Empire; the Dark Ages; the early medieval period, during which the only guardians of literature were monks and when hand-written manuscripts had to be transported from monastery to monastery on the backs of mules; the burning of the great library at Alexandria in AD 640, when many original Greek texts which had survived up to that time were finally lost. You could say that the most remarkable thing about *The Republic* is the simple fact of its survival. Against many odds, and after almost 2,400 years, you can now go along to any reasonably good bookshop and find a translation, in paperback, produced with the help of the most up-to-date technology.

The Republic is, thus, the earliest available text relevant to my subject. Therefore, there are at least two good reasons for beginning my narrative proper with an account of its main arguments (as I shall in the next chapter). I have already given one, namely that Plato's work is the earliest known. The other is that it is still available. This means that *The Republic*'s argument confronts us just as directly as it confronted Plato's contemporaries. It demands our attention, just as it demanded theirs. We cannot ignore it. We have to come to terms with its arguments for ourselves and figure out where we stand in relation to them.

The availability of a text also accounts for why I have chosen to start with Plato rather than with his mentor, Socrates. By most accounts, Socrates was unusual and charismatic. He inspired the younger Plato to such an extent that his influence remained with Plato for the rest of his life. Moreover, Socrates is certainly a good candidate for the title 'first great philosopher', and an even better one for 'first political philosopher'. From

7

our point of view, however, the problem with Socrates is that he never wrote anything. This means that he spoke more directly to his fellow Athenians than he ever could to us. Even so, I should give a brief account here of Socrates' approach to philosophy, and his life, because it is with the story of Socrates that the story of Plato really begins. Without some knowledge of the former story, it would be impossible to fully appreciate *The Republic*'s point.

Socrates the philosopher

The fact that Socrates never put his thoughts down in writing distinguishes him from every later philosopher. Whereas the others are remembered mainly through their books, Socrates practised philosophy by means of a purely 'word of mouth' technique. To the Athenians he was a familiar figure. They would encounter him in the marketplace as he debated philosophical questions with anyone prepared to engage in a discussion with him. This can make Socrates appear truly remarkable to present day philosophers.

However, it doesn't really make him as remarkable as all that, for Socrates was a contemporary of the *sophists*, wandering scholars who would, in the typical case, move from place to place, providing tuition in return for a fee. There were many sophists and, like Socrates, all tended to work through speech rather than writing. So, it wasn't the simple fact that Socrates practised his teaching orally, in public, which made him so exceptional. If we are to understand what it was, we must consider how Socrates and the sophists differed.

There were a number of differences. One was that, unlike most sophists, Socrates made no charge for his services.[1] Another was that, whereas most sophists travelled from place to place in the course of their work, Socrates left Athens only once in his life.[2] More significantly from our point of view, Socrates and the sophists differed in the reasons they had for working as they did. On the one hand, it was Socrates' opinion that philosophy could only be properly taught and practised orally. 'Dialectic' was the route to truth. As this suggests, it would be wrong to think that Socrates just never found the time to write, or – perhaps – that he never managed to make the effort. On the contrary, he considered writing an inappropriate technique. (I think most present day philosophers would agree with him that discussion is central to philosophy, although they would be less dismissive of the written text.) It is consistent with this interest in truth that Socrates should have insisted, as he did, on the primacy of reason and logic, on *rationality*. His approach would be to challenge the person with whom he was arguing to formulate a definition of the thing – usually a virtue – they were discussing. Socrates would then call the definition into question, forcing his opponent to defend it. (This has come to be known as 'the Socratic method'.)

By contrast with Socrates, the sophists tended to attach more importance to the arts of rhetoric and persuasion than they ever did to seeking truth through the use of reason. The opinion of one sophist – a contemporary of Plato's called Isocrates – is on record. According to him, 'likely conjecture about useful things is far preferable to exact knowledge of the useless' (Isocrates 1954–6: 63). Socrates strongly disapproved.

In fact, it is easy to appreciate why the sophists took this attitude in favour of rhetoric. It is what they were hired to teach. There was a demand for their services, partly because anyone who lacked the skill of speaking persuasively in public could never succeed in getting his[3] way at meetings of the Assembly, Athens' supreme legislative institution. The Assembly passed laws, and decisions of policy were made there. It met every ten days or so, and any citizen could attend and speak. When you think that citizens composed roughly a quarter of the population, you can imagine how large the more well-attended meetings must have been. (There were about 30,000 citizens in all and, out of that number, about 6,000 regularly attended meetings of the assembly.) Moreover, if a citizen took out a case against you, the legal system required that you should be tried before a court of fellow citizens, usually numbered in hundreds. You would have to defend yourself. No wonder it was so important to the Athenian citizen that he should master the skill of persuading others by rhetoric, and that sophists were able to command high fees for teaching it. Some sophists may also have been experts in this or that field of learning but, if they taught that too, it came secondarily, as a bonus.

To sum up, then, one difference between the typical sophist and Socrates was this. Whereas the sophist taught rhetoric and sometimes claimed specialist knowledge, Socrates sought truth through the use of reason. More than that, far from claiming to know anything, Socrates professed ignorance. At his trial, in his address to the jury, Socrates related a story about it. He claimed that an old friend of his, Chaerophon, once visited the oracle at Delphi and asked the god whether there was anyone wiser than Socrates himself. Apparently, the god replied that there was not. According to the story, when he heard of this Socrates was so puzzled that he set about interviewing those with a reputation for wisdom. It turned out that no one's pretensions to knowledge could survive Socratic interrogation. Therefore – and here is the moral – only Socrates knew that he knew nothing, and it was this knowledge which made him wiser than everyone else (Plato 1954a: 49ff].

For a further distinctive feature of Socrates' approach we need to consider how he differed, not from the sophists, but from other philosophers. Of course, philosophers had lived and worked in Greece long before Socrates appeared on the scene. Examples of other Greek philosophers are Thales, who thought that everything was made from water;

Empedocles, who explained natural change with a theory of the four elements, earth, air, fire and water; Pythagoras, who believed that history repeats itself in an endless cycle; Heraclitus, who believed that everything is an eternal, ever-changing modification of fire; and Democritus, who thought that matter was composed of atoms. But, as these examples make clear, those philosophers were mainly interested in the fundamental nature of the universe. They were trying to answer questions which, nowadays, would more often than not be raised by scientists – cosmologists or physicists. By contrast, Socrates was primarily interested in moral questions. Like the others, he sought fundamentals, but in the defining characteristics of *virtue* – love, for example, or justice.

Socrates and Athens

In addition to the distinctive features of Socrates' approach to philosophy, we should consider the remarkable events of his life. It is well known that in 399 BC he was brought before the Athenian court having been charged with heresy and corrupting the minds of the young. There is general agreement that these were pretexts rather than credible, serious charges. Socrates was found guilty, sentenced to death, and executed (by poison). Plato thought this a wicked and shameful act, a reaction which was only to be expected from one of Socrates' disciples, and, ever since, there has been a tendency to portray Socrates as a hapless martyr for reason and truth (not least because a great deal of what we know about Socrates is based on Plato's testimony). For example, the nineteenth century philosopher John Stuart Mill ranks his execution with Christ's crucifixion. In the second chapter of his *On Liberty* – a celebrated defence of free speech – Mill describes Socrates as the 'acknowledged master of all the eminent thinkers who have since lived' and 'the man who probably of all then born had deserved least of mankind to be put to death as a criminal' (Mill 1991a: 29). But it could be that Mill was painting a rosy picture here and, as so often, there is another side to the story. We should consider this, beginning with events which took place when Plato was quite young, and Socrates the mentor and inspiration to a circle of young men which included Plato's elder brothers, Glaucon and Adeimantus. (It is here, then, that Plato first appears on the scene.)

At this point, perhaps I should re-emphasise that I am not out to write the history of Athens. My subject is philosophy, not history, and philosophy's central subject matter is ideas and arguments – the relations between them, the presuppositions on which they are based, and so on – not the sequence of past events. However, sometimes it is only possible to fully appreciate a philosophical argument, or a text, if you know something of the historical context in which it was first formulated or written, and that is why I am giving a brief outline of certain historical events here.

In fact, quite a number of the texts I shall be discussing are associated in one way or another with a political upheaval – a war or a revolution. In the case of *The Republic* the upheaval in question was a terrible war, the Peloponnesian War, between a league of city-states led by Athens and, opposing them, the armies of Sparta. This lasted for twenty-seven years and came to an end in 404 BC, when Socrates was 66 and Plato 24 years old. For our purposes, the most relevant facts are as follows.

First of all, Athens was a democracy whereas Sparta was not. To see just how democratic Athens was you need only recall my earlier account of how the Assembly functioned. (Of course, there were some respects in which it was less democratic than a modern 'representative democracy'. For example, the franchise did not extend to slaves or women. Nor did it extend to residents of Athens who lacked an Athenian pedigree, which is why even Aristotle was denied the vote. But you could certainly argue that, on the other hand, the degree to which citizens participated in decision making made it far more democratic.) Moreover, on the whole the Athenians were proud of their constitution. In his *History of the Peloponnesian War* – published in 410 BC or thereabouts – Thucydides records a funeral speech given by the great Athenian statesman Pericles at the end of the war's first year. Pericles says this:

> Here each individual is interested not only in his own affairs but in affairs of the state as well: even those who are mostly occupied with their own business are extremely well-informed on general politics

And he adds,

> this is a peculiarity of ours: we do not say that a man who takes no interest in politics is a man who minds his own business; we say that he has no business here at all

> (Thucydides 1954: 145)

This was the Athenian ideal, a system in which every citizen has a right to participate and take an interest in public affairs, and, moreover, where there is an expectation that each citizen will do just that. Sparta was completely different. It was a repressive dictatorship run by an elite military caste.

Second, during the closing years of the war, Athens suffered a period of political instability. The democracy was twice overthrown, the first time, in 411 BC, by disaffected pro-Spartan conspirators. Then it was restored after a four month period known as the Reign of the Four Hundred. It was overthrown again in 404 BC, when Athens was finally defeated by the Spartans. There followed an eight month period known as the Reign of the Thirty Tyrants. These were not mere changes in the system. Each tyranny – that of the Four Hundred and that of the Thirty – was a reign of terror. Thucydides records that during the time of the Four Hundred, although the Assembly and the Council whose members it chose by lot continued to meet,

11

they took no decisions that were not approved by the party of the revolution; in fact all the speakers came from this party, and what they were going to say had been considered by the party beforehand. People were afraid when they saw their numbers, and no one now dared to speak in opposition to them. If anyone did venture to do so, some appropriate method was soon found for having him killed, and no one tried to investigate such crimes or take action against those suspected of them. Instead, the people kept quiet, and were in such a state of terror that they thought themselves lucky enough to be left unmolested even if they had said nothing at all.

(1954: 575)

It is a picture which has remained depressingly familiar. A further attempt to overthrow the democracy looked likely in 401 BC – just two years before Socrates' trial – but this never materialised. It is easy to appreciate that, for most Athenians, the twelve year period prior to the trial must have been insecure and jittery.

In connection with these events, we should bear in mind – third – that the democracy was not equally popular with all elements of the population. It was popular with the ordinary people, the poor. It was also popular with middle class traders and merchants, some of them quite wealthy. (In a cosmopolitan seaport like Athens, which depended for its wealth on trade with the outside world, this class would have been particularly strong.) However, it was far less popular amongst the hereditary aristocracy, many of whom would have regarded it as a threat to their own power and influence. The crucial points to note here are, first, that Plato's family and associates were members of this class; second, that – as a teacher – Socrates was closely associated with the same class; and, third, that in both 411 and 404 groups of young aristocratic males, much like the ones Socrates used to teach, were instrumental in bringing about the democracy's fall. In the nervy atmosphere of post-war Athens, it could be that the activities of the philosopher in the marketplace – once apparently harmless and eccentric – came to take on a more sinister, conspiratorial, aspect. Perhaps it was this that inspired the charge of 'corrupting the youth of the city'.

So, was Socrates really a martyr, someone who suffered for the stand he took on behalf of freedom of thought? Or, were the suspicions that he was deeply involved with subversive, anti-democratic, elements justified? If I were to pursue these questions any further, I really would be straying from the point. So, let us now move on to consider *The Republic*'s argument.

2

Plato: The Republic

One of Socrates' major legacies to Plato is evident throughout *The Republic*. It is a certain view of philosophy's purpose. As we have seen, the purpose of Socrates' interrogations was to arrive at all embracing definitions. ('Socratic ignorance' was the usual result, because these turned out to be rather elusive.) Quite similarly, Plato thought that the job of the philosopher was to search out the unity which, as he supposed, underlies apparent diversity.

This is a good point at which to mention another of Socrates' legacies too, namely the idea that philosophy should proceed by argument, dialectically. Nearly all Plato's books are written as dialogues, with Socrates as the leading participant. The other characters tend to be figures who would have been known to Plato's Athenian readers. For example, in *The Republic*, the main characters – Socrates apart – are Plato's older brothers, Glaucon and Adeimantus; Polemarchus, a rich Athenian citizen; Polemarchus' father; his two brothers, one of them a well-known orator; and Thrasymachus, a sophist and orator. (Most of them have little to say, so I haven't listed them all by name.) There is some disagreement amongst scholars over the extent to which the 'Socrates' of the dialogues resembles the real Socrates. The consensus appears to be that, in the earlier dialogues, he does. However, as *The Republic* was written during Plato's middle period, we can safely take it that the 'Socrates' of that work is just a mouthpiece for Plato's ideas.

Plato's perfect state

So, what does *The Republic* say? Well, as the book's purpose is to define and justify a certain conception of the perfect or 'ideal' state, it would be a good idea to start by summarising Plato's description of that state. I shan't spend too long on the details. So far as I am concerned, it is the principles that underlie his description which count, and I shall eventually want to focus on those. In any case, if you want the details, you can always read *The Republic* itself.

Briefly then, Plato's state's most fundamental feature is its system of administration. There is a pyramidal class structure, with a ruling group of 'philosopher rulers' or 'guardians' at the pyramid's peak. It is their job, and theirs alone, to rule. That is because they are philosophers which means that they – and they alone – know what is good and will therefore do what is best. Everyone is supposed to 'mind their own business' and concentrate on what they are best at, leaving the philosopher rulers to get on with the job of ruling. (In many translations the rulers are called 'philosopher kings' but there is no especially good reason for describing them as 'kings'. For one thing, Plato explicitly states that women are capable of becoming philosopher rulers.[1] For another, Plato's rulers do not inherit their positions, as kings normally do. Plato's state is a meritocracy.) Immediately subsidiary to the guardian class is a class of 'auxiliaries'. Their job is to ensure that the rulers' directives are carried out. You could think of them as 'middle management'. Alternatively, since Plato clearly thinks of them as exhibiting military virtues, you could think of them as junior officers, with the philosopher rulers as the generals. Finally, at the base of the pyramid, the largest class is composed of everyone who is not a guardian. It is the class of ordinary people.

With certain further assumptions, the rest of Plato's description follows. For example, Plato has to make sure that the guardians are capable of doing their job. Given this, together with the assumption that talent is to some extent innate rather than acquired – that is, that we are born with it – it makes sense that some guardians should be charged with the responsibility of selecting infants for training as future guardians. If you assume, further, that the talent you are born with is inherited from your parents, then it makes sense to think people with an improved talent for guardianship can be produced by means of selective breeding, just as dogs with a keener sense of smell or hearing can. Plato imagines that, in his ideal state, there will be statutory festivals at which young male and female guardians select sexual partners by drawing lots. He supposes that, although the selection process will appear random to the participants, in fact it will have been orchestrated behind the scenes by older guardians who are making sure that the right couples breed in order to produce the best stock (*Republic* 459e.ff).[2] That might strike you as fanciful, sinister, or just fun, but – however it strikes you – I think you will appreciate the point that it is a logical consequence of Plato's idea that the state should be run by a class with specialist expertise.[3] Again, once selected at infancy, the young guardians have to be trained for their future role. For that reason, there is a lengthy section of *The Republic* in which their education is described. Within it, there is, for example, a long section devoted to a discussion of why they should not be permitted to read certain literature. '[We] cannot have any poet saying that the gods disguise themselves as strangers from abroad, and wander round our towns in every kind of shape' says Plato (through his mouthpiece, 'Socrates'). 'We must stop all stories of this kind, and stop mothers being misled by them and scaring their children with harmful myths' (*Rep*: 381d). Later, he lists a string of passages he would excise from the work of Homer (383a.ff) and there is a great deal more in the same vein. This is reasonable enough if you assume that the literature to which a child is exposed can influence the way his or her character develops. It is the same logic which can lead a modern parent to deny a young child access to certain violent movies and video games. As for other arts, such as music, Plato writes, for example, that the 'Ionian and certain Lydian modes, commonly described as "languid" should be prohibited for the way they foster, drunkenness, softness [and] idleness'. The young guardians are only permitted to listen to music in the 'Dorian and Phrygian modes' as these tend to foster military and civic virtue (*Rep*: 399a).

Or again, if you assume – quite reasonably – that the way people live can affect their attitude to the wider community, then you will take care over the way you design their living conditions. That is what Plato does. In his state, the guardians live communally, in special compounds. They live frugally. The little property they have is held in common and 'they eat together in messes and live together like soldiers in camp' (*Rep*: 416e). They are certainly not permitted to own land, houses or money, and nor are they allowed marriage and family life. The purpose of all this is to ensure that the interest of any individual guardian is closely identified with that of the community as a whole. Nothing else must get in the way as guardians should be 'partners in their dealings with their fellow citizens' (417b).

All this illustrates the extent to which the administration of Plato's state lies in the hands of a specially trained ruling class. One good way to summarise the vision which lies at the core of his view is with the 'foundation myth' he proposes for it. This is the famous 'myth of the metals'. 'We shall tell our citizens the following tale', says Socrates (knowing very well that it isn't true; so far as the rulers are concerned, the point is that people will be easier to control if they believe it).

> You are, all of you in this community, brothers. But when God fashioned you, he added gold in the composition of those of you who are qualified to be rulers (which is why their prestige is greatest); he put silver in the Auxiliaries, and iron and bronze in the farmers and other workers. Now since you are all of the same stock, though your children will commonly resemble their parents, occasionally a silver child will be born of golden parents, or a golden child of silver parents and so on. Therefore, the first and most important of god's commandments to the Rulers is that in the exercise of their function as Guardians their principal care must be to watch the mixture of metals in the characters of their children. If one of their own children has traces of bronze or iron in its make, they

must harden their hearts, assign it its proper value, and degrade it to the ranks of the industrial and agricultural class to which it properly belongs: similarly, if a child of this class is born with gold or silver in its nature, they will promote it appropriately to be a Guardian or an Auxiliary. And this they must do because there is a prophecy that the state will be ruined when it has Guardians of silver or bronze.

(*Rep*: 415a–c)

Plato's intentions

The question of justice

What are we to make of this? Because *The Republic* has a sort of 'double aspect', there is no simple answer. As I commented earlier, the very fact of its survival means that its argument confronts us just as it confronted Plato's contemporaries. Like them, we have to come to terms with it. However, that does not mean that anyone reading the paperback nowadays will automatically find its meaning clear. If philosophy is a conversation across the generations then – sometimes – trying to understand the others can be like trying to follow the words of a stranger from a far and distant land very different from your own. You have to make an effort. This is especially so in the case of Plato, whose ideas, out of all those I discuss in this book, have taken the longest journey to reach us.

For one thing, there is the question of reading a philosopher's intentions correctly. Take the way Plato's state (supposedly) embodies the 'virtue' of 'justice' to a perfect degree and is, thus, 'ideal' in the sense that we are intended to treat it as a measuring rod. The idea is that actual states are the more just, the more they resemble his ideal and the less just the less they resemble it. At first sight, Plato's intention appears more or less equivalent to the intention expressed by John Rawls when he introduces his *A Theory of Justice* (Rawls 1972) as follows:

> Justice is the first virtue of social institutions, as truth is of systems of thought. A theory however elegant or economical must be rejected or revised if it is untrue; likewise laws and institutions no matter how efficient and well-arranged must be reformed or abolished if they are unjust.
>
> (Rawls 1972: 3)

Rawls goes on to argue that there are 'principles of justice' which would be chosen by fair-minded people who stand to gain from cooperating with each other, at least when those people are placed in conditions so arranged that their judgement cannot be biased. He thinks that a social, legal or political arrangement is the more just the more it satisfies those principles, and the less just the less it does so. So, like Plato's ideal state, Rawls' famous 'two principles of justice' are meant to serve as a template.

But we must be careful here. It is true enough that modern people – our contemporaries – do have a tendency to think of justice in terms of the satisfaction of certain principles. That is because, like Rawls, they tend to associate justice with *fairness*. Indeed, Rawls sometimes describes the subject of his work as 'justice as fairness', and it is a great strength of his philosophical position that he tries to work this idea out in a logical, systematic, way. Clearly, if a just arrangement is one in which everyone affected by it can be treated fairly then 'the philosophical problem of justice' will have been solved once correct principles have been arrived at; that is, principles which, if followed, would result in everyone's being treated fairly, or at least in their being treated as fairly as is humanly possible. Notice also that, when the problem is conceived this way, the question of how goods which are scarce ought to be distributed usually comes well to the fore. This is inevitable given that, in modern times, the justice – and, indeed, the competence – of a government or regime's behaviour tends to be judged by the way it distributes scarce resources which are in great demand. Philosophers who broadly share this way of thinking about justice can still disagree over precisely what the correct 'principles of justice' are. For example, Rawlsians hold that, under just arrangements, the worst off people are better off than they would be under any alternative set-up. (This is required by Rawls' 'second principle of justice'.) They disagree with utilitarians who hold that justice requires satisfaction of the 'principle of utility' according to which 'the greatest good is the greatest happiness of the greatest number'.

Utilitarianism and Rawls' theory are discussed in later chapters. For the present, the question at issue is this: Are these more recent treatments of justice really addressing the same question with which Plato was concerned? Here, the fact that Plato never refers to anything resembling Rawls' second principle, or the principle of utility, should be enough to put us on our guard. So should the fact that he shows no interest in the question of fair distribution. On the contrary, and as we have seen, Plato thinks of 'justice' in the state as a matter of its having a certain structure, and of there being a balance or harmony between the structure's parts, these being the three classes, the guardians, the auxiliaries and the rest. At one point, Plato even draws a parallel between justice in the state and justice 'in the individual'. According to him, the soul, like the ideal state, also has three parts. In the case of the soul, these are 'reason', 'spirit' and 'appetite', and a person can only be happy when these are in harmony (*Rep*: 441c.ff). This comparison is more than a poetic flight of fancy. It is so integral to Plato's political vision, that, in *The Republic*, he introduces his description of the just state on the pretext that it will help us to understand what justice in the individual is. 'Justice can be a characteristic of an individual or of a community', he writes, but adds that, because 'a community is larger than an individual' we may find it 'on a larger scale in the larger entity, and so easier to recognise' (368e).

The way John Rawls conceives the question of justice, such talk of 'justice in the individual' would make no sense. So, it is fair to ask whether Plato and Rawls have come up with different answers to the same question, or whether they give different answers because they were trying to answer different questions in the first place. And here the problem of reading intentions correctly is compounded by a further problem, that of translation. In Plato's case, this arises because the word 'virtue' is the most accurate translation anyone can think of for the Greek word *aretē*, and because, even so, 'virtue' and *aretē* do not mean quite the same thing. So, although you could easily gain the impression that Plato, like Rawls, believes that 'justice is the first virtue of political institutions', that is not what he believes – or not precisely. What Plato believes is that *dikaiosynē* (the Greek word translated as 'justice') is the state's *aretē*.

The difference between 'virtue' and *aretē* is that the latter is connected much more closely to notions of function and status. In fact, *aretē* is sometimes translated, not as 'virtue' but as 'excellence'. You demonstrate *aretē* by showing that you are especially good at something – fighting in battle, for example, or speaking in the assembly. In the early, 'heroic' period of Greek history – the period of the Trojan War, of Homer's *Iliad* and *Odyssey* – *aretē* seems to have been a question of excellence in being the sort of person you were, and 'the sort of person you were' would, in turn, have been a matter of your social rank. Much as an axe demonstrates its peculiar excellence by cutting swiftly and cleanly, so nobles and warriors would have demonstrated *aretē* by doing what is expected of nobles and warriors – showing authority, acting courageously in war, and so on. Some scholars have argued that there was nothing we would recognise as 'morality' during that period; that there were only individuals demonstrating, or failing to demonstrate, the qualities appropriate to their caste.[4] By the time Plato was writing, the meaning of *aretē* was far less strictly tied to social class, but it still meant 'excellence' at this or that particular activity. This explains why *aretē* can sometimes be translated as 'skill'.

The inexact match between the meanings of 'virtue' and *aretē* shows just how careful you sometimes have to be if you want to know what a writer is really trying to say. It also helps us to understand why Plato defined 'justice in the state' as he did, so let us now consider that definition.

Plato's definition of 'justice in the state'

Without a definition of 'justice' – or, at least, without some account of the word's meaning – we would have no reason at all for believing Plato's claim that the state he describes in *The Republic* is perfectly just. Plato supplies a definition about half way through the book. 'Justice', he says, 'consists in minding your own business and not interfering with other people' (*Rep*: 433a–b). A little later he adds that, 'when each of our three classes . . . does its own job and minds its own business that . . . is justice, and makes our state just' (*Rep*: 434c).

Here, it is important to emphasise that the phrase 'minding your own business', although it is the one conventionally used in translations of Plato, is a slightly unfortunate choice for what Plato had in mind. In English, to 'mind your own business' is to keep your nose out of other people's affairs. It is to not interfere where you have no right. But all Plato means is that, *in a just state, everyone concentrates on doing what he or she is best at*. This is a definition of 'justice' which would have come fairly naturally to someone who was thinking, not in terms of 'virtue', but in terms of *aretē*, as the latter is tied far more closely to notions of function and purpose. Plato is asking what the particular purpose, point or 'excellence' of the state is and, so far as he is concerned, this is pretty much equivalent to asking for the purpose or point of living in a community or a society.

Incidentally, this is a good point at which to note yet another example of how you have to go quite carefully if you want to understand what Plato is really trying to say. In Plato's time a Greek would have lived in a 'city-state', or *polis*, consisting of a city and its outlying area. The 'city' in question would be a centre at which people could meet and trade and, if the *polis* was a democracy, attend meetings of the assembly. Typically, it would consist of a tract of land with an acropolis (citadel). Clearly, the Greek city bore little resemblance to the great cities of our own time. Plato is asking how the *polis* should be organised, a fact which becomes even clearer if you consider that *The Republic* was not even the original title of his work. It was originally entitled *Politeia*, which translates as 'constitution'. Nowadays, we tend to think of the state as a particular set of institutions – the legislative assembly or parliament, the courts, the police and the armed services, and so on – but that is not quite what Plato had in mind. I would say that 'state', 'community' and 'society' all cover something of what he had in mind, but that none of them captures it accurately.

It is Plato's view, then, that every member of a community benefits when each specialises in the task he or she is best at doing. That is what gives communal living its point. In line with this, his definition of 'justice' is preceded, much earlier in the discussion, by a speculative account of how society could have originated. 'Society originates', says the 'Socrates' character, 'because the individual is not self-sufficient, but has many needs which he can't supply himself' (*Rep*: 369b). He then goes on to argue that, at an absolute minimum, a state or community would have to consist of four or five men. 'It will need a farmer, a builder, a weaver, and also, I think, a shoemaker and one or two others' (369d). This is the number required to satisfy our basic needs for food, shelter and clothing, and it obviously makes sense that each of these men should concentrate on a single activity and share his product with the others. It would be silly to expect the farmer, say, to 'devote a quarter of his time to producing a quarter the amount of food, and the other three quarters, one to building himself a house, one to making clothes, and another to making shoes'. Not only that, but 'We have different natural aptitudes which fit us for different jobs' (370b). Of course, there is a great difference between this simple, rather idyllic, community and something as sophisticated as Athenian society, so Plato presents a scenario in which more specialists are needed as tastes develop and become more complex. Even his simple society will soon come to need smiths and other craftsmen to make and repair tools, shepherds and cowherds to guard livestock, merchants and other types of trader. As for a fully civilised society, which Plato portrays as 'unhealthy' because it is marked by a taste for more than bare necessities, it will need a great deal more. 'It will want couches and tables and other furniture, and a variety of delicacies, scents, perfumes, call-girls, and confectionery.' 'We shall have to enlarge our state again', he writes.

> Our healthy state is no longer big enough; its size must be enlarged to make room for a multitude of occupations none of which is concerned with necessaries. There will be hunters and fishermen, and there will be artists, sculptors, painters, and musicians; there will be poets with their following of reciters, actors, chorus-trainers, and producers; there will be manufacturers of domestic equipment of all sorts, especially those concerned with women's dress and make-up. And we shall need a lot more servants – tutors, wet-nurses, nannies, cosmeticians, barbers, butchers and cooks. And we shall need swine-herds too; there were none in our former state, as we had no need of them, but now we need pigs and cattle in quantities too, if we are to eat meat.
>
> (*Rep*: 373b–c)

Plato adds that, with this luxurious lifestyle, more doctors will be needed – and so on and so forth. Finally, and of course, a guardian class whose special skill is ruling will be needed to administrate and take decisions. In this way, the tripartite class structure of Plato's ideal state follows smoothly and quite logically from his definition of 'justice'.

There is quite a lot wrong with Plato's definition, but there is something right about it too, so let us take that first. Plato is right to suppose, then, that everyone benefits where there is division of labour and people specialise in doing things they are good at. You could say that this gives the community a certain function and communal life a certain point, so he is right on that score too. However – turning now to where his definition goes wrong – it does not follow that the benefits of specialisation give communal life its *only* point, so much so that everything must be organised to satisfy that particular end. Nor does it follow that society cannot come to serve new and different requirements as it develops. More than that, the original reason for something's existence can become quite irrelevant to the way it is now. For all we know, social organisation evolved because tribal life made it easier for women to concentrate on childrearing while men hunted, or perhaps it meant that people could have sex more often, with the result that individuals with a 'social gene' succeeded where others failed. Perhaps so but, so far as I can see, the fact would be of absolutely no relevance to the way modern societies like those of Europe and North America ought to be run. It is a mistake to suppose that there must always be conclusions to be drawn from an account of how a thing originated. (This is sometimes called 'the genetic fallacy'.) So, Plato's story of how the first state might have developed is really beside the point.

Actually, you don't have to push Plato's definition very hard before it falls to pieces in front of your eyes. It's a mess. In addition to the difficulty I have just mentioned, there are plenty of other things wrong with it. Here are just three examples. First: Although it is undoubtedly true that we have different natural aptitudes, these are only preconditions for the talents and skills we eventually have once we are mature. Talents and skills are things you work on and develop. Just for example, it could be that some people are congenitally incapable of becoming pianists. It could be that others are born with a 'natural talent' but, out of the latter, only those who learn the piano and practise hard at it will become good pianists. Therefore, Plato is wrong to assume that each of us is suited, from birth, to fill a specific social slot. (Given the effort he puts in to describing the education of the philosopher rulers, you would think he would have noticed this.) Second: Plato's idea that we should specialise in what we are best at assumes that everyone is absolutely hopeless at doing anything other than the thing he or she is best at. Without this assumption, there would be no reason for stopping people doing things they are good at, even if those things are not what they are best at. For example, someone could be a brilliant software engineer and a very good, but not one hundred per cent brilliant, cook. If this person was a useless cook, then he would be well advised to concentrate on the software. But I am supposing that he is not useless. He is very good, which means that if he wants to open a restaurant and give up software engineering, there need be no reason why he shouldn't. One thing is for sure: there would be no social collapse of the sort that would ensue if farmers were forced to spend three quarters of their time building, weaving and making shoes. Third: Plato's definition assumes that, for each person, there is an economic slot conveniently waiting to be filled; for example, that, for a society of exactly one hundred people, there will be exactly one hundred jobs to be done. (Either that, or there is some unmentioned method for disposing of those unfortunates who find themselves classed as 'spare capacity'.) This is completely implausible.

I could continue, but by picking away at the shortcomings of Plato's definition in this detailed way, we run the risk of overlooking something else. I have not yet mentioned that definition's most striking feature. This is not a detail. It is the definition's remarkably *un-Athenian* character. In the previous chapter I quoted from Pericles' funeral oration, the speech with which that great statesman celebrated the Athenian ideal at the end of the first year of the Peloponnesian War. There is a direct contrast between his proud boast that 'we do not say that a man who takes no interest in politics is a man who minds his own business; we say that he has no business here at all' and Plato's claim that 'Justice consists in minding your own business and not interfering with other people'. The very feature Pericles celebrates as his city's crowning glory, Plato denigrates as its deepest vice. This is a contrast which takes us to the heart of Plato's position, so let us now explore it.

Democracy and the totalitarian menace

So far, I have repeatedly emphasised that there are differences between Plato's world and our own, and that you have to take these into account if you want to understand what he was really trying to say. There is another side to the coin, though, for there are also similarities which lend his arguments a certain urgency, even in present day circumstances. For example, in his time as in ours – in Athens at least – democracy was widely held to be superior to other systems of government. If you forget that Athens had a strong democratic tradition then you are likely to miss the point of *The Republic*. But, more than that, just as the Athenians would have recognised in Plato's argument a sustained critique of their democratic ideals, so we can treat it as embodying a critique of our own. If you value democracy, then, one way to approach *The Republic* is by trying to answer its anti-democratic case.

There is a relatively short, but sustained and direct, attack on democracy itself in *The Republic*, Part IX (*Rep*: 555b.ff). There, Plato argues that the typical 'democratic character' is superficial, feckless and easily led (this being a result of too much liberty and the prevailing idea that all are equal). People with this type of character are said by Plato to be easy prey for the manipulative and power-hungry, with the inevitable result that democracy degenerates into tyranny. For the most part, this train of reasoning merely reveals Plato's hostility to the Athenian system, as well as his aristocrat's contempt for the common people. For example, he claims that, in a democracy, practically all leaders are drawn from a class of 'thriftless idlers' whom he compares to drones in a beehive: 'their energetic leaders to drones with stings, the more inert mass of followers to drones without stings' (*Rep*: 364b).

Remarks like that contain more prejudice than argument, and we can safely ignore them. However, there is one thread running through these passages which we do have to take seriously, namely Plato's insistence that democracy cannot be relied upon to produce the best leaders or decisions, or even very good ones. Democracy – be it Athenian democracy or modern 'liberal democracy' – is (at the very least) a system or method for choosing leaders or making decisions. The leaders and decisions it yields are – as Plato says – the most popular, 'most popular' being defined with reference to a given voting procedure (some would say rather arbitrarily, but that is a point we can set to one side for the moment). This being so, there is no guarantee whatsoever that it will produce leaders who are 'the best' in the sense of being wise, or good, or efficient, nor that the operation of democratic procedures will result in wise or sensible policies. Sometimes the 'democratic decision' will turn out in retrospect to have been quite foolish. So, if you want to defend democracy against Plato, you can't do it with an argument that, despite appearances, democracy really does produce 'the best' leaders and decisions. It doesn't, there is no point in trying to think of such an argument, and you have to come up with a different way of defending democracy.

Before considering how this might be done we should note something else which would have been all too familiar to Athenians, just as it is to us, and that is his state's centralised, authoritarian, structure. To Athenian readers of *The Republic*, Plato's state would have been immediately recognisable as an idealised portrait of their city's great enemy, Sparta. As I noted in the previous chapter, this was a dictatorship run by a military caste. As in Plato's state, the ruling class – the 'Spartiates' – lived collectively in fairly harsh, simple and disciplined conditions, men and women alike. Likewise, in both Sparta and Plato's state, the purpose of this 'Spartan' lifestyle was to ensure the closest possible identification of the individual's interests with those of the community. As in Plato's state, orders were passed down from the top to those who formed the base of the pyramid. Plato idealises this in at least two ways. First, although he doesn't describe the way the lower classes live in his state, we can assume that, thanks to its just constitution (or rather its *aretē*), their conditions will be the best possible. By contrast, the Spartan *helots* lived the harsh and brutalised life of serfs. Second, whereas Plato's state is benignly ruled by philosophers, the Spartan ruling group were nothing more than a military caste.[5]

Twentieth century commentators have drawn other parallels. For example, Karl Popper has described Plato as a defender of 'totalitarianism'. Whatever the precise meaning of 'totalitarianism' may be – there is some dispute amongst scholars over whether the word denotes a new phenomenon or whether it is just a new word for something much more ancient – this is, in one way, fair enough, for all are agreed that Stalin's Soviet Union and Hitler's Germany were examples of totalitarian systems at work. Under these regimes, a small group (the party elite, this time with a 'leader' at its helm) strove to exert total control over a passive and compliant population. As in Plato's state, everyone, but especially members of the dominant party, was expected to put the interest of the nation, the race or the community first. And there are other similarities. For example recent totalitarian regimes have striven to monopolise the media, and so to exert control, not only through censorship – which certainly exists in Plato's state – but through the dissemination of propaganda. Some commentators have drawn parallels between this and the propagation of 'the noble lie' (the myth of the metals) by Plato's philosopher rulers.

This suggests another way to answer Plato. Rather than attempting the impossible, by trying to show that democracy always produces 'the best' results, we can try to undermine his case for the centralised state. And, whatever you may think of his ideal state, that case is so powerful that it is worth trying to answer it. That is one reason why Plato remains an interesting challenge. After all, between his time and the present there must have been plenty of disgruntled reactionaries who have produced this or that more or less eccentric argument for some form of state with a central authority. Our own times have witnessed quite a few dictators, each spinning a line on 'preserving the national identity', 'eliminating undesirable elements', 'running things efficiently', 'making the country safe before democracy is restored', and so on. But Plato does something a lot more interesting than that. The position he takes is a forceful illustration of the way understanding a political philosophy can sometimes require understanding much more than its approach to 'the political' narrowly conceived. To fully appreciate the argument of *The Republic*, we must consider how Plato answers questions which, at first sight, appear to have nothing to do with politics. They are questions about the nature of the universe; about meaning and knowledge; appearance and reality.

The theory of forms

Appearance and reality

At the heart of Plato's world view there lies his 'theory of forms'. According to that theory, the world revealed by our senses – the world of objects, shapes, colours, sounds and smells – is a mere appearance. It is the distorted reflection of a deeper, 'true', reality. The latter is the world of forms ('patterns' or 'paradigms'). It is from these that the reflections are held by Plato to derive the secondary reality they have. Plato also thinks that most of us are fated to spend our lives labouring under the deluded belief that the world of mere appearance is, in fact, the real world. For the next few pages, I shall try to explain the theory in a certain amount of detail.

But *how*, according to the theory, is the appearance supposed to reflect the reality, and by what process is the deception supposed to come about? After all a reflection, the thing it reflects, and the person deceived into mistaking one for the other can be related in a number of ways. The way the reflection in an ordinary plane mirror is related, on the one hand, to the object it reflects and, on the other, to the person seeing the reflection is just one. (It is safe to say that, where this relationship holds, we are not usually deceived into confusing the reflection with the thing itself. However, I am sure that all of us have been on occasions, for example where a mirror is used to great effect by a professional magician.) This variant contrasts with the way the image on a cinema screen is related to that on the translucent film in the projector. It seems right to call the former a 'reflection' of the latter, and you could say that the latter is, in its turn, itself a reflection of the real events which were originally filmed. Again, I doubt that many of us are often deceived into confusing the image on the screen with reality itself – certainly not these days – but it is easy to see how someone unfamiliar with the cinema could be.

Here is yet another possibility. Suppose you are standing on a piece of dry land, but that all around you are pools of water. Some are quite brackish; others less so, and their surfaces are rippled by the breeze. Now try to imagine how you would appear to a creature living near the bottom of one of the pools. Even if it were looking directly up at you, its perception of you would be distorted by the ripples moving across the intervening surface. Also, because light entering water is refracted, you would appear to be in the wrong place. Moreover, it is quite likely that your image would be further reflected and distorted by objects within the pool, as well as by movements of the water itself – currents, eddies and suchlike disturbances. This creature will be surrounded by fractured and distorted images – as if it were living within a warped kaleidoscope – and it could hardly avoid confusing these images with the 'real' world (that of the surface).

Plato sometimes portrays the relation between the world of forms and the world of appearances in a manner which resembles this. Consider, for example, the beliefs he expresses (through the medium of the 'Socrates' character) towards the end of his dialogue, *Phaedo*. The dialogue is represented as taking place in the death cell during the night on which Socrates will swallow poison and die, so fulfilling the sentence of the Athenian court. A few disciples are present, and Socrates comforts them by outlining his belief in the survival of the soul after death. After briefly stating his belief that the earth is spherical and set at the centre of the universe, he continues as follows.

I believe that it [the earth] is vast in size, and that we who dwell between the river Phasis and the Pillars of Hercules inhabit only a minute portion of it; we live round the sea like ants or frogs round a pond; and there are many other peoples inhabiting similar regions. There are many hollow places all round the earth, places of every shape and size, into which the water and mist and air have collected. But the earth itself is as pure as the starry heaven in which it lies,

25

and which is called Ether by most of our authorities. The water, mist, and air are the dregs of this Ether, and they are continually draining into the hollow places in the earth. We do not realise that we are living in its hollows, but assume that we are living on the earth's surface. Imagine someone living in the depths of the sea. He might think that he was living on the surface, and seeing the sun and the other heavenly bodies through the water, he might think that the sea was the sky. He might be so sluggish and feeble that he had never reached the top of the sea, never emerged and raised his head from the sea into this world of ours, and seen for himself – or even heard from someone who had seen – how much purer and more beautiful it really is than the one in which his people lives. Now we are in just the same position.

(Plato 1954b: 172)

Socrates continues in this vein for some time. He then goes on to assert his belief that his departed soul will migrate, first through the upper air and then into the Ether, onwards and upwards to yet purer and more beautiful regions.

It is Socrates' belief that, once he has reached these, he will gain a clearer view of how things really are. It would be interesting to pursue this argument to its final destination. I shan't, though, because the point I am trying to make here has nothing to do with the soul's alleged immortality. It relates, rather, to the cosmology embodied in this passage. I mean the way Plato represents the earth's structure and its relation to the rest of the universe. My point is that, with the assumption of the cosmological picture given here, you can see how someone really could – quite genuinely and sincerely – believe that the world we perceive is a pale reflection of a different, 'higher' reality. That is because it is equally possible to appreciate how a creature in a pond who actually thought about these things could form a similar belief. The belief may not be true, but – with the assumption – it makes sense, so much so that you could, if you wanted, represent the relation which is supposed to hold between appearance and reality here with the help of a diagram.

Without the background assumption, a thesis such as the theory of forms can be mystifying. Believe me. I speak from experience here because I know that when I first encountered Plato I had real trouble figuring out what the forms were supposed to be. (I was in my first year as a philosophy student.) When I tried to picture the forms, I tended to imagine nebulous, cloud-like entities, wobbling like jellies as they hovered in the sky. As for their connection with earthly things, the best I could do was imagine invisible wires or strings running between tables and chairs and the forms themselves. (In fact, I recollect that, when lecturing on the subject, the professor drew a diagram on the board which illustrated the connection in pretty much that way.) The whole thing struck me as faintly ridiculous – even though, at the time, I was completely unable to discover any fault in Plato's argument itself. Of course, I now realise that I only gained such an impression because I was approaching his thesis with the wrong background assumptions. Any modern person, reading Plato for the first time, would find it equally difficult to work out where the forms are supposed to be located, for example, how they connect with other things. However, with different background assumptions, it makes a lot more sense.[6]

The forms, meaning and knowledge

Plato's theory of forms supplies him with answers to a number of difficult philosophical problems. To illustrate the theory I shall concentrate on just two: first, a problem about how words acquire meaning; second, a problem about knowledge. Plato's solutions to these are closely related, and each is directly relevant to his political theory. I shall eventually say how, but let me first outline the problems and the way Plato handles them.

First of all, then, there is the question of what distinguishes a mere sound or mark on paper (papyrus, stone or the computer screen) from a word. When we express ourselves in language, we normally do so in speech or writing – so, of course, there is a sense in which words are sounds or marks – but they are not *just* that. How come? You can answer the question by pointing out that, unlike mere sounds and marks, words carry *meaning*. That is true enough, but it only raises a further question, namely, by virtue of *what* do words carry meaning? Plato's answer is that a word has meaning when it is a name; that is, when there is a certain one-to-one relationship between the word and the thing it 'stands for'. This is clearly true in the case of some words. For example, the words 'Socrates' and 'Plato' mean what they do because they stand for Socrates and Plato themselves. Plato believes that what goes for words such as these goes for meaningful words generally.

In some respects this is an appealing and quite persuasive answer. (At any rate, it has certainly persuaded a lot of intelligent people, for Plato is only giving his own version of an answer which, after his time, had a long and distinguished history.) To appreciate its power, all you need to do is think about what happens when an infant first learns to speak. The first thing a child learns is to associate words with the things they stand for – 'Mummy' with its mother, 'dog' with the dog, and so on. If this isn't naming, then it is something very like it, and it would be easy to assume that, as the child learns increasingly more language, it is just continuing to do the same thing. Nevertheless, the idea that all words are names gives rise to some fairly intractable difficulties. For example, how is it to account for general terms such as 'dog' where this is used, not as the infant uses it, to refer to a specific dog, but to dogs in general (as in 'man's best friend is the dog')? Whereas there is only one Socrates (for whom 'Socrates' is the name) there are many dogs; and, not only that, dogs can differ greatly. There are big dogs, little dogs, shaggy dogs, short-haired dogs, lap-dogs, hunting-dogs, guard-dogs, brown dogs, white dogs, red setters, Scots terriers, mongrels, and so on. If the general term 'dog' is a name, then *what* does it name?

Note also that the same difficulty is raised in the case of abstract terms such as 'justice' and 'beauty', for, just as there are many dogs, so there are many just acts and many beautiful things. If 'justice' and 'beauty' are names then, again, the question of what they name is forced upon us. If these words name objects, then those objects can't be ordinary, visible things, like Socrates discussing philosophy in the marketplace.

Faced with such challenges, any philosopher attracted by the thesis that all words are names is now forced to choose between two alternatives. One is to abandon the thesis and go in search of a completely different theory of meaning. The other is to stick with it, but argue that the objects named by general and abstract terms are no ordinary objects. Plato takes this second alternative and, in terms of his theory, the objects in question are the forms. So, for example, he would say of 'dog' that the word has meaning because it names that which all dogs have in common; 'that which all dogs have in common' being that all dogs 'share in' or 'partake in' or imperfectly reflect the ideal form of dog (or maybe that should be 'dogginess'). Likewise, he holds that the things we (correctly) describe as beautiful reflect or 'partake of' the form of beauty – or, as he also puts it, 'beauty itself'.

With all that said, we can now deal more briefly with Plato's solution to the second philosophical problem I said I would mention. This is the problem of defining knowledge. According to Plato, to have knowledge is to be directly aware of an object. Now, there is a certain 'common sense' to this answer, just as there was in the case of his solution to the question of meaning. That is because there are everyday cases in which knowing something really is nothing more than being directly aware of an object. For example, in broad daylight you know that the objects in front of you are there, just because you can see them there.[7] To put the same point slightly differently you have knowledge because the objects – the tables and chairs, say – are directly present to one of your faculties. In this case it is sight.

However, the idea that to know is to be aware of an object also raises difficulties and – just as he did in the case of meaning – Plato attempts to solve these by assuming the existence of a special type of object. And, in the case of knowledge he assumes something else too, namely a special faculty with which each type of object is perceived. As an example, take his account of knowledge in geometry. Like other branches of mathematics, this poses a problem for Plato's account because students of geometry do not take objects as their subject matter. Or, at least, if they do the objects are no ordinary objects, not in the way tables and chairs are ordinary objects. If, at first, you find that point difficult to grasp, that is probably because you are picturing your old schoolteacher drawing a triangle on the board and showing that the sum of the triangle's internal angles is 180° or, if not that, drawing a circle and proving that the circumference is equal to πr^2. However, the drawings on the board are really only visual aids. That is the point. If you were to measure the 'triangle' roughly drawn by the teacher on the board you would almost certainly find that the sum of its internal angles was nothing like 180°, but geometry is not really concerned with the properties of *that*. It is only concerned with the properties of perfect figures – the 'ideal' triangle for example – and the drawings on the board are a mere approximation to these. As Plato puts it, students of geometry 'make use of and argue about visible figures, though they are not really thinking about them, but about the originals which they resemble'. And, as he adds,

> it is not about the square which they have drawn that they are arguing, but about the square itself or diagonal itself, or whatever the figure may be. The actual figures they draw or model, which themselves cast their shadows and reflections in water – these they treat as images only, the real objects of their investigation being invisible except to the eye of reason.
>
> (*Rep*: 510d)

Notice the way Plato introduces a special object of knowledge in this passage, not the drawing but 'the square itself' or the 'diagonal itself'. ('The triangle itself' would fall into the same category.) Notice too his introduction of a special faculty. These intellectual objects are not present to vision, as ordinary objects can be, but to the faculty of reason. Plato's phrase 'the eye of reason' is significant here. He clearly believes that both the 'eye of vision' and 'the eye of reason' scan objects, but that there is a different type of object for each type of eye. Indeed, there is a well-known section of *The Republic* in which Plato invites us to think of his theory of knowledge as represented diagrammatically (*Rep*: 509d.ff).[8] Picture a line. On one side, there is a list of (supposed) faculties. It moves in descending order of importance from 'intelligence' to 'mathematical reasoning' to 'belief' to 'illusion'. On the other, there is a corresponding list of the objects appropriate to each faculty. The forms come right at the top. Like the objects of mathematics these are intelligible, objects for the 'eye of reason' to peruse. 'Shadows and images', the objects of illusion, are placed right at the bottom. Interestingly, our awareness of physical things is relegated by Plato to the status of 'belief', but I suppose that is what it would be for deluded inhabitants of a murky pond.

The escape from the cave

When taken in conjunction, Plato's account of meaning and his account of knowledge help explain quite a few of *The Republic*'s features. For example, take the structure of Book One. In this section of the book a number of characters advance definitions of 'justice', each in his turn. As each definition is produced, Socrates refutes it with the help of counter-examples. For example, one character, Polemarchus, claims that to act justly is 'to give every man his due' (*Rep*: 331e). Socrates points out that this cannot be right, as 'giving a man his due' could mean repaying money to someone who has gone mad, and who will only do harm with it as a result. This contradicts Polemarchus' real guiding thought, which is that 'one friend owes it to another as a due to do him good, not harm'. Again, if 'giving a man his due' means helping one's friends and harming one's enemies then, as Socrates points out, a doctor, a cook, a navigator, a farmer or a shoemaker can be in a better position to give someone his due than a just man can (332c.ff). It depends on the circumstances. Another character, the bad tempered Thrasymachus, argues both that 'justice or right is simply what is in the interest of the stronger party' (338c) and that it is 'obedience to the ruling power' (339b.ff). Socrates refutes him by pointing out that – because a ruling power can be mistaken about what is in its interest – these claims contradict each other.

I shan't go through these arguments in any detail. What I would like you to notice, however, is the general structure of Plato's argument here. Plato is assuming that all things called by the same name have something in common, its 'essence'; that there is, as he explicitly states, 'a single form for each set of particular things to which we apply the same name' (596a). Without this assumption, there would be no point in trying to capture that common element with a single definition. Plato's procedure would be pointless. (Just to make it clear that Plato's account is not the only possibility, it may be worth mentioning an alternative at this point. Suppose, then, that, contrary to Plato, Wittgenstein was right to say that there are 'family resemblances' between the things to which the same word applies; that there is 'a complicated network of similarities overlapping and criss-crossing', but – as with members of the same family – no single feature common to all of them. If this is right then Socrates' counter-examples would not refute his opponents' definitions. They could simply retort that their definitions only apply to *some* cases of justice, and that he is thinking of others.)

Plato's theories of meaning and knowledge also help us to understand some otherwise difficult passages. For example, take Plato's argument that 'since beauty and ugliness are opposites, they are *two*'. So that, '[And], as they are *two*, each of them is single'. And,

> The same is true of justice and injustice, good and evil, and all qualities; each of them is in itself single, but they appear everywhere

as a multiplicity because they appear everywhere in combination with actions and material bodies and with each other.

Plato uses this principle 'to distinguish your sight-lovers and art-lovers and practical men from the philosophers in the true sense', as follows.

> Those who love looking and listening are delighted by beautiful sounds and colours and shapes, and the works of art which make use of them, but their minds are incapable of seeing and delighting in the essential nature of beauty itself.
>
> (*Rep:* 476b)

None of this could make any sense until you realise that Plato is assuming (i) that 'beauty' and 'ugliness' name distinct properties which can coexist in the same thing (where this is something visible, or otherwise directly apprehended by our senses); (ii) that we are able to recognise these properties in something because that thing 'partakes' both of 'beauty itself' and of 'ugliness itself'; and (iii) that there is an 'essential nature of beauty itself' (a 'form of beauty') lying behind and beyond the world of appearances.

At this point, I think it is worth emphasising that, for all its far-reaching, otherworldly, ambition, Plato's theory of forms rests on assumptions which it is very natural to make. I mean that you can easily see how someone could make them, even if they are wrong. (Again, you only have to think of how an infant's first efforts at language can be so easily construed on the model of naming.) Even so, a great deal of philosophy, especially philosophy since around the time of the Second World War, has been devoted to dismantling the view of language on which Plato's world view, like that of many others, rests. Here too a quotation from Wittgenstein is appropriate.

> Think of the tools in a tool-box; there is a hammer, pliers, a saw, a screw-driver, a rule, a glue-pot, glue, nails and screws. The functions of words are as diverse as the functions of these objects. (And in both cases there are similarities.)
>
> Of course, what confuses us is the uniform appearance of words when we hear them spoken or meet them in script or print. For their *application* is not presented to us so clearly.
>
> (Wittgenstein 1953: section 11, p.6)

If Wittgenstein is right, then Plato is wrong to construe meaning primarily on the model of naming. Finally on this point, though, there does seem to be one quite striking difference between Plato and ourselves. It is this. Modern people are much more used to making a distinction between 'language' on the one hand and 'the world' on the other. We are used to thinking of the former as a system of rules and conventions, something we bring to the world. On this view meanings are, in part, a function of our linguistic system. By contrast, Plato appears to think of meanings as part of the natural world, that they are 'out there', just as stones and trees are. (Here, it is worth noting a difference between Plato's use of *idea*, the Greek word from which 'form' is translated, and our own. We think of an idea as part of a person, that it is something 'inside the mind' for example. Plato locates ideas in the real world.) When reading Plato, it is sometimes worth bearing this in mind.

I could continue this discussion of the theory of forms for some time. There is plenty more to say. Still, the literature on the subject is already vast and, in any case, my subject is Plato's political philosophy. It is now time to consider the relevance of the theory of forms to that. Here, the key is the relationship between theory and the programme of education Plato requires his philosopher rulers to undergo. This begins with the study of mathematics. As we have seen, it is Plato's view that mathematicians study objects whose true nature is available only to the intellect, not to the senses. After that they are led, through dialectic, to knowledge of the forms. These are also known only to the intellect. The culmination of the process is that the philosopher ruler achieves knowledge of the form of the good. This is the highest form of all, there being no point in having any knowledge without knowledge of what is good and valuable (*Rep*: 505b). Plato compares the form of the good with the sun. As the source of light, it is the sun which makes it possible for us to see the visible world. It also 'causes the processes of generation, growth, and nourishment'. Like-wise, or so Plato thinks, the form of the good is 'the source not only of the intelligibility of the objects of knowledge, but also of their being and reality' (509b).

There is a very famous passage in which Plato compares achieving knowledge of the form of the good with escape from 'an underground chamber like a cave, with a long entrance open to the daylight and as wide as the cave'. Within this chamber, there are people who 'have been prisoners there since they were children, their legs and necks being so fastened that they can only look straight ahead of them and cannot turn their heads'. Behind them and higher up there is a fire, and other people are carrying wooden cut-out figures of men, animals and other things. Shadows of these are cast on the opposite wall. The prisoners mistake these for real objects. (It is like mistaking the image on a cinema screen for real life.) Of course, our own situation is supposed to resemble the predicament of the prisoners, and the philosopher ruler who finally achieves knowledge of the truth is like the person who finally escapes from the cave and sees the sun directly. Plato writes,

> Suppose one of them were let loose and suddenly compelled to stand up and turn his head and look and walk towards the fire; all these actions would be painful and he would be too dazzled to see properly the objects of which he used to see the shadows.

And,

> And if . . . he were forcibly dragged up the steep and rugged ascent and not let go until he had been dragged out into the sunlight, the process would be a painful one, to which he would much object, and when he emerged into the light he would be so dazzled by the glare of it that he wouldn't be able to see a single one of the things he was now told were real. . . . Because, of course, he would need to grow accustomed to the light before he could see things in the upper world outside the cave. First, he would find it easiest to look at shadows, next at the reflections of men and other objects in water, and later on at the objects themselves. After that he would find it easier to observe the heavenly bodies and the sky itself at night, and to look at the light of the moon and stars rather than at the sun and its light by day.
>
> (*Rep*: 515c–516b)

According to Plato, it is when 'one has grasped by pure thought what the good is in itself' that 'one is at the summit of the intellectual realm as the man who looked at the sun was at the visual realm' (*Rep*: 532a–b).

To appreciate the relationship between the theory of forms and Plato's political outlook you need only consider how this celebrated parable carries us to the truly authoritarian heart of his vision. The point is that if all real knowledge is direct awareness of an object, just as vision is direct awareness of an object, then only a specially initiated elite can have real knowledge. Imagine trying to explain what it is like to see a red object to someone who can only see in black and white. I have never tried, but I guess that, if you were resourceful, there are quite a few things you could explain – that red is a colour, for example, and that it forms part of a spectrum. However, one thing you could never do is show that person what red is, that is, to have the same experience you have when you see something red. (To do that you would have to get him or her to see in colour – the very thing I have just supposed you cannot do.) Your difficulty would exactly parallel that of the person who, having once escaped from the cave, has now returned and is trying to explain to the others what it is like to see the world outside. And likewise, the philosopher rulers could never explain their knowledge to us, the uninitiated. There would be no point in our asking questions, so we might just as well carry on with our lives, 'minding our own business' as we go.

Conclusion

How shall I summarise this discussion of *The Republic* and draw it to a close? Well, earlier I raised the question of how a supporter of democracy might try to answer Plato's anti-democratic case. The outline of the theory of forms I have just given suggests a way of doing so, one which draws attention to just how much you have to believe if you are to accept Plato's argument.

Here is an analogy. Suppose that, one day, a huge space-ship from extra-terrestrial regions lands in a well-known public space. For the sake of the story, suppose that it lands in Central Park, New York City. The visit has been anticipated for some days, and a crowd has gathered. There is a reception party which includes all the world's major political leaders. The doors of the ship slide silently open, and the aliens' leader appears. Here is what the leader says.

> Greetings Earthpeople. We come from a distant planet with a civilisation far more advanced than your own. Our knowledge of science is also much more advanced. Scientists based in our Astronomical Institute's Department of Political Sociology have been studying you for a long time now. We see that you have problems. That is why we are here, for our mission is to travel the universe doing Good Things. We have the answer. Just do what we say and your problems will be solved. All will be well from now on.

Should the earth's leaders resign, having first abolished all political institutions, and should they then put themselves, and us, entirely in the hands of the aliens? The answer is clear. They would be crazy to do any such thing. Just think how much you would have to believe if you decided to let the aliens take over. You would have to believe at least the following:

1. That the 'space-ship' really is a space-ship and the 'aliens' really aliens; i.e. that this isn't just an elaborate stunt someone is pulling.
2. That even if the aliens are who they say they are, they are really as altruistic as they claim to be; that is, that they don't have sinister motives which they are not going to tell you about.
3. That even if the aliens are as altruistic as they claim to be, their science really is so highly developed that they can achieve what they say they can achieve.
4. That, in the case of social and political life here on earth, there really is a single problem – or a single set of problems – to which there is a straight, once-and-for-all solution.

Of course, it could be that the aliens' claims are true. It might even be that there are good reasons for suspecting that they are, but you would *still* be crazy to trust them so far as to put ourselves entirely in their hands. My point is that it is possible to think of *The Republic* as a classical Greek version of this science fiction fantasy, for there would be no more reason for trusting someone who claimed to be an especially qualified philosopher ruler. Suppose this person claims to have been through the educational process Plato describes, with the result that he now has direct access to the form of the good. To believe this, you would have to be persuaded that the theory of forms is true, but, even if you suspected that there could be some truth in it, it seems to me that it would be a big mistake to submit yourself to his authority once and for all.

Now note that, for a pro-democratic argument, all we have to do is change this last example slightly. Suppose that a self-styled 'philosopher ruler' comes knocking on your door asking you to vote for him. (You are living in a present day, liberal democracy.) This person claims to have been educated in a special way, to have access to the form of the good, and so on, but the difference now is that, if elected to power, his party will leave the electoral system intact. If it makes a hash of things, you will be able to vote against him next time. Would you now vote for him? Well, if you thought there could be something in his argument – i.e. in the theory of forms – you might. In this case, you don't have to submit to his domination forever, you can just give him a run for his money.

Here, then, is one virtue of democracy, namely that it gives people with ideas on how things should be done a chance to prove those ideas without your having to accept their arguments fully, or your having to place yourself irrevocably under their control. (And, of course, the person knocking on your door need not be claiming to be qualified as a philosopher ruler. He or she could be an advocate of the latest, fashionable, economic theory.) Notice that this is *not* the argument that democracy tends to produce the best solutions, whereas other systems do not. On the contrary, it is an argument that democracy is a protection against anyone who thinks that there can be such a thing as 'the right' or 'the best' solution. It is not an argument which sits easily with the idea that the perfect state is like a well-oiled machine of which we are, each of us, a specific moving part. In *The Republic* we find one variant of that idea – and in the course of this book we will encounter others – but it could be the wrong way to think of the relation between the state and ourselves.

3

Aristotle

In 347 BC Aristotle left Athens and set sail for distant shores at the Greek world's outer rim. Fifty-two years had elapsed since the execution of Socrates, but only months – if that – since the death of Aristotle's great teacher, Plato. (Plato had died earlier that same year at the age of 80.) Aristotle and Plato had first met when the former joined the latter's renowned foundation for the promotion of learning and scholarship – 'The Academy', as it was called. On learning of its existence, Aristotle had travelled to Athens from Stagira in Thrace, just so that he could join. He was 17 at the time. The Academy's reputation had grown to such an extent that it had come to attract talented intellectuals from throughout the known world (and, of course, not the least of its attractions was the fact that Plato continued to teach there himself). But there can be little doubt that Aristotle was Plato's most gifted pupil, and no doubt at all that he was to become the most famous.

By 347 Aristotle must have enjoyed a certain standing in Athens. And yet, as the dates make clear, he can have wasted no time in preparing for his departure. Why the haste? The most likely explanation is that the Athenians were feeling threatened once again, not by Sparta this time, but by Macedonia, whose ruler, Philip II, had ambitions to dominate the region. Aristotle was a notable member of a high-ranking family whose Macedonian connections were well known. Hadn't his father been Philip's doctor for a time? It is more than likely that Aristotle was leaving Athens at a time when he could feel neither welcome nor secure there.

Having crossed the Aegean Sea, Aristotle settled first at Aterneus on the coast of Asia Minor (in what is now Turkey) and later at Assos, another town on the same coast. At this time, Aristotle and a small community of other scholarly exiles were supported by the local ruler, or 'tyrant', Hermias. Later still, in 345 BC, Aristotle moved to the nearby island of Lesbos. Aristotle was away from Athens for twelve years. It was a period during which he had many adventures[1] and during which he also produced one of his most remarkable works. *The History of Animals* (Aristotle 1910) is not a work of philosophy at all – at least, it is not what you or I would recognise as such. It is a work of comparative zoology. The work is so systematically constructed, and it contains so many detailed and accurate observations, that it once prompted Charles Darwin himself to remark of his own contemporaries that they were 'mere schoolboys compared to old Aristotle' (Darwin 1888: Vol. 3, 252). *The History of Animals* is especially remarkable for its treatment of marine life. Aristotle must have spent a great deal of time walking the shore, searching the beach and the rock-pools for specimens he could dissect and analyse. There was an accompanying text – the *Dissections* – which consisted of diagrams and drawings. Tragically, this is now lost. It was during this same period that Aristotle produced the *Nicomachean Ethics* (so named after his son, Nicomachus)[2] and the *Politics* (Aristotle 1976 and 1981). It is the latter which forms this chapter's main subject.

The foregoing brief account should give you some idea of how Aristotle approached philosophy. So should a comparison with Plato. For example, consider how widely the two philosophers differed in their main interests. As we have seen, Plato followed Socrates in being largely, though not exclusively, concerned with questions of value.[3] By contrast, Aristotle was interested in much else besides, including what we would now call 'science'. I say 'what we would now call' because our distinction between science and philosophy would not have been drawn by the Greeks. In its original meaning 'philosophy' is simply the love of wisdom and a 'philosopher' someone who seeks to know and understand – and you only have to list the titles of the books by Aristotle which have survived to appreciate that he was certainly that. There are works on logic, psychology, botany, astronomy, physics, poetry and many other subjects, all this in addition to the work on ethics, politics and zoology I have already mentioned. As Jonathan Barnes, one of today's leading Aristotle scholars, has observed, 'Choose a field of research, and Aristotle laboured in it; pick an area of human endeavour, and Aristotle discoursed upon it. His range is astonishing' (Barnes 1982: 3). And so it is.

Another difference between Plato and Aristotle is this. It was Plato's ambition to direct our minds away from the world of 'mere' appearance towards the deeper reality which, as he thought, lies behind it. By contrast, Aristotle is a great observer. As with zoology, so in the case of philosophy generally, he approaches his subjects by recording and systematising numerous observations. In this respect, Aristotle's method is far more 'empirical' than Plato's. And yet another difference is that, when it comes to politics, Plato is the far more *engaged* of the two. As we saw in the previous chapter, Plato's *Republic* is more than a description of an ideal state. It is an idealised version of a real constitution, Sparta's, drawn up by a man who had sympathised with a particular side in the recent war, and who took a particular stance in criticism of contemporary Athenian institutions. By contrast with this – and as we shall see – Aristotle tends to write of the differences between constitutions rather as he writes of the difference between the squid and the crawfish; that is, as the dispassionate observer of interesting phenomena. Perhaps we should not find this surprising in someone who spent the greater part of his life as an immigrant and a *metic* – that is, a non-citizen resident of the city to whose life he contributed so much.

Let us now take a closer look at his arguments, beginning with his treatment of a theme which has tended to recur throughout the history of political thought.

Aristotle's political science

Taking the scientific approach

You could say that Aristotle was the first 'political scientist'. Read the following passage through and you will see what I mean. It occurs in Part Four of *The Politics*, about half way through the book.

> We agree that every state is composed of many parts, not just one. Now if our chosen subject were forms of animal life, we should first have to answer the question 'What is it essential for every animal to have?' And among those essentials we should have to include some of the organs of sense perception, and something for the processing and reception of nourishment, such as mouth and stomach, and in addition parts of the body which enable the animal in question to move about. If these were all that we had to consider and there were differences between them (several different kinds of mouth for instance, of stomach, of sense-organs, and of parts to do with locomotion), then the number of ways of combining these will necessarily make a number of different kinds of animals. For it is impossible for one and the same animal to have several different kinds of mouth or ear. So when you have taken all the possible couplings of these one with another, they will produce forms of animal; and the number of forms of animal will be equal to the number of essential parts.
>
> (*Pol.*: 1290b21)[4]

Aristotle then goes on to say this:

> We may apply this to the constitutions mentioned, for states are made up not of one but of many parts, as has often been said.
>
> (1290b38)

In other words, good practice in comparative zoology and good practice in the comparative study of political constitutions are equivalent. In both cases, you should apply the same techniques. The passage embodies a frequently made assumption, namely *the assumption that correct procedure in science is, equally, the correct procedure to follow when seeking to understand political phenomena.*

I should add that you can hardly blame Aristotle for having made the assumption. It isn't just that, as I have said, he would not have distinguished 'philosophy' from 'science'. More than that, we have to bear in mind that, in later periods, when political philosophers have followed the examples set by the leading scientists of their time – by Galileo, for example, by Newton, and more recently by Darwin – they were following examples set by *other people*. Aristotle could have done no such thing because he was *himself* the leading 'scientist' of his generation. He can only have pictured himself as an inquisitive individual applying techniques of rational analysis to every category of phenomenon which interested him. From our standpoint in time, the idea that 'scientific method' can be applied with equal success outside science can appear open to question, but if you try to see things from Aristotle's point of view, it is difficult to see what else he could have believed.

Is the assumption at issue correct? Well – so far as I can see – there is no straight 'yes or no' answer to the question. When philosophers borrow from scientists it all depends on who is borrowing what from whom and on the purpose for which the loan is used. We shall encounter further examples later. For the present, we must now consider what Aristotle thought scientists actually do (for, like many others, conceptions of what counts as good scientific practice can vary over time).

The parts of animals and the constitutions of states

The passage quoted above was drawn from *The Politics*, but it should give you a good idea of how *The History of Animals* is constructed. In the latter, Aristotle painstakingly categorises the way forms taken by parts of animals vary from species to species. The discussion opens, quite appropriately, with a discussion of the concept of 'part' itself; that is, with a distinction between different types of part. For example, Aristotle notes that, 'Of the parts of animals some are simple: to wit, all such as divide into parts uniform with themselves, as flesh into flesh' and that, 'others are composite, such as divide into parts not uniform with themselves, as, for instance, the hand does not divide into hands nor the face into faces' (*History of Animals*: 486a).[5] (Incidentally, the opening chapter of the *History* also contains a brief discussion of the distinction between *genera* and *species*. It was Aristotle who introduced this method of categorisation – and it is still used.)

The following passage is quite representative of the exhaustive and detailed account Aristotle goes on to provide.

Of swimming creatures that are destitute of feet, some have winglets or fins, as fishes: and of these some have four fins, two above on the back, two below on the belly, as the gilthead and the basse; some have two only, to wit, such as are exceedingly long and smooth, as the eel and the conger; some have none at all, as the muraena, but use the sea just as snakes use dry ground – and by the way, snakes swim in water in just the same way. Of the shark-kind some have no fins, such as those that are flat and long-tailed, as the ray and the sting-ray, but these fishes swim actually by the undulatory motion of their flat bodies; the fishing frog, however, has fins, and so likewise have all such fishes as have not their flat surfaces thinned off to a sharp edge.

Of those swimming creatures that appear to have feet, as is the case with the molluscs, these creatures swim by the aid of their feet and their fins as well, and they swim most rapidly backwards in the direction of the trunk, as is the case with the cuttle-fish or sepia and the calamary; and, by the way, neither of these latter can walk as the poulpe or octopus can.

(ibid.: 489b)

And so on and so forth. This discussion of locomotion in marine life is followed by an account of flight in different animals – insects, birds and so on – which is followed in its turn by an account of the differences between 'blooded' and 'non-blooded', 'oviparous' and 'viviparous', animals. Later still, comparative zoology is replaced with anatomy. 'To begin with', writes Aristotle when introducing these sections of his work, 'we must take into consideration the parts of Man' and a few lines later that 'The chief parts into which the body as a whole is subdivided, are the head, the neck, the trunk (extending from the neck to the privy parts), which is called the thorax, two arms and two legs' and a few lines later still that 'Of the parts of which the head is composed the hair-covered portion is called the "skull". The front portion of it is termed "bregma" or "sinciput", developed after birth – for it is the last of all the bones in the body to acquire solidity' and so on (ibid.: 491a). Later still, Aristotle notes that, 'taking size for size of animal, the largest brain, and the moistest, is that of man. Two membranes enclose it: the stronger one near the bone of the skull; the inner one, round the brain itself, is finer' (494b).

The History of Animals demonstrates Aristotle's extraordinary – wonderful – genius for observation and classification. And I have been quoting only from the first book of *The History*. There are nine in all. There are mistakes, of course, but the truly remarkable thing is just how much Aristotle got right.[6] No wonder Darwin was impressed.

Still, my subject is not Aristotle's comparative zoology but his treatment of politics. As the foregoing account of *The History of Animals* shows, it was Aristotle's belief that science proceeds by observation and categorisation. Hence the wealth of detail and the exhaustive lists. But the point is that he also believed that the same method applies equally to both zoology and politics. Sure enough, open *The Politics* at random and you are almost certain to find passages very similar to that section of the *History* in which he categorises different types of 'swimming creature'.

Here is an example. In it, Aristotle is categorising people by occupation and social class.

> There is on the one hand the people, on the other the notables, as we call them. Of each of these there are several kinds. For example, of the people one kind is engaged in agriculture, another in crafts, and yet another in commerce, in buying and selling. Another kind takes to the sea, and there they fight or trade or carry passengers or catch fish. (In many places the sections of the population engaged in one or other of these occupations are large: fishermen are numerous at Tarentum and Byzantium, traders at Aegina and Chios; at Athens many are engaged on triremes, at Tenedos in passenger traffic.) To these we may add the labouring class and those whose possessions are so small that they cannot have any time off, also those who are not of free birth on both sides, and any other similar kind of multitude. The distinguishing marks of the notables are wealth, good birth, virtue, education and the other things listed under the same heading.
>
> *(Pol.*: 1291b14)

So, rather as species of fish can be distinguished in terms of the number and position of their fins, so the 'city-states' or *poleis* of Greece can be distinguished in terms of the way they divide into socio-economic classes. (City-states were numerous and small, so Aristotle had a great deal of material on which to draw for his comparative study.)

And now for an absolutely crucial point. Just as science proceeds by categorising its objects of study according to the parts of which they are composed, so – according to Aristotle – parts themselves tend to be differentiated, one from another, in terms of their *function*. Fins or feet are for movement, eyes for seeing, and so on. 'Nature', says Aristotle, 'does nothing without some purpose' (*Pol.*: 1253a7). Every modern evolutionary biologist would concur – or almost. (Modern evolutionary biologists would insist that 'purpose' does not imply 'deliberate intention'.) Likewise, when it comes to the parts of states rather than animals, Aristotle tends to distinguish groups of individuals in terms of the specific functions they perform. Quite often they are categorised according to the specific skill they exercise. For example, farmers are distinguished from skilled artisans, traders and merchants, labourers and the military (see, for example, *Pol.*: 1290b38). Sometimes they are categorised more generally. For example, the slave is distinguished from the free man by his function as a mere tool for the latter.

If you pursue this line of thought you are likely to draw two implications. The first is that, just as people can be classified according to the functions they perform, so they can be *further* classified according to whether they perform that function well or badly. The second is that, since 'nature does nothing without some purpose', so that (for example) each social class has a function, it is most likely the case that 'man' the species has its own peculiar (or 'proper') function, something 'over and above' the 'particular functions' of particular individuals. Aristotle draws both implications in the following passage.

> If we take a flautist or a sculptor or any artist – or in general any class of men who have a specific function or activity – his goodness and proficiency is considered to lie in the performance of that function; and the same will be true of man, assuming that man has a function. But is it likely that whereas joiners and shoemakers have certain functions or activities, man as such has none, but has been left by nature a functionless being? Just as we can see that eye and hand and foot and every one of our members has some function, should we not assume that in like manner a human being has a function over and above these particular functions? What, then, can this possibly be? Clearly life is a thing shared also by plants, and we are looking for man's *proper* function.
>
> (*Ethics*: 1097b22)

The general direction of Aristotle's argument should be clear by now. For one thing, if a social class has a function just as a bodily organ has a function and – moreover – if each has a 'proper' function, doesn't this imply that the best state is the one in which each class performs its proper function as well as it can? For another, if even 'man', or the human being 'as such', has a function, doesn't it follow that the best constitution for a state is the one which best enables man 'as such' to fulfil his proper function? Well, Aristotle certainly draws both conclusions. But, before considering them, let us first take a closer look at his idea that the state is a natural phenomenon.

The political animal

One of Aristotle's best-known remarks occurs quite early on in *The Polit-ics*, in the course of a discussion of different kinds of 'association'. After describing how (he thinks) the village develops from the household, and the state from the village, he concludes that, 'while the state came about as a means of securing life itself, it continues in being to secure the *good* life'. Shortly after that, he adds, 'It follows that the state belongs to the class of objects which exist by nature, and [that] man is by nature a political animal' (*Pol.*: 1253a1). The point of this remark – or a *part* of its point – is to emphasise what he takes to be a feature of our biology. (Incidentally, as is usual, I have used the word 'man' here, although what Aristotle means is that *humans* are political animals. In fact, the Greek word of which 'man' is a translation – *anthropos* – is not gender specific.)[7] When Aristotle says that the state exists by nature and that we, also 'by nature', are political 'animals' he is not employing the expressions 'by nature' and 'political animal' as figures of speech. He means them quite literally. That is why you can find parallel remarks in *The History of Animals*; for example, when he defines 'social creatures' as creatures which 'have one common object in view' and then states that 'this property is not common to all creatures that are gregarious. Such social creatures are man, the bee, the wasp, the ant, and the crane' (*Animals*: 488a).

In such passages, Aristotle is trying, very carefully, to state how we differ from other species. On the one hand, as above, he distinguishes animals which are genuinely social – bees, wasps, ants and ourselves – from those which are merely 'gregarious'; that is, which swarm together in flocks, like birds, or in shoals, like fish. On the other, he takes pains to stress that the precise *character* of our social life is very different from that of ants, bees and the others. For example, in *The Politics*, he goes on to stress that, 'obviously man is a political animal in a sense in which a bee is not, or any other gregarious animal'. This is because nature 'has endowed man alone among the animals with the power of speech' which 'serves to indicate what is useful and what is harmful, and so also what is just and what is unjust', the real difference between man and other animals being that 'humans alone have a perception of good and evil, just and unjust, etc.' (*Pol.*: 1253a7).

This view merits at least three comments, the first being that if Aristotle means, quite simply, that humans are by nature social creatures then he is surely right. All the scientific evidence we now have supports it. We humans did not have to learn to be social – that is, to live as members of communities. We have been social creatures from the start, as were the earlier primates from whom we are directly descended. Studies of our nearest living relatives, the chimpanzees, only confirm this.[8] One way to highlight the distinctiveness of Aristotle's position is to contrast it with that taken by the eighteenth century philosopher, Jean-Jacques Rousseau. In his *Discourse on the Origins of Inequality*, Rousseau imagines our pre-historic ancestors to have been 'solitary, idle' and living, like animals, 'always close to danger' (Rousseau 1984: 86). According to Rousseau, it was only later that humans had 'sociability' thrust upon them. In the mid-eighteenth century, when he was writing, Rousseau's portrait of the 'noble savage' became fashionable and popular for a time. It was how Europeans liked to imagine the life of people indigenous to North America, which was, of course, still quite unknown and unexplored. But Rousseau was wrong about Native Americans, and he was wrong about our early ancestors too.

Related to this, and secondly, Aristotle's view that 'the state belongs to the class of objects which exist by nature' (*Pol.*: 1253a1) contrasts not just with views of human nature like Rousseau's, but with the view that the state is an artificial construct with a particular purpose. We have already encountered one version of the latter in Plato's work. As you will recall from the previous chapter, it is his view that a 'just' state is one in which everyone specialises by concentrating on doing what he or she is best at. The farmer concentrates on growing food, the builder on constructing houses, the shoemaker on making shoes, and so on. That way, everyone benefits from everyone else's skills. To depict the state, or 'community', as Plato does is, thus, to portray it as a useful device for helping us to satisfy our needs and wants more effectively. If you were to remove individuals from Plato's 'just' state then, for all he says to the contrary, they would remain more or less unchanged. It is just that they would find life much more inconvenient because the farmer would have to make his own shoes, for example, the builder grow his own food, and the shoemaker construct his own house. Contrast this with Aristotle's view that 'Anyone who by his nature and not simply by ill luck has no state is either too bad or too good, either subhuman or superhuman' (Pol.: 1253a1). For Aristotle there is more than mere inconvenience at stake. On his view, the stateless individual is scarcely recognisable as genuinely human.

Thirdly, to fully understand Aristotle's view that we are political animals it is important to realise that 'the state' of his time was nothing like the state of our own. The state with which we are most familiar is the 'nation-state' with a large population, the latter being tens of millions in the cases of, say, Britain or France and hundreds of millions in the case of a 'superstate' such as the USA. By contrast, the Greek *polis* (or 'city-state') was minute. Only three *poleis* ever had populations of more than 20,000 citizens. These were Athens itself, Syracuse, and Acragas in Sicily. So, even in these cases, if you assume that roughly 10 per cent of the population were citizens, that makes a population of 100,000. Most *poleis* were much smaller, and you can see just how small they must have been if you consider some of the strictures Aristotle puts on size. For example, he suggests that a state is becoming too large once a town crier with 'the voice of a stentor' is needed to capture everyone's attention, and he thinks that, if the state is to fulfil its proper function, 'it is necessary that the citizens should know each other and know what kind of people they are' (Pol.: 1326b11). Some Greek *poleis* are known to us only because they are referred to by Aristotle himself, and some of these must have been tiny. (Reading the *Politics* is like time-travel. You glimpse a world which has long since disappeared.)

Not only did the Greek *polis* differ in size from the modern nation-state, it was differently laid out and differently administered. Typically, the *polis* would consist of a city – Sparta, Athens, Syracuse – and its outlying area. The city would be a cultural and administrative centre. There would be a market. Where the *polis* was a democracy, it would be the place where the assembly met. As for the outlying area, *poleis* could vary greatly. At one extreme, Sparta possessed 3,200 square miles of territory – enormous by Greek standards. At the other, the small island of Ceos was divided into four *poleis*. In his book, *The Greeks*, H.D.F. Kitto points out that 'It had therefore four armies, four governments, possibly four different calendars,

and, it may be, four different currencies and systems of meas
this is less likely' (Kitto 1951: 66). (The area of Ceos is 6¹
that is 160 square kilometres.) Of course, there would hav
resembling the modern nation-state we call 'Greece'. WI
Greek would be the fact that you shared a language, a culture anu a ..
with other Greeks.

It transpires, then, that when Aristotle describes us as political animals,
he doesn't just mean that we are social creatures by nature. He means that
our natural home, the setting in which we are most likely to flourish, is a
particular type of association, the *polis*. To understand why he should say
that, we have to consider his ethics, and – most especially – his account of
virtue.

The city, virtue and happiness

An isolated piece in a game of draughts

There is a sentence in *The Politics* in which Aristotle compares the situation of a person with no city, or state, to that of 'an isolated piece in a
game of draughts'. It occurs shortly after his remark that the state exists by
nature and that man is by nature a political animal. Having said that,
Aristotle continues as follows:

> Anyone who by his nature and not simply by ill luck has no state is
> either too bad or too good, either subhuman or superhuman – he is
> like the war-mad man condemned in Homer's words as 'having no
> family, no law, no home'; for he who is such by nature is mad on war:
> he is a non-co-operator like an isolated piece in a game of draughts
> (*Pol.*: 1253a1)

What are we to make of this analogy? To appreciate Aristotle's point, I
suggest that you imagine a chequered board on which there is only one
piece, that is, a piece which is not only 'isolated', as in Aristotle's example,
but solitary. In that situation, the conditions required if the piece is genuinely to count as a 'piece in a game' would be absent. To count as such,
there would have to be other pieces present, and it would have to stand in
certain relationships to the other pieces. More than that, the rules which
define the game, and the piece's role in it, could not apply. In fact, you
could say that the solitary piece has lost its very identity, for what makes a
bit of wood or plastic a piece in a game is less a question of its having a
certain colour or shape – of its being round like a draughts-piece or horse-
shaped like the knight in chess – than it is a question of its having a rule-
defined role. Of course, that is why it can make perfect sense to say 'Let the
salt-cellar be the king, the pepper-pot the queen, and these tap-washers
pawns'. If it is a piece's proper and, in that sense, 'natural' place to be

deployed in a game – that is to be moved around a board in ways which are conditioned by its rule-governed relationship to the other pieces on the board – then it follows that the situation of the solitary piece is both wrong and, in the same sense, 'unnatural'.

In Aristotle's analogy, the piece is not entirely solitary, but it has become isolated. It has been cut off from its fellows and it can play no further part in the game. But, either way, there is the same moral to draw, namely that, since 'man is by nature a political animal' – that is, since a person can only function in the right and natural way in the context of a state – then to find yourself without a city 'by ill luck' is to have suffered a great misfortune, a tragedy even. By the same token, anyone who is without a city 'by nature' – who experiences no need for a city – really would be, as Aristotle says, 'subhuman or superhuman', a beast or a god.

The analogy is powerful. Even so, it is only an analogy. To grasp Aristotle's point, we need to put analogy aside and ask *exactly what* it is we are supposed to lose through becoming stateless. To put it roughly, Aristotle believes that it is only within the context of a state that the citizen can find opportunities for the exercise of *virtue*. On this view, what you lose is, therefore, the opportunity to live well. Without the state, you cannot develop and flourish in the manner appropriate to a human. (Likewise, the isolated piece cannot move in the appropriate ways.) Happiness also has a role to play here. That is because Aristotle thinks that happiness consists in the exercise of virtue – if you like, that happiness *is* the exercise of virtue. If he is right, it follows that it is only within the context of a state – more accurately a *polis* – that anyone has a chance of finding happiness. At one point, he summarises his position as follows: 'The state is an association of persons whose aim is the best life possible' (*Pol.*: 1328a33).

Virtue

At this stage, I am sure that many readers will be wanting to raise objections to Aristotle. (Haven't explorers, lost in the frozen Antarctic wastes, demonstrated patience, courage, fortitude and self-sacrifice? Well, of course they have, so why suppose that virtue can only be exercised in the context of a state? As for the alleged relation between virtue and happiness, don't we all know from experience that bad behaviour can sometimes be fun?) But, before dealing with difficulties, let me first try to put the case *for* Aristotle as forcefully as I can.

To start with, here is a list of fairly obvious points, each of which relates to the concept of virtue in one way or another: (i) Virtue, or virtuousness, can be a property of an individual action. An action can be courageous, for example, or it can manifest patience, modesty, generosity, tact, and so on for many other virtues. (ii) People, too, can be virtuous – and not just single actions. There is a relationship between these first two points, namely that (iii) the people we call virtuous are those who tend – as a rule and on the whole – to do virtuous things; that is, the people we describe as courageous are those who tend to act courageously, the ones we describe as generous are those who tend to act generously, etc. Of course, even people who are not very virtuous – even those who are not at all virtuous – can do virtuous things on occasion, but (iv) it's a fair assumption that virtuous people find it much easier to do virtuous things than non-virtuous people do. When the latter do virtuous things they find it difficult; they have to struggle.

Now, if all that is as obvious as I think, the fact is all well and good because it shows how hard it is to quarrel with the way Aristotle describes virtue in the *Nicomachean Ethics*. According to Aristotle, a virtue is a *disposition* to act in certain ways and not others. You can also see why he thinks of a virtue as something that you have to develop by practising it; that is, as a skill, like harp-playing, building or any other craft. These are things you can do well or badly, and the person who has developed a given skill is the one who can practise it with ease. On Aristotle's view, the person who lives well is, thus, the person who has developed the skill (or skills) of acting virtuously.

One well-known feature of the *Nicomachean Ethics* is, thus, the 'Table of Virtues and Vices', in which Aristotle lists the appropriate virtue for each 'sphere of action or feeling', together with that virtue's corresponding vices. For example, we are told that courage is the virtue appropriate to the sphere of 'fear and confidence', that an excess of the disposition we call courageous is 'rashness' (or foolhardiness) and that a deficiency of the same disposition is cowardice. The virtue is thus presented as the 'mean' or mid-point between two vices, so this is an illustration of Aristotle's famous 'doctrine of the mean'. Similarly, when it comes to money, 'liberality' is portrayed as the mean between 'prodigality' (an excess of the same type of behaviour) and illiberality or meanness (the corresponding deficiency); the virtue of modesty is portrayed as the mean between shame and shamelessness, and so on. As the 'Table of Virtues and Vices' illustrates, so far as Aristotle is concerned, acting virtuously is rather like negotiating an obstacle course. It is like steering a wobbly bicycle between strategically placed traffic cones; and that is just what you would expect really, given that the English word 'virtue' is a crude near-equivalent for the Greek *aretē*. (As we saw in the last chapter, *aretē* is somewhat closer in meaning to 'skill' and 'function'.)

Aristotle and contemporary 'virtue ethics'

As it happens, there are quite a few philosophers writing at present who believe that modern moral philosophy has got it all wrong and that the only possible remedy is a revival of Aristotle's approach. So, in order to highlight the strengths of Aristotle's account, let me now give a brief outline of some of their main arguments. According to 'neo-Aristotelian' proponents of 'virtue ethics', then, modern moral philosophy's basic mistake is to portray morality as a matter of *rule-following*. (In fact, the mistake in question – if it is one – is supposed to have been made by pretty well every moral philosopher since Immanuel Kant, whose *Groundwork of the Metaphysic of Morals* was first published in 1785. Fortunately, it would be irrelevant to dwell on that claim here (cf. Kant 1948).)

To illustrate their argument, let us take simple utilitarianism as a case in point. Simple utilitarianism states that 'the greatest good is the greatest happiness of the greatest number'. If this is right then, clearly, doing the right thing is a question of following a rule, namely, 'When faced with a choice between two or more courses of action, always choose the alternative which – in your opinion – is most likely to contribute to the greatest happiness.' (Actually, it would be a very crude utilitarianism which left it at that, but it will do for our purposes.) Against this 'rule-following' account, the objection from virtue ethics points out that it misrepresents the way people really think about morality. To see how, imagine that some person is on the point of choosing a career. Call this person P. P has the makings of a competent administrator, and has the opportunity to take a low paid job in the head office of a charity. But suppose that P is also a talented artist. If he were to take the job, P would fail to develop further as a painter, although he would also be certain to increase the sum of human happiness. On the other hand, even if P were to succeed as an artist – having declined the opportunity – only a specialised minority would appreciate P's work, because it is so avant garde. What should P do? According to simple utilitarianism the answer is obvious. It follows directly from the greatest happiness rule that P should take the job. According to the objection this misrepresents moral thinking, because it could be that P has a *calling*, and that taking the job is absolutely the wrong thing for P to do. In this case, *virtue* enters the picture because you could say that P's *integrity* requires that P concentrate on painting.[9] Moreover, what goes for P might not go for someone else who is, in many respects quite similarly placed. Simple utilitarianism entails that it must, but this is wrong – or so the objection runs. For example, suppose that you refuse to enter a burning building, at great risk to your own life, in order to save those inside. If you succeeded in saving them, you would increase the sum of human happiness. You would also be praised as a hero. However, if the risk is great, no one would blame you for refusing. Simple utilitarianism entails that everyone in your situation would be equally blameless. But this is wrong because if you are a trained firefighter – even an off-duty firefighter – you would (morally) have to enter the building. We have different moral expectations of trained firefighters. We expect them to exercise the *virtues* appropriate to firefighters. So it can be objected that simple utilitarianism misrepresents real moral thinking here too. In fact, it is arguable that utilitarianism gets things completely back-to-front because – in reality – we more often blame people for following, rather than ignoring, rules such as the greatest happiness rule. As one neo-Aristotelian writer, Susan Wolf, has put it, 'I don't know whether there are any moral saints. But if there are, I am glad that neither I nor those about whom I care most are among them' (Wolf 1982: 419). In other words a 'moral saint' – someone who always tried to do the morally right thing (as defined by utilitarianism or some other rule-following ethic) – would just be a sanctimonious prig.

Aristotelian moral philosophy, which portrays moral behaviour as the exercise of virtues, avoids such objections – or so the argument goes. Now, I am sure that readers will have realised that there is plenty to be said against the arguments I have just outlined, and quite a lot more to be said in favour of them. Still, I think I have made the point that Aristotelian ethics is worth taking seriously – that it is more than an anachronism – and that is all I set out to do here. That said, it is with his account of *happiness* that Aristotle's moral philosophy really comes into its own.

Happiness

In fact, the Greek word is *eudaimonia*. This is normally rendered as 'happiness' in English, although the translation is not quite exact. Still, having issued that warning I'll stick to 'happiness' anyway, if only because it is less awkward.

As with his account of virtue, so a good way to highlight the merits of Aristotle's account of happiness (as I shall continue to call it) is to contrast it with the account given by simple utilitarianism. As we have seen, the latter is founded on the principle of utility – the principle according to which 'the greatest good is the greatest happiness of the greatest number' – and this is a *distributive* principle. By this, I mean that it treats happiness as something which can be divided between people, rather as cake or money can be divided. You could say that it treats happiness as if it were kind of *stuff*. Examples of parallel principles are 'So divide the cake that the greatest number of people get the greatest possible amount of cake', or 'So divide the money that the greatest number of people get the greatest possible amount of money'. Unlike these, the principle of utility instructs us so to divide happiness that the greatest number of people get the greatest possible amount of happiness. In fact, you could have a parallel principle for pretty well anything divisible – not just cake or money but (more plausibly) freedom or rights. It follows that utilitarianism must face the following question: Why make *happiness* the value on which your ethical system is founded, and not some other value?

One very plausible answer to this is that people really do treat happiness as more fundamental than other values. Some people want cake and some don't. Some desire great wealth, and others lack expensive tastes – and so on for many other things – but *everyone* desires happiness. Moreover, the reason why people want cake, money or other things is their belief that cake/money/those other things will make them happy. It seems that everyone desires happiness *for itself*, and not because it is productive of something further. (You can want cake because it makes you happy, but can you want happiness because it brings you cake?) In fact, the last point is made by Aristotle himself. Of 'happiness', he says, 'we always choose it for itself and never for any other reason' (*Ethics*: 1097a15-b2).[10] Utilitarians would agree.

So, what is it about happiness which makes it so desirable to everyone? It is here that the utilitarians differ, for the latter philosophers tend to portray happiness as a *state of mind*, as if it were a kind of sensation or a sort of euphoria. So far as they are concerned, it is the state of mind everyone desires to be in. For simple utilitarianism, then, 'maximising happiness' means maximising the number of people who are experiencing that state of mind, the amount of time during which they experience it and – assuming that it can be experienced more or less intensely – maximising the degree of intensity with which they experience it. (Perhaps I should stress once again that I am dealing with a very simple form of utilitarianism here. However, Jeremy Bentham, the 'classical' nineteenth century utilitarian, comes quite close to it (see Bentham 2000b, especially chapter 4).)

In the hands of the right utilitarian philosopher, this type of view can be put quite persuasively. However, there is a big problem which comes with it, and to see what it is note – first – that a state of mind can be drug-induced. For example, you can induce torpor or euphoria in someone by giving them the right sort of pill. It follows that, if happiness were literally a state of mind – in just the same way that torpor and euphoria are states of mind – it ought to be possible, similarly, to devise a 'happy pill' made from the drug which induces the state of mind called 'happiness'. Now try the following thought experiment. Suppose that someone were to present you with a bottle of happy pills and that this person were to say 'Swallow these pills and you will be extremely, incredibly happy, happier than you have ever been, or than you could ever be again, once the effect of the pills has worn off. Then, once the effect starts to wear off, you will drop dead instantaneously and painlessly, without even realising it.'

Would you take the pills? (Of course, you also have to suppose that there is no one who will be made unhappy by your death, at least not to an extent which would counterbalance the extreme happiness you would experience if you took the pills. In short, you have to suppose that 'other things are equal'.) My point is that, if simple utilitarianism's account of happiness were correct, the only rational thing to do would be to swallow the pills. Given that everyone desires happiness, everyone who was offered a pill would take it and, if there were enough pills to go round, the human race would soon be wiped out. However, I am pretty sure that most of us would *not* choose this option. (Certainly, when I put this example to others they tend to say that they wouldn't, although they are often at a loss to explain why.) If I'm right, this demonstrates the falsity of simple utilitarianism. Happiness is not something you can achieve just by taking a lot of pills. Therefore, it is not a state of mind (at least, not in the way that euphoria is).

Aristotle's view is very different from the utilitarian's, and it raises a different question. That question is: When you are dying, and you look back over the course your life has taken, what judgement will you form? The question arises because, for Aristotle, happiness (or, rather, *eudaimonia*) is not a matter of being in any sort of state of mind. It is a matter of 'living well or doing well' (*Ethics*: 1095a7). On this view, asking 'Was I happy?' is not at all like asking, 'How did I feel?' It is asking, 'How did my life go?' For Aristotle, then, 'happiness' is an *evaluative* term. It is *the concept in terms of which you assess the course of a life*. Once you think of it that way, some of the things Aristotle says – things which can seem strange when you first encounter his work – fall into place. For example, it is obvious that your life could go badly, not through any fault of your own, but through simple bad luck or misfortune. Therefore, it is quite natural that Aristotle should think that 'a man is scarcely happy if he is very ugly to look at, of low birth' or that a person is 'presumably even less so if he has children or friends who are quite worthless, or if he had good ones who are now dead' (*Ethics*: 1099b20). (Contrast this with simple utilitarianism, which implies that even ugly, friendless, people can be happy, provided they take the right pills.) Again, in judging the course your life has taken, it will be important to decide whether you have lived rightly. There is even a short section of the *Nicomachean Ethics* in which Aristotle raises the question of whether only the dead can be truly happy (*Ethics*: 1100a10ff). This will strike you as an absurd question if you think like a utilitarian and suppose that happiness is a state of mind. (The dead cannot be conscious.) It is not so absurd if you think like an Aristotelian, for whom looking back over the course of a life must be a key activity.

I think that Aristotle gives a far better account of the way 'happiness' is actually used than the utilitarians do, and that he gives a far better explanation of why 'happiness is something we always choose for itself and never for any other reason' (*Ethics*: 1097a15-b2). More than that, 'When you look back, how will you judge your life to have gone?' strikes me as a 'real' question. I mean that it is one most of us will find ourselves asking, irrespective of its relation to any philosophical theory. It is, therefore, quite unlike, 'would you take the happy pills?', which is an artificial 'philosopher's example'. This is also a reason for preferring Aristotle's account.

But is he right? Well, there are contemporary neo-Aristotelians who certainly think that he should be taken very seriously. For example, one such, Alasdair MacIntyre, has compared the 'unity of an individual life' with 'the unity of a narrative', so that asking 'What is the good for me?' is asking, 'how I might live out that unity and bring it to completion' (MacIntyre 1981: 218–19). He adds,

51

The unity of a human life is the unity of a narrative quest. Quests sometimes fail, are frustrated, abandoned or dissipated into distractions; and human lives may in all these ways also fail. But the only criteria for success or failure in a human life as a whole are the criteria of success or failure in a narrated or to-be-narrated quest . . .

(ibid.)

This is not Aristotle's theory precisely, but it is a contemporary ethical theory which is very Aristotelian in spirit.

An association whose aim is the best life possible

So where does this leave Aristotle's claim that 'The state is an association of persons whose aim is the best life possible' (*Pol.*: 1328a21)? In English, this is usually rendered as the claim that it is only within the context of a 'state' that 'virtue' can be exercised and 'happiness' consequently achieved. But this is a puzzling claim which begs some fairly evident questions. (Why can't lonely explorers, out in the Antarctic, demonstrate virtue? Why can't bad behaviour make you happy?) Earlier, I postponed dealing with these in order to emphasise the strengths of Aristotle's moral philosophy. Let us now return to them. Trying to make sense of Aristotle's claim is, in any case, a good way to bring this chapter to a close, as it will involve drawing some threads together.

Polis, aretē, eudaimonia

For a start, recall that 'state', 'virtue' and 'happiness' are inexact translations of Greek words. What Aristotle really says is that it is only within the *polis* that a person can demonstrate *aretē* and so achieve *eudaimonia*. By way of summary, let us take each word in turn.

First: *polis* refers to the small Greek city-state. Second: the word *aretē* is more functional in its connotation than 'virtue'. Anything which performs its function well has *aretē*, which means that an inanimate object – a tool such as an axe – can, literally, demonstrate *aretē* if it is sharp, easy to handle, and so on. (True, it is acceptable English to speak of an axe's 'virtues', but this is a metaphorical usage. When we speak of a person's virtues, we do not use 'virtue' with quite the same functional sense.) We have already seen the notion of *aretē* at work in Plato's idea that a 'just' state is one in which everyone concentrates on what he or she is best at – in other words, a state in which everyone performs the function to which they are best adapted. And third: The meaning of *eudaimonia* is also related to function, unlike that of 'happiness' which is not. (In line with this, *The Concise Routledge Encyclopaedia of Philosophy* defines *eudaimonia* as 'the state of having an objectively desirable life, universally agreed by ancient philosophical theory and popular thought to be the supreme human good'. The *Encyclopaedia* adds that 'This objective character distinguishes it from the modern concept of happiness: a subjectively satisfactory life' (Taylor 2000). To have lived *eudaimonically* is, thus, to have lived well, and – as noted a moment ago – it would be natural for the person who valued *eudaimonia* to ask, 'How has my life gone so far?' By contrast, that is not the question which will automatically arise for a modern happiness-valuer, such as a utilitarian.

Substitute the Greek terms for the English, and Aristotle's claim turns out to resemble the claim that a spark-plug can only function properly when it is set within an internal combustion engine, or that a musician whose skill lies in accompanying others – a bass-player, for example – can only demonstrate his or her talents to the full when working as a member of a band. In the terms of Aristotle's own analogy, it is like saying that a draughts-piece can only perform the function for which it has been designed when it is actively deployed in a game. How else could the spark-plug, the musician, the draughts-piece, perform their 'proper' functions and so demonstrate their appropriate virtues? Likewise, how else could a person perform his or her 'proper' function without a *polis* within which to operate? Substitute *polis, aretē* and *eudaimonia*, for 'city', 'virtue' and 'happiness', and Aristotle's claim becomes almost self-explanatory.

'Proper' function and social function

That should help explain Aristotle's conception of the relationship between the state, virtue and happiness. But is he right? The answer is that he would be right, only if certain assumptions were correct. One is that just as a tool has a 'proper' function – a screwdriver to insert or to remove screws, a saw to cut wood, and so on – so each person has a proper function, one for which he or she is best fitted. Another is that, for each person, that person's proper function is to fulfil a given social role. You can see these assumptions at work in the following passages. They are drawn from early chapters of *The Politics* in which Aristotle attempts to justify slavery.

> [Again] in any special skill the availability of the proper tools will be essential for the performance of the task; and the household-manager must have his likewise. Tools may be animate as well as inanimate; for instance, a ship's captain uses a lifeless rudder, but a living man for watch; for a servant is, from the point of view of his craft, categorised as one of its tools. So any piece of property can be regarded as a tool enabling a man to live, and his property is an assemblage of such tools; and like any other servant is a tool in charge of other tools.
>
> (*Pol.*: 1253b23)

And,

> those whose condition is such that their function is the use of their bodies and nothing better can be expected of them, those, I say, are slaves by nature. It is better for them, just as in the cases mentioned, to be ruled thus [i.e. by a master]. For the 'slave by nature' is he that can and therefore does belong to another, and he that participates in reason so far as to recognise it but not so as to possess it (whereas the other animals obey not reason but emotions). The use made of slaves hardly differs at all from that of tame animals: they both help with their bodies to supply our essential needs.
>
> (ibid.: 1254b16)

In short, the proper function of the 'natural slave' is to serve as the free man's tool. And women are also compared with tools, rather as slaves are. Aristotle writes that 'Nature has distinguished between female and slave: she recognises different functions and lavishly provides different tools' (*Pol.*: 1252a34) and, later, that 'as between male and female the former is by nature superior and ruler, the latter inferior and subject' (ibid.: 1254b2). As for the 'lower orders' generally, there is no escaping the fact that Aristotle takes an aristocrat's elitist view of the social order. Even when he argues for the superiority of democracy over oligarchy, it is only because he thinks that the former is the best decision procedure for the ruling group of citizens to adopt. In the end, his argument for the *polis* turns out to be the argument that it is the only environment in which a privileged elite can find the leisure and the opportunity to live the good life – if you like, that it is the only soil in which the flower of the citizenry can truly flourish. That is why he insists, for example, that 'the citizens must not live a mechanical or commercial life' as 'such a life is not noble, and it militates against virtue' (*Pol.*: 1328b33). Also, it explains why, in the *Ethics*, he should define 'the happy man' as 'one who is active in accordance with complete virtue, and *who is adequately furnished with external goods*, and that not for some unspecified period but throughout a complete life' (*Ethics*: 1101a20) (my italics). In other words, to be happy you need (at least some) wealth.

Science, virtue and social hierarchy

It is clear that Aristotle was no believer in equality or in freedom for all. Some readers will think this forgivable. Why expect modern 'political correctness' in a philosopher who lived so long ago? Others will be less forgiving. (To be fair, perhaps I should add that in ancient Greece, the slave was, typically, a member of the household – a farm labourer for example. The system under which slaves worked in huge gangs and in dreadful conditions, in mines or on plantations – as in Rome or the pre-Civil War USA – was a horror yet to come.) Still, this is meant to be an introduction to philosophy, so whatever your reaction to Aristotle's conclusions may be, what I would really like you to appreciate is the relationship between these conclusions and the underlying philosophical positions he takes.

That said, let me now summarise the basic features of Aristotle's philosophy as I have outlined it up to this point. So far, I have concentrated on two major features of Aristotle's work, his approach to science and his account of virtue. As I have pointed out, it is the conception of *function* by which these are united. Thus, it is Aristotle's view that science proceeds by analysing its subject matter into parts, and in classifying those parts according to their function. As for virtue, Aristotle believes that virtue consists in performing your social function well.

These philosophical views condition and reinforce Aristotle's attitude to social hierarchy. To see how this happens in the case of the former, take a passage from *The History of Animals*; for example, take the passage in which Aristotle writes of fish that 'of these some have four fins, two above on the back, two below on the belly, as the gilthead and the basse; some have two only, to wit, such as are exceedingly long and smooth, as the eel and the conger' and that 'some have none at all, as the muraena, but use the sea just as snakes use dry ground' (*Animals*: 489b). Now compare it with the following passage from *The Politics*. In it Aristotle discusses the difference between free men and slaves.

> [For] the 'slave by nature' is he that can and therefore does belong to another, and he that participates in reason so far as to recognise it but not so as to possess it (whereas the other animals obey not reason but emotions). The use made of slaves hardly differs at all from that of tame animals: they both help with their bodies to supply our essential needs. It is, then, nature's purpose to make the bodies of free men to differ from those of slaves, the latter strong enough to be used for necessary tasks, the former erect and useless for that kind of work, but well suited for the life of a citizen of a state, a life which is in turn divided between the requirements of war and peace.
>
> (*Pol.*: 1254b16)

Just as some fish have four fins and some only two, so – Aristotle notes – slaves are less adept in their use of reason than are free men and, more than that, *even their bodies* are different.

What are we to make of this? Well, for a start, I think we can take it that Aristotle's description of what he observed was accurate. Out of slaves and free men, we can be pretty sure that slaves would have been less rational and articulate, and that, for each slave, that slave's physical development would have reflected the nature of the particular menial task in which he or she was primarily engaged. (Slaves who spent their lives tending crops would be stooped, those whose task it was to carry great weights would be very strong and so on.) However, and to put it mildly, modern readers will be unwilling to accept the explanation Aristotle gives. This is that it was 'nature's purpose' to produce physically different types of people, just as it was nature's purpose to produce different species of animal. Modern readers will want to insist that there were, undoubtedly, social factors which played a major role in the explanation of the physical differences. If slaves were less good at reasoning, that must have been the result of poorer education. If they were stronger, that can only have been the result of having to do more physically demanding work. To a modern reader, that must seem obvious. But it evidently wasn't obvious, even to someone as intellectually gifted as Aristotle.

How come? As the passage illustrates, the trouble with proceeding descriptively – that is by simply observing and recording – is that it gives you no way of differentiating something's essential components from its less essential features; for example, between components which perform a genuine function and features which just happen to be present at the time you are looking. Now if you are doing marine biology – at least, if you are trying to categorise fish and other marine species by *species* and *genus* – this may not matter too much. Where some fish have four fins and some only two, you can classify the fish accordingly. It could be that the difference in the number of fins reflects a genuine difference in their function, or it could be purely accidental, like the difference in colour between tabby and ginger cats. For Aristotle's purposes it wouldn't really have mattered. (Of course, you can *assume* that 'nature does nothing without a purpose' – you can take it as axiomatic – in which case you will think that even the specific colour of a cat's coat will be functional for the cat, but you will have no way of really knowing.) The reason why it wouldn't have mattered is that species evolve so slowly that from an observer's point of view – even from the point of view of generation upon generation of observers – they might as well not change at all. Aristotle lived in pre-Darwinian times, of course, but even if the theory of evolution had occurred to him[11] it would not have affected the conclusions he draws in *The History of Animals*, because all he was trying to do there was classify animals in terms of their observable characteristics. However, and by contrast, when the same technique is applied to social and political institutions, all this matters a great deal. It isn't just that political forms change far more rapidly than zoological forms do. The absence of a criterion for distinguishing the essential from the inessential – the genuinely functional from the purely accidental – means that you risk justifying relatively temporary features, specific to some particular political form, as somehow 'natural' and right. That is how Aristotle comes to justify slavery.

So, this is a good example of how a method which serves perfectly well in the scientific study of natural phenomena can let you down when you are studying political institutions. Moreover, Aristotle's perception of the way things were would have been reinforced by that fact that, for every *polis* described in *The Politics*, the class structure is similar. In each, there is a (male) group within which decisions are taken – either democratically, by vote or lot, or by oligarchic command. There is a class of women within which there are various gradations – educated *hetairai* or courtesans, the wives who manage the household, female domestic servants, slaves, and so on. Members of either sex could be householders (though with duties divided according to sex), servants, or slaves. In short, there may have been great differences between *poleis* in the way they were organised, in their constitutions, but in other ways they weren't as different as all that.

Turning, now, from Aristotle's scientific method to his account of virtue, Aristotle was apparently blind to a difficulty which must seem glaring to any modern reader. This is the difficulty of deciding *what* qualities or dispositions count as virtues. Put it this way: If you were to make a list of virtues, on what basis would you make your selection? Would you include courage and patience? If so, why? Would you include cunning, say, or meekness? (What, if anything, would you count as 'womanly virtues'? It's pretty clear that, if you are a social conservative, your answer will be different from the one you would give if you were a radical feminist.) This is a difficult question, but – my point – it is far easier to compile lists of virtues where there is a social hierarchy such that people are born to certain positions, to fulfil certain roles, and where, as a result, certain things are expected of them. For example, in a world where some men are members of an hereditary caste of warrior nobles, such men will be expected to demonstrate courage and physical strength. Even callousness could be a virtue in members of this caste. Again, where it is a noblewoman's unquestioned role to manage the household and the estate, patience and domestic competence will be considered virtues in a noblewoman. Likewise, in a world where people are born to be slaves, there will be virtues appropriate to a slave. (Aristotle mentions obedience and having a strong body.)

Aristotle's blindness to the difficulty in question is – I think – underpinned by the relative stability of the social hierarchy throughout the period during which he lived. His world was much more like the one I have just described. We do not live in a world like that. We do not consider the sons of soldiers or the daughters of housewives to be little soldiers or housewives, poised to fulfil their given roles, well or badly. When we try to compile lists of virtues we try to decide what we would count as virtues in *a person as such*, not what to count as a virtue in someone who happens to hold a given position. But, by contrast with our own, in Aristotle's world people did not just 'happen to' hold their social positions. It was more rigidly structured, and there would, therefore, have been a relationship of mutual reinforcement between Aristotle's account of virtue and his perception of the social order within which he lived and moved. Just as the former supplied a rationale for the latter, so his perception of the latter can only have reinforced the idea that morality is to be accounted for primarily in terms of virtue.

Aristotle's legacy

Here is an analogy: Suppose that you are looking through an album of old photographs; photographs taken in – say – the early years of the last century. Certain differences between the people in the photos will be immediately apparent. Some will be women, of course, and others men, but I don't mean just that. Class differences will be obvious too. You will recognise that the men wearing cloth caps and boots are workers, and that the ones with top hats are upper-middle or upper class. (If it is an English album) you will know that those men in bowler hats disembarking from the train are middle class office workers. Now suppose that you can climb into a time machine and travel back to the year in which the photographs were taken. You would now become aware of yet more differences. People would speak differently, both from yourself and from each other. They would have different accents and mannerisms. Perhaps they would smell a little different, and, even as a casual observer, it is likely that you would notice some of the physical differences between them, differences resulting from more fundamental differences in diet, accommodation and working conditions.

And now suppose – further – that you can climb back into your time machine and travel all the way back to the Greece of Aristotle's time. It was a time when class divisions were far less fluid, and when differences between members of different classes would have been even more striking. Of course, *you* will explain these differences as the effects of social factors which can vary as history progresses. But then you will have a privileged perspective, for you will have travelled back there from the twenty-first century, and you will know that things can change. This shouldn't lead you to underestimate how easy it must have been for someone like Aristotle, rooted in the period as he was, to treat them as permanent natural features.

But if that is a graphic way with which to summarise the drawbacks of Aristotle's method, we shouldn't be misled into treating his contribution to political thought dismissively. On the contrary, Aristotle's influence has been so profound that there can be no simple way of summing it up, although it should be clear that any attempt to do so would have to mention at least the following. First of all, just as Aristotle single-handedly invented the science of comparative zoology, so he invented the science of comparative politics. (For Aristotle, both were aspects of the same enterprise.) Secondly, it was Aristotle who first introduced the (profoundly influential) idea that the method scientists used to study natural phenomena can also be applied in the field of politics. Thirdly, there are elements of Aristotle's moral philosophy – his account of virtue and its relation to happiness – which continue to demand serious consideration. Fourthly, with his account of the relationship between the state and the individual, Aristotle introduced an important theme into political philosophy. Unlike Plato, who tends to treat the state as an instrument for the satisfaction of individual ends, Aristotle contends that there is an organic relationship between the state and the individual. The subsequent history of both conceptions is long and chequered.

As for Aristotle himself, the story of his life is laden with ironies. There is the irony that the philosopher who celebrated the life of the citizen, the life of full participation in the affairs of the *polis*, should have spent his own life as a non-citizen outsider, a *metic*. More than that, he was twice compelled to leave Athens by hostile, anti-Macedonian feeling, once in 347 and again in 325. (In the interim, Aristotle had established the Lyceum, an institution to rival Plato's Academy.) On the great chequerboard of Greece, it seems that Aristotle was, himself, something of an isolated piece. There is another irony too. Between 343/2 and 340, Aristotle had served as tutor to the son of Philip, the Macedonian king. (There is no evidence that Aristotle managed to teach his pupil much. So far as Philip was concerned, it seems that Aristotle was there mainly as a status symbol.) After Philip's death, the son grew up to become Alexander the Great, the ruthless general whose empire stretched throughout the known world, into Persia and southwards into Syria and Egypt, eastwards across the Himalayas, and into northern India. The destruction of the world Aristotle celebrated – the world he portrayed as the most hospitable natural environment for naturally political creatures – had begun at the hands of his own pupil. When Aristotle died in 322 BC, it would not be long before that world, the world of the independent *polis*, had vanished from the face of the earth.

4

—·◦☉◦·—

What happened next?

It is usual for histories of political thought to move quite directly from Greek times to the sixteenth or even the seventeenth century. At most, what you get is a sideways glance at what happened in the interim. This means that a period of getting on for two thousand years is more or less ignored. As this book is an introduction to the subject – not a work which claims to be breaking new ground – it is no exception to the rule. Even so, I realise that blindly following custom is not enough and that readers unfamiliar with the history of political philosophy are owed some sort of explanation here. Such readers will be wondering why it should be so usual to leave such a long gap. Can it really be true that nothing happened in the intervening period? Was there really no one with interesting things to say?

These questions can be answered – though partially – with the help of the 'conversation' analogy I drew in my introductory chapter. Interesting philosophers do not turn up, over time, at regularly spaced intervals, any more than interesting guests arriving at a party do. Sometimes the most interesting guests arrive quite late, and all in a group. Since our purpose is to understand arguments and ideas – to hear what the guests have to say for themselves – we have to concentrate on the contributions they make to the discussion; not on the sequence of events as they unfold, one after the other, over time.

That answer is fair enough, but only so far as it goes. It is partial and inadequate because it only raises the further question of *why* it should have taken so long for anyone interesting to arrive. (After all, two thousand years is no mean period.) I wouldn't blame readers for being puzzled by this. Perhaps some will be suspecting me of selectivity and bias. Could it be that the 'interesting' philosophers I am referring to are no more than the philosophers I happen to find interesting? Or, to take an objection which is quite often raised, could it be that I am adopting a peculiarly 'Western' cultural perspective and ignoring developments which took place elsewhere?

I think not. The truth is that, within political philosophy, there were no major developments throughout the period in question. Of course, this doesn't mean that nothing happened at all. Outside philosophy, plenty happened. After all, these were years which witnessed events of some significance – the rise and the subsequent decline of the Roman empire, for example, and the rise of two major religions, Christianity and then Islam. Nor does it mean that there were no developments in other areas of philosophy itself. There were times when Stoics, Epicureans, neo-Platonists and many others came to prominence and whose influence then waned. The names of these schools and movements will be familiar to some readers. But, although argument over questions of logic, meaning, ethics and metaphysics continued to take place, philosophers took little, if any, interest in political questions.

Why not? Part of the explanation is that, when it came to politics, the prevailing conditions could only have been hostile to philosophical specu-lation. Some of those conditions are detailed by Bertrand Russell in his *History of Western Philosophy* (Russell 1991). One is that Alexander's depradations signalled the beginning of a centuries-long period of tur-moil and political instability. This tended to discourage political specula-tion by robbing it of its point. In the world of the *polis*, where a citizen could be an active, useful, participating member of an association, it was only natural that a thoughtful person like Aristotle would ask what the true nature and function of the *polis* can be, how it should be organised, how its individual members are related to it, and so on. By contrast, under the new conditions the most anyone could hope for was to be spared the attentions of this or that warlord's marauding army. As a result, it was inevitable that philosophers would turn their attention inward, away from the social and political. To put it in Russell's words, philosophers 'no longer asked: how can men create a good state? They asked instead: how can men be virtuous in a wicked world, or happy in a world of suffering?' (Russell 1991: 240).

Another factor is that, throughout the period in question, there was never a time when the dominating culture could have encouraged the development of original social and political ideas. In Roman times, this was because the Romans took nearly all their cultural clues from Greece. (It even happened that some educated Greeks, when captured and made into slaves, were employed in Roman households as educators.) It is worth quoting Russell on this point too.

> To the end, Rome was culturally parasitic on Greece. The Romans invented no art forms, constructed no original system of philosophy, and made no scientific discoveries. They made good roads, system-atic legal codes, and efficient armies; for the rest they looked to Greece.
>
> (1991: 283–4)

In fact, Russell is exaggerating slightly, and, to see by just how much, you only have to consult Cicero's *Republic* (Cicero 1998a [AD 52]). Cicero was a high-ranking Roman official, a consul, who wrote in his spare time. (He discussed the art of rhetoric, as well as philosophy, and he was especially known for his political speeches.) His debt to the Greeks is more than apparent throughout the *Republic*. Even the title is borrowed from Plato, as is another of his titles, *The Laws* (Cicero 1998b). Not only that, like Plato's *Republic*, Cicero's is written in dialogue form. In Cicero's version, the main participants are prestigious Romans who lived a generation or so before Cicero himself, and – moreover – there are some evident parallels between passages in Cicero's text and sections of its Greek predecessor.[1]

But there are differences too. For example, whereas Plato's ideal state is ruled by philosophers, Cicero's is ruled by public-spirited 'great and good men'; and whereas Plato's state supposedly reflects the absolute perfection of the world of forms, Cicero harks back to a golden age through which Rome had passed – or so he thought – in the century before his own. Most strikingly, whereas Plato's *Republic* contains no discussion of his ideal state's constitutional structure – it is simply assumed that the philosopher rulers will know how to direct us – Cicero is far more pragmatic. He argues for a system of checks and balances based on a separation of powers. As this shows, although Cicero's work is modelled on Plato's, it is no slavish copy. On the contrary, it is designed to address the practicalities of contemporary Roman life. Even so – and the example of Cicero notwithstanding – it is fair to say that a culture which paid such deferential respect to a prior culture, looking back instead of forward, could not have been expected to produce much by way of original work.

About four hundred years after Cicero, Saint Augustine published his *City of God* (Augustine 1963). This was written in response to those pagans who argued that Rome would never have been sacked if the Romans had stuck with their original gods and if Christianity hadn't been made the official Roman religion. And, as the inclusion of the word 'city' in its title suggests, it is a work of political thought. More precisely, it is a discussion of what our relationship to the state (or 'city') ought to be. However, unlike Plato, Aristotle or even Cicero, Augustine has no observations to offer on the form the state ought to take; on who should rule or on whether democracy is preferable to other systems. Quite the contrary. Augustine argues that there are, on earth, two coexisting cities, 'the earthly city' and 'the city of God'. Every person is loyal either to one or to the other. (Clearly, these are not cities in the literal sense, each with a precise geographical location. Augustine's 'cities' are, rather, categories into which we fall, each of us into one or the other.) It is Augustine's thesis that, after Christ's second coming, only the city of God will survive. His advice to members of the latter city (i.e. Christians) is to concentrate on making themselves ready for this event. In the meantime, Christians should tolerate the authorities and obey the law, whoever those authorities may be and whatever laws they pass. Politically, this is a gospel of quietism, one interpretation of Christ's injunction to 'Render [therefore] unto Caesar the things which are Caesar's; and unto God the things that are God's' (*Matthew*, xxii, 21). It follows that the example of Augustine only tends to confirm Russell's claim that, during the period under discussion, philosophers tended to turn their eyes inward or heavenwards (or both) and away from the social and political.

As the medieval period progressed, conditions became still more unfavourable to the production of new political theory. It became increasingly the case that the institutions in which learning took place – the monasteries and, later, the universities – were theological institutions. Throughout the period, philosophers were men who had taken holy orders. Frequently, they were bishops or archbishops. At a time when it was generally held that even monarchs owed obedience to the Pope, and that the Pope owed obedience only to God – that is, when the prevailing rationale for the status quo accorded such an important place to the clergy – such individuals would have been unlikely to challenge it.

Even so, it would be wrong to say that absolutely no work of political philosophy was produced during the long period which began with the decline of the Greek *polis* and which came to a close in the sixteenth century; that is, with the dawn of the 'modern' age. The examples of Cicero and Saint Augustine are enough to make the point. However, it would be equally wrong to exaggerate. These are isolated cases, and what does appear to have been missing is a sustained public debate to which many individuals contributed, many with very different points of view from others. In this respect our own period is markedly different from earlier times. Just consider how thoroughly political argument pervades our own existence. In our own time, literacy – the ability to read – is the norm rather than the exception. Most people have access to radio and television. Moreover, communications technology is now so well developed that we can be aware of events taking place thousands of miles away, even on the other side of the world and even as they happen. We can gather the opinions of different politicians, 'experts' and others, as they are broadcast by the news channels (this being the culmination of a process which began at least as far back as the eighteenth century, when the first newspapers were published). One result of such developments is that we are, most of us, exposed to a diversity of political attitudes on a regular basis, and that most of us have the opportunity to contribute at some level to some political argument. We swim in a sea of ideas. Of course, I don't mean to say that the argument is always high level or sophisticated, only that political argument is all around us, in the workplace, in the café and the bar, in the newspapers (even the tabloids), on every 'phone-in programme', in the bulletins which regularly interrupt the flow of sound broadcast by every music station.

Now consider how different things must have been at the height of the medieval period, when intellectual speculation was confined to a small Latin-speaking elite, when government was the province of another elite, and when the illiterate majority simply got on with their lives; their horizons bounded geographically by the borders of their village or city courtyard, and intellectually by a single, all embracing world picture imposed from above. (And the situation in 'the East' seems to have been much the same. Just as the philosophy which came to dominate Western Europe was a sort of Christianised Aristotelianism, so philosophy in the Muslim world consisted largely of the attempt to reconcile the teachings of Plato and Aristotle with the Koran. In any case, talk of 'East' and 'West' – with its suggestion that there are two separate, hermetically sealed, cultures each oblivious to the other – is misleading.)

It is easy to underestimate the significance of such differences. If you are puzzled by the relative absence of developments in political philosophy from the post-Alexandrian ('Hellenistic') period through Roman and then medieval times, then I would simply ask you: Why think of this absence as something which needs explaining? I suggest that any puzzlement arises only through viewing the past from a certain perspective. Sustained political argument, at all levels, is such an all-pervasive feature of our own times that, looking back at the past, we expect to find it there as well. When we fail to detect it we naturally assume that something has gone wrong, that we are looking in the wrong place, even that something is being hidden from us (because of, say, 'cultural bias'). But the simple truth is that there is nothing to see.

Finally, political philosophy was no exception to a general rule which applied elsewhere. In cosmology or 'natural philosophy' (science's predecessor disciplines) Aristotle's influence was just as dominant by the end of this two thousand year period as it had been at the beginning. Part of the explanation – or so it is reasonable to assume – is that there was no good reason for rejecting his description of the universe. Aristotle held that the universe consists of a serious of concentric spheres, with (the) earth at the centre. What reason could there be for thinking otherwise? Don't the stars appear to move round the earth, and as for the planets, which appear to move independently of the stars, isn't their movement quite well accounted for by the fact that they lie at the interface of spheres? Again, Aristotle held that there are four elements – Earth, Air, Fire and Water – and that each seeks a natural level at which it comes to rest. Well, doesn't observation confirm that earth does fall, that water tends to rest on earth, and that fire does rise? Yes, of course. That is exactly what we see.

One idea which remained influential throughout the period was the idea of 'The Great Chain of Being'. (This is also expressed by Aristotle, in certain of his writings.) According to the 'chain of being' thesis, every entity in the universe can be ranked in a hierarchy. In the late medieval version, God is placed at the apex of the hierarchy. God's lieutenants – his angels and archangels – are ranked immediately below God. Next come humans who – being both spiritual and physical by nature – are accorded a special place. Animals are ranked beneath us and, below them, beings with merely 'vegetative souls'. Inanimate things – metals, stones, dirt – are ranked lower still. Hierarchy also prevails within each category. Within the class of animals lions are, thus, ranked above dogs, which are, in their turn, ranked above shellfish. Likewise, within the class of metals, gold is ranked above silver, which is ranked above iron.

For the student of political thought, the 'chain of being' thesis is striking, mainly for the way it combines a cosmology – that is, an account of the way the physical universe is constructed – with a rationale for the political order; for – as you would expect – the chain of being also ranks persons in terms of their class and the authority they are subsequently held to wield. The Pope is, thus, ranked above the king; the king above the baron; the baron above the serf. Each owes allegiance to those further up the chain, with the Pope owing allegiance only to God.

What happened to shake this ordered view of the world? The short answer is that a whole set of seismic movements took place. The earth was circumnavigated. America was discovered. Trade increased and, with it, a new middle class developed. Important scientific discoveries were made. There were devastating religious wars. If this were a conventional history book, I would now go on to detail these changes, and to discuss the question of which, if any, were the more fundamental. However, for us the main point is that along with all this there came a new way of thinking about the political realm.

I should not like to give the impression that the change from medieval to 'modern' was instantaneous, or even that it was sudden. By the sixteenth century, things had already moved quite a long way. It was as early as 1532 that Niccolo Machiavelli's notorious *The Prince* (Machiavelli 1961) was published. Machiavelli argues that, rather than exercising the Christian virtues, the successful prince must practise violence and deception – a thesis which clearly represents a severe disruption of an ordered world view in which everything has its rightful place. (I shan't spend too much time on *The Prince*. It is more a handbook for the newly arrived political opportunist than it is a worked out exercise in political philosophy.) The breakdown of an ordered, hierarchical, world picture is also a recurring theme in Shakespeare's more serious plays. 'This goodly frame, the earth, seems to me a sterile promontory', says Hamlet; 'What a piece of work is a man! . . . in action how like an angel! In apprehension how like a god!' But he adds, 'And yet, to me what is this quintessence of dust?' (*Hamlet*, II, ii). 'Unaccommodated man', says King Lear, 'is no more but [such] a poor, bare, forked animal' (which is precisely what 'man' would not be if the chain of being hypothesis were true) (*Lear*, III, iv).

But it was not until the following century – the seventeenth – that the modern argument within political philosophy was to really get going. By contrast with what had gone before, the new approach was assertively rationalistic, radically individualistic and morally egalitarian.

Part II

---◦⬭◦---

Reason and Revolutions

5

———·◦☉◦·———

Hobbes goes to Paris

John Aubrey, the seventeenth century biographer, gives the following account of how it was that Thomas Hobbes first became inspired by geometry.

> He was forty years old before he looked on geometry; which hap-
> pened accidentally. Being in a gentleman's library Euclid's *Elements*
> lay open and 'twas the forty-seventh proposition in the first book.
> He read the first proposition. 'By G – ‡' said he, 'this is impossible!'
> So he reads the demonstration of it, which referred him back to such
> a proof; which referred him back to another, which he also read. And
> so forth, that at last he was demonstratively convinced of that truth.
> This made him in love with geometry.
>
> (Aubrey 1982: 151–2)

I am sure that mathematically-minded readers will empathise with Hobbes' reaction, as reported. One source of geometry's capacity to excite is the way it moves so assuredly from the obvious to the not-at-all obvious. It begins with self-evident truths, propositions which are so patently obvious that it can seem hardly worth making the effort to state them. Take Euclid's 'axiom' that 'things which are equal to the same thing are also equal to one another', or his 'postulate' that 'all right angles are equal to one another' (1989: 155, 145). Such statements are undoubtedly true, but you could hardly call them headline news. (Who could doubt that, if A equals C, and B equals C, then it must be the case that A equals C, which is what the axiom implies. Or, to take the postulate, you would have to be strange indeed not to see that every angle of 90° exactly resembles every other angle of 90° in being an angle of 90°.) But geometry then proceeds to build impressive structures on such modest foundations. It moves, step by logical step, to demonstrate further truths, truths which are new and surprising. For example, take the proposition whose truth is established by Euclid in his *Elements*, Book One, proposition 32 (Euclid 1989). This is the now familiar proposition that for any triangle, the sum of its internal angles must equal two right angles. There must have been a time when this was not known, so Euclid is stating what was once a new –

and striking – truth; a truth which it took geometry to discover. It is not at all surprising that Hobbes should have been 'in love with geometry', just as Aubrey says (Aubrey: op. cit.).

Paris, 1634–7: Descartes

Aubrey tells such a good story that it's a pity it isn't true. At least, we can be fairly sure that it isn't, for it is far more likely that, however it may have originated, the major stimulus for Hobbes' interest in geometry came some time between 1634 and 1637 with a tour of mainland Europe. As part of the trip, he spent some time in Paris, where he became acquainted with some of Europe's leading intellectuals including, most significantly from our point of view, Marin Mersenne, who put him in touch with René Descartes.[1] There is absolutely no doubt that Descartes was his generation's leading thinker, and it is unlikely that nothing would have come from the encounter. Therefore, it is worth a brief digression to consider the latter's achievement, and to reflect on what Hobbes may have learnt from him.

These days, Descartes is mainly remembered as the author of a short work, usually known as the *Discourse on Method*. However, its full title is *Discourse on the Method of Rightly Conducting the Reason and Seeking for Truth in the Sciences* (Descartes 1954a). When Descartes wrote it, it was his intention that it should appear as the preface to a longer work, *The World*, in which Descartes was to present the conclusions he had reached, as a scientist, on astronomy, optics and geometry. As its title indicates, the subject of the *Discourse* itself is scientific method. In fact, its purpose is to justify Descartes' own account of correct scientific procedure. (As things turned out, *The World* was never published in its entirety.)[2]

So, what was this 'method' meant to be? Just briefly, the story is that the intellectuals of Descartes' time believed themselves to be living at the beginning of a new age of scientific discovery. As more was found out, the Aristotelianism which had dominated philosophy throughout the medieval period was increasingly perceived as irrelevant. As an example, take the circumnavigation of the earth by adventurers such as Ferdinand Magellan and Sir Francis Drake. It is true enough that Aristotle himself had argued that the earth is round, but this time the conclusion had been established once and for all, not by ratiocination – that is, not through skeins of argument drawn from the head of some monk in the privacy of his cloister – but by a direct, straightforward, observational test.[3] You simply pointed your ship westward and kept going in the same direction until you arrived back at your starting point. Or, take William Harvey's discovery that the blood circulates around the body. This, too, was made with the help of observation, this time through anatomy, in which people were taking an increasing interest. Moreover, there were some discoveries which actually conflicted with Aristotle's world picture and called it into question. One celebrated example is Galileo's discovery, in 1610, that the planet Jupiter has moons.[4] This demonstrated, again by simple observation, that the prevailing world picture, according to which the earth is at the centre of the universe, just could not have been true. (If there are celestial bodies which orbit another planet, then it can't be true that all celestial bodies orbit the earth.)

The search for a *method* resulted from the optimistic hope that the rate of discovery could be increased – and the progress of humanity accelerated – if the process of discovery could be systematised. Like many philosophers, Descartes felt that the discoveries of his time had been made fortuitously, almost by accident. As he saw it, his contemporaries tended to 'conduct their minds along unexplored routes, having no reason to hope for success, but merely willing to risk the experiment of finding whether the truth they seek lies there' (Descartes 1931: 9). To this, Descartes added the dry comment that, 'As well might a man burning with an unintelligent desire to find treasure, continually roam the streets, seeking to find something that a passer-by might have chanced to drop' (ibid.). Procedures were needed. In Descartes' version, these were to take the form of a codified set of 'certain and simple rules, such that, if a man observe them accurately, he shall never assume what is false as true' and 'will always gradually increase his knowledge and so arrive at a true understanding of all that does not surpass his powers' (ibid.).

However, it is one thing to believe in the desirability of employing a method in science, but quite another to figure out what the correct procedure actually is. It is here – significantly from our point of view – that geometry enters the picture. For our purposes, the most relevant feature of Descartes' philosophy is his recommendation that scientists should follow the methods employed by *mathematicians*, as exemplified especially in the study of geometry. Why? The answer is that Descartes, and the 'Rationalist' philosophers[5] who followed his example, were inspired by the *certainty* mathematicians can achieve. For example, once it has been demonstrated that, for any triangle whatsoever, the sum of its angles *must* equal two right angles, you can be absolutely sure of the fact. Mathematics is thus unique in the way it can demonstrate new, previously unknown truths which are henceforth known for sure. At least, that is how it seemed. It was Descartes' optimistic belief that the method which had turned out to be so successful in mathematics could also be deployed elsewhere – in cosmology, in biology, even in morality.

In fact, the rules Descartes attempts to justify with the argument of the *Discourse* are intended to describe the mental acts a mathematician performs when attempting to work out the solution to a problem. (You could say that they supposedly describe 'what goes on in someone's head'.) The art is to begin with simple, self-evident components –

components which can be grasped by mental 'intuition' – and to proceed, like a geometer, to the discovery of more complex, more interesting, truths. Of course, none of this would make sense unless you believe that the natural world – the world studied by science – can be described by a set of propositions, each of which is logically linked to others, as if in a chain; which is just what Descartes did believe. He once put it in the following, almost poetic, terms:

> The sciences now have masks on them; if the masks were taken off they would appear supremely beautiful. On surveying the chain of the sciences one will regard them as not being more difficult to retain in one's mind than the number series is.
>
> (1954a: 3)

Still, having reached this point we need follow Descartes no further. It only remains to note that Hobbes' masterpiece, *Leviathan* (1981), is imbued with a similar vision. In *Leviathan* Hobbes attempts an explanation of human nature, beginning with the simplest elements and proceeding to the most complex and, from that foundation, he attempts an explanation of the state in terms of *its* elements – i.e. ourselves. Notice how this idea of a movement from simple to complex underlies the rhetorical opening paragraph of *Leviathan*'s 'Introduction'.

> For seeing life is but a motion of Limbs, the beginning whereof is in some principal part within; why may we not say that all Automata (Engines that move themselves by springs and wheeles as doth a watch) have an artificiall life? For what is the *Heart* but a *Spring*; and the *Nerves*, but so many *Strings*; and the *Joynts*, but so many *Wheeles*, giving motion to the whole body, such as was intended by the artificer? *Art* goes yet further, imitating that Rationall and most excellent work of Nature, *Man*. For by Art is created that great LEVIATHAN called a COMMON-WEALTH, or STATE, (in latine CIVITAS) which is but an Artificiall Man; though of greater stature and strength than the Naturall, for whose protection and defence it was intended.
>
> (Hobbes 1981: 81)

And it isn't just the idea of a method which proceeds from simple to complex in which we find an echo of Descartes. It was Descartes who believed that the human body is just a machine, and Descartes who compared the universe to a clock. The whole passage is modishly Cartesian.

Paris, 1640–51: Exile

And that was just one Paris visit. Hobbes returned to England in 1637 – as it happened, it was the year in which Descartes published his *Discourse*

– but in 1640 he was back, this time for a very different reason. In England, there had been serious tension between Parliament and the monarchy for some time. Sensing trouble ahead, Hobbes had gone into exile. Sure enough, civil war broke out in 1642. There followed one of the most turbulent periods of British history. The war itself ended with the surrender of the king, Charles I, to the parliamentary forces, led by Oliver Cromwell, but the constitutional crisis itself persisted for some time after that. It was not until 1649 that Charles was executed. (He was beheaded.) Cromwell became 'Lord Protector' in 1652 and, for the only time in its history so far, Britain was a republic.

This time, although Hobbes maintained his intellectual contacts, he was also constrained to keep less intellectual company. However, it was also more exalted in its social status, for Hobbes was to serve as mathematics tutor to the young Prince of Wales, the boy who would later become Charles II of England. Along with Hobbes, the queen (herself French) and most of the English court were also living in Paris, in exile. In the course of day-to-day conversation, I don't suppose Hobbes would have come across much to contradict his own staunchly royalist view of events. Hobbes returned to England in 1651, having judged it safe enough to do so. (By then, Cromwell himself had started to behave like a sovereign.) The monarchy was eventually restored in 1660.

The disturbing events of the civil war period left a profound impression on those who lived through them. These were violent and terrible years during which – according to one authoritative estimate – a greater percentage of the British population lost their lives than during the First World War of 1914–18.[6] The title of a contemporary popular song, *The World Turned Upside Down*, captures a prevailing view of events. (As an idea, Aristotle's Great Chain had obviously fallen well out of favour.) Hobbes' own recorded comment was that between the years of 1640 and 1660, anyone who 'as from the Devil's Mountain, should have looked upon the world and observed the actions of men, especially in England, might have had a prospect of all kinds of injustice, and of all kinds of folly that the world could afford' (Hobbes 1969: 1). They were events which prompted Hobbes to revise his philosophical project. Originally, it had been his intention to construct an entire philosophical system. This was to appear in several volumes, with a treatment of political questions occurring quite late in the series; but he now decided to focus on the political work. The result was *Leviathan* (Hobbes 1981). Its argument forms the subject of the next chapter.

Leviathan is named after a terrible monster described in the Bible's book of *Job*. According *Job*, 'Out of his [Leviathan's] nostrils goeth smoke, as out of a seething pot or caldron; His breath, kindleth coals, and a flame goeth out of his mouth' (ibid.: 20–1). And, if that isn't scary enough, 'The flakes of his flesh are joined together: they are firm in themselves; they cannot be moved; His heart is as firm as a stone; yea, as hard as a piece of the nether millstone' (ibid.: 23–4). Most importantly, though, 'Upon earth there is not his like' and 'he is a king over all the children of pride' (ibid.: 33–4). This means that only Leviathan is a match for Behemoth, the monster described in the previous chapter of *Job*. Behemoth is also terrifying. 'His strength is in his loins, and his force is in the navel of his belly', says *Job*. 'He moveth his tail like a cedar: the sinews of his stones are wrapped together' and 'His bones are as strong as pieces of brass; his bones are like bars of iron' (ibid.: XL, 16–18).

Just as *Leviathan* was the title of Hobbes' defence of absolute sovereignty, so *Behemoth* was the title of his history of the civil war (Hobbes: 1969). Leviathan wrestles Behemoth: Picture this clash of titans – the awesome devastation and turmoil – and you get some idea of the awful dread which the events of the civil war period inspired in Hobbes and so many of his contemporaries.

6

—·◦☉◦·—

Hobbes: raising the great Leviathan

Leviathan contains one of the English language's best-known, most frequently quoted, lines, the line in which Hobbes describes the life of 'man' in the 'state of nature' as 'nasty, brutish, and short'. The phrase is so well known that we may as well begin with it, and – rather than taking it in isolation – we ought to start with the full text of the paragraph in which it occurs. Here it is.

> Whatsoever therefore is consequent to a time of Warre, where every man is Enemy to every man; the same is consequent to the time, wherein men live without other security, than what their own strength, and their own invention shall furnish them withall. In such condition there is no place for Industry; because the fruit thereof is uncertain: and consequently no Culture of the Earth; no Navigation, nor use of the commodities that may be imported by Sea; no commodious Building; no Instruments of moving, and removing such things as require much force; no Knowledge of the face of the Earth; no account of Time; no Arts; no Letters; no Society; and which is worst of all, continuall feare, and danger of violent death; And the life of man, solitary, poore, nasty, brutish, and short.
>
> (Hobbes 1981: 186)

The way Hobbes portrays it, life in the state of nature is indeed a fearsome thing. It isn't just fear and danger of violent death that you have to contend with. As the full quotation shows, pretty well every activity you can think of – anything you might want to count as a component of a civilised existence – is absent.

But what is this terrifying 'state of nature'? Well, in the passage quoted Hobbes says that it is a state in which people have only their own strength and ingenuity to rely on for protection. That is because the state of nature is, by definition, a situation in which there is no political authority. This means that there is no civil or criminal law and, obviously, nobody to enforce the law. And why should Hobbes think that life in such a state would be so terrible? We can't just take it for granted that it would be, as there are – no doubt – anarchists and others who would disagree. Anarchists would argue that life without any (political) state at all, even a benignly run state, must always be preferable to submission to any sort of political authority. To objections along such lines Hobbes would reply, as he does in the subsequent paragraph, that experience can only confirm his description. The doubter (or anarchist) need only remind himself that 'when taking a journey, he armes himselfe, and seeks to go well accompanied; when going to sleep, he locks his dores; when even in his house he locks his chests' (ibid.: 186–7). Hobbes' point is that, even where there are law making and law enforcing authorities, we have to take such ordinary precautions because other people are, as he thinks, intrinsically untrustworthy.

However, he also regards such evidence as subsidiary. So far as he is concerned, observation can only provide additional support for a conclusion which has already been reached by *reason*. Perhaps there was once a state of nature. Perhaps there has never been any such thing. Again, perhaps our condition has, at times, approached the state of nature as Hobbes describes it, but perhaps we have always managed to pull back from the brink of the abyss in the nick of time (which is, no doubt, the way he would have thought about the civil war). All that is beside the point. For Hobbes, the crucial point is that his conclusion is, as he puts it, an '*Inference*, made from the passions' (ibid.: 186) (my emphasis). That is, his description is meant to be a description of the way a state of nature would, logically, have to be, given the truth of certain prior assumptions.

The comparison with geometry is more than apposite here. Take the statement that the sum of the internal angles of a triangle is equal to that of two right angles (or, if you prefer, 180°). In this case too, observation lends support to Euclid's conclusion, just as it (supposedly) does to Hobbes' description of life in a state of nature. In the case of the triangle, 'observation' means taking your protractor, measuring the internal angles of a given triangle and adding them together. If you measure carefully enough, you will always find that they total 180°. But, likewise, observation is secondary to reason here, for Euclid's conclusion that, for any triangle, its angles *must* total 180° would hold true even if there were no triangles actually in existence. That is because its truth is derivable by reason – in this case by means of Euclid's proof – from certain prior assumptions, just as Hobbes' description of life in the state of nature is supposed to be.

As the comparison shows, Hobbes' description forms part of a deductive argument; that is, an argument which relies on reason rather than observation, and attempts to proceed logically, step by step, from premise to conclusion. In fact, it is more than that. It is part of a very particular sort of deductive argument, namely a *social contract* argument. In this respect, the argument of *Leviathan* stands at the beginning of a long and distinguished line. In the hands of the right philosopher, a social contract argument can be a powerful tool. So, we shouldn't let Hobbes' elegant seventeenth century English fool us into thinking that his philosophical argument is just as archaic as his spelling. Far from it.

What is a social contract argument?

As Part II of this book is devoted to the work of the great, 'classical' social contract theorists – Thomas Hobbes (1588–1679), John Locke (1632–1704) and Jean-Jacques Rousseau (1712–1778) – I should explain what a social contract argument is before I go any further.

To start with, then, we should note that the arguments of the classical theorists share a basic structure and – with it – a terminology. To begin with, people ('men') are pictured as inhabiting a 'state of nature'. This is defined by the absence of any form of political authority. In the state of nature there is no one to make law and, consequently, no civil law. As Hobbes puts it, there are no 'publike Officers, armed, to revenge [all] injuries' (ibid.: 187). Had there been such things as police forces back in the seventeenth century, the state of nature would no doubt have been defined, in part, by the absence of police. Life in the state of nature is portrayed as less than ideal. It has its 'inconveniences' (Locke's word). Therefore, people are pictured as seeking a means of escape, and the means they employ is a 'social contract'. When someone, as it were, 'signs up' to the contract, that person agrees to set aside certain liberties and to respect the liberties (or 'rights') of others. The contract is also the means by which a 'sovereign' is established. After the contract, everyone is supposed to obey the sovereign, with the result that the state of nature's inconveniences are overcome. After the social contract, when people are no longer living in a state of nature, they are said to inhabit 'civil society'.

It is important to bear in mind that, in the technical terminology of this type of theory, the word 'sovereign' does not necessarily refer to a single individual. It refers to the ultimate law making authority, and each philosopher I discuss in Part II can be distinguished from the others in terms of the form of authority he prefers. Thus, so far as Hobbes is concerned, a single individual – a monarch, say – is preferable to any other form; although even Hobbes is prepared to entertain the possibility that an assembly, such as a parliament, can be sovereign. For Locke, authority must be limited in the sense that it can remain in place only with the consent of the governed. (Otherwise, Locke is less concerned with the precise form a constitution takes, although he most prefers a 'mixed' system in which the power of a monarch is checked by parliament.) For Rousseau – an ultra-democrat – true sovereignty can only reside in an assembly of the whole people.

Anyone new to social contract theory could be forgiven for interpreting the foregoing story as an attempt at history. There is an apparent narrative: Once upon a time people lived in a state of nature. Then they became parties to a social contract. After that they lived under a sovereign in civil society (happily ever after?). On a first reading, you could easily gain the impression that the social contract theorists believed in the literal truth of this story. Indeed, there is some textual evidence that at least one of them, Locke, actually did.[1] But, whatever the classical theorists themselves may have believed, it is clear that no one living at the beginning of the twenty-first century can treat social contract theory as literal history. (There are plenty of social contract theorists writing now, but none who would present his or her argument as real history.) As things presently stand the consensus view of social contract theory is as follows: In order to appreciate the full explanatory power of this type of theory you must first strip it of any quasi-historical baggage with which it may be encumbered and treat it as a form of *rational choice theory*. To see what this means, suppose – first – that you have to give the reason for something's existence, or the reason why some event has occurred. That something has to be the sort of thing which can be brought into existence through human agency. It may be an institution, such as 'the state' or 'the market', or a series of events, such as a war. Now – secondly – try to imagine a world from which the thing whose existence you are trying to explain is absent. On this view, that is just what the 'state of nature' is. It is a purely imaginary, hypothetical, situation from which whatever it is you are trying to explain is missing. In Hobbes' case this means trying to imagine living without a state and without a sovereign, not because humans ever lived in such a condition, but because it is the existence of a state and a sovereign for which Hobbes is trying to give a rationale. (If you prefer, you could call the 'state of nature' the 'no-state situation'.)[2] The next step in the procedure – the third – is this: Having imagined away whatever it is you are trying to explain, you then try to figure out what reasons people would have for introducing it. By this criterion, Hobbes qualifies as a rational choice theorist because, having imagined away the state, he thinks he can justify its existence in terms of what people who found themselves in a no-state situation would choose to do if they were rational. If he is right, then he can claim to have accounted for the form of state he favours in terms of its *purpose* or *point*.

That should explain the basic principle underlying social contract argument, construed as an exercise in rational choice theory. To appreciate the force this type of theory can carry, note that justifying an institution such as the state in terms of the reasons people would have for choosing it from a no-state situation if they were rational is not the same as justifying every state which actually exists. It's possible that rational people would choose states of a certain type. For example, they might only choose states with constitutions which guarantee certain basic rights. Again, like Locke, they might insist that a government must be removable once the people have withdrawn their consent. Actually existing governments – which have more often than not been established by means of war, revolution and bloody violence – may not satisfy such criteria. It is for this reason that a social contract theory can be a powerful *critical* weapon. You can use it to justify certain forms of state, but you can also use it to argue for the removal of others.

Finally, at this point it is also worth noting one of rational choice theory's more interesting features. It can so often be used to demonstrate that, when every individual makes the most rational choice he or she can make in the circumstances, the overall outcome can be something no one could rationally want. For example, no one could rationally want there to be an economic recession, and yet a recession is, in the main, the outcome of a huge number of individual choices, each made in a perfectly rational way. Again, a destructive war is something no one could seriously want, and yet a war can be the outcome of individual decisions, each made for the best of reasons. You could say that the state of nature, as Hobbes describes it, most resembles the last of these. In fact, we have already seen how he compares it to 'a time of Warre, where every man is Enemy to every man' (1981: 186). *Leviathan*'s purpose is to show us the escape route.[3]

Hobbes' conclusion: the great Leviathan

It follows that understanding Hobbes' argument means following the steps by means of which he tries to derive his conclusion from his initial premises. In other words, it means understanding why he should think that people who find themselves in a state of nature would, if they were rational, subject themselves to a sovereign of the type he describes. We shall be tracing those steps shortly. However, before we do, let me first outline the conclusion Hobbes sets out to establish. It could be helpful to have an idea of where his argument is meant to be taking us.

In fact, many readers will already know that Hobbes advocates absolute sovereignty; but then, 'absolute sovereign' is a rather vague phrase, and if we are to understand him we need to be more specific. So, to begin with we should note that what Hobbes fears most is sovereignty which is *divided*. Here, it is useful to contrast Hobbes' view of things with the conventional account of modern liberal-democratic constitutions, according to which they rely on a system of checks and balances. On the latter view, the power of – say – the US President can be checked by Congress, the power of Congress by the Senate, the judiciary can act to check any of these, and all decisions have to be measured against the requirements set out in a written constitution. Similarly, in the UK, Parliament can act as a check on the power of the sovereign, who can in turn (and, at least, in theory) act as a check on the excesses of the former. Hobbes' preferred 'commonwealth' also contrasts with the supra-national institutions which have risen in influence during our own times – the United Nations, for example, or the European Court of Human Rights. These are not states themselves, but they can act in ways which check the power of individual nation-states.

Hobbes would have none of this. So far as he is concerned, there can only be a single ultimate *locus* of power and authority. For Hobbes, it is a matter of the relationship between different *wills*. As he sees it, there can be no more than one dominant will within any state (or 'common-wealth'). Where there is more than one, only political collapse and terrify-ing anarchy can result. *Leviathan*'s central idea is, thus, the uniting of many wills into one. This is what is supposed to happen at the time of the social contract. According to Hobbes, it is for reasons of self-defence that, at the time of the contract, people erect a 'Common Power' by conferring 'all their power and strength upon one Man, or upon one Assembly of men, that may reduce all their Wills, by plurality of voices, unto one Will' (1981: 227).

The latter vision permeates *Leviathan* throughout, and in more than the book's formal argument. For example, you will find it expressed in the original cover illustration, which depicts an enormous artificial person (looking a lot like Charles I) who is composed of a vast number of much smaller, natural persons. You will find it in the grudging reluctance with which Hobbes acknowledges that it is just about possible that an assembly could be sovereign, an arrangement which he nevertheless com-pares with a game of tennis in which the player 'is carried to the ball, though by good Players, yet in a Wheele-barrough' which many people are trying to steer, each in the direction he judges correct (ibid.: 310). You will also come across it in the repeated comparisons Hobbes draws between 'diseases of the commonwealth' and diseases of the human body; for example, when he writes of a system which purportedly relies on a threefold division of power that:

> [But] I have seen a man, that had another man growing out of his side, with an head, armes, breast, and stomach, of his own: If he had had another man growing out of his other side, the comparison might then have been exact.
>
> (ibid.: 372–3)

Another feature of the absolute sovereignty preferred by Hobbes lies in the sovereign's power to make law. All contract theorists agree that it is the sovereign's job to *interpret* law. It has to be, for society would be unable to function without a settled standard. But on Hobbes' account, he/she/it (depending on whether the sovereign is a person or an assembly) does far more than that. The sovereign simply decides what the law is going to be, and that settles things. Law is simply the command of whoever has the power to enforce it – nothing more. Here, too, there is a contrast between Hobbes' doctrine and a prevalent modern orthodoxy, this time the view that people are the bearers of fundamental 'natural' or 'human' rights. If the latter view is correct then, morally speaking, there are certain things you just cannot do to other people because, if you did, then you would be violating those other people's rights. Human rights – if there are such things – place limits on the power of the sovereign.

Such a doctrine would be anathema to Hobbes. Take his attitude to private property. According to Hobbes, the doctrine that there is an absolute right to private property, 'such as excludeth the Right of the Soveraign' (1981: 367) is one of those things which weaken and tend to the dissolution of a commonwealth (by limiting the sovereign's ability to raise taxes, for example). Against it, Hobbes insists that the property you have a right to hold is simply the property the sovereign lets you hold, nothing more, nothing less. Or, consider Hobbes' attitude to what we would now call the rights to 'free speech' and 'liberty of conscience', the latter being the right to follow your conscience in matters of morality and religion. These days, such rights feature as significant items on every list of human rights. By contrast, Hobbes is all for censorship. 'It is annexed to the Soveraignty', he writes, 'to be Judge of what Opinions and Doctrines are averse, and what conducing to Peace.' Likewise, it is the sovereign's prerogative to judge 'how farre, and what, men are to be trusted withall, in speaking to Multitudes of people; and who shall examine the Doctrines of all bookes before they be published' (ibid.: 233). As for private conscience, Hobbes insists that the doctrine according to which 'every private man is Judge of Good and Evil actions' is just sedition and 'poyson' (ibid.: 365). (It is easy to appreciate why he should have held such views. As he saw it, a major cause of the civil war was that Parliament had become just as powerful as the king, so that there were, in fact, two centres of power and authority, and an inevitable tension between the two. You can see why he would have insisted on the sovereign's indivisibility. Likewise, the doctrine of private conscience – especially favoured by the Puritans of the Parliamentary side – was an obvious culprit.) That said, now for the argument itself.

Hobbes' argument

The premises: Human nature and life in the state of nature

When examining an argument which claims to proceed from true premises to a true conclusion via a sequence of logically valid steps, it is often a good idea to start with the premises. Take the standard example of a logically valid, three stage 'syllogism', the one you will find in pretty well every introductory textbook on logic. This states that 'all men are mortal' (first premise); that 'Socrates' is a man' (second premise); and 'therefore' that 'Socrates' is mortal' (conclusion). The logic is impeccable, but it doesn't yield a true conclusion if 'Socrates' is, in fact, your pet name for your desktop computer (in which case, one premise – the second – will be false).

In Hobbes' case, examining the premises of his argument means taking a closer look at his account of life in a state of nature. The state of nature, you will recall, is an *apolitical* condition from which law and authority are absent. As you will also recall, he compares it with a state of war. It is, he says, a 'warre of every man against every man' (1981: 186), a situation in which everyone has to be constantly on guard against the incursions of the others, and in which life is, as a consequence, fairly terrible. But why should this be? If life in the state of nature is so terrible, that can only be as a result of the way others behave. In fact, if other people were, in general, caring and altruistic – if everyone automatically regarded everyone else as their brother or sister, and if each person was always prepared to help the others out – then the state of nature might not be so bad. In fact, there would probably be no reason for quitting it in favour of life under a sovereign at all. For Hobbes, life in a state of nature is nasty, brutish, and short, precisely because people are *not*, as a rule, so caring and altruistic.

Why aren't they? Well, right at the core of Hobbes's philosophy there lies a particular view of human motivation. On that view we are, each of us, motivated by desire (or appetite) and aversion. We desire those things which, so far as we can see, tend to our own preservation, and we try to avoid those things which, so far as we can see, tend to our own destruction. In addition to this we are creatures of limited sympathy. (Hobbes' word is 'diffidence'.) We find it difficult to empathise with the plight of others, which means that, when it comes to the crunch, we tend to prioritise our own desires over those of other people. We are also rational creatures, but the function of our reason is simply to help us figure out how best to obtain those things we desire. Says Hobbes, 'the Thoughts are to the Desires, as Scouts, and Spies, to range abroad, and find the way to the things Desired' (1981: 139). In short, it is Hobbes' view that we are strongly egocentric by nature.

Is Hobbes right? In fact, it is possible to call Hobbes' account of human nature into question, as it is the inferences he draws from it. However, before criticising Hobbes, I think it is worth tracing his argument through to its conclusion. There is quite a lot to be learnt from seeing how it works.

So, now note that Hobbes' account of motivation (supposedly) has two corollaries (or logical implications) to which he attaches special emphasis. One takes the form of a thesis concerning the meanings of moral terms. According to Hobbes, in the state of nature these are used subjectively. Thus, 'whatsoever is the object of any man's Appetite of Desire; that is it, which he for his part calleth *Good*'. Likewise, the word 'Evill' is reserved for 'the object of his Hate, and Aversion' (ibid.: 120). The relevance of this 'subjectivist' thesis really becomes clear after the contract, when the sovereign is in place. As we have seen, it is a function of the sovereign to supply a settled standard of right and wrong. The second corollary is that the desire for power is *insatiable* in the sense that, however much power a person has, that person will always desire more.

For future reference, note that 'power' is defined by Hobbes as a 'present means to obtain some future apparent Good' (ibid. 150). Note also that 'power', thus defined, covers a lot more than brute physical ability – the strength to beat someone in a fight, or to run fast. There are also what Hobbes calls 'instrumental' powers, namely, those powers which are 'means and Instruments to acquire more: as Riches, Reputation, Friends, and the secret working of God, which men call Good Luck' (ibid.). Power is, thus, the ability to get what you desire, *by whatever means*, and the more you are able to influence others – to get them to do what you want them to – the more power you have. The conclusion that each of us constantly desires more power over the others is directly implied by the thesis that we are motivated by desire for those things which tend to our own preservation *plus* the assumption that, however much a person may achieve what he or she desires, there is always something else to be desired. As Hobbes puts it, 'Nor can a man any more live, whose Desires are at an end, than he, whose Senses and Imagination are at a stand' (ibid. 160). Moreover, you often need extra power if you are to hang on to the power you already have. It is, therefore, 'a generall inclination of all mankind' that there should be 'a perpetuall and restless desire of Power after power, that ceaseth onley in Death' (ibid.).

If all this is true – and if it is also true, as Hobbes claims, that everyone is pretty well equal in power – his description of life in the state of nature (as being nasty, brutish, and so on) follows – or so he contends. This is how: When there is a conflict of interest between egocentric, power-seeking people who are 'diffident' towards others, they will inevitably come into confrontation. 'When any two men desire the same thing, which nevertheless they cannot both enjoy', says Hobbes, 'they become Enemies'. He adds that 'in the way to their End' they will 'endeavour to destroy, or subdue one another' (ibid.: 184). Given that no one is strong or cunning enough to subdue the others – 'the difference between man, and man' being 'not so considerable, as that one man can thereupon claim to himself any benefit, to which another may not pretend, as well as he' (ibid.: 183) – everyone will be constantly on their guard against 'invasion' by others. Bearing in mind that war 'consisteth not in Battell onely, or the act of fighting; but in a tract of time, wherein the Will to contend by Battell is sufficiently known', it is accurate to describe this condition as a war 'of every man, against every man' (ibid.: 185–6). Hobbes' conclusion that 'whatsoever is consequent to a time of Warre, where every man is Enemy to every man' is also 'consequent to' the state of nature follows (ibid.: 186).

Or so he claims. In fact, it is possible to question this reasoning, but, as I have already said, I am postponing critical analysis of Hobbes' argument for a later section. For the moment, let us just note that there are, in fact, *two* major questions raised by Hobbes' account of life in the state of nature. The first relates to his unflattering description of humans as ego-centric, power-hungry creatures, and it is simply, is it true? The second is: Would life in the state of nature be as nasty as he claims, *even if his description of human nature is true?*

From premise to conclusion: contracts

Let us now turn to Hobbes' claim that the only way to escape the state of nature is to establish an absolute sovereign by means of a social contract. On this point, one thing I would particularly like you to appreciate is just how crucial the notion of a contract is to Hobbes' philosophy. It shows up in his account of the social contract itself, of course, but for Hobbes there are more contracts at stake than just that. In fact, *Leviathan* is shot through with talk of contracts. Take his description of the state of nature itself. As we saw at the beginning of this chapter, it isn't just 'continuall feare, and danger of violent death' (1981: 186) which make life in the state of nature so intolerable. It is the absence of everything which makes existence civilised. In the passage I quoted, Hobbes also mentions industry, agriculture, trade, building and construction, 'knowledge of the face of the earth', the arts, literature and 'society' (ibid.). None of these is supposed to be possible in the state of nature. Why not? Hobbes' answer is that such activities are only possible where people can draw up agreements and make contracts with each other and where, having done so, they can be relied upon to keep their side of the bargain. As this is not possible in the state of nature then – or so Hobbes argues – neither are the activities he lists. The concept of a contract is, in this way, central to Hobbes' argument.

The centrality of contracts to Hobbes' argument appears especially striking if you contrast him with earlier thinkers. In the theories of Plato and Aristotle, for example, contracts hardly figure. It could be argued that there is a reason for this difference, one which is connected with Hobbes' 'atomised' representation of human existence. In the idealised *poleis* of the Greek philosophers – where 'virtue' or *aretē* is the rule – each person fulfils the social/political role he or she is best fitted by nature to perform. By contrast, in Hobbes' world there is no such natural order. On his view, we are – by nature – self-interested centres of desire and aversion, each of us constantly jostling for position with the others. There is no natural social order and no naturally ordained role for any of us. A theory which represents human relations in the latter way requires some sort of device for reconciling interests which would otherwise conflict – but a more artificial one. For Hobbes, that device is the contract. Think of it that way and it seems practically inevitable that he should have attached such prominence to contracts.

That said, let us now ask why Hobbes should have thought it so impossible to become party to a contract in the state of nature. To this, his answer is that, in the normal case, agreeing to a contract is a matter of committing yourself to a *future* action. For example, suppose that you and I agree to a contract. I agree to do such-and-such a job for you if you agree to pay me such-and-such a sum of money. The point is that, when we make the agreement, the things we agree to do remain to be done. This means, in turn, that each of us has to *trust* the other. However, if he is right about human nature – that is, if the most rational thing for each of us to do is to pursue our self-interest (as defined by him) – then neither of us can trust the other. In the example, I can't trust you to pay me because, for all I know, you might find an opportunity to do something else with the money, something which is more likely to help you achieve your self-interested ends. Likewise, you can't trust me to do the work because, for all you know, self-interest might lead me to do something else. As Hobbes puts it,

> If a Covenant be made, wherein neither of the parties performe presently, but trust one another; in the condition of meer nature, (which is a condition of Warre of every man against every man,) upon any reasonable suspicion, it is Voyd.

(ibid.: 196)

In fact, 'voyd' is too weak a term. It isn't just that contracts agreed in the state of nature are automatically rendered void. In the state of nature, conditions are such that agreeing to a contract would be *pointless*, because no one could ever trust anyone else.

From premise to conclusion: the laws of nature

The actors in Hobbes' 'state of nature' drama are playing a 'noncooperative, nonzero-sum game', as 'rational choice' terminology would have it. In this type of game there is a best outcome, one which a rational person must prefer to other possibilities, but the best outcome is actually ruled out where every individual, judging the world from his or her own standpoint, acts rationally. (Quite often, such theorists illustrate their point with the help of a particular example, the example of 'the prisoner's dilemma'.)[4] Earlier, I remarked that the application of rational choice theory to particular situations quite often demonstrates just this; that although every individual is making the most rational choice he or she can make in the circumstances, the outcome is something no one could rationally want. An economic recession, a war, a fuel shortage – all can result from individual decisions, each rationally made. Rather similarly, in the state of nature, the (absolutely) best outcome would result if everyone were to lay down his or her arms and agree not to 'invade', deceive or act aggressively towards the others. No one could rationally want the state of

85

nature to persist. However, so long as no one can trust anyone else to keep an agreement – and chooses, quite rationally, on that basis – that is exactly what it does.

Hobbes summarises this, and related, points in terms of a set of 'Lawes of Nature' which – in line with my characterisation of him as a rational choice theorist – he describes as 'dictates of Reason' and 'Conclusions, or Theoremes' (ibid.: 216–17). Hobbes defines 'law of nature' as follows:

A LAW OF NATURE (Lex Naturalis) is a Precept or general Rule, found out by reason, by which a man is forbidden to do, that, which is destructive of his life, or taketh away the means of preserving the same; and to omit that, by which he thinketh it may be best preserved.

(ibid.: 189)

Hobbes's first law of nature is this:

That every man, ought to endeavour Peace, as farre as he has hope of obtaining it; and when he cannot obtain it, that he may seek, and use, all helps, and advantages of Warre.

(ibid.: 190) (Hobbes' italics)

It is noticeable that there are two elements to this formulation. First, it describes a best possible outcome, namely 'peace', which – as Hobbes tells us – 'every man ought to endeavour'. But second, it also contains a statement of what it is rational to do when the best possible outcome is foreclosed by the behaviour of others. In the latter circumstances, it is rational to 'seek and use all helps and advantages of war'.[5] An equivalent pairing of 'best possible outcome' with 'most rational course to pursue in the circumstances' is contained in the way Hobbes formulates his second law of nature, which is this:

That a man be willing, when others are so too, as farre-forth, as for Peace, and defence of himselfe he shall think it necessary, to lay down this right to all things; and be contented, with so much liberty against other men, as he would allow other men against himself.

(ibid.: 190) (Hobbes' italics)

This tells us – first – that the best possible outcome would result if everyone were to 'lay down [this] right to all things' (which everyone has in the state of nature) but that – second – this can only be done 'when others are so too'. Where they are not, the best possible outcome is foreclosed. The third law of nature is simpler and more direct. It is just:

That men performe their Covenants made

(ibid.: 201) (Hobbes' italics)

In other words, 'keep your contracts'.

I shan't itemise and discuss every single one of Hobbes' laws of nature

– there are nineteen, and things could get very tedious were I even to try. Instead, let us now consider the role played by the sovereign in this scenario.

Contracts enter the picture here too, for once the sovereign has been instituted, so have the conditions which make it possible to make and keep contracts. As we have seen, in the state of nature making contracts would be a pointless activity because no one could trust other parties to a bargain to keep their word. The introduction of the sovereign changes this. This is not because the sovereign's appearance on the scene is followed by a radical improvement in everyone's moral character. People remain just as egocentrically motivated and 'diffident' as they were before. It is because the sovereign is prepared to use *force* against anyone who steps out of line (that is, if he is doing his job properly, unlike Charles I). This means that, if I now make a contract with you, I can trust you to keep your word, because I know that you are scared of the sovereign who will, in any case, force you to stick to it. For the same reason, you can now trust me. Hobbes summarises his position as follows:

> For the Lawes of Nature (as *Justice, Equity, Modesty, Mercy*, and (in summe) *doing to others as wee would be done to.*) of themselves, without the terrour of some Power, to cause them to be observed, are contrary to our naturall Passions, that carry us to Partiality, Pride, Revenge, and the like. And Covenants without the Sword are but Words, and of no strength to secure a man at all. Therefore notwithstanding the Lawes of nature, (which every one hath then kept, when he has the will to keep them, when he can do it safely,) if there be no Power erected, or not great enough for our security; every man will and may lawfully rely on his own strength and art.
>
> (ibid.: 223–4) (Hobbes' italics)

'Covenants without the Sword are but Words, and of no strength to secure a man at all' and, a little later, 'Covenants being but words, and breath, have no force to oblige, contain, constrain, or protect any man, but what it has from the publique Sword' (ibid.: 231). It is in such pronouncements that the distilled essence of Hobbes' position is contained. Given the role his sovereign is required to play, it is easy to appreciate Hobbes' insistence that the sovereign should have unbridled power and be prepared to use it.

From premise to conclusion: how the sovereign is established

To complete the picture of Hobbes' argument, we must now consider what he thinks people do when they submit themselves to the authority of a sovereign and thereby move from the state of nature to civil society. By what process is this achieved?

To appreciate Hobbes' account, we need to understand a distinction he draws between 'natural' and 'artificial' persons. The former conception is relatively unproblematic. To explain it, it should be sufficient to point out that you and I are both natural persons. An artificial person, in Hobbes' sense, is created when one natural person authorises another to act as his or her representative, or – to put it another way – in his or her *person*.[6] In this sense of 'represent', a lawyer represents you, or acts in your person, when in court and defending your case. The lawyer is your 'stand-in' so to speak. Likewise, a politician represents the persons of those in his or her constituency when speaking at meetings of the governing assembly. It is in this way that people, having tired of the state of nature's 'inconveniences', are pictured as authorising a sovereign – be that sovereign a single (natural) person or an assembly – to '*Present* the person of them all, (that is to say, to be their *Representative*)' (ibid.: 228) when they establish a commonwealth by *institution* (one of the two methods Hobbes describes). This is the point in Hobbes' narrative at which all people lay down the 'right to all things' and allow themselves only so much liberty as they would allow others against themselves, as required by the second law of nature. Having done that, they 'conferre all their power and strength upon one Man, or upon one Assembly of men, to beare their Person' (ibid.: 227). The great Leviathan is, thus, born. (The other form of contract described by Hobbes is what he calls *contract by acquisition*. This is a deal made by a defeated people with the leader(s) of a conquering power. The sovereign power is acquired by force. But it makes little difference. Hobbes remarks that sovereignty acquired in this way, 'differeth from Soveraignty by Institution onely in this, That, men who choose their Soveraign, do it for fear of one another, and not of him whom they Institute: But in this case, they subject themselves, to him they are afraid of' [ibid.: 252]. Even so, the contract is just as binding in both types of case – or so Hobbes would have us believe.)

Does Hobbes' argument work?

Having completed my brief outline of Hobbes's argument, I now propose to go back over it, this time examining it for weak spots. As I shall show, there are several points at which Hobbes fails to make the logical connections he wants to establish. It has to be said that, as philosophers go, this hardly makes him unusual; and nor is my purpose entirely negative and critical. You could say that I am treating Hobbes as a case study. In what follows, I shall concentrate on difficulties with his argument which arise from the fact that it is an exercise in rational choice theory; and understanding where such an argument can go wrong seems to me a very good way to deepen our understanding of this type of argument.

The premise: Is Hobbes' account of human nature true?

Are we essentially power-hungry and egocentric, as Hobbes says we are? Well, it was Hobbes' own belief that he could derive the truth of his premise from a theory according to which the fundamental components of the universe, the units out of which everything else is constructed, are small, imperceptible, motions. When it is applied to human behaviour, it is supposed to follow from this theory that each of us is a kind of machine, appetite being a movement towards something, aversion a movement away from something, and so on. Bear in mind that, when Hobbes was writing, there was nothing unusual about such ambition. In Hobbes' time, many philosophers and philosopher scientists were trying to explain the nature of the universe in terms of fundamental components. For example, just as Hobbes thought that all is motions (or 'endeavours') so Newton was to claim, later in the century, that everything is composed of small hard corpuscles or atoms. Hobbes' theory of motions may well appear archaic these days, but in his own time such all embracing explanations were the stuff of up-to-the-minute scientific theory.

Unfortunately, though, that is not a reason why *we* should accept Hobbes' description of human nature. However, I would like to suggest here that it is possible to accept Hobbes' description while rejecting his own argument for it. In other words, you don't have to believe any sort of cosmological theory – old-fashioned or otherwise – to take his account of human nature seriously. All you need to do is recognise that his portrait is sufficiently accurate as a representation of the way people behave *in political situations* for it to figure in explanations of what happens *in those situations*. There is a parallel here between the Hobbesian 'political man' (or person) and the 'economic man' (or person) who figures in textbooks of economic theory.[7] Economic man behaves with 100 per cent economic rationality. When faced with a choice of alternatives, economic man always does his utmost to maximise benefits and minimise costs. (For example, however wealthy he may be, given the choice between purchasing a tin of beans at thirty-five pence and another at thirty-four pence, economic man will always take a fifteen minute walk to purchase the latter, provided – of course – that in taking the walk itself he does not incur a quantifiable cost of more than one penny.) Economic man is such an unattractive character that were you or I to meet him we would hate him on sight. But fortunately – or so I hope – there is nobody exactly like economic man. That is not the point, however. Economic man is not so much a fiction as an abstraction, and the point is that, in *the situations with which economic theory is concerned*, our behaviour does resemble economic man's. In fact, it resembles it so closely that theorists are able to formulate viable theoretical principles with its help, as well as predict the behaviour of actual markets. Now, if Hobbes' description of human nature is accurate, the same goes for the relation between that description, treated as an abstraction, and human behaviour in the situations with which political theory is concerned. At least, that is how we should treat it – or so I suggest. (Of course, whether people really do behave like Hobbesian 'political man' even in those situations is a *further* question. I leave it to you, the reader, to decide about that.)

To illustrate the point, take Hobbes' claim that everyone is pretty much equal in power. (I mentioned this earlier. See page 83, above.) Here is what he says:

> Nature hath made men so equall, in the faculties of body, and mind; as that though there bee found one man sometimes manifestly stronger in body, or of quicker mind than another; yet when all is reckoned together, the difference between man, and man, is not so considerable, as that one man can thereupon claim to himself any benefit, to which another may not pretend, as well as he.
>
> (ibid.: 183)

Now, if you take what Hobbes says here at face value, it is actually false. Imagine a group of three people and suppose that one of them has much more physical strength than the other two, that he is the Incredible Hulk, say. In this situation, and contrary to what Hobbes says, it is obvious that the Hulk would have the power to subdue the others if he wanted to. Or, suppose that ten people are competing for a prize in a quiz. The subject is nuclear physics. One competitor is Albert Einstein and the other nine have been selected that afternoon, at random, from amongst the shoppers at the local supermarket. Unless something funny is going on, Einstein will win hands down. No one will be so much 'of quicker mind' that he or she will be able to 'outwit' Einstein, so Hobbes would be wrong about this case too. But the point is that politics – the subject – takes little if any interest in such small groups. Typically, politics is concerned with the relationships which hold between social classes, nation-states, supporters of political parties, and groups of suchlike size; that is, with groups which tend to be thousands, tens of thousands, millions, tens or hundreds of millions strong. And, when it comes to groups of that size, Hobbes is absolutely right. Not even the Incredible Hulk could control an entire population with only the help of his own strength or cunning. In such cases, it is true, as he says, that 'as to the strength of body, the weakest has strength enough to kill the strongest, either by secret machination, or by confederacy with others, that are in the same danger with himselfe' (ibid.). As a generalisation, then, Hobbes' statement is sufficiently accurate to describe human behaviour in the contexts to which it is meant to apply.

From premise to conclusion? The decision to quit the state of nature

But if Hobbes' portrait of human psychology is accurate – or accurate enough – if his premise is true, what of the move from premise to conclusion? Because Hobbes' argument is a social contract argument, assessing the validity of its internal structure means assessing the credibility of his claim that people really would make the choices he says they would. In fact, it is not so obvious that they would, not even if human nature is just as he describes it.

As I see it, there are several claims at issue here. To start with, there is the claim that Hobbesian people really would choose to leave the state of nature, rather than remain in it. Even this is questionable. To see why, bear in mind that a social contract argument relies on a contrast between two conditions: life in the state of nature and life under a sovereign. To justify the existence of the state, such an argument, if it is to persuade us, must show that the former condition is *worse* than the latter. Only then would people have a reason for moving from one situation to the other. If it cannot persuade us of the point, then we may as well embrace anarchism and reject the state altogether. The point is that 'worse' and 'better' are relative terms. It could be that neither situation is terrific. But that is irrelevant. All that matters is that one is worse, relative to the other one. So, even if life in the state of nature were just as terrible as Hobbes portrays it, it could still be the case that life under a sovereign – especially an absolute sovereign – would be even worse. (Would the former really be any worse than life under . . .? Fill in the blank with the name of your least favourite tyrant.)

But – to move on – we needn't even suppose that life in the state of nature would necessarily be as terrible as Hobbes makes it out to be. Even if his account of human nature is true, life in the state of nature might not be as bad as all that. That is because a lot depends on the 'background conditions' we assume to prevail. For example, what if there are relatively few people, and what if resources are relatively plentiful? For example, suppose you are a member of a small group living at the edge of a vast, fertile plain and another group lives at the other edge. There is little reason for thinking that a war of all against all would arise in this situation, as there would be little or nothing for people to compete for. Ferocious competition of the sort Hobbes envisages would arise only when resources became relatively scarce in relation to the number of individuals.

A contradiction? Rational choice and power

Now for a further question: Even if the most rational course of action for Hobbesian individuals to take is to quit the state of nature, does it follow that the only remedy for the state of nature's 'inconveniences' is subjection to the rule of an absolute sovereign of the type Hobbes prefers? Related to this, it is noticeable that Hobbes tends to present us with a choice between two stark alternatives. The way he tells his story, *either* we live in a state of nature *or* we are ruled by an absolute sovereign. There are no intermediate possibilities. Even systems in which power is limited or divided are portrayed by Hobbes as steps on the slippery slope which can only lead us back to the abyss. The consequence of the want of absolute power – he repeatedly tells us – is 'perpetuall warre of every man against his neighbour' (ibid.: 260).

Now, if the choice facing them were as clear cut as Hobbes suggests then it is, at least, arguable that his individuals would, if they were rational, choose subjection to an absolute sovereign. But if things are not so stark, then the latter option looks distinctly unattractive when compared with other possibilities. For example, if it were open to them to choose a system based on the division of powers, boundaries could be drawn beyond which the sovereign was not permitted to step. If there were, in addition, democratic controls – periodic elections, for example – then the sovereign could be changed if that is what people wanted. This looks far more attractive than the system preferred by Hobbes, where the sovereign's rights are unlimited,[8] and under which the sovereign, having been chosen, cannot be removed. (Why make a commitment from which you could never escape?) Not only that, a division of powers is just one possibility. Rather than quitting the state of nature, it is arguable that rational individuals would choose to join 'mutual protection agencies', rather like insurance companies, whose function was to protect their members and to resolve disputes on their behalf.[9] As we have seen, it is Hobbes' view that such possibilities are closed off. He thinks that only an absolute sovereign would be strong enough to keep others 'in awe', and thereby ensure that contracts are kept and civilisation preserved. But Hobbes could be wrong. In fact, it can be argued that his insistence that only absolute sovereigns are capable of doing the job sovereigns are supposed to do involves him in a logical contradiction, in which case his argument fails a test every purportedly logical argument must pass.

Let me spell this out in more detail. According to the objection, there is a contradiction between Hobbes' conclusion – that *only* absolute sovereigns can do the job – and one of his premises. This is the premise which states that everyone is fairly equal in power, so much so that 'the weakest has strength enough to kill the strongest, either by secret machination, or by confederacy with others, that are in the same danger with himselfe' (ibid.: 183). (We discussed this earlier, but for a different reason.) The objection states that if the premise is true, political power can only arise where many people act in agreed and predictable ways. From this, it is held to follow that less centralised systems are no less viable than the system Hobbes advocates. If this is right, it follows that Hobbes' conclusion is inconsistent with one of his premises.

To appreciate the objection's force, imagine what would happen if you were to go along to your nearest major road, stand in one of the traffic lanes, and raise your hand in an authoritative gesture, clearly signalling that you want the traffic to stop. If you were lucky, cars and trucks would swerve to avoid you, although you would no doubt be treated to some abuse. If you were unlucky, you would be run over. Now compare this with what would happen if you were to go down there in a uniform, and travelling in a white car with the word 'POLICE' inscribed on the side. Police officers do just that, and are able to make the traffic come to a halt, just by making the same gesture. So how is it that a police officer can stop the traffic just by raising a hand, whereas you can't? There is no reason to believe that the average police officer is any stronger than the average person generally, and certainly no police officer is physically strong enough to stop a speeding truck, so it can't be a question of brute strength. Can it be that police officers have magic powers, then?

No, of course they don't. Drivers stop when signalled by the police because they know what will happen if they don't, and what will happen if they don't is that other people, a whole multitude, will behave in certain ways. For a start, the officer who made the 'stop' gesture will call up other officers who will chase the motorist and who *are* capable of using physical force to stop him. When arrested he can be taken before a magistrate, whose authority is supported by a bureaucratic apparatus for making sure that people pay their fines. Supporting this, there will lie, in its turn, a system of prisons, and offices and prisons only function as such because those who work them operate in certain ways (by sending out reminders and warnings to non-payers, for example, and by keeping inmates locked up). Otherwise, they would just be rooms. As this shows, the police officer has power only because he or she can rely on a whole network of others to behave in a regular and predictable manner.

Now, the same goes for political power, including the power of a sovereign. In fact, Hobbes is well aware of this. 'The Greatest of humane Powers', he says,

> is that which is compounded of the Powers of most men, united by consent in one person, Naturall or Civill that has the use of all their Powers depending on his will; such as is the Power of a Commonwealth

(ibid.: 150)

Actually, Hobbes' use of the word 'consent' here is too strong, and we should note this. It is an exaggeration to describe the power of the sovereign as resting on the 'consent' of others, as Hobbes does here, just as it would be an exaggeration to describe the police officer's power as arising from the 'consent' of others. At least, it is an exaggeration if 'consent' is taken to mean 'express consent'; that is, consent which is openly and consciously given. But in my example, the prison officers and others who behave in regular and predictable ways, and who therefore support police officers in the exercise of their power do not have to give their express consent to, say, a police officer's having such-and-such a power (for example, the power to stop traffic). They only have to behave in regular and predictable ways, and where consent is involved it need only be 'weak' consent to, e.g., work in a prison in return for such-and-such a wage.

Still, even with that reservation, the objection is left unaffected. It states that, because it relies on the predictable behaviour of others, the power of an absolute sovereign is, in that respect, no different from any other political power arrangement. Thus, if people can consent to an absolute sovereign – if only in the weak sense of 'consent' just outlined – then they can equally well 'consent' to a system in which power is divided. Because both types of system rest on agreement, there is no reason for thinking that the former is any more or less prone than the latter to disintegration. So, either Hobbes rejects his premise – that all power rests on 'consent' – or he rejects his conclusion, that the only rational thing to do is choose an absolute sovereign. That is where the inconsistency lies. (Personally, I would go for rejecting the conclusion.) If this objection is right, things are serious for Hobbes, for it is an objection which affects the very basis of his position.

The contract: real or hypothetical?

By now, I have said enough to suggest where weaknesses in the internal structure of Hobbes' argument may lie. Now for a more general question, one which relates to the *type* of theory this is. That question is: What are we to make of the 'social contract' on which so much of Hobbes' argument (and so much subsequent theory) hangs?

Broadly speaking, there are two possibilities. On the one hand, it could be that we are intended to take the social contract story *literally*; that is, it could be that we are supposed to believe that there really was a past event at which real people really did make an agreement to establish a sovereign authority. (Or – a variant on the same theme – we could be meant to believe that there have been a number of such events.) On the other hand, perhaps there was never a real contract and – perhaps – we are meant to accord the contract a purely theoretical role; that is to say, perhaps we are meant to believe in a *hypothetical* contract. Let us take each possibility in turn.

So – first – what if there was a real social contract? Hobbes' 'geometrical' approach makes it unlikely that he intends us to think of it this way, but it is still worth noting that, had this been his intention, then his argument might well have contained the potential to establish one of the conclusions he wants. This is the conclusion that we are *morally* obliged to obey a law when it is the command of an absolute sovereign, even if – on independent grounds – we may dislike or disapprove of the law in question. (This is Hobbes' proposed answer to one of political philosophy's traditional problems – 'the problem of political obligation' as it is sometimes called.)

Let me explain the point with the help of a story. Suppose that P and Q are next door neighbours. Every so often, P, who is in business, has to spend a week or so travelling abroad. Each time P goes away, P asks Q to look after and feed P's beloved cat. Q agrees, and after each trip, P returns with a present for Q. (This is a token of gratitude – a bottle of wine, or whatever.) This is a regular occurrence. It has been going on for years, so much so that Q has come to expect a present each time P comes back. Now suppose that, one day, P returns without a present. Q objects, and exclaims, 'Where is my present?!' To this, P's indignant response is, 'We don't have a *contract* you know!'

Now, P's response is – surely – correct. To see why, consider just how different the situation would have been if P and Q had actually agreed a contract. Suppose that each of them had signed a piece of paper stating, 'I, P, agree with you, Q, that in the event of my going on a trip . . .', and so on. In this case, P is under an *obligation* to return with a present for Q, an obligation which would not exist if there were no actual contract. That is because it is the very fact of P's having signed – the fact that the contract is therefore real – which creates the obligation. Signing the contract is like saying, 'I promise . . .'. As for the relevance of the example to Hobbes' argument, it is this: If there is an obligation to obey the law, then there must be a reason why I (like everyone else) ought (morally) to obey the law – by paying my taxes, for example – even when I am inclined to break it. Now, Hobbes is claiming that there is such an obligation. Moreover, he is claiming that I ought to pay my taxes where the law stating that I should is the command of an absolute sovereign. But from where does this obligation arise? If it is meant to arise *from a contract* – if that is Hobbes' claim – then, as the example shows, it could only arise from a real contract. It follows, as I am claiming, that it would help him a great deal if the social contract were, itself, a real contract.

However, it is worth adding here that it wouldn't really help him *that much*. There is a further major problem with social contract theory, the following. Even if it could be established that a group of our ancestors had at a point in the remote past made an agreement which could be described as 'a social contract' – and there is no evidence whatsoever that any such thing ever happened – there would remain the problem of explaining why, and how, such an agreement should be binding on *us*. Suppose that my great-great-great-great-grandfather died owing your great-great-great-great-grandmother money. Does that mean I owe you money? Or, suppose that we can both trace our ancestry back to the Norman Conquest in

1066. I am a direct descendant of the Norman aristocrat who confiscated land which, as it turns out, belonged to the Saxon from whom you are directly descended. Does that mean that I should give you my house? Does it mean that I should give you my ball-point pen? It is by no means obvious that I should do either, because it is by no means obvious that a moral obligation – including the obligation to keep a contract – is transmitted genetically from generation to generation. As the philosopher David Hume, who was sceptical of the whole 'social contract' idea, put it, 'this supposes the consent of the fathers to bind the children, even to the most remote generations' and, as he added, 'it is not justified by history or experience in any age or country of the world' (Hume 1953: 47).

What of the other possibility, the possibility that, for Hobbes, the social contract is hypothetical in its status. (As I have suggested, out of the two views I distinguished, it would certainly be fairer to attribute this one to him.) To return, for a moment, to the story of P and Q, you could say that with their regular behaviour – P going away, Q feeding the cat, P coming back with a present – P and Q are behaving *as if* there was a contract between them. If you wanted to, you could add that it is in the *rational self-interest* of each to behave that way – Q's reason for feeding the cat is to get the present; P's reason for bringing the present is to keep Q sweet, so that Q will feed the cat next time. By analogy, if *Leviathan* is mainly an exercise in rational choice theory, then perhaps it would be fairer to Hobbes' intentions to think of him as stating that, if people act rationally, they will behave *as if* there had been a social contract?

Well, perhaps it would, but the trouble with interpreting Hobbes that way is that it enmeshes his argument in a different set of difficulties. For example, it faces him with the problem of explaining why any one should obey a law (i.e. a command of the sovereign) when it seems quite apparent that there is no good reason arising from self-interest for doing so. Take an example of a trivial misdemeanour. Suppose that it is late at night. You have been visiting friends and you are walking home. You urgently need to sleep as, the next morning, you will have to get up and go to work. The shortest route home involves cutting through the park, but there is a bylaw: 'KEEP OFF THE GRASS – BY ORDER, THE SOVEREIGN'. Should you obey? There is no one around to see you, so you won't be setting a bad example, and just one person walking across the grass just once is hardly likely to damage it. You would be breaking the law if you did, but why not go ahead and walk across the grass anyway? If there had been a real contract, and one which is binding on us, Hobbes could claim that we morally ought to obey the law, even in this case. But what if there is no real contract? Behaving *as if* there was a contract means keeping off the grass even so, but why should you? Hobbes thinks that we are rational creatures who are motivated by self-interest, so he would have to show that, despite first appearances, it would nevertheless be in your self-interest to keep off the grass and take the long way home. And, so far as I can see, he could only demonstrate the point by assuming that every law breaking act is a step on the slippery slope back to the state of nature; and, as he constantly reminds us, no worse calamity could possibly befall us.

But if that is Hobbes' argument, it is unconvincing. To persuade us, Hobbes would have to demonstrate that if you walk across the grass you would increase the likelihood of society's collapsing into barbarism, that a war of every man on every man would ensue, and so on. In short, Hobbes would be forced to fall back on (what I call) a 'what if everybody did it?' argument, and the trouble with such arguments is that they usually fail through making false factual assumptions.

In other words, for such an argument to work it has to be reasonably certain that people really will do it (whatever 'it' may be). In the case of my 'crossing the park' story, this means that Hobbes would have to convince us that by crossing the grass you increase the likelihood that everybody (or at least a considerable number of people) would do the same as you. Of course, something could hang on what 'doing the same thing' means here. In crossing the grass you both 'cross the grass' and 'break the law'. It makes little difference in this case, though. To take the first possibility. It is no doubt true that if everybody, or a substantial number of people, turned up at your local park and started walking about on the grass, the lawn would suffer. But, in the story as I told it, it is pretty certain that this is not going to happen. (It is late at night. There is no one around to see you, so others will not be encouraged.) Likewise, we can be equally confident that if everyone were to break any law they felt like breaking, whenever they felt like it, civilisation would collapse. But, if we are to believe Hobbes we need a reason for thinking that your walking across the grass will encourage a general disrespect for the law. However, there is no such reason. Hobbes' pro-'law and order' argument assumes that most people are incapable of distinguishing trivial misdemeanours such as walking on the grass – or, say, exceeding the speed limit by 5 mph on a sunny day when there is hardly any traffic on the motorway – and 'rapine', 'revenge', and suchlike serious and evil deeds. But there is no reason to assume any such thing.

Hobbes' legacy

In this chapter, I have concentrated on displaying the way Hobbes' argument – construed as an exercise in rational choice theory – is structured. As I think I have just shown, out of the two most sympathetic interpretations to which that argument is open, neither allows Hobbes to establish the conclusion he wants.

Does this mean that his philosophy can be ignored or dismissed? Absolutely not. Let me add that I am only too well aware of how easy it can be for some smartypants philosophy teacher to show off to a crowd by taking a classic argument, such as Hobbes', and ostentatiously tearing it into little pieces. Everyone is left wondering why anyone ever bothered to read Hobbes in the first place. This approach is guilty of several falsifications. For one thing, it misrepresents philosophy by treating certain arguments – smartypants' own – as conclusive when, in reality, they are just as provisional as every other argument. It also ignores the fact that a major work of philosophy like *Leviathan* is more than just a set of arguments. It is also a work of imagination, and specific arguments, or groups of them, can quite often be subsidiary to a work's guiding conception.

That said, what have we inherited from Hobbes? I would say that the most valuable items in his legacy are, first, an approach to political philosophy and, second, a vision. The former is the social contract approach. Hobbes may have been the first writer to present a lengthy, developed, social contract argument; but his gift to later generations is not just that. It is that, in *Leviathan*, we have a working example of a method which is pregnant with possibility. The point is amply demonstrated by the ways in which later philosophers were to work and rework the social contract idea. As for the vision, along with the social contract approach there goes a way of representing fundamental aspects of the relationships which hold between individuals themselves, and between individuals and institutions such as the state. One way to think of the state of nature is as a schematic, almost a diagrammatic, representation of the form those relationships take. Different philosophers will represent them differently, of course, but – as we have seen – for Hobbes the basic form of human relationship is *contractual*. In *Leviathan*, individuals are portrayed as having 'desires', wants, needs, interests and so on which inevitably conflict, and as seeking resolutions through contractual agreement. It is not the only way to portray the human condition, but nor is it silly or patently inaccurate. Arguably, it is a portrait of our condition which is peculiarly appropriate to modern (i.e. post-medieval) times.

Finally, something which has *not* survived over time is Hobbes' notoriety. It is hard for modern readers to appreciate but, during his lifetime, his work was regarded as shocking by many, scandalous even. Why should this have been? The answer is *not* that he advocated rule by an absolute sovereign. That view would have been commonplace in a period when monarchs routinely claimed to rule by divine right. (In this connection, it is noticeable that Hobbes says a great deal to suggest that, so far as he is concerned, the sovereign's absolute power is distinct from *arbitrary* power; that the sovereign cannot single an individual out for special punishment – or for preferential treatment – simply for convenience, or on a whim, or just because he happens to have taken a dislike to that individual.)[10] On the contrary, to the extent that Hobbes scandalised public opinion, he did so by subverting a received, conventional, view; the view that the actions of the sovereign are limited by an independently determinable natural law, instituted by God. (This is the view outlined in the work of 'natural law theorists' such as Samuel Pufendorf and Hugo Grotius.)[11] In England, this conventional picture of things was further reinforced by a constitutionalism according to which the power of a sovereign should be held in check or balanced by the people. Hobbes subverted this in a number of ways. For example, by making the sovereign the interpreter of God's law he appeared to deny the former's subservience to the latter. No doubt, it was this which led to the suspicion of atheism under which Hobbes fell. Then again, Hobbes' royalism notwithstanding, there was the fact that his argument could easily have been used to support Cromwell's rule. (What did it matter who was in charge, provided that person behaved as a strong sovereign should?)

In the next chapter, we turn to a text in which the more conventional view of the relationship between natural law and political authority is revived and reworked. Ironically, it is also a progressive work in which the foundations of the modern world view are laid. More than that, it deserves to be ranked, for its influence, with a small number of world-historical texts: the Bible, the Koran, Marx's *Capital*, Darwin's *Origin of Species*, and a handful of others. The text in question is John Locke's *Second Treatise of Civil Government*.

7

—◦◡◦—

Locke and the modern order

For a rough indication of John Locke's importance to the history of political thought, you need only list the conclusions he sets out to establish. First, Locke holds that we are fundamentally equal. No one is anyone else's natural superior or natural inferior. Second, and closely related to this, Locke holds that we have certain fundamental rights. Third, he claims that these rights crucially include the right to life and the right to liberty. (Nowadays, such rights tend to be labelled 'human rights'. Locke calls them 'natural rights'.) Fourth, Locke holds that no government is legitimate unless it remains in place with the consent of the governed, so much so that when that consent is withdrawn the people have a right to rebel, to overthrow the government (using violence if necessary), and to replace it with another.

By now, such views are orthodox. There can be few who do not claim to respect principles similar to Locke's – who do not claim to recognise the 'human rights' of others, for example – even amongst those who flout them in practice. But in Locke's time there were many who would have considered his *Second Treatise of Civil Government* to be dangerous and subversive (Locke 1993). Locke's political philosophy is important because it is one of the first serious attempts to articulate the principles I just listed within the context of a philosophical theory, thereby supplying them with a particular interpretation and supporting them with an intellectual defence. It would be no exaggeration – or not much of one – to describe him as the political philosopher who laid the moral foundations of the modern world view.

Nor should we forget that Locke was one of the first philosophers to elaborate an argument in defence of private property. This is a theme which frequently recurs within political arguments taking place in our own time. Not all modern political philosophers believe there is a right of private ownership, or a 'natural right to property' as Locke calls it. Nevertheless, one rough-and-ready way to distinguish modern 'isms' – liberalism from, say, socialism or conservatism – is in terms of the way supporters of those positions think property ought to be distributed. (To put it broadly, socialists tend to favour the redistribution of property, whereas conservatives do not.) More than that, there are, even now, philosophers who take Lockean and anti-Lockean positions on the subject of property.[1] (Locke's defence of property is, in some ways, separable from the rest of his argument. I have made it the subject of a separate chapter, the following.)

In short, we have plenty of very good reasons for paying attention to Locke's political philosophy; and because – in addition to everything I have mentioned so far – the *Second Treatise* is an exercise in social contract theory, the right place to start is with Locke's account of life in the state of nature.

The state of nature

Like Hobbes, Locke portrays the state of nature as a condition from which political authority and the power to enforce it are absent. That has to be so for, within the context of a social contract theory, it is true *by definition* that the state of nature is apolitical. But that is where the similarity between the two philosophers ends. For example, whereas Hobbes thinks that life without authority can only be insecure and bleak, Locke is more inclined to stress its positive features. 'The state all men are naturally in', he writes, is 'a state of perfect freedom to order their actions, and dispose of their possessions and persons as they think fit, within the bounds of the law of nature, without asking leave, or depending upon the will of any other man' (Locke 1993: II, 4).[2] Nor does Locke equate the state of nature with the state of war, the 'plain difference' between the two being, in his opinion, 'as far distant, as a state of peace, good will, mutual assistance, and preservation, and a state of enmity, malice, violence, and mutual destruction are one from another' (II, 19). So, whereas for Hobbes the state of war is simply the condition of defensive mutual suspicion which results when authority is absent, so far as Locke is concerned you only get a state of war when one person deliberately sets out to destroy another's liberty and life. War is 'a declared design of force upon the person of another' (II, 19). Unlike Hobbes, Locke clearly believes that, *generally speaking*, people are capable of 'living together according to reason, without a common superior on Earth' (ibid.).

The law of nature

But one of the most striking differences between Locke and Hobbes is that, so far as Locke is concerned, people have rights, duties and obligations, even in the state of nature, where there is no civil authority. '[But] though this be a state of liberty', he writes, 'yet it is not a state of licence' for 'the state of nature has a law of nature to govern it, which obliges everyone' (II, 6). This contrasts sharply with Hobbes' view that, within the state of nature, there is only a 'right of nature' which is 'the Liberty each man hath, to use his own power, as he will himself, for the preservation of his own life'. In other words, everyone is entitled to what they can grab and hold on to, by force if necessary (Hobbes 1981: 189). Hobbes might as well have stated that there are, in nature, no rights at all.[3] Locke's idea – that we are morally bound by a 'law of nature' – is quite different, and before we go any further we should consider its main features.

To begin with it is crucial to grasp the distinction between the *natural law*, as it is conceived by Locke and others, and the *civil law*.[4] Civil law is, quite simply, the law as we all know it. It is the law you will find transcribed in statute books, or embodied in the decisions made by magistrates and judges as they follow precedent. The content of the civil law is whatever the law making authorities decide that it should be. It may specify that, as a citizen, you have certain rights, but these will be (mere) legal rights; that is the rights which, as it happens, the civil law specifies you should have. Likewise for obligations. This being so, it is clear that the civil law can vary over time, or from state to state. To take a contemporary example, for most roads in the UK and Australia you have a right to drive on the left and a duty not to drive on the right. By contrast, in France and the USA, things are the other way round. There is no real point to these differences. It is just that – for whatever reason – the relevant authorities happen to have decided that things should be that way. Notice, too, that – because the civil law is, in this respect, a matter of *convention* – there is no reason for thinking that your legal duties, as specified by that law, must coincide with your moral duties. To take an obvious example: Under Nazi law you had a legal duty to reveal the whereabouts of anyone Jewish who you knew to be in hiding. However, there is no way this could be counted a moral duty. In this case, it would be your *moral* duty to *break* the civil law.

By contrast with the civil law, the natural law (if there is such a thing) is binding on everyone equally, wherever they live and under whatever authority. It is held to apply even where there is no civil authority and, hence, no civil law. The natural law is the measure of the civil law, and where the former is violated by the latter, you may be entitled to break the civil law. You may even be morally obliged to break it, for your rights and duties as defined by natural law are your moral rights and duties. The natural law is, thus, the moral law. To put it another way, it is *morality construed on the model of law.*

From this, I think it should be clear how the idea that there is a law of nature – a law which transcends the civil law – can serve as a powerful critical weapon. Thus, if there is some objectionable regime which is, say, denying votes to blacks, or education to women, or ill-treating an ethnic minority group, it helps you criticise it if you can argue that it is guilty of violating a law of nature by which we are all bound. (Likewise, should you prefer the contemporary rhetoric, it helps you criticise the regime if you can argue that it is guilty of human rights violations.) Of course, such behaviour may be perfectly legal so far as the regime's (civil) legal system is concerned. It may even be considered acceptable by a sizeable proportion of the population. But, if you can argue that it violates a law of nature, you can condemn it even so.[5]

However, that said, the idea that morality can be construed on the model of law also has its difficulties. This becomes apparent once you start to press the analogy between civil and natural law. For example, there is the fairly fundamental question of how we can know what the law requires. In the case of civil law it is a relatively straightforward matter to find this out. You can consult the relevant lawbook. Failing that you can phone a lawyer. But how do you find out what the natural law requires? If, like Locke, you think that the natural law is the command of God, then you could try consulting a holy text. But holy texts are notoriously open to interpretation, and, in any case, only the followers of the religions to which they are holy regard them as authoritative, so you would be faced with the problem of explaining to those who do not share your beliefs why they should take any notice of them – and you can't phone God either.

Equality, liberty, and rights

How does Locke resolve this difficulty? Well, Locke believes that the content of the natural law can be discovered *by reason*. For example, take the following crucial passage. Locke opens by writing of the state of nature that it is:

> a state also of equality, wherein all the power and jurisdiction is reciprocal, no one having more than another: there being nothing more evident, that creatures of the same species and rank promiscuously born to all the same advantages of nature, and the use of the same faculties, should also be equal one amongst another without subordination or subjection, unless the lord and master of them all, should by any manifest declaration of his will set one above another, and confer on him by an evident and clear appointment an undoubted right to dominion and sovereignty.
>
> (II, 4)

In this passage, Locke is arguing that there is no natural characteristic sufficient to distinguish one person from another, *from which it follows that the former is entitled to exert authority over the latter*. Of course, there are plenty of natural differences between us. When it comes to the exercise of certain skills – philosophy or football – some of us are better or more adept than others. This is not to mention obvious natural differences in age, sex, colour and so on. But Locke's point is that, when it comes to moral status, these just don't count. We are 'equal one amongst another without subordination or subjection'. As Locke sees it, it is partly a question of what God must have intended. There is no 'manifest declaration of his will' by which the 'lord and master' of us all has set 'one above another'. Still, you don't have to believe in God to accept his fundamental point.

Further, since it is the law of nature's foundational principle that we are each bound to recognise others as equals, it follows quite directly that we each have certain fundamental 'natural' rights, notably a right to life and a right to liberty. In fact, you could say that the two statements – the statement that we are basically equal and the statement that we have natural rights to life and liberty – are just two different ways of making the same point; for what can it be to respect others as equals, if it is not to recognise that they have lives of their own to live? And what can it be to interfere with someone's liberty or life, if it is not to subordinate that person to one's own arbitrary will? (As Locke reminds us later, to be free is 'not to be subject to the inconstant, uncertain, unknown, arbitrary will of another man' (II, 22).)

The core of Locke's argument, as I have outlined it so far, is well summarised by Locke himself, as follows:

> The state of nature has a law of nature to govern it, which obliges every one: and reason, which is that law, teaches all mankind who will but consult it, that being all equal and independent, no one ought to harm another in his life, health, liberty or possessions.
>
> (II, 6)

But is he right? To speak personally, I don't see how anyone can seriously deny that he is. At least, I don't see how a modern person could seriously deny Locke's central point, which is that a simple natural characteristic cannot, just by itself, entitle its bearer to claim any special status. (Whether you choose to express it quite as Locke did, in terms of rights, may be a different matter.) In our time the point has become integral to many a progressive belief system, most noticeably in the arguments of those who campaign against racism, sexism and other forms of discrimination. For example, most modern feminism is premised on the claim that a simple biological feature cannot be used to justify treating a person in certain ways. In the case of feminism, the biological feature is the fact of being female, and most feminists argue that this is not something which automatically justifies consigning a person to a subordinate status or role. The particular version of the fallacy in question to which Locke himself was especially opposed was the doctrine of the 'divine right of kings'. This is the doctrine that a biological feature – in this case, the fact of having a given ancestry and sex – entitles someone to exercise supreme authority. Specifically, Locke wanted to deny that James II's 'natural' relationship to the rest of the Stuart family, taken together with the fact of his having a penis, were sufficient to endow him with a God-given right to rule the country.

Admittedly, Locke's view is peculiarly modern. You only have to consider just how different it is from Aristotle's. As we saw (in Chapter 3) Aristotle believed that some people are naturally inferior to others. For example, he believed that women are inferior to men and – even – that some people are born to be slaves. But then, he was able to view a certain form of state – the ancient Greek *polis* – as a natural phenomenon; a kind of organism in which everything must have its right place if it is to function properly. He could also think of Greece's rigid class system as an unalterable given. All this would have helped maintain him in his inegalitarian view, but no such thing was possible for Locke. It is true that in Locke's time it was still far easier to believe that some are the natural superiors of others, far easier than it is in our own. As he insisted, 'Though I have said above ... that "all men by nature are equal", I cannot be supposed to understand all sorts of equality. Age or virtue may give men a just precedency; excellency of parts and merit may place others above the common level', and so on. And yet, as he goes on to stress, 'all this consists with the equality which all men are in, in respect of jurisdiction or dominion one over another' (II, 54). And *that* is the point.[6]

From the state of nature to civil society

But however persuasive Locke's argument may be up to this point, we are still faced with problems; for it is one thing to establish the fundamental principle that we are free and equal under the law of nature, but quite another to determine exactly how that principle applies in particular cases. Like every law, the law of nature will sometimes require interpretation. In civil society, where civil law prevails and where there is authority and a legal system, the job of interpretation is done by lawyers. It is for judges to determine how the civil law applies in difficult cases, and thereby set precedents for the future. A second difficulty relates to the sanctions which accompany breaches of the law. In the case of ordinary, civil, law these can be specified: 'if you do such-and-such you will be fined such-and-such'; 'if you do such-and-such the police will arrest you and you may go to prison', and so on. However, in the case of the law of nature, it is difficult to see what the parallel could be. Even if there is such a law, there seems to be no tariff of 'natural punishments' to accompany it. And, compounding this, there is a third difficulty, the difficulty of how sanctions are to be carried out. For all his belief that we are, generally speaking, capable of getting along, Locke leaves us in no doubt that there will be law breakers, and his rhetoric becomes quite harsh when describing how they should be dealt with; for example, when he writes that the criminal has 'declared war against all mankind, and therefore may be destroyed as a lion or a tiger, one of those wild savage beasts with whom men can have no society nor security' (II, 11) or that 'such men are not under the ties of the common law of reason, have no other rule, but that of force and violence, and so may be treated as beasts of prey' (II, 16). But the question is, *who* is to hunt down and destroy such 'dangerous and noxious creatures' (ibid.). There are – by definition – no police in the state of nature.

It is Locke's view that, in such conditions, everyone has to be his or her *own* magistrate and law enforcement officer. He writes:

> if anyone in the state of nature may punish another, for any evil he has done, every one may do so. For in that state of perfect equality, where naturally there is no superiority or jurisdiction of one, over another, what any may do in prosecution of that law, every one must needs have a right to do.
>
> (II, 7)

In summary, Locke's argument is this: Because (i) it is necessary for our preservation that the law of nature should be observed (the law would be 'in vain' otherwise') (ibid.) and because (ii) we are equals, with equal rights, it follows (iii) that *everyone* has the right to interpret the law of nature and to punish those who break it. You are entitled to seek reparation from those whom you believe to have harmed you, and you are even entitled to punish those who commit crimes of which you are not, yourself, the victim. As Locke sees it, there is an 'executive power of the law of nature' such that 'every man hath a right to punish the offender, and be executioner of the law of nature' (II, 13, 8).

By now, it should be clear why it is that Locke thinks people would quit the state of nature. In the *Second Treatise*, Chapter 9, he lists the latter's main 'inconveniences' (II, 124–6). There are three. The first is that the state of nature lacks a settled standard or 'common measure' of law. As a result, there will be constant quarrel and disagreement. For 'though the law of nature be plain and intelligible to all rational creatures', writes Locke, 'men' will be 'biased by their interest' when applying it to their own cases (II, 124). The second reason is that in the state of nature there is no settled, recognised, judicial authority. There lacks 'a known and indifferent Judge'. In that state, everyone is 'both judge and executioner of the law of nature' and 'men being partial to themselves, passion and revenge is very apt to carry them too far' in their own cases; lack of concern to 'make them too remiss', when it comes to other peoples (II, 125). Thirdly, enforcing the law of nature requires a centralised power, a power the state of nature lacks (II, 126).

We are meant to conclude that life in the state of nature would be insecure and uncertain, so much so that people would inevitably surrender their rights to interpret and enforce the law of nature to a centralised authority, a 'sovereign'. Locke puts it this way:

> If man in the state of nature be so free, as has been said; If he be absolute lord of his own person and possessions, equal to the greatest, and subject to no body, why will he part with his freedom? Why

will he give up this empire, and subject himself to the dominion and control of any other power? to which 'tis obvious to answer, that though in the state of nature he hath such a right, yet the enjoyment of it is very uncertain, and constantly exposed to the invasion of others. For all being kings as much as he, every man his equal, and the greater part no strict observers of equity and justice, the enjoyment of the property he has in this state is very unsafe, very unsecure. This makes him willing to quit this condition, which however free, is full of fears and continual dangers. And 'tis not without reason, that he seeks out, and is willing to join in society with others who are already united, or have a mind to unite for the mutual preservation of their lives, liberties, and estates, which I call by the general name, *property*.

(II, 123)

There can be no doubt that Locke's account of the transition from the state of nature to civil society is open to criticisms and questions which parallel those I raised against Hobbes in his account of the same transition. For example, it could be that something hangs on the numerical ratio of 'noxious' law breakers to law abiding others. If the number of law breakers is relatively few, and therefore relatively controllable, then perhaps it could be argued that people would have no reason at all for leaving the state of nature.[7] Again, there are, conceivably, methods for controlling law breakers which fall short of a fully fledged state. Like Hobbes', Locke's argument is open to the objection that – perhaps – 'mutual protection agencies' would do the trick. However, I shan't bore you by repeating the same arguments in a different context and in any case I am sure that readers are capable of working out the parallels for themselves here. Instead, let us move on to one of the arguments for which the *Second Treatise* is best known; the argument that government must rest on consent.

Consent

The role played by consent in Locke's argument

Consent enters Locke's argument at a number of points. One is the point at which people decide to move out of the state of nature and form a community. Each 'devests himself of his natural liberty, and puts on the bonds of civil society' by 'agreeing with other men to join and unite into a community'; this being 'one body, with a power to act as one body' (II, 95, 96). The particular system of government under which people are ruled is also said, by Locke, to rest on consent. So far as Locke is concerned, the fact of consent is more important than the precise nature of the system itself. There are many possible 'forms of commonwealth', and people can even consent to a system in which decisions are made by a single individual (II, 151). However, Locke himself prefers what he calls a 'moderated monarchy' (II, 159); that is, a system in which the power of a sovereign is limited by an assembly, such as a parliament. This was the system that became securely established in England with the 'Glorious Revolution' of 1688, in which Locke played a prominent role (of which more shortly). Consent plays an important role in Locke's defence of property too. This will be discussed in the following chapter.

By now, it should be clear why Locke thinks that government must rest on the consent of the governed. The conclusion follows directly from his premise that we are all equal under the law of nature, and fundamentally free (or 'autonomous'); creatures for whom freedom is the 'Foundation of all the rest' (II, 17). It is difficult to see how anything *other* than consent could legitimise authority for such creatures. On this view, it can be permissible for you to make rules for me to obey, or to give me orders, but only if you have my *permission* to do these things.

The problem of tacit consent

So far, so good. However, things start to go rapidly downhill once you start to ask: What is it that people *actually do* when they give their consent to a political system, or to a government? On this, Locke's unhelpfulness is notorious, thanks to his attempt to distinguish 'express' from 'tacit' consent. The former is relatively unproblematic. Express consent is consent freely, openly and knowingly given. The trouble starts with the notion of tacit consent, which Locke attempts to explain as follows:

> The difficulty is, what ought to be look'd upon as a *tacit consent*, and how far it binds, *i.e.* how far anyone shall be looked on to have consented, and thereby submitted to any government, where he has made no expressions of it at all. And to this I say, that every man, that hath any possession, or enjoyment, of any part of the dominions of any government, doth thereby give his tacit consent, and is as far forth obliged to obedience to the laws of that government, during such enjoyment, as any one under it; whether this his possession be of land, to him and his heirs for ever, or a lodging only for a week; or whether it be barely travelling freely on the highway; and in effect, it reaches as far as the very being of any one within the territories of that government.
>
> (II, 119)

What are we to make of this? For a start, it is pretty obvious that – as stated above – Locke's definition of tacit consent is not much good. Suppose that you live in a modern liberal democracy, and that you voted with the minority at the last election; i.e. that you did *not* vote for the government presently in power. If asked, you would probably say that you did not consent to that government's existence; and it would be no use telling you that, really, you did because this morning you drove to the supermarket and purchased some groceries (i.e. that you went 'travelling freely on the highway'). Or, suppose that you spend a holiday in a country ruled by a ruthless military dictator. You stay in a hotel ('a lodging only for a week'). Some of your friends may tell you that you shouldn't have gone there, but it would be a ridiculous exaggeration to say that, simply by going, you *consented* to the dictator's regime and his policies. On the face of things, Locke's definition of 'tacit consent' would appear to have these and other similarly absurd implications.

The passage quoted has persistently baffled commentators on Locke. Could a powerful intellectual like Locke really have expected his readers to swallow such a hopeless definition?[8] However, it has to be recognised that *any* attempt to justify a political system with the claim that it rests on the consent of the governed has to recognise that it is never true that everyone consents expressly. For modern readers, the point is especially pressing, because it is sometimes claimed that the liberal democratic systems with which we are familiar are based on consent; or, if not quite that, that the electoral machinery by which they are typified ensures that the 'will of the people' prevails. But in modern liberal democracies governments are usually elected with only around 40–50 per cent of the total votes cast. Therefore, we can take it that the other 50–60 per cent of the voters do not consent to the government which gets elected, or not expressly. To that, you have to add the number of people qualified to vote, but who don't. (Some of these just don't bother. Perhaps there are others who are not attracted by the alternatives on offer at election time.) It follows that, even in liberal democracies, most people do not consent to be ruled by the government in power – or, at least, not at election times, not openly, and not literally. If, despite all this, you want to persist with your claim that democratic government rests on the consent of the people, you have to account for such facts. Perhaps you will try to argue that simply by voting people give their consent, not directly to a government but to the electoral *system*, and therefore to its outcome.[9] Or perhaps – like Locke – you will try to argue that everyone consents, but some only tacitly.

Tacit consent reconsidered

In short, it is worth taking a closer look at the notion of tacit consent because – in our own times – the idea the government must rest on consent is so widespread. So, is it possible to reach a definition of 'tacit consent' which represents a useful improvement on Locke's? In this section I shall suggest that it is. In the following, I shall suggest how an improved definition can be used to help Locke's argument. I suggest that it is and, to explain how, let me first define 'consent'. (Up to this point, I have tried to keep technical-seeming, rather formal, definitions out of my discussion; but in this case, I think a definition would be helpful.)

Here, then, is a definition of 'consent':

> Person, P, does action, x, with the consent of person Q if P's right to do x *is conditional upon* Q's expressing the wish that P should have that right.[10]

This definition captures the sense of 'consent' by which a boy can only marry a girl if he first gets the consent of her father, as happens in stories. (In this case the boy's right to marry the girl *is conditional upon* the father's expressly stating that he can, which is in accordance with the definition.) It also captures the sense of 'consent' in which those who vote with the majority can be said to consent to a government's having power. In such cases, the government's right to hold office is conditional upon the majority's expression of the wish that it should do so. (Perhaps there are other senses of 'consent', but this is the one relevant to our enquiry.) Now, here is my suggested definition of 'tacit consent':

> Person, P, does action, x, with the tacit consent of another person Q, if both (i) the context is such that Q would normally be expected to express the wish that P refrain from doing x, and (ii) Q refrains from expressing that wish.[11]

This is consistent with the definition of 'consent' I gave a moment ago, but it applies only in cases *where a person's failure to make the absence of a wish explicit can itself be taken as the expression of that wish*. To take an example (borrowed from Jean-Paul Sartre):[12] suppose that a woman is invited to a social gathering where she meets a stranger, a man she has not met before. Suppose that, during the course of conversation, he takes her hand. There is a normal expectation that she will withdraw it, but suppose that – instead – she continues to let it rest in his. In this case, it would be fair to take her inaction as an indication of her tacit consent to whatever is likely to come later. (To put it in terms of the definition, she has not made explicit the wish that he should not have the right to do whatever he seems likely to do.) Or, if you don't like that example, here is another, borrowed from A. John Simmons.

> Chairman Jones stands at the close of the company's board meeting and announces, 'There will be a meeting of the board at which attendance will be mandatory next Tuesday at 8.00, rather than at our usual Thursday time. Any objections?' The board members remain silent.
>
> (Simmons 1979: 79–80)

According to Simmons, 'In remaining silent and inactive, they have all tacitly consented to the chairman's proposal to make a schedule change' (ibid.). I think this is right.

There are three features of this account of tacit consent to which I would especially like to draw your attention. The first is that it is an improvement on Locke's view, at least as it is stated by Locke in the passage I quoted earlier. My definition does not entail that you give your tacit consent to a government simply by travelling on the highway, or lodging somewhere for a week. Secondly, the definition entails that what counts as an indication of tacit consent must be a function of context. This can vary. Sometimes it can vary with culture or convention. For example, a woman who leaves her hand resting in a man's may be lending her tacit consent to whatever is likely to happen later in the evening, but only where there is an expectation that she will withdraw her hand otherwise. Where the expectation is absent – as it might be if holding hands became nothing out of the ordinary – her action (or, rather, her inaction) would lose its significance. Thirdly, it is clear that, in this type of case, *consent given tacitly can only be withdrawn explicitly.* (The woman has to make a point of withdrawing her hand. The board members have to say that they don't like the proposed time.)

So far as I can see, the above definition accurately captures what people quite often mean when they use the expression 'tacit consent'. But, although it is an improvement on Locke's stated view, the question of whether it is an improvement which could actually help him remains open. I think its answer depends on the second and third features just listed (the fact that tacit consent requires a context and the fact that it can only be withdrawn explicitly). So, let us now ask: For Locke, was there a context within which certain actions (or failures to act) could be taken to indicate tacit consent, and others as its explicit withdrawal?

Tacit consent and the events of 1688

I chose 'Reason and Revolutions' as the title for Part II because every text on which I concentrate in this part of the book is related, in one way or another, to a major political upheaval. As we saw in the last chapter, Hobbes' *Leviathan* (1981) is a response to the English civil war, that series of upheavals which culminated in the execution of Charles I and the rule of Oliver Cromwell. The text I discuss in the following chapter – Rousseau's *Social Contract* (Rousseau 1968) – embodies ideals which helped fuel the French Revolution of 1789. Likewise, Locke's *Second Treatise* is closely associated with events which subsequently became known as 'the Glorious Revolution of 1688'.

Briefly, what happened was this: In 1685 Charles II died, and he was succeeded by his brother, James. (James thus became James II of England.) For the British – or most of them – this was bad news indeed. For one thing, James was sympathetic to Catholicism. More than that, he had actually converted to the Catholic religion, and – in those times – this indicated more than adherence to a particular set of religious beliefs. It meant that you tended to take a particular side in the power struggles which were then going on throughout Europe, the side of centralised, authoritarian, government. In the British context, it meant that you would be hostile to popular rule and, specifically, to attempts by Parliament to compromise the sovereign's power. For the largely Protestant British, for whom such a compromise had been the outcome of decades of unrest – a bloody civil war, a revolution, a military dictatorship – this can only have represented a retrograde step. True, Charles II had, himself, been sympathetic to Catholicism and hostile to Parliament, but he had come to power, post-Cromwell, on a tide of popular support. Also, throughout his easygoing reign he had tried to rule in a spirit of compromise, maintaining religious toleration and with a grudging respect for Parliament. Even so, he had been treated with considerable hostility and suspicion by certain sections of the population. But when James came to power, things rapidly deteriorated, for James soon proved himself to be rigidly-minded, ruthless and tyrannical.

Here are some of the things that happened next. A rebellion led by the Duke of Monmouth was viciously put down (1685). The defeated rebels were put through a show trial at the 'Bloody Assizes' held in the west of England and presided over by the infamous Judge Jeffreys. About 800 were dispatched to Barbados, as slaves, and the rest – about 200 – were brutally executed. A witness describes how Jeffreys 'was perpetually either drunk or in a rage' and how, having 'required the prisoners to plead guilty', he 'ordered a great many to be hanged up immediately without allowing them a minute's time to say their prayers' (see Lee 1998: 157). In September 1685, poor Lady Alice Lisle, an elderly woman who had given refuge to two fleeing rebels, was publicly beheaded in the square at Winchester (even though she may well have been ignorant of their true identities). While all this was going on, James was forcibly removing senior political figures from their positions of influence. The Lord Privy Seal, holder of one the highest state offices, was dismissed (1685) as were six of the country's twelve senior judges (1686). The Bishop of London found himself summoned to appear before the newly created Court of High Commission and suspended from his position. At the same time others, sympathetic to James' ambitions, were promoted to influence, including the aforementioned Judge Jeffreys.

That is a brief, selective, list of events of course, but it should give you an idea of how things were. The way James was behaving, it was inevitable that he would encounter increasing resistance; and so he did, from all levels of society. In 1688 seven bishops refused to co-operate with James in issuing a Declaration of Indulgence. (This was a declaration suspending laws against dissidents and Catholics. The bishops refused to allow it to be read in churches throughout the land.) The king had them brought before a court but – in another act of defiance – the court acquitted them. That same day (30 July 1688) a group of conspirators dispatched a letter to the

Dutch king, William of Orange, in which they invited him to invade. This he did. In November, William landed in England with his army. In cities throughout the land, the population rose in his support and, about a week later, James was chased from the country.

So that was the 'Glorious Revolution of 1688'. (Was the period really turbulent enough to qualify for the title 'revolution', or was it a continuation of much that had gone before? That is a question I shall leave to the historians.)[13] Now what has this got to do with Locke? More specifically, what has it to do with his *Second Treatise*? More specifically still, what does it tell us about his definition of tacit consent? Let me take each question in turn.

The answer to the first is that, prior to revolution, there were various ways in which Locke became implicated in political events. His involvement dates from the period, beginning in 1672, during which he served as secretary to Anthony Ashley-Cooper, Earl of Shaftesbury. Shaftesbury was a powerful figure who played an instrumental role in various plots and intrigues, and it seems unlikely that Locke – who was not just an employee but a close friend and a pillar of Shaftesbury's household – would not have done likewise. In 1683 Locke was actually forced to flee the country. He took refuge in Holland, where he lived for a time under the assumed name of Dr van der Linden; and in 1688, when he returned, it was on board a ship of the fleet which carried William's army.

What of my second question, that of the relationship between these events and the *Second Treatise* itself? Well, because it was published in 1690, two years after the revolution, it was thought for a long time that the book was a kind of *apologia*; that is, a justification for the events which had recently taken place. However, more recent evidence suggests that it was written well before the revolution, in or around the year 1680, in which case we should think of it more as a manifesto. Either way, it is clear that Locke's prime intention was to defend the right to resist those with pretensions to absolute power, and to rebel where necessary. For example, and as the title of the *Second Treatise* suggests, there is also a *First Treatise of Civil Government* (1964b: 135–263). This is a critique of *Patriarcha* (Filmer 1949), a work in which Sir Robert Filmer defends the claim of absolute monarchs to rule by divine right. One of Filmer's arguments is the contention that monarchs stand in the same relation to their subjects as parents do to their children. As you would expect, Locke is opposed to this conclusion, and it is this which explains why he takes pains, in the *Second Treatise*, to distinguish the parental form of authority from other forms, especially political authority. The latter's final chapter is entitled 'Of the Dissolution of Government'; and, in his closing paragraph, Locke concludes that where the people have 'set limits to the duration of their legislative' or else 'when by the miscarriages of those in authority it is forfeited', it 'reverts to the society, and the people have a right to act as supreme' (II, 243).

How are these events relevant to Locke's conception of 'tacit consent' (the third question I raised, above)? Well, earlier I proposed a definition of 'tacit consent' which applies in cases where a person's failure to withdraw consent can itself be taken as the expression of consent. (The woman leaves her hand in the man's. The board members remain silent.) I also drew your attention to two implications of this definition. One was that it applies only in certain contexts. (There is an expectation that a woman who did not consent would withdraw her hand. The rules permit the members to object.) The other was that, where it applies, consent, if it is to be withdrawn, must be withdrawn *expressly*. (The woman must make a point of withdrawing her hand. Board members must speak up.) Now, my suggestion is that events such as those which took place between 1685 and 1688 provide a context in which the people's failure to act would count as an indication of tacit consent, and in which rebellion would count as its explicit withdrawal.

Of course, if the *Second Treatise* was written as early as 1680, then the events Locke had in mind can't have been the events of 1688 itself. But we can be sure that, in 1688, people did pretty much what he would have wanted them to when faced with arbitrary and tyrannical government. In other words, if we assume that people who are naturally free and equal (and 'autonomous') would object to tyrannical rule there is an expectation that they will make their objection clear, or – to put the point in terms of consent – that they will expressly withdraw their consent. If they do not, they can be assumed to have consented tacitly. If they do, then precisely how they do it will depend on the means they have available to them, and this will vary across levels of society. And that is what happened in 1688. A rich and powerful group wrote a letter to William of Orange. They proceeded to raise an army. The bishops refused to permit the reading of the Declaration of Indulgence. The court refused to find them guilty. As for the people, 'City after city rose in rebellion. By one spontaneous, tremendous convulsion, the English nation repudiated James' (Churchill 1956: 324). In its own way, each group signified its refusal to consent to James' rule. That is a scenario of the type Locke had in mind.

Where does this leave Locke's argument for government based on consent?

To summarise: I have suggested an interpretation of 'tacit consent' which is (i) in line with one way in which the phrase is ordinarily meant and (ii) in line with the political position Locke was out to defend. Perhaps it is what Locke had in mind all the time. After all, the *Second Treatise* is a revolutionary manifesto – it is not meant to be a scrupulously argued philosophical text – so we should not expect Locke's every point to be elaborated in detail and defended against every objection he could think of.

Moreover, it is important to remember that Locke was *not* out to defend the claim that, by voting at election times, the electorate lends its consent to the actions of the incoming government. As noted earlier, the problem of defining tacit consent arises for such a view because it is necessary to explain how consent can be given, if it is, by those who vote with the minority. It must also face the question of what electoral system, if any, is best equipped to produce an outcome which reflects 'the will of the people' – 'first past the post' or some form of proportional representation. But such questions were of no concern to Locke. In fact, he only draws on the idea of majority consent at one point, and that is the point at which he discusses the way people move from the state of nature by forming a community. Majority consent is necessary, he says, because 'it being necessary to that which is one body to move one way; it is necessary the body should move that way whither the greater force carries it' (II, 96). This is different from the point at which the community establishes a system of government, or at which it puts a particular governing party, or individual, in power. (As we saw, Locke most prefers the system in which the monarch's powers are limited by parliament, but, in his time, the franchise on which parliament was based was far more limited than anything with which we are familiar.) In short, although Locke favoured government *by consent*, it does not follow that he favoured government by, say, a democratically elected representative government. This is contrary to what a modern reader, coming to Locke for the first time, is likely to expect.

But does this mean that the *Second Treatise* is of no relevance to more recent concerns? Certainly not. On the contrary, it is a good example of the way a work of political philosophy can take on a double aspect, for there are two different audiences to bear in mind here. One is the late seventeenth century, post-revolutionary, audience for whom the book was intended. As noted, this audience would have understood it to be a defence of the right to rebel, as indeed it was meant to be understood. The other audience is the present day audience. There is no getting away from the fact that you and I can, if we like, go to a bookshop and buy a copy; and we can't just treat it as a 'period piece' as if it were an exhibit in a museum. As modern readers, we will tend to equate 'government based on consent' with democracy. Locke may not have been especially concerned to do this, but that does not absolve us from trying to find ways of bringing Locke's arguments to bear on the idea that the institutions of liberal democracy are mechanisms for securing government with the consent of the people.

Certainly, the authors of the United States' *Declaration of Independence* were not slow to see the connection. Here are its famous opening lines:

We hold these truths to be self-evident, that all men are created equal, that they are endowed by their Creator with certain unalienable Rights, that among these are Life, Liberty and the pursuit of

Happiness. – That to secure these rights, Governments are instituted among Men, deriving their just powers from the consent of the governed.

(US *Declaration of Independence*, 1776)

The authors of the *Declaration* go on to state that 'whenever any Form of Government becomes destructive of these ends, it is the Right of the People to alter or to abolish it, and to institute new Government', all of which is entirely in the spirit of Locke, as is the rest of the second paragraph. It was just over a decade later that the Constitution of the United States – the blueprint for a major democratic *system* – was signed. Locke's *Second Treatise* became a manifesto for not just one, but two, major revolutions.

8

---·○◎○·---

Locke: the argument for property

Present day philosophers, looking back at Locke, are sometimes apt to describe him as a defender of 'capitalism' or the 'free market economy'. Such expressions would not have been available to Locke himself. Their origins lie in the nineteenth and twentieth centuries. Even so, there is something right about the description, for the key elements of the position he takes on property are as follows. First, Locke holds that the bearer of rights over a given item of property must always be a specific, identifiable, individual – you or me, this person or that person. He is, as we would now say, an advocate of 'private' property. Secondly, he holds that, when a property right is transferred from one person to another, this should only happen when both parties *consent* to the transfer. Normally, consent is involved when one person sells, or gives, an item of property to another, or when one person leaves it to the other in his or her will. Thirdly, and by the same token, Locke is opposed to the transfer of property by force, as happens when one person steals from another, or when the state – or, as Locke would say, the 'sovereign' – imposes a tax without permission.

It is possible to think of a 'free market economic system' in operation as nothing more than the repeated transfer of property from individual to individual by sale, gift or inheritance. In such a system, the state's only function is to make sure that everyone's ability to engage in consensual, 'free', transactions is not interfered with. The state must be a 'minimal' state, with the job of preventing theft and fraud, and that's all. So, if that is a fair characterisation of a free market economy then – fair enough – Locke is a defender of a free market economy.

However, we should not be misled by this into misreading Locke's intentions. In our own time, anyone supporting a position such as Locke's would be self-consciously placing himself, or herself, on the political 'right'. Note that the system advocated by Locke contrasts with the type of system under which property (or a sizeable amount of it) is 'collectively' or 'commonly' owned. Under systems of the latter type, every member of the community or group has rights of access to and use of the property provided that certain conditions are fulfilled. (If you would like an example, think of the rights of access and use you have, as a member of the public, to a local park.) These days, the most prominent advocates of collective and/or common ownership tend to be socialists. It is also worth remarking that Locke's view contrasts with the 'redistributivism' according to which a democratically elected state is, indeed, entitled to raise taxes from the relatively better off in order to help the relatively worse off; either that, or to finance projects generally thought to be public goods. This is the 'welfare state' system with which most readers will be familiar, or so I guess. In our time, a pro-capitalist, anti-socialist, anti-welfare state philosopher would immediately qualify as a supporter of the right. (I mean the anti-state right, not the fascist, nationalist or racist right. That's different.)

But just as Locke could not have described himself as 'pro-capitalist', so the distinction we so readily make between 'right' and 'left' was equally unavailable to him. (It originated with the French Revolution.)[1] Not that 'collectivist' views were unknown to him. Only forty or so years before the *Second Treatise* was published, the 'True Levellers' or 'Diggers' had argued that the earth was, by right, commonly owned, that private property is theft, and put their ideas into practical action by uninvitedly setting up communities and starting to cultivate the land. Not only that, throughout Locke's time, private landowners had been steadily 'enclosing' land which had previously been commonly held. As for taxation by the state, this had been claimed by monarchs, such as Charles I, who believed themselves entitled to rule absolutely. (In connection with this, we have already encountered Hobbes' view that a property right derives 'only from the Sovereign Power' (Hobbes 1981: 367).) But, in opposing this claim, Locke was taking the attitude of a revolutionary, not a reactionary, and standing up for the individual against arbitrary power.

If that matters it is because this book is, in part, a history of thought, which makes it important to get Locke's intentions right. However, as philosophers, it is vital to grasp the essentials of Locke's argument whatever his intentions may have been, and wherever we may happen to stand on the political spectrum. That is because his argument for property remains one of the most influential there is.

Locke's argument in perspective

For the rest of this chapter, I shall be trying to represent Locke's property argument, in outline, as clearly and accurately as I can. As I go, I shall indicate where (in my opinion) its major strengths and its major weaknesses lie. However, before getting down to details, it would be helpful to stand back a little and try to get Locke's argument into a broader perspective.

First of all, then, exactly what conclusion is the argument designed to establish? Well, anyone who has read the previous chapter will know what to expect. Locke holds that the right to property (by which he means private property) is specified by the law of nature. It is one of our three most fundamental natural rights (the other two being life and liberty). As readers will also know, Locke also holds that the civil law must reflect the natural law; to put it another way, that the legal order must reflect the moral order. In the case of property this means that, for any actual property distribution – that is, where specific items of property are owned in specific ways by specific individuals or groups – that distribution must not violate anyone's natural right. Since we have a natural right to *private* property, it follows that only systems based on private ownership are in accordance with the law of nature, or so Locke holds.

Secondly, *what sort* of argument is Locke offering for that conclusion? In raising this question, I am thinking particularly of a very useful distinction which is drawn by the 'neo-Lockean', pro-free market philosopher Robert Nozick in his *Anarchy, State, and Utopia* (Nozick 1974). This is the distinction between 'historical' and 'patterned' justifications for specific distributions of property (ibid.: 153ff). Locke is advancing (what Nozick calls) a historical argument. In other words, it is Locke's view that the rightness or wrongness of a person's claim to own a given item of property is a matter of how the ownership *came about*. For Locke (as for Nozick and similar free marketeers) consent must have been involved each time the item changed hands. For example, suppose that you own something as property. (If it helps, suppose that it's a building – a house – or a piece of land.) If you bought it from someone who – in turn – bought it from someone else, who inherited it from a parent, who was given it by a friend . . . and so on, then your ownership is rightful. (The justification is 'historical' in the sense that it looks back through time.) On the other hand, if you stole the property, or if you bought it with money extorted from some innocent victim, then it is not.

According to a 'patterned' justification, a person's ownership of an item is morally justified if that ownership is consistent with a wider arrangement under which property is distributed in accordance with *a certain pattern*. In philosophy, patterns tend to be specified by principles, so a good example of a patterned justification would be the utilitarian argument that property ought to be distributed in accordance with (some version of) the greatest happiness principle. On such a view, your ownership of something is morally justified if it is in accordance with, or if it promotes, 'the greatest happiness of the greatest number'. (It seems to me that, in ordinary life, people sometimes appeal to one sort of justification, and sometimes to another. For example, if you say 'So many people are prepared to hear that rock star play that he *deserves* to be rich' you are invoking a historical principle. At any rate, you are appealing to how it came about that he is so much richer than others. On the other hand, if you say 'It must be wrong that so-and-so should have so much when others are so poor' you are implicitly appealing to a pattern, e.g. 'discrepancies in wealth should not exceed a certain limit'.)

Now, so what? For future reference, it is worth placing a special emphasis on two points here. The first concerns the relation between the two forms of justification. It is that justifications of one form are logically inconsistent with those of the other.[2] That is because, where people exercise their rights over time, and thereby acquire legal rights to property in morally acceptable ways, there is no guarantee that a specific pattern will be the outcome. On the contrary, anything could happen. For an analogy, take the game *Monopoly*. At the start of a game, every player is dealt a set number of 'title deed' cards and the same amount of monopoly money. The game begins, and each player takes turn to roll the dice and move his or her counter around the board. The rules of the game are systematically applied throughout – although some play with more skill and cunning than others, and some have more luck. Someone eventually wins. Notice, though, that the systematic application of the rules carries with it no guarantee that there will be a specific outcome. If the same person always wins, or always loses, there is no point in complaining that it's not fair. On the contrary, it's just too bad. So it is with historical justifications for given property distributions.

The second point relates to historical justifications only, and it is this. Political philosophers who give historical justifications for, say, property or the state are not doing real history. They are doing something quite different, namely justifying the existence of private property, the state, or whatever with an account of how it *could* have come into existence. How the phenomenon *in fact* came into being is – supposedly – neither here nor there. You may recall that I made this point earlier, when introducing social contract theory as a form of rational choice theory.[3] Social contract theorists such as Hobbes and Locke justify their preferred form of state with an account of what rational people would have chosen from an initial no-state situation (the state of nature). This is different from relating the history of how real states actually came into being. By the same token, we have to think of Locke as attempting to justify the institution of private property with an account of how it could have come into being. (For reasons we shall eventually come to – and whatever Locke thought he was doing himself – it is impossible to credit him with having described the real origins of the institution.)

So, let me just summarise the upshot of this 'stage-setting' discussion, as follows. First: Locke's argument is designed to establish that the private ownership of property is a fundamental right embodied in the natural law (i.e. the moral law). Second: His conclusion is supposed to follow from an account of how the institution of private property could have arisen, even though it did not arise that way. In fact, Locke tries to show how the institution could have arisen by morally legitimate steps. Third: As you already know, Locke's argument is a social contract argument. Let us now follow it through, starting from the beginning.

Locke's argument

From the common stock to private ownership

A social contract argument must begin with a situation, real or imaginary, from which the phenomenon it is trying to explain or justify is absent. Accordingly, Locke begins with a situation in which there is no private property. In the beginning there was only common ownership, or so Locke holds. We are, supposedly, taught this by reason, 'which tells us, that men, being once born, have a right to their preservation, and consequently to meat and drink, and such other things as nature affords for their subsistence' (II, 25) and by revelation, from which we (supposedly) learn that God gave the earth to 'mankind in common' (ibid.). (This gets interesting already. Note that Locke could have started with a 'no ownership situation'; that is, a situation in which nobody owns anything. But he doesn't. Instead, he imagines a situation in which there *is* property ownership, but in which all such ownership is common ownership. It could make a difference, and I'll come to the point later on.)

Locke then sets himself the task of explaining how the institution of property could have arisen from this initial situation. He explains the procedure this way:

> I shall endeavour to shew, how men might come to have a property in several parts of that which God gave to mankind in common, and that without any express compact of all the commoners.
>
> (II, 26)

In the initial situation, where common ownership prevails, people face a problem, one which can be summarised in a word – 'survival'. Even if you don't agree with Locke that it is a fundamental principle of the law of nature that 'every one' is 'bound to preserve himself', this being a command of God (II, 6), you have to agree that, in most of us, the drive to survive is strong. But the trouble with nature in its raw state is that it is, in most cases, useless. To survive, people in the initial situation will need to convert it to a usable form if they are to supply themselves with food, shelter, clothing and other necessities. They will have to hunt animals, grow crops, build houses or huts, and so on. In short, they will have to *work*. 'The earth, and all that is therein' may have been 'given to men for the support and comfort of their being', he writes, but 'though all the fruits it naturally produces, and beasts it feeds, belong to mankind in common' there must 'of necessity be a means to appropriate them some way or other before they can be any use, or at all beneficial to any particular man' (II, 27). Now, as Locke's use of the word 'appropriate' indicates, it is at this point – when a person first labours on a piece of raw nature – that he or she acquires a right of private ownership in the thing worked on.

What of other people? If you have a right to remove something from the common stock by your labour – that is, a private right to something which was previously owned by everyone in common – how come you don't have to ask permission from everyone else in the world first? Locke's answer is pragmatic: 'If such a consent as that was necessary, man had starved, notwithstanding the plenty God had given him' (II, 28).

I have already pointed out that consent has a crucial role to play in Locke's argument for property. As the passages under discussion show, the concept of labour is equally crucial. In fact, you could say that *labour* and *consent* are the argument's two operative concepts. Labour justifies initial acts of appropriation, those with which things are removed from the common stock and taken into private hands. Consent justifies the transfer of property rights in things which are already owned from one person to another.

From persons to property

Locke is assuming that the *fact* of your having laboured on a previously unowned something gives you a *right* to what you have produced. But is it so obvious why this should be? You may go into the wilderness – into a forest, say – cut down trees, make a clearing, plough the land, grow crops, and so on. You may also be powerful enough to keep out intruders. But although that will give you control as a point of *fact*, it does not follow – or not without further argument – that you have a *right* to the fruit of your labours. Similarly, suppose that some future explorers land in some previously unoccupied wilderness, that they land on Mars, for example. Suppose that they then put in a great deal of work, excavating for minerals. Such technologically sophisticated explorers would have the edge. They would have *de facto* control of the planet, but it is not so obvious that they, or the nation from which they came, would have the right to own it. (I surmise that there would be a chorus of objections were any such thing ever to happen.)

Locke answers the question of how the fact of labour can create the right of ownership with an account of what he thinks work essentially is. According to Locke, when you work you 'mix your labour' with nature. The following passage is crucial.

> Though the earth and all inferior creatures be common to all men, yet every man has a property in his own person. This nobody has any right to but himself. The labour of his body, and the work of his hands, we may say, are properly his. Whatsoever, then, he removes out of the state that nature hath provided and left it in, he hath mixed his labour with, and thereby made it his property. It being by him removed from the common state nature placed it in, it hath by this labour something annexed to it that excludes the common right

of other men. For this labour being the unquestionable property of the labourer, no man but he can have a right to what that is once joined to, at least where there is enough and as good left in common for others.

(II, 27)

Here is a step-by-step summary of the argument:

1. Everyone has a property in his or her own 'person'. This property is 'inalienable'; that is, nobody can transfer the ownership of his or her person to somebody else, by, say, giving it away or selling it. (For example, you can't sell yourself into slavery.)
2. Your body is part of your person. Therefore, you have an inalienable property in your body. Labouring is something you do with your body. Therefore, you have an inalienable property in your labour, just as you do in your body. (It is – as Locke almost puts it – the labour of *your* body and the work of *your* hands and therefore properly *yours*.)
3. When you work you mix your labour with a part of nature. (For example, when you plough a field, your labour and that part of the earth you have ploughed become inextricably mixed.) Because you have an inalienable property in your labour it follows that you must now have an equally inalienable property in that part of nature with which your labour has become all mixed up.

What are we to make of this famous argument? Well, first, the crucial notion that you and I have 'an inalienable property in our own persons' is clearly related to, if not quite equivalent to, other fundamental Lockean principles. It goes hand-in-hand with the idea that we are equals under the law of nature, that – in nature – no one is entitled to exert authority over anyone else, and that everyone has natural rights to life and liberty. For Locke, these are not much more than different ways of saying the same thing.

Secondly, Locke's argument has one great strength. (You won't be surprised to learn that it has its faults too, and that after three hundred years of criticism these have been pretty well documented. I shall mention some of these in a moment, but let me emphasise the positive first.) The strength of Locke's argument at this point lies in the way it tries to account for a deep moral conviction many people have. Perhaps it is a conviction we all have. This is the conviction that it is the person who produces something – the person who has actually done the work – who most deserves to benefit from that which he or she has produced. There can be few readers, if any, who would want to deny that the farmer who has laboured to grow the wheat has a far greater right in it than does some idle passer-by, who chooses to help himself. (*Why should* that person get anything?) Or, to take a parallel example, few would disagree that it is the student who actually wrote the essay who deserves the 'A' grade (not the plagiarist). Locke's argument takes account of this conviction by placing a particular construction on it; you have 'a property in your own person', etc.

But there is plenty wrong with the latter. Even if Locke's moral convictions (or 'intuitions') are in the right place, his argument raises quite a few difficulties. Let me outline just three. I will try to be brief.

First of all, there is the difficulty of specifying a relevant sense of the term 'labour'. This can be more difficult than Locke makes it look. For example, how is Locke's argument to deal with the 'mental labour' of, say, writers or architects? Such individuals play no part in the printing or binding of the books they write – or in the building of the structures they design – but don't our 'moral intuitions' tell us that they should have some sort of right in the things they have taken such a decisive hand in producing? (Mine do.) Consider the following example, which features a physically disabled, but intellectually talented, inventor. This inventor lives a long time ago, before the invention of the plough. In fact, he is the person who invented the plough. In his area, the soil is rich in nutrients. His tribe could live well by agriculture, if only they had a plough – but they don't, so they are forced to eke out a meagre existence by foraging. Then, one day, the inventor thinks up the plough. Being disabled, he can play no part in its construction himself, so he explains the design to the others, who then go on to do all the physical things – cut down trees, saw wood, construct the plough, till the fields, and so on. I think you will agree with me that the inventor is just as entitled as the others to a share in the plough and the crops it is used to grow. But now ask: Has the inventor created the plough by his *labour*? Here, you have a choice of answers. You could say that he has, although not with labour as Locke thinks of it; not with 'the labour of his body, and the work of his hands' (ibid.). This might lead you to conclude that Locke emphasises *physical* labour at the expense of other forms of labour, such as 'intellectual labour'. On the other hand, you could say that he has not, in which case you will have to conclude that Locke has not given a complete or an adequate account of how the entitlement to property arises.

Secondly, there is the question of *how much* your labour entitles you to. By Locke's account, as you remove things from the common stock, your labour entitles you to no more than you have mixed it with. 'He that is nourished by the acorns he picked up under an oak, or the apples he gathered from the trees in the wood, has certainly appropriated them to himself. Nobody can deny but the nourishment is his.' This small act of labour is enough to 'put a distinction between them and the common' (II, 28). Again, 'Though the water running in the fountain be everyone's, yet who can doubt but that in the pitcher is his only who drew it out? His labour hath taken it out of the hands of nature' (II, 29). Likewise, 'this law of reason makes the deer that Indian's who hath killed it; 'tis allowed to be his goods who hath bestowed his labour upon it, though before it was the common right of everyone' (II, 30).

As for agriculture, the form of productive activity which lies at the forefront of Locke's concerns, it is meant to follow – equally – that 'As much land as a man tills, plants, improves, cultivates, and uses the product of, so much is his property' because 'He by his labour does, as it were, enclose it from the common' (II, 32). But now suppose a farmer decides to let a field lie fallow with a view to improving its fertility. For a whole year, this farmer invests no labour in the field. Does this mean that the land must return to the common stock, so that others can take it away from him and use it for their own purposes? By Locke's 'labour-mixing' argument it appears that it should. However, this is not the conclusion Locke wanted. What he *wants* to show is that agriculture is an activity from which those who carry it out derive a right to the land on which they work (provided that it is not first owned by someone else). As this illustrates, Locke's bucolic examples oversimplify things by focusing on activities which involve physical labour and nothing else – picking up an acorn, drawing water, shooting a deer. But most productive activities – even those which involve a great deal of physical labour – are not like that. In most cases, physical labour is just one component in a repertoire of techniques which, together, make up the activity in question. My example of letting a field lie fallow is a case in point. (Of course, if farming, the activity, is to continue, it is sometimes necessary that fields should be left fallow. But notice that it would not help Locke to respond along such lines, for the Native American in his example could point out that if hunting, the activity, is to continue, it is equally necessary that there should remain deer, roaming the prairie and available to hunt. It seems that Locke would have to concede either that *both* the farmer's field and the remaining deer remain in the common stock, to be claimed by anyone, or that *neither* do.)

Locke's examples oversimplify things in another way too, by focusing on activities which are carried out by *just one* person. But most productive activities are not like this. Most of them involve the co-ordinated actions of more than one individual. This is probably true of modern agriculture, except for the most primitive. It is true of operating a fishing boat, and it is certainly true of, say, car production in a factory employing many thousands of people, each concentrating on a single task. It's a good question whether Locke's argument can explain exactly how much each person becomes entitled to own after having contributed labour to the process.

The third difficulty on my list relates to Locke's idea that when you work you 'mix your labour with nature'. The core problem here is that labour is not something you 'mix' at all – not literally. It is not like a spoonful of instant coffee granules, something to be mixed with boiling water; or like fertiliser, to be mixed with the soil. Locke's talk of 'mixing' can only be metaphorical. In philosophy, the use of metaphor is – I

125

suppose – fair enough. However, trouble can start once you take a metaphor too literally, and, in Locke's case, that is what happens; for the logical step by means of which he seeks to move from 'this person has laboured' to 'this person has a right to the fruits of his/her labour' would be impossible without it. And it is a metaphor which raises all kinds of awkward questions for Locke. For example, it raises the question of why mixing something you own with something unowned should mean that you come to own the latter rather than that you lose the former. In a well-known example, Robert Nozick has put the objection this way: 'If I own a can of tomato juice and spill it in the sea so that its molecules (made radioactive so I can check this) mingle evenly throughout the sea, do I thereby come to own the sea, or have I foolishly dissipated my tomato juice?' (Nozick 1974: 175). The latter seems the more sensible answer, even though the tomato juice and the sea become 'inextricably mixed'. There is no good reason for thinking that things should be any different where 'labour' is mixed with 'nature', or so the objection goes.

So much for the first stage of Locke's property argument, the stage at which he pictures individuals acquiring an initial right of ownership by labour, thereby removing things from the common stock. There is plenty more I could say, but it is time to move on. Just to summarise: The general conclusion I would draw here is that, although Locke tries to do something interesting and worthwhile with his argument – by trying to explain why those who actually do the work should have a special entitlement to, or 'stake' in, what they produce – his 'labour-mixing' metaphor is a misleading construction. The criticisms I have raised here suggest that he goes wrong by overemphasising the role played by physical labour in the productive process, as well as by oversimplifying the nature of that process itself. He also underplays the way different forms of production can differ; agriculture from fishing or manufacturing, for example.

This raises an obvious question: If the weaknesses in this part of Locke's argument can be so apparent to philosophers writing now, how come he didn't notice them himself? After all, Locke was no fool. Well, when one person fails to notice something which is perfectly apparent to another, quite often the explanation lies in a difference of perspective. Each is standing in a different place. I would hazard an explanation along such lines here. Locke was writing in pre-industrial times, when agriculture was the dominant mode of production. Moreover, it was an agriculture based on an inherited technology, which had been passed down over generations. Nobody knows when the plough was invented, or who invented it. In fact, that person stands in the same relation to generations of farmers – including those of Locke's time – as Bill Gates does to users of Microsoft Windows. Even so, his or her contribution is scarcely recognised by Locke. Of course, this is quite unsurprising if you consider that, in Locke's time, it would have seemed that ploughs had always been around. Their existence must have seemed 'natural' in a way, almost as natural as that of the earth and the grass.

From primitive self-sufficiency to the developed economy

Although you acquire a right to the elements of raw nature you have mixed your labour with, the law of nature also places restrictions on the amount you are entitled to acquire. There are two. First, you must let nothing spoil or go to waste. 'As much as anyone can make use of to any advantage of life before it spoils, so much he may by his labour fix a property in. Whatever is beyond this is more than his share, and belongs to others' (II, 31). We are subject to this requirement because the world was a gift from God, to mankind in common, and intended for our use and preservation, so 'Nothing was made by God for man to spoil or destroy' (II, 31). Second, you must leave enough, and as good, over for others to use. 'For he that leaves as much as another can make use of, does as good as take nothing at all' (II, 33). Locke thinks that, in the first stages of appropriation, when the population was small and resources plentiful, it would have been impossible *not* to observe this restriction. 'Nor was this appropriation of any parcel of land, by improving it, any prejudice to any other man, since there was still enough – and as good – left; and more than the yet unprovided could use' (ibid.).

To imagine the world as it would have appeared as the first stage of Locke's narrative progresses is to picture an idyllic, pastoral, scene. It is to imagine a world in which resources are more than sufficient to meet everyone's needs, and in which conflict is at a minimum. In terms of their economic activity, the early tillers of the soil he invites us to picture are on much the same level as the acorn-pickers, water-drawers and primitive deer-hunters of his examples. But the economic world so pictured is *not* the economic world of Locke's time. (Still less is it the economic world of our own.) Nor does it represent the economic set-up it was Locke's intention to justify. The difference is that in the former world people can do little more than produce enough to satisfy their immediate needs (including, I suppose, the immediate needs of their immediate dependants). It is, as I just put it, a world of 'primitive self-sufficiency'. By contrast, the latter is characterised by a developed system of trade and industry by means of which the activities of numerous individuals – often separated by vast distances – are co-ordinated. Under this system, mere self-sufficiency drops out of the picture, for it is also characterised by the fact that nature is exploited *to the full*. Locke approves and writes, for example, that although God gave the world to men in common, 'since he gave it to them for their benefit, *and the greatest conveniences of life they were capable to draw from it*, it cannot be supposed he meant it should always remain common and uncultivated' (II, 34) (my emphasis).

To reach his desired conclusion, Locke has to show how it is possible for people to move from the former situation to the latter. He does this by introducing *money* into his story. As we noted right at the beginning of this chapter, in a developed free market economy, based on consent, property is normally transferred from one person to another by sale, gift or inheritance. Now, of course, the transfer of property by consent is also possible in an economy of primitive self-sufficiency, but to a far more limited extent. Gift is possible. Having picked up my acorn or shot my deer, I can give it to you. Inheritance is also possible. Having ploughed up my piece of land, I can leave it to my son. However, from it, I will have been able to produce little more than I require for the satisfaction of my immediate needs, and he will be able to do no more than that. Sale and purchase (as opposed to barter) are completely impossible, for these require money, and money has yet to be introduced.

So, let us now consider how Locke thinks money makes a difference. First, as any textbook of economics will tell you, money is a 'medium of exchange'. Locke would concur, and – as you should expect by now – he insists that it was first introduced by consent. It doesn't much matter what money is made of provided that its use is a matter of mutual agreement. (A banknote is, after all, 'just a piece of paper'.) Locke imagines our early ancestors using pieces of metal, shells, pebbles or diamonds (II, 46). But whatever the material used, so far as Locke is concerned it is most important that money should be made of something which does not rot or perish. On his account, it is this feature which makes it possible to accumulate wealth without violating the law of nature's first restriction, the injunction not to let things spoil. This is because *things which do not rot can be stored*. For example, suppose that someone grows a plum tree. Before the introduction of money, then, once the plums have ripened, this person (and his immediate family) must either consume the entire crop – which could be a tall order given that it will only last for about a week – or he must consume part of it, and barter the remainder in exchange for things which will, themselves, only last for a limited period. After money has been introduced, things are quite different, for the plums can now be exchanged for durable tokens of metal or stone. More than that, it will now be possible to grow many plum trees, tens or hundreds, and exchange their fruit for such tokens. All these tokens (this money) can be stored with a clear conscience – that is, without violating the first restriction – 'the bounds of his [the grower's] just property not lying in the largeness of his possession, but the perishing of anything uselessly in it' (II, 46).

This explains how money makes it possible for people to accumulate wealth. It also explains how a fully developed economy can emerge by legitimate steps, for individuals who have become relatively wealthy will eventually pass their property on. They will sell it, give it away, or – most likely – leave it to their children. Those to whom it is transferred will, in their turn, increase its value with their own labour – at least the 'industrious and rational' among them will (II, 34). Over the generations, industry and trade will develop and nature will become increasingly exploited for the benefit of humanity as a whole. And, with that, we reach the end of Locke's story.

Two objections from inequality

Inequality of resources

So much for the step by step details of Locke's narrative. I should now like to consider a couple of objections to Locke which tend to be raised at the more general level. These arise from the fact that Locke quite evidently rationalises and condones economic and social inequality. Within his scenario, as generation succeeds generation, the quantity of land which has been taken into private hands will progressively increase. Even the great uncultivated wilderness of America (as Locke believed it to be) would eventually become parcelled into plots. There would remain no 'raw' uncultivated parts of nature for those who came along later to mix their labour with; not even for the rational and industrious among them. To survive, such latecomers would have no alternative but to put their labour out to hire in return for a wage. Society would soon become significantly divided into two classes: the class of those whose ownership of private property was such that they could derive a living from it, and the class of those who had nothing to sell but their own labour (the 'bourgeoisie' and the 'proletariat' as Marx was later to call them).

Of course, there will be some readers who will see nothing wrong with Locke's conclusion. (They will say, 'And what's wrong with *that*?') However, others will find it troubling. I am not thinking especially of readers who will consider the very fact that Locke defends inequality a sufficient reason for dismissing him outright. (There will be some.) There will be others who perceive an inconsistency between the premise on which Locke's political philosophy is founded and this implication of his property argument. As you will recall, the former is radically egalitarian. Locke insists that we are equals under the law of nature; that we have equal natural rights. Such readers will be wondering how he can say this and, at the same time, rationalise economic inequality. Moreover, in our own times many of the objections most commonly raised against free market systems invoke the fact that markets, left to themselves, operate in ways which create and increase inequality. So, there is another reason for considering this type of objection. As the philosopher who originally formulated an articulate defence of the natural right to property, it is instructive to consider how he might have dealt with objections of this type.

As for the specific objections I have in mind, the first can be put in terms of fairness and unfairness. Everyone needs resources, so it is plain unfair that some should have much more than others. That is how the objection runs. As this objection has it, it isn't just that Locke's conclusion is apparently inconsistent with his premises. It also relates to the second restriction he places on the right to appropriate. This is the injunction to leave 'enough and as good' for others. How can Locke permit some to have more than others and insist, at the same time, that everyone should have enough and as good as everyone else?

It is plain from the text of the *Second Treatise* that Locke would respond to this objection by insisting that, in a developed economy based on private ownership, it is possible to exploit nature far more efficiently, with the result that everyone benefits – property owners and non-property owners alike. In short, it is Locke's claim that, in a system based on private property, even the worst off are better off than they would be under any other system. Take the following passage:

> he who appropriates land to himself by his labour, does not lessen but increase the common stock of mankind. For the provisions serving to the support of human life produced by one acre of enclosed and uncultivated land are (to speak much within compass) ten times more than those which are yielded by an acre of land, of an equal richness, lying waste in common. And, therefore, he that encloses land and has a greater plenty of the conveniences of life from ten acres, than he could have from an hundred left to nature may truly be said to give ninety acres to mankind.
>
> (II, 37)

To which Locke adds:

> I ask whether in the wild woods and uncultivated waste of America, left to nature, without any improvement, tillage, or husbandry, a thousand acres yield the needy and wretched inhabitants as many conveniences of life as ten acres of equally fertile land do in Devonshire, where they are well-cultivated.
>
> (ibid.)

But is Locke right? I shall restrict myself to three comments. The first is that a pure uncultivated waste and a world divided between private owners may not be the only alternatives. Other more 'collective' systems of ownership are also conceivable. It seems to me that the question of which, out of the various possibilities, most efficiently promotes the situation of the least well off is a question for economic analysts and historians to answer. Most likely, a lot depends on circumstances. For example, it is certainly arguable that a free market, left to itself, can sometimes work to the *disadvantage* of the worst off; for instance, that this happens in times of recession. Again, it is arguable that a system based on private ownership is unlikely to deliver the best railway system (so disadvantaging the worst off, who can't afford their own cars) or help us deal with global warming (which threatens everyone). There is much to be said on these issues, but I don't think it takes a philosopher to sort them out, so I shan't pursue them.

Secondly, even if Locke is right, it is not so obvious that he can take this line and, at the same time, observe the 'leave enough and as good' restriction. Even if the worst off people are better off where private ownership prevails than they would be under other arrangements – and even if they have enough – it has to be true by definition that, being 'worse off', they can't – at the same time – have 'as good as' the others. Locke may well have been right to say of Native Americans that 'A king of a large and fruitful territory there [America] feeds, lodges, and is clad worse than a day-labourer in England' (II, 41), but he could not deny, either, that the same labourer had a worse diet, worse housing and less adequate clothing than his equally English landlord, with whose material values he would have had far more in common.[4] It is interesting to speculate on how Locke could have answered this, apparently obvious, objection.

Related to this – my third comment – there is a point which certainly does deserve mention in a book such as this, for it concerns the fundamental structure of Locke's philosophical argument. It is that, by claiming that a system based on private property most improves the situation of the worst off, Locke is invoking a *pattern*. He is appealing to the distributive principle that an arrangement which ensures that the worst off people are better off than they would be under any other system is better than any other. (In effect, he is appealing to something like John Rawls' second principle of justice, of which more in a later chapter.) Now, if something I said much earlier in this chapter is right, it follows that Locke's argument is logically broken backed, for his defence of property is essentially historical and – if I was right – patterned and historical arguments are logically inconsistent with each other. You can't have it both ways. (Would anyone have found his argument acceptable if it had been *purely* historical; that is, if he hadn't introduced this patterned element? It's an interesting question, but one I can't follow up here.)

Labour and consent

What of the second objection from inequality? This concerns the relationship between labour and consent; the values by means of which Locke legitimates the acquisition of property. The question is, what happens when the two conflict? To illustrate the problem, take the case of rational and industrious person P. In the early period of primitive self-sufficiency, P mixes his labour with nature, and so acquires the land with which he has mixed it. Previously, this was under common ownership. When P dies, the land is inherited by his equally rational and industrious son P2, who further improves it with his labour, as does P3, P's rational and industrious grandson. In fact, P3 becomes so rich that he retires, having first sold the property to P4, a charismatic and imaginative entrepreneur. P4 converts the agricultural land to industrial use, and so becomes richer still, so much so that he can give away some of the property to hardworking P5 . . . and so on. Eventually, we come to wastrel playboy PN who has purchased a large country estate with his inherited wealth. Picture PN, as he idles away his time in his castle; drinking, gaming and whiling away time with his mistresses. Actually, it doesn't matter what you imagine him doing, provided that – whatever it is – it is quite obviously *not labouring*.

And now picture honest and hard-working day labourer Q, who enters the story at this point. There, at another part of the estate, Q is labouring hard and long, with his spade and his hoe, as he tills the soil. Now, who is entitled to the land? If it is consent which legitimates ownership, then the land should belong to PN. Every step of the process as a result of which he has come to own the estate has involved nothing but consent. On the other hand, if it is labour, then – by that yardstick – shouldn't the land fall into the hands of Q? There appears to be a conflict of criteria. Locke *wants* to say that whereas it is labour which legitimates initial acts of acquisition, it is consent which legitimates subsequent transfers of property from one person to another. The conclusion he wants to draw is that, as a result of the transfers in question, the land should remain the property of PN. Indeed, he is insistent that 'the turfs my servant has cut' become my property, not the servant's (II, 28). But why be so restrictive? Why not say that the ownership rights in the land must gravitate from the landlord to the day labourer? According to the objection, Locke's prioritisation of consent over labour in this type of case is no more than the expression of an arbitrary prejudice in favour of inherited wealth.

This is a powerful objection, but I think the *Second Treatise* contains a potential answer to it. However, unlike Locke's answer to the first objection from equality it has to be teased from between the lines. It is an answer which invokes the idea that labour is something which can be mixed and stored. Recall the example of the person who exchanges the plums he has grown for tokens made of stone or metal. If labour is something you can mix with nature, you could say that just as the plums contain his labour before the exchange has taken place so, afterwards, it becomes invested, or 'contained' in the stones. Over a period of years, say ten years, as the stone-tokens are repeatedly saved, so – by this argument – the man will have saved stones within which ten years worth of labour is stored. This stored labour will then be transferred to whatever he purchases with them, or so you could argue. If it is a piece of land, this land will now contain the ten years worth of labour which was originally put into growing plums. Any further labour invested in the land will be added to that, and, when subsequent transfers take place, this labour will move from one medium of containment to another. If you follow this line of argument through, then you have to conclude that, when PN buys the estate, he does more than exchange some money for some land. You have to say that the money contains many generations-worth of stored labour and that, after the purchase, this labour is transferred to become stored in the land. If this is right, it means that Locke can remove the contradiction between his preferred criteria and argue that *both* PN *and* Q have invested labour in the estate; indeed, that both have, in a sense, actually laboured on it.

To this, I will only add the following: Look what you have to do to reach this conclusion. Ordinarily, we think of labour as physical work. But to reach the conclusion (with Locke's 'labour theory of value') you have to stretch the notion so far that labour becomes a mysterious and ghostly fluid; something which can be mixed with the soil, with plums, stones, even with industrial machinery, but without anyone's being able to see or detect it. Exactly where this leaves the argument is a good question.

Locke as a social contract theorist

I shall bring this chapter to a close with a few observations on the strengths and weaknesses of social contract theory as an approach to questions in political philosophy. This is a theme to which I have returned more than once during the course of this discussion of Hobbes and Locke. For example, in my discussion of Hobbes I raised the question of whether the contract is meant to be real or hypothetical.[5] Some of Locke's arguments supply good illustrations of further difficulties by which this approach can be beset. That apart, this is a good point at which to look back over the last two chapters, and to try to reach an overview.

Just to remind you, to take a social contract approach is – in essence – to try to figure out what rational people would do when placed in an imaginary situation (the state of nature). In the hands of the right philosopher, this can be a powerful way to proceed. For example, if you can give a convincing account of how rational people, finding themselves in a situation where there is no state, would then set up a state of a certain type, you will have given an equally convincing answer to the question of what the point of having states is. You will also have a critical weapon to wield against those who claim legitimacy for states which do not match your preferred description. The art is to begin with a description of human life in the state of nature which, in crucial respects, accurately reflects human nature and the human condition as they really are. In short, people in the state of nature must be just like us, only rational.

However, the relationship between the imaginary, rational people of social contract theory and real people like you and me can vary, and this can affect a social contract argument. As an example of how, take the argument discussed in the foregoing chapter, Locke's argument that legitimate government must be founded on the consent of the governed. Locke tells us that rational people, being fundamentally free and equal, would only agree to be governed on such terms. He also tells us that rational people, with natural rights to protect, would erect a government to avoid the insecurities of the state of nature, so rendering their rights more secure. In fact, you could put his conclusion this way: *Rational people would only consent to a government which respects their natural rights.* But the trouble is the 'consent' criterion and the 'natural rights' criterion can move independently. Unlike the rational beings hypothesised by social contract theory, real people – you and I – can consent to anything. Real people can consent to governments which violate their rights. I won't give any, but I am sure that a history of democracy would supply plenty of examples. Conversely, governments not based on consent can respect rights – the 'benevolent dictator' is certainly a possibility, if only a logical one.

So, what happens when the two criteria conflict? Where a government respects natural rights, but rules without consent, must it remain in place even so, or must it go? More crucially, where the people consent to a government which violates rights, is it, or is it not, entitled to remain in place? It is at least arguable that this problem is obscured by the fact that Locke is primarily concerned with the right to rebel. It is Locke's opinion that 'the people are not so easily got out of their old forms, as some are apt to suggest'; that it is only when 'the people are made miserable, and find themselves exposed to the ill usage of arbitrary power' that they are inclined to rebel (II, 223, 224). He is probably right and, if he is, it follows that people will usually withdraw consent only from governments which violate their rights. However, the converse claim – that people will only consent to governments which respect rights – does not hold. The problem is a real one, and it must become especially pressing for anyone who tries to use an argument like Locke's to, say, legitimise representative democracy with the claim that even rights-violating governments are entitled to remain in power until the next election, because the people consented to their rule at the last one.

A further difficulty for social contract theory arises from something I mentioned earlier, the claim that a social contract argument can be used to justify the existence of an institution – such as a state of a certain type – with an account of how it *could* have come into being, even though it did not *in fact* come into being that way. As it happens, where the institution in question is the state, or a certain type of state, this claim is quite in order. If it can be shown that rational individuals would choose to establish a state of that type, then fair enough, that is what you and I would agree to if we were rational; and, if the rational thing is the right thing, then it follows that you and I should agree to it. But problems can arise where the same type of argument is applied to other institutions, the institution of private property being a case in point.

'Historical' justifications of the way property is distributed, such as Locke's, score over 'patterned' accounts because they attach property rights securely to specific individuals. For example, if you want to know why Lord Such-and-Such should be the owner of the Such-and-Such estate, then a historical account which traces the transactions through which the estate's title has passed can tell you. (By contrast, appeal to a pattern, such as a utilitarian pattern, might yield the conclusion that the general happiness is best served when some people own more than others, but it won't tell you why those people over there should have the wealth, and not you.) However, this is an advantage a historical account derives from its ability to show how a given distribution came about *in fact*.

If – by contrast – you interpret Locke's property argument as an account of how an actual distribution could have come about, even though it didn't, you hit a problem. To illustrate it take the well-known fact that all property in England originated with a massive theft. I mean that, for every piece of English land, even if you can trace its ownership back a thousand years (itself a tall order in most cases) – and even if it can be shown that every time it changed hands it did so legitimately, with the consent of those involved – you eventually get back to the Norman Conquest of 1066, when all property in land was systematically stolen by the Normans from the Saxons. (You can think of the *Domesday Book* as a record of who stole what from whom.) Does Locke's argument entail that no one in England is legitimately entitled to own anything, even the property they think they have a clear title to? To me, that seems an absurd conclusion. If I am right, it follows that, in the case of the institution of property, an explanation of how it could have come about is not so obviously relevant to an explanation of how it did. (To be honest, I have not yet figured out why the conclusion should be so absurd, but I think it is. Perhaps time has something to do with it. I don't think it would seem so absurd if the Norman Conquest had happened more recently – last year, perhaps, or even three or four generations ago. For the moment, that is something I can leave to you.)

What else shall I say about Locke? Well there is so much. For example, just as the Norman Conquest raises a problem for Locke's argument, so – maybe – does the colonisation of North America. Just as the Normans took property from the Saxons, didn't European settlers steal from Native Americans? Perhaps; but Locke would say not, and his argument could easily be pressed into service as a justifying rationale for what happened. (It is no accident that so many of his examples involve the 'wild indians' of that continent.) This is something on which I have hardly touched, and – I am sure – there is more besides. However, I think I have said enough to give you an idea of why it is worth taking an interest in Locke's philosophy. He is the philosopher who first lent full theoretical articulation to some central themes which have, since his time, continued to structure political thought; most especially, the idea that government should be based on consent, and the idea that property ownership is something which needs to be defended with an argument. It would be hard to describe the *Second Treatise* as a model of disciplined logical rigour, but

– contrary to popular belief – logical rigour is not the only philosophical virtue, or even the most important one. Locke's major virtues are his inventiveness and his imagination. That said, it is time to move on.

9

---⋅◦◎◦⋅---

Rousseau

The subject of property is also discussed, though briefly, by Jean-Jacques Rousseau in his *Discourse on the Origins of Inequality*. This is what he says:

> The first man who, having enclosed a piece of land, thought of saying 'This is mine' and found people simple enough to believe him, was the true founder of civil society. How many crimes, wars, murders: how much misery and horror the human race would have been spared if someone had pulled up the stakes and filled in the ditch and cried out to his fellow men: 'Beware of listening to this impostor. You are lost if you forget that the fruits of the earth belong to everyone and that the earth itself belongs to no one'
>
> (Rousseau 1984: 109)

As the passage demonstrates, Rousseau's attitude to property was quite different from Locke's. The point is confirmed a little later when Rousseau expresses a sentiment Locke could never have shared as he reproaches the (property/slave) owner in the following terms:

> Do you not know that a multitude of your brethren perish or suffer from need of what you have to excess, and that you required the express and unanimous consent of the whole human race in order to appropriate from the common subsistence anything beyond that required for your own subsistence?
>
> (ibid.: 121)

The Discourse on Inequality is a speculative account of how humanity reached its present 'civilised' condition. Rousseau's narrative begins with a portrait of the first humans as solitary forest dwellers. In this condition, as Rousseau portrays it, human needs were few and simple, and human passions correspondingly so. Of 'the savage man', he writes that 'the only good things he knows in the universe are food, a female, and repose, and the only evils he fears are pain and hunger' (ibid.: 89). According to Rousseau, the human condition changed over time. From this solitary, nomadic state there arose, first, a more communal, and then a more settled way of life. It was with agriculture that property came on the scene and, as Rousseau sees it, it was with the latter that the rot really started to set in, for rules of property bred economic and social inequality. This is how:

> The stronger did more productive work, the more adroit did better work, the more ingenious devised ways of abridging his labour; the farmer had greater need of iron or the smith greater need of wheat, and with both working equally, the one earned plenty while the other had hardly enough to live on.
>
> (ibid.: 118)

And, as Rousseau goes on to explain:

> It is thus that natural inequality merges imperceptibly with inequality of ranks, and the differences between men, increased by differences of circumstance, make themselves more visible and more permanent in their effects, and begin to exercise a correspondingly large influence over the destiny of individuals.
>
> (ibid.)

As people fall into relations of domination and subservience, it soon becomes necessary to dissimulate and pretend. 'Being and appearance became two entirely different things, and from this distinction arose insolent ostentation, deceitful cunning and all the vices that follow in their train' (ibid.: 119). Eventually, we reach a condition in which despotism prevails. Rousseau describes this as follows:

> This is the last stage of inequality, and the extreme term which closes the circle from which we started. It is here that all individuals become equal again because they are nothing, here where subjects have no longer any law but the will of the master, nor the master any other rule but that of his passions, here that notions of the good and principles of justice vanish once more. Here everything is restored to the sole law of the strongest, and consequently to a new state of nature different from the one with which we began only that one was the state of nature in its pure form and this one is the fruit of an excess of corruption.
>
> (ibid.: 134–5)

Liberty, law and Rousseau's reputation

The foregoing passage embodies one of the most striking differences between Rousseau's version of the social contract argument and the work of his predecessors. (There are plenty of others, and these should become apparent as this chapter progresses.) That difference lies in his conception of the relationship between the social contract and the political conditions of his own time. The point is that we are not intended to take his description of 'despotism' as a gloomy prediction, an account of how things are likely to turn out if we aren't careful. So far as Rousseau is concerned, despotism has already arrived. In the form of rule by an absolute monarch, despotism had prevailed in France for some centuries. Rousseau goes on to say that 'the contract of government is so fully dissolved under despotism that the despot is only master for so long as he is strongest' (ibid.: 135). Add to this Rousseau's view that a genuinely political association can only be established with a 'true contract between a people and the chiefs that people chooses, a contract whereby both parties commit themselves to observe the laws' (ibid.: 128) and you have to conclude that no existing government is legitimate, or, as the famous opening sentence of *The Social Contract*'s first chapter would have it,

Man was born free, and he is everywhere in chains.

(1968: 49)

It follows that, if there is to be a true contract, it must lie in the future. In the meantime, 'The insurrection which ends with the strangling or dethronement of a sultan is just as lawful an act as those by which he disposed the day before of the lives and property of his subjects' (ibid.: 135). If anything is a recipe for revolution, this is.

The Social Contract (1968) is the work in which Rousseau sets out the positive side of the equation. With it, he prescribes a remedy for humanity's servile condition. To understand the book properly, there are two points on which it is essential to be clear from the outset, so let me now mention them. The first is that Rousseau is no 'back to nature' enthusiast for some idealised, pastoral simple life. He does not imagine for a moment that the life of early humans, as he portrays it in the *Discourse on the Origins of Inequality*, is something to which we could return. He does not even invite us to regard it as especially enviable. Rousseau's point is just that, because their lifestyle was simple, the emotions and needs of early humans were correspondingly simple; nothing more than that. It is true that Rousseau has been held responsible – by his contemporaries and subsequently – for romanticising 'the noble savage', but this is based on a misreading of Rousseau. More than that, there are, in his view, advantages to living in communities, governed by law. We are 'perfectible' creatures, and given the right conditions we could thrive. It is just that, having reached our present fallen condition, we have yet to be redeemed, but a return to the solitary existence of the primitive, nomadic, forest-dweller is not an option.

The second point is that, for Rousseau, the most important thing – the fundamental value – is *freedom*. 'The worst thing that can happen', he says, is 'to find oneself at the mercy of another' (1968: 125). Rousseau believes that the instinct for liberty is so deeply ingrained by nature that one can even observe it at work in animals, although, in 'civilised' humans, it has become subdued. 'Even as an unbroken horse erects its mane, paws the ground, and rears impetuously at the very approach of the bit, while a trained horse suffers patiently even the whip and spur', says Rousseau, 'savage man will not bend his neck to the yoke which civilised man wears without a murmur' (1984: 125) and 'When I see animals, born free and hating captivity, breaking their heads against the bars of their prison . . . I feel that it is not for slaves to argue about liberty' (ibid.: 126).

So, whereas the 'savage' had liberty but lacked the advantages derived from living socially under law, so 'civilised' humanity has lost the former in the process of gaining the latter. Therefore, the problem is to reconcile the two, and that is what Rousseau sets out to do with the community, or 'form of association', he describes in *The Social Contract*. There is a key passage in which he describes the task as follows:

> How to find a form of association which will defend the person and goods of each member with the collective force of all, and under which each individual, while uniting himself with the others, obeys no one but himself, and remains as free as before.
>
> (1968: 60)

This is certainly a worthwhile aim to set yourself. It is even a noble aim, so how come Rousseau's posthumous standing has so often been so disreputable? Well, the French Revolution had something to do with it. In his lifetime Rousseau was an immensely popular writer. After his death, in 1778, his status in the eyes of the French public became saintlike. This makes it unsurprising that he should have become cast as the revolution's philosopher, even though eleven years were to pass before the storming of the Bastille in 1789. In fact, Rousseau's attitude to violence was ambivalent, and there is nothing in his work you could describe as a detailed manifesto for an uprising. (In fact, he was less popular for his strictly political writings than he was for his other work.)[1] But it was Rousseau who set the tone. As Simon Schama puts it in *Citizens*, his history of the revolution, 'What he invented was not a road map to revolution, but the idiom in which its discontents would be voiced and its goals articulated' (Schama 1989: 161). As things have subsequently turned out, the association has done Rousseau's reputation no good at all, for, unlike the American Revolution which shortly preceded it, the French degenerated into a prolonged orgy of bloodletting – 'The Terror' as it became known. There is, at least, guilt by association.

And there is something else too; something associated with far more recent – equally, if not more terrible – events, and which is more closely related to the argument of more strictly political works. A charge frequently levelled at Rousseau is that he laid the foundations of a philosophical position which would later become the ideology of 'totalitarianism'; that is, the belief system which informed the actions of (amongst others) Hitler and Stalin, and in the name of which so much terrible damage was done in the twentieth century. According to one version of this accusation, J.L. Talmon's, Rousseau is guilty of advocating 'totalitarian democracy' (Talmon 1952: 38–49). In a similar vein, Sir Isaiah Berlin imputes a 'sinister paradox' to Rousseau:

> This is the sinister paradox according to which a man, in losing his political liberty, is liberated in some higher, deeper, more rational, more natural sense, which only the dictator or only the State, only the assembly, only the supreme authority knows, so that the most untrammelled freedom coincides with the most rigorous and enslaving authority.
>
> (Berlin 2002: 48–9)

Berlin adds that 'For this great perversion Rousseau is more responsible than any thinker who ever lived' (ibid.: 49).

What I should now like to do is examine this charge in more detail. I am not especially out to defend Rousseau against it, although I am not out to attack him either. That is not my present concern. As it happens, I think the charge is overstated, but I also think there is *something* right about it, even so. What is true is that his interpretations of certain key political concepts – the concept of freedom, for example – are very different from those advanced by many other philosophers. It is worth examining the difference more closely, because to understand it is to understand, not just Rousseau, but a great deal of subsequent political thought.

From freedom and democracy to totalitarianism?

A 'totalitarian' system is a system in which a single group – such as a party or a gang of generals – seeks to impose its will on the population, absolutely, by every available means. The aim is total control, hence the word 'totalitarianism'. Stalin's Soviet Union and Hitler's Germany usually crop up in discussions of totalitarianism, mainly because the term was initially coined, in the earlier part of the twentieth century, with them in mind. They were thought by many to exemplify a new phenomenon. Of course, there are others who think that there is nothing at all new about them, and that 'totalitarianism' is just a new-fangled name for good old-fashioned dictatorship. Scholars disagree, and it is an interesting question.[2] However, it is not a question I shall discuss here. I shall just carry on talking about 'totalitarianism', and I shall assume – I think, quite reasonably – that everyone will know what I mean.

For us, the subject is Rousseau's argument, and the question presently at issue must be: How can someone so committed to the ideals of freedom and (as we shall see) democracy lay himself open to the charge of having advocated totalitarianism? Let us take freedom first.

From freedom to totalitarianism?

The answer to the question depends – of course – on how you define 'freedom'. According to Rousseau, freedom is *'obedience to a law one pre-scribes to oneself'* (1968: 65) (my italics). Is this an accurate definition? Well, it certainly looks fair enough at first glance. There is nothing obviously wild or pretentious about it. More than that, it is a definition which recognises that, when a person is made to obey laws prescribed by someone else, that is usually a reason for describing that person as *lacking* freedom. The slave must obey the slave owner's rules, the captive must follow the captor's instructions, the menial worker must do as the boss says. In these cases the slave, the captive, the worker lack freedom because each is 'subject to the will of another'. It seems to follow, quite directly, that if each of them could make his or her *own* rules, each would be free. If it is a test of a definition that it should accurately reflect the way words ordinarily apply to simple, clear cut, cases, then Rousseau's definition appears to pass the test.

But this is where it starts to get interesting. Notice, now, that there are other ways to define 'freedom', and that these *also* pass the test. For example, many philosophers think of freedom as the absence of obstructions to action. If this is right, you are free to perform an action *if, and only if, there is no obstruction, standing in your way, sufficient to prevent you from doing it.* This definition also applies, quite clearly, to simple clear cut cases. For example, if the police were to erect a barrier across my street, then – obviously – I would lack the freedom to drive along the street as a result. This is the definition of 'freedom' (or 'liberty') which underpins the argument of John Stuart Mill's *On Liberty* (Mill 1982). '[T]here is a sphere of action', he wrote, 'in which society, as distinguished from the individual, has, if any, only an indirect interest.' The individual liberty Mill wants protected is the unimpeded freedom to move around inside the sphere. (Incidentally, perhaps I ought to point out that I am using the words 'freedom' and 'liberty' interchangeably.)[3]

In his famous essay, 'Two Concepts of Liberty' (1969), Isaiah Berlin draws a distinction between what he calls 'positive' and 'negative' conceptions of freedom. The former definition, Rousseau's, exemplifies a positive conception. It qualifies as such because it defines freedom in terms of self-control, or 'autonomy'. 'The "positive" sense of the word "liberty" derives from the wish of the individual to be his own master', writes Berlin. He continues:

> I wish my life and decision to depend on myself, not on external forces of whatever kind. I wish to be an instrument of my own, not of other men's, acts of will. I wish to be a subject, not an object; to be moved by reasons, by conscious purposes, which are my own, not by causes which affect me, as it were, from outside. I wish to be

somebody, not nobody; a doer – deciding, not being decided for, self-directed and not acted upon by external nature or by other men as if I were a thing, or an animal, or a slave incapable of playing a human role, that is, of conceiving goals and policies of my own and realising them

(ibid.: 131)

'I feel free to the degree that I believe this to be true, and enslaved to the degree that I am made to realise that it is not' (ibid.), or so Berlin adds. By contrast, Mill's conception of liberty is, in Berlin's terms, 'negative'. Berlin outlines 'the notion of "negative" freedom' as follows:

I am normally said to be free to the degree to which no man or body of men interferes with my activity. Political liberty in this sense is simply the area within which a man can act unobstructed by others. If I am prevented by others from doing what I could otherwise do, I am to that degree unfree; and if this area is contracted by other men beyond a certain minimum, I can be described as being coerced, or, it may be, enslaved.

(ibid.: 122)

And so on. According to Berlin, political philosophers can be roughly categorised as falling into one or the other of two groups, depending on which conception of freedom, out of the two, they tend to endorse. (Perhaps he is right, but I shan't go into that question.)

Does any of this matter? According to Berlin it does, for – as he contends – this apparently small difference between definitions has far-reaching implications. At first glance, they may appear 'no more than negative and positive ways of saying much the same thing', but they represent notions of freedom, which 'historically developed in divergent directions not always by logically reputable steps, until, in the end, they came into direct conflict with each other' (ibid.: 131–2). According to Berlin, it is the 'positive' conception of liberty which lends itself to the support of repressive, authoritarian doctrines. Berlin holds that, by contrast, the true friends of liberty have tended to interpret liberty in a 'negative' way. (In Berlin's view, one of liberty's true friends is John Stuart Mill. There is a full discussion of Mill below, in Chapter 11. I mention him from time to time here, mainly because his arguments provide a good contrast with Rousseau's.)

Now, Berlin's argument raises plenty of interesting questions, but our subject is Rousseau, so I shan't raise them here.[4] I have introduced his positive/negative freedom distinction into the discussion only because it will help me explain how, given the importance Rousseau attaches to liberty, he can nevertheless be represented as a totalitarian at heart. So, let us now get back to the definitions of 'freedom' at issue – Rousseau's and Mill's. Earlier, I pointed out that, for each, there is a range of simple cases to which it clearly applies, and that there are, therefore, good reasons for accepting either. But now note that when applied to certain, equally simple, cases, the two definitions yield contradictory implications.

A simple example will help me explain. Suppose, then, that some person is heavily, but not hopelessly, addicted to some drug. Following my usual practice, let me call this person P. For the purposes of my argument, it doesn't especially matter what the drug is, but let us suppose that it is tobacco. In short, suppose that P is a heavy smoker. Now suppose that, one day, P decides to give up cigarettes. For my purposes, this is a good example, because deciding to give up cigarettes can be portrayed as a matter of prescribing a rule to yourself. P, as it were, says 'From now on I shall not smoke cigarettes. Even when I have a strong craving for a cigarette, I shan't have one'. That is the rule. Now suppose that, for three days, P manages to stick to the rule and refrain from smoking. Recall that, according to Rousseau, freedom is 'obedience to a law one prescribes to oneself' (1968: 65). If this is right, it follows that, at this point in the story, P's actions are quite free. (And so they are. Of course, the 'negative' definition also entails that P's actions are free at this point. It is a clumsy way to put it – but true – that nobody is preventing P from not smoking.) So far, so good. But now suppose that, after three days, P attends a social gathering – that P is in a bar with some friends, say – and that someone offers P a cigarette. At this point, P finds it impossible to stick to the rule any longer, takes the cigarette, and smokes it. Now ask: Is P's action in taking the cigarettes a free action? My point is that, according to Rousseau's definition it is *not* (P has broken the rule) whereas according to the 'negative' definition it *is*. (Nobody stopped P from taking the cigarette.)

At this point, some readers will be wondering what any of this has to do with 'totalitarian' political theory. To see what, notice now that it is quite natural to use the language of freedom and unfreedom when describing P's behaviour. For example, you could say that P 'is no longer in control', that P has 'given in' to a craving, even that P is a 'slave' to an addiction. But notice, too, that although P is – in a sense – a slave here, P is not a slave *to another person*, as a real slave would be, but to one of P's *own* wants, in this case the craving for tobacco. This shows that, to describe P as a 'slave' here (or, at least, as 'lacking freedom') you have to distinguish two classes of want or desire; you have to say that to satisfy one type of want is to act as a free agent, and that to satisfy the other type is to act as a slave. (In the story P both 'wants to give up smoking' and 'wants a cigarette'. In satisfying the former want, P, by sticking to the rule, acts freely. In satisfying the latter, P acts unfreely.)

Let me summarise it this way: For philosophers who interpret the concept of freedom in a 'positive' way, *real* freedom is action in accordance with wants (desires, etc.) of one type; phoney freedom, unfreedom, even 'slavery', is action in accordance with wants of another type. Now, clearly, a great deal hangs on how you categorise wants. Which are wants of the first type, and which of the second? Here, I should say that, so far as I am concerned, the fact that positive conceptions of liberty must invoke a fairly complex conception of the self actually counts in their favour. (We are complex beings. We do have different types of want, and we do make distinctions between our own wants, thinking of some as wants we should not 'give in' to.) I am fairly sure that it is possible to hold such a conception without falling into the traps against which Berlin warns us. But that's another story. Berlin is surely right to say that a conception of freedom which rests on a distinction between different types, or 'levels', of want is open to exploitation by those who seek to control us, in one way or another. If 'real' freedom means following those wants and desires which form part of the 'true' self, then it all depends on what you count as the latter. The religious ascetic can say that real freedom is the service of God; the hippy mystic can say that real freedom is tuning in, turning on and dropping out; the fascist can say that real freedom is quickening the progress of the master race to its historic destiny; and the authoritarian, or 'totalitarian', can say that real freedom is the service of the party, or the state. Is Rousseau guilty of this last, dubious, manoeuvre? To see, we must turn to a different aspect of his argument.

The general assembly and its place in the ideal community

Like Plato's *Republic*, Rousseau's *The Social Contract* is a description of an ideal state; but, whereas Plato's state is supposed to be the most perfect realisation of the virtue of justice there can be, for Rousseau, the supreme value is freedom. As noted already, it is Rousseau's aim to describe a 'form of association' the members of which are both subject to law and yet free. As we have also noted, Rousseau believes that freedom is a matter of following a rule, or law, you prescribe to yourself. It follows that Rousseau's ideal 'form of association' must be one in which the subjects – or, rather, 'citizens' – only follow rules of which they are, themselves, the originators.

Is this possible? Well, according to Rousseau it is, thanks to the way decisions are made in the general assembly. This is his ideal state's central institution. Rousseau stipulates that its meetings must be 'fixed and periodic' (1968: 137) and that every citizen must be present. On this view, a parliamentary system, in which the assembly consists of representatives or 'deputies' elected by the people at large is not legitimate. Even the English system, which was the most progressive and democratic in the Europe of Rousseau's time, won't do. Says Rousseau, 'The English people believes itself to be free; it is gravely mistaken; it is free only during the election of Members of Parliament', and he adds that, 'In the brief moments of its freedom, the English people makes such a use of that freedom that it deserves to lose it' (ibid.: 141). In this version of the social contract argument, then, 'the sovereign' – i.e. the source of all legitimate authority – is a meeting at which every citizen is present; 'the sovereign can act only when the people is assembled', says Rousseau (ibid.: 136). (So, here is another difference between Rousseau and his predecessors in the social contract tradition, Hobbes and Locke, each of whom defines 'the sovereign' quite differently.)

One thing which will be apparent from this is that Rousseau's ideal community would have to be small, so small that all the citizens can meet together. This is, indeed, how he portrays them. In certain respects, Rousseau's community is an idealised version of a democratically run Greek *polis*. (You may remember Aristotle's insistence that once a town crier 'with the voice of a stentor' is needed to capture everyone's attention, a *polis* is getting too large (Aristotle 1981: 1326b11).)[5] Two other communities also mentioned by Rousseau with approval are Geneva and Corsica. It was in the former that Rousseau had his upbringing.[6] The Geneva of his time was an independent, walled city. To an extent, it was democratically run, and the citizens were, in the main, relatively independent tradesmen and artisans. Rousseau liked to sign himself 'Citizen of Geneva', so, rather as he idealises the *polis*, you could say that he idealises Geneva too. As for Corsica, the small, mountainous, Mediterranean island is, according to Rousseau, 'the one country in Europe which is still fit to receive laws', and he adds 'I have a presentiment that this little island will one day astonish Europe' (1968: 96). (He was right – though not quite in the way he intended to be. As things turned out, Europe's next great dictator, Napoleon, was to come from Corsica.)

One potential objection to which Rousseau is exposing himself here – I should have thought quite obviously – is the objection that his proposal is impracticable. Aren't the populations of the modern states which actually exist far too large to permit a meeting which every citizen attends? On the other hand, isn't it unrealistically idealistic to imagine that those states will eventually resolve themselves into assemblages of smaller communitarian units, the size of an ancient *polis* or Corsica? Rousseau's own response to this objection is, I think, unconvincing. He insists that just as it was possible for the people to assemble and enact laws two thousand years ago, so it must be possible now. 'Has human nature so much changed?' he asks (ibid.: 136). But the evidence he cites to support this argument is unpersuasive. The decision procedure followed at meetings of the Roman assembly was nothing like the procedure he envisages for his own general assembly. (We shall consider the latter more closely in a moment.) Moreover, if the population of Rome was as large as Rousseau claims – 'more than four million citizens without counting subjects, foreigners, women, children, or slaves' (ibid.) – it would have been impossible for the Roman assembly to adopt Rousseau's procedure. More recently, it has been suggested, in Rousseau's defence, that with modern information technology size of state is no longer a problem for his argument. If every citizen has access to the web, via a PC, then a voting procedure of the sort Rousseau advocates is possible, however large the population. We are, so to speak, all members of a 'virtual general assembly'. (For this suggestion, see Wolff 1998: 34ff.)

This argument strikes me as equally unconvincing. (I shall say why shortly.) In answer to the objection, it seems to me that Rousseau would have been far better advised to insist that the point of describing an ideal state is to set a standard against which actual states can be measured. He could have argued that actual states can approximate to the ideal, even though the ideal itself is unattainable (just as some machines can create less friction than others, even though no machine can be completely frictionless). He should then have left it at that.

In Rousseau's ideal community, when the general assembly meets, votes are taken, and those proposals for which the majority votes become law. So what has all this to do with totalitarianism? It may be impracticable to envisage a world of small communities, in which decisions are made by majority vote at a general assembly of all the citizens, but such a world seems about as far from the early twentieth century world of repressive totalitarian dictatorships as you can get. So, how can Rousseau possibly be open to the accusation that he is a covert apologist for a system which prefigures the latter? The answer lies in the fact that there are different ways to describe exactly what happens when people take a majority vote. Let us now consider this.

The general will

This is what Rousseau says happens:

> When a law is proposed in the people's assembly, what is asked of them is not precisely whether they approve of the proposition or reject it, but whether it is in conformity with the general will, which is theirs; each by giving his vote gives his opinion on this question, and the counting of votes yields a declaration of the general will.
>
> (1968: 153)

The passage has to be read carefully. It is important to see that what Rousseau is actually saying is very different from what a modern reader might easily take him to be saying. For example, he is *not* saying that, when a vote is taken, the point of the procedure is to allow each member of the assembly to express a preference (such as a want, a desire, or an attitude of approval). In fact he explicitly rejects such a view, saying 'what is asked of them [the voters] is not precisely whether they approve of the proposition or reject it'. On the contrary, in Rousseau's assembly, the majority vote is used to determine the answer to the question 'What is the general will?', and this is meant to be a question of *fact*. Rousseau's contention that 'When, [therefore], the opinion contrary to my own prevails' – i.e. when I vote with the minority – '*this proves only that I have made a mistake*, and that what I believed to be the general will was not so' makes it plain (ibid.: 153, my emphasis).

The former view – that votes express preferences – is pretty much the view which underpins the classical utilitarian defence of 'representative government', as first outlined in James Mill's *Essay on Government* and later refined by John Stuart Mill in his *Representative Government*. For example, it is the presupposition on which the argument of James Mill's *Essay on Government* is based (see James Mill 1955 and John Stuart Mill 1991c). On this view, the representative system is the best available mechanism for reconciling conflicts of 'interest' between members of the electorate. This view is also the 'received' version of democracy; the view with which most readers of this book will have been brought up and with which they will be most familiar. This makes it especially important to stress just how different Rousseau's is. One difference is this: On the received view, it *just makes no sense* to say that, if you vote with the minority, you are mistaken. If you think that votes express preferences (wants, desires or whatever) then your voting with the minority only signifies that more people than you happened to want something different from what you happened to want – and that's all there is to it. For example, if you and a group of friends decide to go for a meal one evening, and if everyone except you votes to visit an Italian restaurant, whereas you would prefer a trip to the local curry house, that only signifies that you most prefer a different kind of food. It would be absurd to insist, against this, that you are mistaken, and that you really want an Italian meal just like everyone else (and that it's just that you haven't realised it). By contrast, on Rousseau's view it makes perfect sense to say that what you really want and what you think you want are two quite different things. That is because, where any given 'proposition' is concerned, the nature of the general will is, as I have said, a fact, and it is the task of the people as a whole, convened as the general assembly, to determine what it is. So, when Rousseau says that 'the general will is always rightful and always tends to the public good', he means that it is always rightful *by definition*. The general will is, thus, something quite different from what everyone wants, or from what most people happen to want. Rousseau calls the latter 'the will of all'. (As we shall see later, he thinks that, in less than ideal conditions, people will vote on the basis of the latter, rather than consider the general will.)

If that isn't puzzling enough, then there are plenty of other perplexing questions just waiting to be asked here. For example, isn't there something highly questionable about the very idea that a majority vote can determine a question of fact? In the thirteenth century a vote on the questions of whether the earth is at the centre of the universe, of whether there are angels, or of whether God created Adam, would no doubt have yielded a great majority in favour. In the twenty-first century there would, most likely, be a majority against. The questionable thing is the suggestion that 'what the majority believe' has any relevance to the actual truth or falsity of such claims. (Aren't they true or false, *whatever* anyone thinks?) Again, it is Rousseau's belief that, on becoming a member of a legitimate community, every citizen acquires an extra will, a 'will as a citizen'. What one wills 'as a citizen' is meant to be equivalent to the general will, and this is supposedly different from that which one wills 'privately', as an individual. But isn't there something mystificatory, and highly questionable, about the idea that there is some sort of 'community will', which is both over and above the wills of individual members of the group and not attached to anyone in particular? In other words, how can there be a will which is not your will, my will, or his or her will? As for the 'common good', likewise, how can there be a good which is not yours, mine, his or hers? At first glance anyway, none of this appears to make much sense. And not only that, isn't there something wrong with the suggestion that you or I might *never* know what we really want; that it could happen that someone else is always the best judge of what we really will 'as citizens'. Ordinarily, we tend to regard individuals themselves as the best judges of what their preferences really are. (What if one of your friends were to say, 'You may think you want a curry, but what you really want is an Italian meal'?) Rousseau's thesis appears to deny the obvious. In summary, it seems pretty clear that there is a serious question as to whether any real sense can be made of Rousseau's conception of a 'general will'.

Totalitarian logic at work?

Before considering how Rousseau might respond it would be a good idea to summarise the objection under discussion, that his philosophy is a defence of 'totalitarian democracy'. We are now in a position to see how that objection is lent support by the way he interprets two concepts, each of which is fundamental to his argument. One is the concept of freedom and the other is the concept of a 'general will', supposedly the will of the community considered as a whole.

As I have presented it so far, then, Rousseau's position is this. First, he interprets freedom as obedience to a law one prescribes to oneself. As we noted, there is nothing especially wild about this definition. It accurately captures the way 'freedom' is quite often used in mundane, day-to-day contexts. However, as we also noted, it raises the question of what rules count as the rules you have genuinely 'prescribed to yourself'; of when you are following your 'real' will, and of when you are guided by preferences which are – in a sense – 'external'. Secondly, Rousseau presents us with a picture of an ideal community in which the citizens (supposedly) prescribe rules to themselves by voting at a general assembly. It is by taking a majority vote that they discover the general will, or so Rousseau holds. Consequently, they remain free, because they follow the wills they have 'as citizens', whatever the preferences which determined their vote may have been. Even citizens who voted with the minority remain free. In short – or so the objection runs – Rousseau's definition of 'freedom' and his conception of the general will, taken together, lead to the conclusion that, if you vote with the minority (or if you, say, change your mind after an election) what you think you want and what you really want are two completely different things. Worse, they mean that what you really want is what those with power and authority tell you you really want. (Never mind what you think you really want.) On this view, the powers that be can tax you, imprison you, even kill you, whilst telling you that (really) it's what you want them to do all the time, so you 'remain free'. This is the sick joke, the 'great perversion' critics such as Berlin have in mind (Berlin 2002: 49). And if that strikes you as a parody, or an exaggeration, those who raise the objection can always summon the following notorious passage in their support.

> [Hence], in order that the social pact shall not be an empty formula, it is tacitly implied in that commitment – which alone can give force to all the others – that whoever refuses to obey the general will shall be constrained to do so by the whole body, which means nothing other than that he shall be *forced to be free*.
>
> (1968: 64) (my emphasis)

Could it be that, with this passage, Rousseau is rationalising state repression by trying to persuade us (and himself) that it is precisely what it is not – liberation. If so, he is guilty of something for which George Orwell coined the term 'doublethink'. That was in *Nineteen Eighty-Four* (Orwell 1954), his famous description of life in an imaginary totalitarian society.

An answering case

Well, that is the case against Rousseau; the case according to which, for all his protestations on behalf of freedom, he is, in fact, an advocate of totalitarianism. (At least, it is a substantial part of the case. There will be a little more to add later.) I think you will agree with me that it is a powerful case, and I have tried to put it as persuasively as I can. However, at this point I must come clean and admit that even I am not entirely convinced by my own efforts. So far as I am concerned, there is something about the argument which does not quite ring true.

In fact, there are several reasons for being suspicious of it. One is that 'totalitarianism' is not a word which would have been available to Rousseau himself. More than that, if it genuinely denotes a distinct phenomenon – something which did not really come into being until the twentieth century – then Rousseau would never have known totalitarianism. Certainly, he could never have been aware of the great twentieth century totalitarianisms, even if 'totalitarianism' is really just a new name for something much older. Such considerations are insufficiently strong to defeat the argument completely. However, they should put us on our guard, for it is all too easy to look back at history and read into it; that is, to mislead yourself into thinking you detect dramas, as they unfold, when those dramas never really took place. Perhaps the story of how, over the centuries, supporters of liberal democracy and negative liberty (good) have slugged it out with supporters of totalitarianism and positive liberty (bad) is a case in point.

Then again, there is the fact that the nearest thing to 'totalitarianism' Rousseau would have known – the 'despotism' exemplified, most especially, by French absolute monarchy – was explicitly condemned by Rousseau. As we saw, he condemns it as the system under which 'notions of the good and principles of justice vanish' (1984: 134). Can Rousseau really have been so blind to the implications of his own argument that he unwittingly defended the very system he set out to subvert? Put like that, the suggestion seems scarcely credible. (And there is absolutely no evidence that he acted as a covert agent for Louis XVI. That would be a still more preposterous suggestion.) Finally, yet another reason for suspicion is that eighteenth century despotisms and twentieth century totalitarian regimes ran large nation-states, whose populations fell into classes and interest groups. By contrast, and as we have also seen, Rousseau's ideal communities have to be small.

It is with this last point that the key to Rousseau's defence lies, or so it seems to me. What I should like to do now is offer a few suggestions as to how an argument designed to counter the objection under discussion might go. To put it broadly, it strikes me that the portrait of Rousseau as an apologist for totalitarianism goes wrong by failing to take the strictures he places on the size of his ideal communities seriously enough. I shan't try to show that, far from advocating totalitarianism, Rousseau was a supporter of liberal democracy (as we know it in the twenty-first century 'West'). That would be an equally bad distortion. However, what I shall suggest is that, if we are to get Rousseau right, we must ask what life in a community run along the lines he advocates would actually be like.

Freedom

Before that, let us return, just briefly, to his definition of freedom. As I have outlined it, one of the claims on which the case against Rousseau rests is the claim that he is guilty of distorting the concept. Against this, there are at least two points to be made in his defence.

The first is that Rousseau's definition of freedom as 'obedience to a law one prescribes to oneself' (1968: 65) is not false. As I pointed out earlier, we do regard the fact that a person is following his or her own rules as a reason for describing that person as free. I used the case of smoker P, who is trying to give up, to illustrate this. Conversely, where someone is 'subject to the will of another' – that is, where someone else is making the rules for a person to follow – that is usually reason for saying that he or she is not free. Rousseau's definition may not apply to all cases in which it is appropriate to use words like 'free' and 'unfree', but it certainly applies uncontroversially to a great many. If Rousseau is guilty of anything, then, it is not so much misdefining the word 'freedom' as stretching the concept beyond its normal range of application. That is what 'totalitarian' thinkers supposedly do when they equate freedom as 'following your own rules' or 'doing what you really want' with 'the service of the state' or 'the destiny of the nation'.

So they may do, but – the second point – there are many definitions and concepts which can be twisted to serve disreputable ends. Take the 'negative' conception, discussed earlier, according to which freedom is essentially the absence of obstructions to action. As we noted, like Rousseau's 'positive' conception this is *also* true for a range of cases. But now suppose that an evil dictator manages to spike the national water supply with some new-fangled drug. The result is a docile population which can be manipulated into doing everything the dictator wants. Then there is an election. There is a full turnout and the dictator wins with 100 per cent of the votes. Were the people voting freely? Well, the dictator can certainly point out that no one prevented them from voting precisely as they wanted to, so – being 'negatively' free – they were free in every important respect. Against this, you or I might feel that his first having subjected them to his will, with the help of the drug, is somehow relevant. (Substitute a press baron for the dictator in this story, and the opinion columns of the tabloid papers he owns for the drug, and the example looks a lot less far-fetched.)

But if Rousseau's definition of the word 'freedom' is unexceptionable, even though philosophers can err by stretching the concept of freedom, 'positively' interpreted, the question remains of whether Rousseau himself is guilty of the latter offence. The answer depends – of course – on whether those who vote at the assembly can really be said to 'prescribe rules to themselves', even those who vote with the minority; and even here there are points to be made in Rousseau's defence. For example, there is the fact that it can be acceptable linguistic usage to say, of a person, that he or she is free 'in a given respect' but not in another. You could say, for instance, that an adult citizen of a democracy, saddled with a huge debt, is 'politically free' (he or she can vote) but 'economically unfree' (he or she is in hock to the bank, and working all hours to service the debt). Perhaps you could say, equally, that citizens in Rousseau's ideal community are politically free; that they are in *that* respect more free than the subjects of a despot. Perhaps it is a point which can be used to support Rousseau. Certainly, it looks all the more plausible the more you imagine the citizens to be lively participants in an assembly which is the governing institution of a small, relatively simple, community. To this, it could be worth adding that we do, in fact, sometimes tend to describe democracies as 'free' and less democratic systems lacking freedom (even now, even when comparing modern nation-states). In modern democracies, there are permanent minorities, but the usage persists, even so.

None of this adds up to an *argument* in Rousseau's defence. It simply suggests that his usage of 'free' and 'unfree' is not entirely perverse. It is possible that the foregoing could be developed into an argument but, as I have said, I am not out to offer a fully developed defence of Rousseau here.

The general will

What of the other claim on which the case against Rousseau rests, the claim that his idea of a general will, distinct from the wills of individual members of the community, is bogus. Contrary to this objection it *is* – I think – possible to make sense of the idea. What you have to do is imagine an association formed for some specific purpose.

Here is an example. Suppose that there are ten individual people, each of whom buys a lottery ticket on a Saturday afternoon. Each knows that he or she has a very slim chance of actually winning anything, but each figures that some chance is better than no chance, so everyone goes on buying the tickets. Then, one day, somebody suggests forming an association, the purpose of which is to increase everybody's chance of winning *something*, however little. The ten agree amongst themselves that, should anyone happen to buy a lucky ticket, the resulting winnings will be divided equally between every member of the group.[7] That way, everyone's chance of winning something is multiplied by ten. We have to suppose, also, that everyone enters on equal terms. (Obviously they do; it would be irrational to enter on any other terms. In a freely entered agreement, why would you agree to anyone else's getting more than you?)

What has this got to do with Rousseau? Well, for a start, notice that there is a way of describing what goes on here which invokes a distinction between two kinds of 'will'. Before the association is formed then – or so you could put it – everyone only has an individual or 'private' will. To be guided by this will is to say, in effect, 'Should I win, let me keep all the money'. After the association is formed, each person acquires a second will, namely a 'will as a member of the association'. This is something very different from his or her private will. To be guided by this second will is to be guided by the maxim 'Should anyone win, including me, let the money be divided between the members'. This is not an arbitrary maxim. It is logically implied by the terms of the agreement by which the association was formed. Now suppose, further, that one member wins some money. Let us say that it is one thousand pounds. A meeting of all the members is held, and a question is put to them: 'How shall the money be divided? What is the will of the association?' Clearly, this is a question of fact, and it has only one right answer, 'Divide the money equally and give everyone a hundred pounds'. In this example, then, it makes very good sense to speak of there being a will of the association, which is something quite different from the will of any individual member; and it also makes sense to describe the question – what is the will of the association? – as a question of fact.

Points of analogy between this example and the argument of *The Social Contract* are as follows. First, just as the gambling association is formed for a specific purpose, so is Rousseau's legitimately run community. Its purpose is to 'defend the person and goods of each member with the collective force of all' (1968: 60). Second, each person enters the covenant on equal terms, for 'the general will is an institution in which each necessarily submits himself to the same conditions which he imposes on others' (ibid.: 76) and 'the social pact establishes equality among the citizens in that they all pledge themselves under the same conditions and must all enjoy the same rights' (ibid.). Third, as in the example, so in *The Social Contract*, each person only has an individual or 'private' will before the agreement is made, but acquires a further 'will' as a consequence of the agreement – in this case a 'will as a citizen'. Fourth, it is because the content of the general will is dictated by the terms of the social contract that it is not to be identified with the private will of any given individual. Fifth, for the same reason, the answer to the question 'what is the general will?' is a rationally determinable question of fact.

With the help of this analogy, it is – I am sure – possible to make sense of the idea of a general will.[8] But at what cost? Clearly, interpreting the notion of the general will with the help of the analogy must mean that it only makes sense to speak of a general will in the context of a community to which the analogy applies. What would such a community be like? Well in Rousseau's time – before the advent of information technology – it would have to have been small, small enough for the entire citizenry to meet in the same place on a regular basis. But, in addition, it would have to *lack complexity*. For example, it would have to be the case that the only questions facing the members of the assembly were questions of fact, easily resolvable with reference to the terms of the social contract. More than that, the citizens would have to be similarly placed. There would have to be few, if any, differences of 'interest' between, say, members of different social classes, town-dwellers and country people, members of different ethnic and/or religious groups, and so on. Without this, it is difficult to see how the social contract could have the same point for everyone, or how everyone could think of themselves as having entered the contract on equivalent terms. (This is my reason for being sceptical of R.P.Wolff's suggestion that information technology would be enough to create a 'virtual general assembly' in a modern state.)

Imagine a community of relatively independent peasant farmers, each more or less equal in wealth and power to the others. Imagine a meeting at which they are trying to decide whose turn it should be to use the combine harvester next week. Imagine that, and you have imagined something like one of the communities Rousseau idealises. ('As long as men were content with their rustic huts, as long as they confined themselves to sewing their garments of skin with thorns or fish bones' writes Rousseau in the *Discourse on Inequality*, 'they lived as free, healthy, good and happy men so far as they could according to their nature', thereby invoking a past golden age. There is a great deal of that kind of thing in his work. (1984: 115–16).) On the other hand, it is clear that no modern society could possibly be construed on the 'gambling association' model. Modern societies are not just large, they are complex. In my view, it is this, rather than his alleged 'totalitarianism', which explains why the utilitarian view of freedom and democracy, and not Rousseau's, has tended to gain currency over the past two hundred years or so. The former is well adapted to the large, plural, societies we have increasingly come to inhabit. Rousseau's is not.

'Perfectibility' and the totalitarian state

In my earlier discussion of the 'gambling association' example, I imagined that one member wins a thousand pounds, that a meeting is held, and that the following question is put: 'How shall we divide the money? What is the will of the association?' As I argued, there is a right answer to this question, namely that the money should be divided equally, with everyone getting a hundred pounds each. But will the members actually come up with the right answer? The answer is that they will, but only if they are correctly motivated; that is, we have to assume that they will be public spirited enough to place the interests of the group before their own 'private' interests, and consider the question soberly and seriously. With this assumption, the probabilities are that each member is more likely to come up with the right answer than the wrong answer. (Or so we have to suppose if we are to agree with Rousseau that taking a majority vote is a good way to determine the general will. The supposition does not seem unreasonable.)

However, what could happen is that the members are too corrupt or self-interested to put the public will of the association first, in which case each person will be motivated by his or her 'private' will. Where this happens, 'the will of all' prevails and 'There is often a great difference between the will of all [what all individuals want] and the general will' because 'the general will studies only the common interest while the will of all studies private interest, and is indeed no more than the sum of individual desires' (ibid.: 72).

Precisely the same thing can happen when motions are put at meetings of Rousseau's general assembly. That is why, within his ideal state, arrangements have to be made to ensure that citizens are public spirited enough to put the common good and the general will before their own, selfish, private demands. One such arrangement is the complete prohibition of what Rousseau calls 'sectional associations'. These are smaller groups formed within – Rousseau says 'at the expense of' (ibid.: 73) – the larger association. With the help of the analogy I have been using, the logic underlying the prohibition should be fairly evident. It is simply that, for every association of which you become a member, you acquire an additional 'will'. For example, in addition to your private will, and your will as a citizen, where there are sectional associations you could find yourself with a 'will as a member of such-and-such a political party', a 'will as a member of such-and-such a trade union', and a 'will as member of such-and-such a pressure group'. With all these extra wills, it will be increasingly difficult for you to coolly contemplate the nature of the general will. The others will get in the way.

Then again, there is Rousseau's insistence that there should be a 'civil religion' designed to reinforce solidarity among the citizens, and their sense of a social bond. With it, there must go 'a profession of faith which is purely civil and of which it is the sovereign's function to determine the articles, not strictly as religious dogmas but as sentiments of sociability' (ibid.: 186). 'The dogmas of the civil religion must be simple and few in number', says Rousseau, 'expressed precisely and without explanations or commentaries'. They must include articles of religious belief in, for example, 'The existence of an omnipotent, intelligent, benevolent divinity that foresees and provides; the life to come', and so on, but also a commitment to 'the sanctity of the social contract and the law' (ibid.). (Otherwise people can believe what they like.)

Modern readers will find it difficult not to detect intimations of totalitarian state control in such a passage. Contrast Rousseau's attitude to sectional associations with that taken by orthodox utilitarian democratic theory, the theory I described earlier as the 'received view'. It is the view with which most of us were brought up. On this view, sectional associations are absolutely essential to the operation of democracy. Without them, it would be impossible for individuals to bring pressure to bear on the decision making machinery; to 'make their voices heard'. By contrast – or so critics can argue – a view such as Rousseau's leaves the individual powerless in the face of a powerful, unchecked, state machine. This is, of course, precisely the end totalitarian rulers seek to achieve. Such critics can draw additional support for their view from Rousseau's claim that the articles of the contract are reducible to a single one, 'namely the total alienation by each associate of himself and all his rights to the whole community' (ibid.: 60), or his remark that, after the contract, the citizen's life 'is no longer the bounty of nature but a gift he has received conditionally from the state' (ibid.: 79).

Then again, there is the figure of 'the lawgiver'. Rousseau imagines that a people can be ready for law but unsure how to establish it; in which 'the general will' needs to be 'shown the good path which it is seeking, and secured against seduction by desires of individuals' (ibid.: 83). At this point the lawgiver – who is, 'in every respect, an extraordinary man' (ibid.:

85) – appears on the scene and shows the people the way. Rousseau has this to say:

> Whoever ventures on the enterprise of setting up a people must be ready, shall we say, to change human nature, to transform each individual, who by himself is entirely complete and solitary, into a part of a much greater whole, from which that same individual will then receive, in a sense, his life and his being. The founder of nations must weaken the structure of man in order to fortify it, to replace the physical and independent existence we have all received from nature with a moral and communal existence. In a word each man must be stripped of his own powers, and given powers which are external to him, and which he cannot use without the help of others. The nearer men's natural powers are to extinction or annihilation, and the stronger and more lasting their acquired powers, the stronger and more perfect is the social institution. So much so, that if each citizen can do nothing whatever except through co-operation with others, and if the acquired power of the whole is equal to, or greater than, the sum of the natural powers of each of the individuals, then we can say that law making has reached the highest point of perfection.
>
> (ibid.: 84–5)

Read in a certain light, such passages can make your blood run cold. How can a modern reader fail to detect in this description of 'the lawgiver' a cult of the leader? How can a modern reader fail to picture Hitler at Nuremberg, having descended from his plane to the strains of Wagner, addressing his assembled acolytes, each transformed 'into a part of a much greater whole' from which each receives 'in a sense, his life and his being' (ibid.). Yet this cannot be what Rousseau himself had in mind, and – so far as I can see – a better explanation for such passages runs as follows.

In the eighteenth century it was fashionable to draw upon classical themes. You can see this fashion at work in the architecture and the art of the time, and, in the above passage, you can also see it at work in philosophy. In reality, Rousseau's lawgiver is no fascist dictator, but a drafter of constitutions. Rousseau is self-consciously evoking such figures as Solon who redrafted the constitution of Athens, and Lycurgus, who gave Sparta its first constitution. As for the talk of 'changing human nature' and 'transforming human nature', well, it was Rousseau's view that our character, human nature itself, is a function of the prevailing social and political institutions. In this respect, he differs from, say, Hobbes, for whom human nature remains the same whatever political conditions prevail. But with this, Rousseau is invoking a tradition which can be traced back to Aristotle – and isn't he right, at least to the extent that you or I would have been very different people had we lived at a different place at a different time?

In short, it makes more sense to think of Rousseau's ideal community as a romanticised *polis* than it does to think of it as a proto-totalitarian state, prefiguring horrors which were to come one hundred and fifty years or so after his death. That said, however, it is important to remember the dual aspect such texts as *The Social Contract* inevitably possess. A lot will depend on where you strike the balance between Rousseau's own intentions and the significance his arguments must inevitably hold for later readers including ourselves.

Kataklusmos

After the French Revolution, life became cheap for a while. Simon Schama relates how, in Lyons in 1793:

> The Terror went into action with impressive bureaucratic efficiency. House searches, usually made at night, were extensive and unsparing. All citizens were required to attach to their front doors a notice indicating all residents who lived inside. Entertaining anyone not on that list, even for a single night, was a serious crime.

And then,

> From early December the guillotine went into action at a much greater tempo. As in Paris, pride was taken in its mechanical efficiency. On the eleventh of Nivôse, according to the scrupulous accounts kept, thirty-two heads were severed in twenty-five minutes: a week later, twelve heads in just five minutes.
>
> For the most eager Terrorists, though, this was still a messy and inconvenient way of disposing of the political garbage. Citizens in the streets around the place des Terreaux, on the rue Lafont, were complaining about the blood overflowing the drainage ditch that led from beneath the scaffold. A number of the condemned, then, were executed in mass shootings on the Plaine des Brotteaux – the field where Montgolfier had made his ascent. Yet another ex-actor, Dorfeuille, presided over some of these *mitraillades*, in which as many as sixty prisoners were tied in a line by ropes and shot at with cannon. Those who were not killed outright by the fire were finished off with sabres, bayonets and rifles. On the fourth of December, Dorfeuille wrote to the President of the Convention that a hundred and thirteen inhabitants of 'this new Sodom' had been executed on that single day and in those that followed he hoped that another four to five hundred 'would expiate their crimes with fire and shot'.
>
> (Schama 1989: 781–3)

Schama adds that, by the time the killings had finished, 'one thousand nine hundred and five people had met their end'. And that was just Lyons.

Schama is describing just one instance of the atrocities which were taking place across the greater part of France.

These were events which traumatised the European consciousness and, like a select number of horrors to follow – 'the war to end all wars' (1914–18), the Holocaust, 11 September 2001 – their infamy was so great that a shorthand expression became sufficient to evoke them: 'the Terror'. It is a sobering thought that, if you are now aged 25 or 30, your generation is only the eighth to have come into being since the old order was despatched in this orgy of hacking, gouging, stabbing and slicing, of gutters running with blood. Imagine eight people in a room. That's not many people.

Part III

Modern Times, Modern Themes

10

After the flood

Reactions to the French Revolution varied. William Wordsworth, who passed the autumn of 1790 in Paris, described his experience this way:

> Bliss was it in that dawn to be alive,
>   But to be young was very heaven!
> (*The Prelude*: Book XI, lines 108–9) (Wordsworth 1932: 736)

As Wordsworth saw it, these were times

> In which the meagre, stale, forbidding ways
> Of custom, law, and statute, took at once
> The attraction of a country in romance!
> When Reason seemed the most to assert her rights,
> When most intent on making of herself
> A prime Enchantress – to assist the work
> Which then was going forward in her name!
>   (ibid.: lines 110–16)

Others were more circumspect. For example, Jeremy Bentham reserved a special contempt for the *Declaration of the Rights of Man and of the Citizen*, issued by the French National Assembly in 1789. With a distinct echo of Rousseau, the declaration opens with a description of the assembly as 'the representatives of the French people, organised as a National Assembly'. Rousseau is echoed still more distinctly in the opening sentence of the declaration's first article. This states that 'Men are born free and remain free and equal in rights'. (Presumably, we are meant to take it that 'men' are no longer 'in chains' thanks to the revolution.) So far as Bentham was concerned, this talk of natural and imprescriptible rights was mere '*bawling* upon paper' which 'proceeds from the same temper and the same sort of distress as produces bawling with the voice' (Bentham 2000c: 391). The line occurs in the 'Preamble' to Bentham's *Anarchical Fallacies*, an essay in which Bentham conducts a piecemeal dissection of the declaration's claims. It is the text which also contains one of Bentham's most famous remarks, the following:

163

Natural rights is simple nonsense: natural and imprescriptible rights, rhetorical nonsense – nonsense upon stilts.

(ibid.: 405)

Bentham: happiness and reason

Not that Bentham was a reactionary: On the contrary, like Rousseau before him, he was a child of the Enlightenment, a fighter on the side of reason and progress. And yet Bentham's intellectual temper is so different. On reading his major work, *The Principles of Morals and Legislation* (2000b), it is hard to believe that it was first published in 1789, a mere eleven years after Rousseau's death. Whereas Rousseau's style is high-flown and declamatory, and his argument prone to abstraction, Bentham's is icily pragmatic. To appreciate the difference you only have to compare the way Rousseau imagines that the assembled citizenry in his (imagined) ideal state will earnestly deliberate over the nature of the general will with Bentham's scornful dismissal of the very idea:

But anywhere – even in France – how can the law be the expression of the universal or even the general will of all the people, when by far the greater part have never entertained any will, or thought at all about the matter; and of those who have, a great part (as is the case with almost all laws made by a large assembly) would rather it had not taken place.

(2000c: 421)

Bentham is widely known as a founder of the utilitarian movement; and, as readers will know by now, utilitarianism is that moral and political philosophy which claims to base its arguments and principles on 'the principle of the greatest happiness' or 'principle of utility'. As Bentham puts it in one place, '*it is the greatest happiness of the greatest number that is the measure of right and wrong*' (2000a: 3) (Bentham's italics).

Here is the opening paragraph of *The Principles of Morals and Legislation*:

Nature has placed mankind under the governance of two sovereign masters, *pain* and *pleasure*. It is for them alone to point out what we ought to do, as well as to determine what we shall do. On the one hand the standard of right and wrong, on the other the chain of causes and effects, are fastened to their throne. They govern us in all we do, in all we say, in all we think: every effort we can make to throw off our subjection will serve but to demonstrate and confirm it. In words, a man may pretend to abjure their empire: but in reality he will remain subject to it all the while. The *principle of utility* recognises this subjection, and assumes it for the foundation of that system, the object of which is to rear the fabric of felicity by the hands of reason and law. Systems which attempt to question it deal in sounds instead of senses, in caprice instead of reason, in darkness instead of light.

(2000b: 87; Bentham's italics)

Utilitarianism was more than a philosophy. It was a political movement, which achieved real prominence in the earlier half of the nineteenth century. Since then, it has continued to wield an influence. It is – if you like – one 'modern "ism" '; so let us begin Part III by asking what it was that originally made utilitarianism so attractive.

I would attribute utilitarianism's success to three factors, two of which can be detected at work in the passage quoted above. The first is utilitarianism's promise to sweep away clutter; to replace muddle and mystification of all kinds with a single – simple and easily comprehensible – criterion. When faced with a choice between actions or policies you simply select the one which, so far as you can tell, will most increase the sum of human happiness. In a loose sense of 'scientific', there is something appealingly scientific about this. Moreover, there is something anti-pretentious about it. One of Bentham's great attractions as a writer is the wicked sense of humour with which he expresses his hostility to all forms of self-importance. This attitude is progressive as well, because the individuals who deal in pomposities, 'in sounds instead of senses, in caprice instead of reason, in darkness instead of light' tend to be those (philosophers and others) who base their reactionary claims on appeals to tradition and intuition.

The second factor is the theory of motivation with which Bentham connects the principle of utility. As the passage shows, Bentham holds that everyone is motivated by the desire for pleasure and the fear of pain (even though some people pretend otherwise). For Bentham, happiness is simply a positive balance of pleasures over pains. This is also appealingly straightforward. To be 'utilitarian' is to value 'usefulness', of course, and what on earth can usefulness be if it is not serving the happiness of humanity. Also, it is easy to appreciate how such an account of motivation could carry a ring of truth with it.

To this, I would add – thirdly – that, when taken together, the principle of utility and the theory of motivation make utilitarianism particularly attractive to those individuals whose job it is to frame and administer policy in plural societies. By a 'plural' society I mean a society composed of many different groups, each with its own wants, needs, characteristic lifestyle and plans. Following the utilitarians, let us call all such wants, preferences and plans 'interests' for short. Throughout the nineteenth century, the societies of Europe and North America were to become increasingly plural. With industrialisation there came a large new class of industrial workers. (Bentham, who lived until 1832, would have been a witness to this.) Alongside this class, there remained a class of agricultural labourers. Mid-nineteenth century society was divided between these, between townspeople and country dwellers, between the old aristocracy and the newly rich aristocracy of 'trade', and in other ways too (and, of course, any individual could belong to more than one of these categories). In addition to all this it is, no doubt, the case that men and women can be categorised, for certain purposes, as falling into separate interest groups and – on top of all that – there are differences between religious and ethnic groups to be considered.

In a plural society, the 'interests' of such groups are more than likely to come into conflict, and – in such a context – 'politics' becomes the art of compromise and conflict resolution. The task can look forbidding – especially to those who want to reach solutions which are fair, and not just pragmatic – but utilitarianism offers a prospect of help. This it does in two ways. First, with its theory of motivation it offers to explain all behaviour in a single way as 'the pursuit of happiness'. This promises to simplify the political task because it suggests that, while members of different interest groups may *appear* to be pursuing different ends, they are *really* pursuing the same end, i.e. happiness. If this is right, then all the administrator has to do is divide that thing – the 'happiness-cake' – between everyone in a fair and just way. Second, the principle of utility tells you *how* to divide the cake. You just arrange things in such a way that 'the greatest happiness of the greatest number' results.

I should add that, with two hundred years of hindsight, utilitarianism's theory of motivation appears open to question, and the principle of utility appears far from easy to interpret and apply. But that is a subject with which I shall deal in the following chapter. For the moment, my only point is that it is easy to see why utilitarianism should have held such a powerful appeal, especially for social reformers, and the leading utilitarians were certainly that. Bentham's own work covered many aspects of social policy, including prison reform. His utilitarian associate, James Mill, wrote a famous defence of democracy, *An Essay on Government* (1955). The aim of Bentham's *Principles of Morals and Legislation* (2000b) was to advocate a reform of the law along utilitarian lines. Every law and legal penalty whose existence could not be justified in terms of the greatest happiness principle should be erased from the statute book, or so Bentham argued. (His great successor, John Stuart Mill, said that Bentham had 'found the law a chaos and left it a science' (1987a: 158).) Even Bentham's funeral – which must have been one of the weirdest ever – had a political point to it. It was Bentham's stated wish that he should be publicly dissected, and so he was. In his time, the only corpses to which trainee surgeons were permitted access by law were those of executed criminals, and the 'ceremony' was part of a campaign, in the name of science and progress, to have this access widened. The remains of his body, dressed in a coat and hat and seated in his favourite chair, are placed on display in a glass cabinet – the 'auto-icon' – in the foyer of University College London.[1]

History and community

Commenting on what he describes as Rousseau's 'contribution to the search for this concept' – i.e. the concept of the state – Hegel has this to say:

> Unfortunately, . . . He takes the will only in a determinate form as the individual will, and he regards the universal will not as the absolutely rational element in the will, but only as a 'general' will which proceeds out of this individual will as out of a conscious will. The result is that he reduces the union of individuals in the state to a contract and therefore to something based on their arbitrary wills, their opinion, and their capriciously given express consent; and abstract reasoning proceeds to draw the logical inferences which destroy the absolutely divine principle of the state, together with its majesty and absolute authority. For this reason, when these abstract conclusions came into power, they afforded for the first time in human history the prodigious spectacle of the overthrow of the constitution of a great actual state and its complete reconstruction *ab initio* on the basis of pure thought alone, after the destruction of all existing and given material. The will of its re-founders was to give it what they alleged was a purely rational basis, but it was only abstractions that were being used; the Idea was lacking; and the experiment ended in the maximum of frightfulness and terror.
>
> (Hegel 1967: 156–7)

Even his greatest admirers concede that Hegel's style can be difficult and obscure – even that he is, on occasions, completely incomprehensible – so don't be surprised if you haven't grasped the meaning of the foregoing passage in its entirety. However, even if you haven't, it will certainly give you an impression of what he thought about the French Revolution. For a start, it is pretty clear that, like many others, he thought of the Terror as a catastrophe; that it was, as he says, an experiment which ended 'in the maximum of frightfulness and terror'. In fact, also like many others – like Wordsworth, for example – Hegel had initially taken a positive attitude towards the revolution, viewing it with optimism and hope. But, as he saw it, things had gone badly sour since then. There is something else too; Hegel attributes the catastrophe to an obsession with intellectual abstractions, an attempt to reconstruct the state *ab initio*, 'on the basis of pure thought alone'. Again, this judgement was widely made, by Bentham, for example, with his suspicion of 'natural rights' talk, and, as we shall see later, by Edmund Burke.

But the passage also contains some more specifically Hegelian elements. Take the way he thinks of Rousseau as engaged in a specific enterprise, namely a search for 'the concept' of the state. That is not quite how I would describe Rousseau's purpose and nor do I think it is how Rousseau would have described it himself. As we saw in the previous chapter, the point of *The Social Contract* (Rousseau 1968), as stated by Rousseau himself, is to describe a form of association in which people are subject to law and yet remain free. It is also, quite clearly, an attempt to solve the problem of political legitimacy through an account of what would be dictated under the terms of a genuine social contract. However, none of this seems to add up to an attempt to grasp the state's 'concept'. In fact Hegel's account of Rousseau, as given in the passage, is inaccurate and rather sketchy. It is just not fair to describe the decisions made in Rousseau's ideal community as resting on 'capriciously given free consent'. Still, given Hegel's own purpose, maybe that doesn't matter, for his thumbnail sketch of Rousseau is part of a great story according to which, as Hegel sees it, all political philosophers, whether they know it or not, are engaged in the same enterprise, the enterprise of trying to apprehend a concept in its entirety. Hegel's point is that Rousseau's efforts only met with incomplete success. As he goes on to say in the next paragraph, a conception such as Rousseau's 'comprises only one moment, and therefore a one-sided moment, of the Idea of a rational will' (ibid.: 157). Rousseau's philosophy, and with it the French Revolution, are thus portrayed by Hegel as a particular 'moment', a milestone event, on the road to philosophy's ultimate goal, and, with it, history's ultimate goal too.

Now, in writing a book such as this, one is forced to be selective. Something has to go, and I have chosen not to devote an entire chapter to Hegel. That means that there would be no point in my even trying to give a full account of his philosophy. I think that's the right decision, because I believe that present day readers will find many of his claims less interesting than those made by the writers on whom I do propose to concentrate. For example, I doubt that many, reading this, will be impressed by Hegel's claim that 'The state is the actuality of concrete freedom' (ibid.: n. 160), or his argument's (apparent) implication that philosophy's final goal has been achieved with the publication of his own work. However, what I should do is say something about Hegel's legacy, for it seems to me that the things of value we have inherited from Hegel are not so much a particular view of what the end of history actually is, or of what the best state actually is, but certain patterns of thinking. It is the latter which have wielded so much influence over subsequent thinkers, and most especially as follows.

First of all, and as you will have gathered, Hegel takes a certain view of history. He believes that it follows a definite course. In his *Philosophy of History* (Hegel 1956) he traces that course from ancient, pre-Greek, times to his own, passing as he goes from the Greeks, to the Romans, to the rise of Christianity, and then to the Reformation. However, unlike conventional histories, Hegel's account is more than a record of events, a description of 'what happened to occur'. Particular historical events are portrayed as the manifestations of an underlying process, working itself through at a more fundamental level. That is what makes it a *philosophy* of history, and not just an exercise in history. A contrast with Rousseau is worth drawing here. As we saw in the previous chapter, in his *Discourse on the Origins of Inequality* (1984) Rousseau also traces the course of history, and, with it, the development of human consciousness. Hegel does the same, so there is a sense in which you could describe Rousseau as one of Hegel's precursors. However, there are differences. Rousseau takes care to emphasise that his history is a purely speculative account, that it consists solely of 'hypothetical and conditional reasonings, better fitted to clarify the nature of things than to expose their actual origin' (ibid.: 78).[2] By contrast, Hegel thinks he is describing what actually happened. Also, you don't get the same sense of inexorable destiny from Rousseau as you do from Hegel. Rousseau makes it clear that, as he sees it, the people are in a state of war with the sovereign, but he doesn't give the impression that a revolution is just around the corner, or even that one is inevitable in the long run. Hegel, however, leaves you with no doubt that events can, and will, only move in one direction. Along with all this, there goes his view that the underlying process, of which particular historical events are the manifestation, will eventually work itself through.

The second feature of Hegel's legacy worth noting becomes apparent once we ask precisely what that underlying process is supposed to be. It is here that grasping Hegel's thought can prove especially difficult. In his work Hegel sets out to chart the progress of what he calls *Geist*. In English translations of Hegel this tends to be rendered as 'mind' or 'spirit'. What can this mean? Well, *Geist*, 'mind' and 'spirit' are nouns, so there is a natural tendency to think that Hegel is talking about a kind of entity here. However, Hegel is really describing the stages through which humanity passes in its attempts to reach some goal; 'mind' is really a sort of collective noun for humanity, considered as a whole as it seeks to grasp the essential nature of reality. (So, you don't *have* to picture a giant brain, galumphing across the landscape as it hoovers up everything in its path.)

The goal itself is specified differently in different Hegelian texts. In the *Phenomenology of Spirit* it is 'absolute knowledge'. This is supposedly achieved once the mind has grasped reality and understood the latter as its own creation, or – as Hegel puts it – 'when consciousness itself grasps this its own essence, it will signify the nature of absolute knowledge itself' (1977: 57). The stages through which humanity passes include forms of awareness (such as 'sense-certainty' and self-consciousness), intellectual and religious movements (stoicism, Christianity) and social forms. (Slavery is said to be unstable because neither master nor slave is able to recognise an equal consciousness in the other.) In the *Philosophy of*

History and the *Philosophy of Right* (1967) the goal is freedom, or rather, 'mind's progress towards consciousness of itself as free'. Not that this is a different goal. It is the same goal, the goal described in the *Phenomenology*, but viewed under a different aspect. The realisation of a certain form of state is the same goal viewed under yet another aspect. Bear that in mind, and it is possible to make some sense of the paragraph with which Hegel brings the *Philosophy of Right* to a close:

> In the state, self-consciousness finds in an organic development the actuality of its substantive knowing and willing; in religion, it finds the feeling and the representation of this its own truth as an ideal essentiality; while in philosophic science, it finds the free comprehension and knowledge of this truth as one and the same in its mutually complementary manifestations, i.e., in the state, in nature, and in the ideal world.
>
> (1967: 222–3)

Actually, I think you should get the general idea, although the details clearly need far more explanation than I can give them here. Two things should be clear though. One is that, whatever Hegel means by 'freedom' it has to be more than the mere 'negative' freedom from obstructions to do this or that action. In fact, Hegel castigates this as 'mere abstract freedom', a 'stage in the development of the idea of freedom' (ibid.: 34). For Hegel, true freedom can only come with mind's consciousness of itself as free. The other is that, whatever the precise meaning of all this may be, it is a story about *self-realisation*. For Hegel, the 'end of history' comes once this has been achieved. So, that is the second feature of Hegel's philosophy to have been inherited by his successors – the idea that history culminates in self-realisation.

The third is a particular account of (what you could loosely call) the mechanism which drives historical change and through which 'mind' supposedly achieves self-realisation. According to Hegel, change is brought about by what could be described (again loosely) as 'the interplay of cultural movements, ideas, and social forms'. Thus, stoicism is replaced by scepticism and then early Christianity. Supposedly thanks to the negative manner in which the latter portrays humanity's relationship to God, the latter is superseded by a Christianity of a more positive (Protestant) form; slavery disappears from the scene, supposedly because master and slave are unable to view each other as equals, and – as we have seen – the French Revolution is succeeded by the Terror, supposedly thanks to the predominance of an abstract mode of thinking.

Now, so far as I can see, there is *something* right about this. Historical change can sometimes be explained in terms of cultural interactions of one sort or another. One part of Hegel's legacy can be traced to Nietzsche, who characterised 'truth' as a 'mobile army of metaphors' (1995: 92). A central thesis of his *Beyond Good and Evil* (1990) is that philosophical

ethics, the attempt to formulate morality in terms of fundamental principles, should be replaced by a descriptive account of moral change. As he
says at one point, 'Philosophers one and all have, with a strait-laced seriousness that provokes laughter . . . wanted to furnish the *rational ground*
of morality – and every philosopher hitherto has believed he has furnished this rational ground' (ibid.: 108). Against this, Nietzsche argues for
the replacement of supposedly 'scientific' ethics with a 'natural history of
morals'. If this is right, differences between moralities, and between cultures, are rather like differences between languages. In fact, learning
another language *is*, in a way, a question of learning another culture. It is
not always possible to translate directly from one to another. Note also –
and crucially – that there is no overarching *meta*-language against which
other languages can be tested. There is just the interplay of different languages, nothing more. (It is no accident that Nietzsche was a specialist in
comparative philology. It seems that, rather as Aristotle construed political philosophy on the model of biological science, and rather as Hobbes
construed it on the model of geometry, so Nietzsche construed moral
philosophy on the model of comparative linguistics.) Think of it like that,
and you can also trace Hegel's influence to the self-styled 'postmodernists'
of our own time, for whom the history of thought is nothing more than
the constant interplay of 'discourses', with no objective standard or 'grand
narrative' against which to assess their relative merits.[3]

But if there is something right about that way of explaining change,
there is – fairly clearly – quite a lot wrong with it too. The trouble is that it
only applies to certain cases. When applied to others, it is unconvincing.
As a case in point, take Hegel's explanation of the Terror. As he portrays it,
this was a consequence of the way thought was dominated by abstractions
– 'natural right', 'abstract liberty' and so on. If this were true, it would be
convenient for Hegel, because it would fit in with his theory so neatly.
However, there is really no reason for thinking that it is true. To raise an
obvious question: Why wasn't the American Revolution (which preceded
the French by a mere thirteen years) also followed by a reign of terror? The
USA's founding documents are its Declaration of Independence and its
written Constitution, each of which lays heavy emphasis on natural rights,
so the American Revolution was framed in terms of pretty much the same
abstractions as the French. This suggests that Hegel's explanation is
wrong. Moreover, so far as I can see there is no reason why we should
confine ourselves to the realm of ideas in our search for an answer. The
answer could just as easily lie in social or economic factors, or in the fact
that certain individuals 'just happened' to behave in certain ways and not
others.

In short, it seems to me that Hegel's account of the mechanism which
drives historical change is unconvincing. Also, many readers will know
that it was precisely this aspect of Hegel's philosophy with which Marx
found himself most dissatisfied. There will be a full discussion of Marx's

thought in a later chapter, but, having mentioned him, let me now briefly describe another development which took place in the early years of the nineteenth century, one which is relevant to our understanding of his ideas.

These were years which saw the rise of a number of communitarian movements. Some – the Amish, the Shakers – were founded on religious principles, but others justified their way of life with socialist arguments. All advocated the abandonment of conventional modes of existence for life in fairly small scale communities, and quite a few communities were, in fact, established. In Europe, the end of the Napoleonic Wars had been followed by a severe economic recession, and their membership was largely drawn from the pool of otherwise unemployed workers which resulted. Given the prevailing economic conditions, and the time, it is no surprise that many of the communities gravitated from Europe to the New World. For example, the Shaker movement – which began life in the industrial British city of Manchester – moved to the United States and is still going strong. It was no doubt with a similar intention that Robert Owen, the industrialist who had made his fortune in Scotland, offered to buy the states of Coahuila and Texas from the Mexican government in 1828. (As you will gather, he was more than ordinarily rich. Even then, not everyone could afford Texas.) His aim was to set up a whole network of ideal 'Owenite' communities in those states.

The intellectual leaders of the socialist communitarians were, in Britain, Robert Owen, and in France, Fourier and Saint-Simon. To take Owen as an example, his communitarian ideas had, in fact, begun life as a rationale for the living conditions with which he provided the workers in his factory at New Lanark, not far south of Glasgow. Owen provided them with housing, and their children with education. In many ways, their existence was spartan. A rigidly organised routine prevailed throughout the working day, meals were taken communally, and so on. Drink was banned. Even so, conditions were clean and healthy, and there was a steady supply of work. It was most likely this, more than idealism, which attracted workers from the Glasgow slums. You can find the system described, together with Owen's proposals for the total reform of society, in his *Report to the County of Lanark* (1970a). You will have gathered that Owen was no liberal. He was a socialist, of course – he envisages a future world divided into small 'villages of co-operation', a world in which competition no longer prevails – and, rather as you would expect, he was also a utilitarian. 'That government [then] is best', he wrote, 'which in practice produces the greatest happiness to the greatest number; including those who govern, and those who obey' (1970b: 163).

Between the years of 1825 and 1845 twenty-three Owenite communities were established, seven in Britain and sixteen in North America (Harrison 1969). But none of them lasted for very long. They were, as Marx was later to say, too 'utopian'. However, the very fact of their having existed meant that everyone knew exactly what Marx and Engels were talking about when they opened their *Communist Manifesto* with the following words:

'A spectre is haunting Europe – the spectre of Communism'

(Marx and Engels 2000: 245).

Burke and conservatism

Reflections and distortions

And then there was Edmund Burke, for whom revolutionary France presented nothing more than 'a monstrous tragi-comic scene' (Burke 1986: 92). Burke's *Reflections on the Revolution in France* was first published in 1790. The Terror had yet to reach its worst excesses. Even so, there had already been some extraordinary violence and mayhem. For example, in the previous year – on 6 October 1789, to be exact – a crowd had forced its way into the royal palace at Versailles, and marched the king and queen the twelve miles or so to Paris, where they were to spend the rest of their days. Burke describes the event in bloodcurdling terms. As he portrays it, the abduction began with a mob setting upon the sentinel guarding the queen's bedchamber: 'Instantly he was cut down.' Then,

A band of cruel ruffians and assassins, reeking with his blood, rushed into the chamber of the queen, and pierced with an hundred strokes of bayonets and poniards the bed, from whence the woman had but just time to fly almost naked

(ibid.: 164)

After that, it seems that the royal pair and their infant children, 'who once would have been the pride and hope of a great and generous people', were 'forced to abandon the sanctuary of the most splendid palace in the world, which they left swimming in blood, polluted by massacre, and strewed with scattered limbs and mutilated carcasses'. Two members of the royal bodyguard were selected at random, beheaded, and their heads 'were stuck upon spears, and led the procession'. Meanwhile (says Burke) the royal captives were moved along, 'amidst the horrid yells, and shrilling screams, and infamous contumelies; and all the unutterable abominations of the furies of hell' (ibid.: 164–5).

A few pages later, Burke describes his own encounter with the queen, Marie Antoinette, as follows:

It is now sixteen or seventeen years since I saw the queen of France, then the dauphiness, at Versailles; and surely never lighted on this orb, which she hardly seemed to touch, a more delightful vision. I saw her just above the horizon, decorating and cheering the elevated sphere she just began to move in, – glittering like the morning-star, full of life, and splendour, and joy. Oh! What a revolution! And what

173

an heart must I have to contemplate without emotion that elevation and that fall!

(ibid.: 169)

But hang on: Let's not get too carried away! Isn't this the very same Marie Antoinette who is reputed to have so callously dismissed the people's cry for bread with her supercilious remark, 'Let them eat cake!'? Indeed it is. The 'let them eat cake' anecdote may be apocryphal, but its very existence suggests that there is another side to the story, and so there is. You can find that other side, or one variant of it, in Tom Paine's *Rights of Man* (Paine 1985), the first part of which was published in 1791. You can find another variant in Mary Wollstonecraft's *A Vindication of the Rights of Men* (Wollstonecraft 1995a).

Rights of Man is a defence of the revolution's ideals, and it was written specifically as a response to Burke's critique. Like Burke, Paine also describes the events of 6 October, and it is interesting to compare the two accounts. For one thing, there is a great difference between the two over what actually happened. For example, whereas Burke portrays the Royal Guard as innocent victims, Paine describes their behaviour as having been deliberately provocative; and whereas Burke describes the king and queen as having been seized by a mob and forcibly marched to Paris, Paine claims that they went of their own accord. He also claims that, far from being accompanied by 'horrid yells, and shrilling screams' (Burke ibid.: 165), 'not an act of molestation was committed during the whole march' (Paine ibid.: 64). Wollstonecraft – whose essay takes the form of an open letter to Burke – also thinks his description exaggerated, and she considers it to be snobbishly one-sided as well. For example, her retort to his statement that the crowd included 'the vilest of women' (Burke ibid.: 165) is: 'Probably you mean women who gained a livelihood by selling vegetables or fish, who never had had any advantages of education' (Wollstonecraft ibid.: 30). The queen may deserve pity, she concedes, but 'I do not like to make a distinction without a difference' (ibid.). Her comment on Burke's attitude to the revolution and the ensuing Terror is simply this: 'that we ought to remain for ever in frozen inactivity, because a thaw, whilst it nourishes the soil, spreads a temporary inundation' is 'sound reasoning, I grant, in the mouth of the rich and short-sighted' (ibid.: 8).

Who is right? As my subject is philosophy, historical events are not my main concern, so I shan't consider the question (although I suppose I should point out that Paine also had his axe to grind). However, it is certainly worth remarking that Burke's style, as evidenced by the passages I have quoted, ought to be enough to put us on our guard. Everything is expressed in value-loaded terms which make Burke's own point of view only too apparent. Take his description of the queen's assailants as 'cruel ruffians and assassins' (ibid.: 164). You can't deny that it rather prejudges the issue. Or, take his statement that the royal children would once have been 'the pride and hope of a great and generous people' (164). It is really nothing more than a statement of opinion. But real historians try to avoid making such opinionated statements, even when they are trying to persuade you to take a certain point of view.

Another thing real historians try to do is constantly refer to evidence, to documentary records, eyewitness accounts and so on. Insofar as they can, they try to let the facts speak for themselves.[4] But Burke does no such thing. We have to take his word for it that events in the queen's bedroom took place just as he describes. Then again, how does he know? He tells us that 'It is now sixteen or seventeen years since [he] saw the queen of France' (ibid.: 169) so we can be sure that he was not there, hiding in the wardrobe or under the bed. And what about that prurient, faintly pornographic 'almost naked', as in 'the woman [Marie Antoinette] had but just time to fly almost naked' (ibid.: 164)? A tabloid newspaper could hardly have done it better. And so it goes on. Paine's assessment of Burke's essay as a series of 'theatrical exaggerations' seems about right (Paine ibid.: 59). Certainly, with his description of a palace left 'swimming in blood, polluted by massacre, and strewed with scattered limbs and mutilated carcasses' and so on and so forth, Burke seems to be striving so hard for effect in these passages that they don't ring true.

But if Burke is a poor historian, and if *Reflections on the Revolution in France* is more rhetoric than history, perhaps we are not meant to treat it as a work of history at all. Or, if we are, perhaps we should treat it as something else as well. Burke's use of rhetoric suggests that it could be so. His reliance on rhetoric is so blatant.

Burke's conservative political philosophy

If there is such a thing as a distinctively conservative political philosophy, then Burke's essay embodies it. Of course, by 'conservative political philosophy' I do not mean the philosophical doctrines which happen to have been embraced by this or that party of the right at given times in history. Those have varied with historical circumstance. For example, conservative philosophy is not equivalent to pro-free market 'economic liberalism', the doctrine of *laisser-faire*. You could be mistaken for thinking otherwise, because the latter has been popular with the right quite recently, most recently during the 1980s; but *laisser-faire* sits just as easily with certain forms of liberalism, and there is nothing specifically conservative about it. Nor is conservatism equivalent to fascism, even though conservative parties quite frequently tend to attract near-fascists and neo-fascists to their extremes.

On the contrary – and as the term 'conservative' implies – that political philosophy which is genuinely conservative is generally resistant to change and supportive of the status quo. Conservatism properly so-called emphasises the importance of tradition and order, not progress and reform; it prioritises instinct and feeling over reason and argument; it values the particular and specific above the abstract and general. All three elements are conspicuously present in Burke's argument, so let us now take a closer look at it.

I shall focus on just three strands of that argument, each of which is characteristically conservative. First of all, then, Burke is suspicious of intellectual abstraction. So far as he is concerned, the doctrine of natural rights, as embodied in the *Declaration of the Rights of Man* (1789), is an abstraction. Of such rights, he says that 'their abstract perfection is their practical defect' (1986: 151). Likewise, he is suspicious of the idea that a constitution can be designed, from scratch, on the basis of abstract first principles (such as the principle that there are 'rights of man'). 'The science of constructing a commonwealth, or renovating it, or reforming it' is, he says, 'like every other experimental science, not to be taught *a priori*' (ibid.: 152). In his view, it is faith in abstractions – notably 'liberty in the abstract' and the rights of man – which has been a major cause of all the trouble. He asks: 'Is it because liberty in the abstract may be classed among the blessings of mankind, that I am seriously to felicitate a mad-man, who has escaped from the protecting restraint and wholesome dark-ness of his cell?' (ibid.: 90), and 'Am I to congratulate an highwayman and murderer, who has broke prison, upon the recovery of his natural rights?' (ibid.). You are supposed to reply: Of course not!

Burke is not a man to hide his prejudices. Giving expression to a pecu-liarly English bias against the French – that they are stylish but superficial – he describes 'the newest Paris fashion of an improved liberty' as a thing 'the people of England will not ape' (ibid.: 111). (I should think that sort of thing has been around since the Norman Conquest.) One especially noteworthy prejudice is Burke's hostility to the project of the Enlighten-ment, the movement of ideas which had come to prominence in the eighteenth century. The Enlightenment nailed its colours to the ideal of reason, and set its face against (what it saw as) ignorance and superstition. There is sarcasm and invective against 'our new light and knowledge' of which the horrors of 6 October are supposed to have been the 'work'; the 'converts' and 'disciples' of Rousseau, Voltaire, and Helvetius; 'the whole clan of the enlightened'; and the 'incantation – "*Philosophy, Light, Liberality, the Rights of Man*"' (ibid.: 167, 181–2, 183 and 218) (Burke's emphasis).

Not that Burke is against liberty. On the contrary, he is all for it – or so he claims. He writes: 'I flatter myself that I love a manly, moral, regulated liberty'. By his own account, Burke is only opposed to 'a simple view of the object, as it stands stripped of every relation, in all the nakedness and solitude of metaphysical abstraction' (ibid.: 89–90) – to 'liberty in the abstract' in other words. This brings us to a second strand of Burke's argument. For Burke, 'liberty', strictly speaking, is a *specific set of liberties* (or rights), and these are the outcome of compromise and negotiation which has taken place over generations within the context of a particular political tradition. On this account, there is really no such thing as 'liberty' *per se*, or in the abstract; but there is English liberty and, for the French, there used to be French liberty. For the English, the history of liberty is – thus – the history of the liberties established by acts such as the signing of the Magna Carta and, later, by the compromise of 1688. The English never had the right to choose or cashier their governors, as claimed by revolutionary groups; but they do have the right to elect Members of Parliament and so check the sovereign's power. By the same token, the French have gone wrong by throwing out the baby of tradition with the bathwater of revolution. 'You had all these advantages in your ancient state', writes Burke, 'but you chose to act as if you had never been moulded into a civil society, and had every thing to begin anew' (ibid.: 122). (Burke's essay is written in the form of an imaginary letter to a Frenchman.)

Burke's position is well summarised in the following passage:

> You will observe, that from Magna Charta to the Declaration of Right, it has been the uniform policy of our constitution to claim and assert our liberties, as an *entailed inheritance* derived to us from our forefathers, and to be transmitted to our posterity; as an estate specially belonging to the people of this kingdom without any reference whatever to any other more general or prior right.
>
> (ibid.: 119)

It follows that political change must always take place within a tradition as 'Our political system is placed in a just correspondence and symmetry with the order of the world' (ibid.: 120). 'People will not look forward to posterity, who never look backward to their ancestors' (ibid.: 119).

In short, Burke's advice is just this: 'If it ain't broke, don't fix it.' As advice goes, that is not such a bad rule to follow, if only sometimes. Even so, there are some fairly obvious questions directly raised by his account of things. One question is: How do you know when the machine – the unwritten constitution, based on inherited tradition and finely tuned by generation after generation – is actually broke. After all, a constitution is not really a machine, designed for a specific purpose, as if it were a car or a phone. You can tell when these need repair: The car won't go; the phone won't pick up messages. But exactly what must a constitution fail to do before we decide that it needs repair? There is no obvious answer. Moreover, conservatives and their critics will, by definition, give different answers – it is part of what makes them conservatives and the others their critics – so the question is politically loaded. The same considerations apply to a related question: Just suppose that compromises and readjustments do need to be made – and that we can tell that they do – how do we know *what* readjustments it is right to make?

It is here that a third strand of Burke's argument comes into play, his emphasis on what he sometimes calls 'natural' wisdom and what he sometimes calls 'prejudice'. Natural wisdom is 'wisdom without reflection, and above it' (ibid.: 119). 'Prejudice renders a man's virtue his habit' (ibid.: 183). So, prejudice according to Burke is a good thing. His thesis is that, just as constitutional change must take place through adjustments made within a tradition, so those raised within a tradition learn to know, as if by instinct, when a change is right and when it is not. All you have to do is avoid being misled by fancy abstractions and follow 'nature'. The English are supposed to be especially good at this sort of thing, thanks to their 'sullen resistance to innovation' and 'the cold sluggishness of [their] national character' (ibid.: 181). In fact, Burke spends a great deal of time lecturing the French on the virtues of the English national character. Apparently, 'the people of England, far from thinking a religious, national establishment unlawful, hardly think it lawful to be without one' (ibid.: 197); 'The English people are satisfied that to the great the consolations of religion are as necessary as its instructions' (ibid.: 201); 'The people of England will shew to the haughty potentates of the world, and to their talking sophisters, that a free, a generous, an informed nation, honours the high magistrates of its church' (ibid.: 202), and so on. (Burke's argument is focused on the English, but – of course – similar considerations will apply to other traditions within other nation-states.)

Burke's ideal citizen – or rather 'subject' – is, thus, a none too reflective individual who instinctively recognises the value of tradition and follows it. The same character, similarly idealised, appears in the work of Burke's twentieth century followers. According to Michael Oakeshott, 'the man of conservative disposition' follows rules of conduct, knowing that 'they are susceptible of change and improvement', but recognising that 'if we were disposed to argue about them and change them on every occasion, they would rapidly lose their value' (Oakeshott 1991: 421). And likewise, according to Roger Scruton, 'argument is not the favourite pursuit of conservatives'. The conservative may be 'for' certain things but, 'he is for them, not because he has arguments in their favour, but because he knows them, lives with them, and finds his identity threatened (often he knows not how) by the attempt to interfere with their operation' (Scruton 1980: 12–13).

But there is a fairly evident problem with this answer, namely that it just pushes the question one step back. In other words, if knowing what is right is a question of following your instincts – if you are a person with the 'right instincts', that is – then you have to ask yourself: 'How do I know that I am a person with the right instincts?' It is here that the rhetoric comes into its own, or so it seems to me.

Earlier, I observed that Burke's use of rhetoric is so blatant that it is hard to treat his descriptions of events as history, or as history only. I think we are now in a position to see that his rhetorical style has a further purpose. It is to leave the reader in no doubt as to where the distinction between 'us' and 'them' lies. 'We' are the people with 'the right' instincts, uncorrupted by mischievous theoretical abstraction. 'We' support the established order. 'We' trust our prejudices and 'we' recognise, for example, that all are not equal and that 'The occupation of an hair-dresser, or of a working tallow-chandler, cannot be a matter of honour to any person' (ibid.: 138). 'They' are the followers of abstract principle, the contemptible 'clan of the enlightened' (ibid.: 183). The following passage is well known. Some would describe it as notorious.

> Because half a dozen grasshoppers under a fern make the field ring with their importunate chink, whilst thousands of great cattle, reposed beneath the shadow of the British oak, chew the cud and are silent, pray do not imagine that those who make the noise are the only inhabitants of the field; that, of course, they are many in number; or that, after all, they are other than the little shrivelled, meagre, hopping, though loud and troublesome insects of the hour.
>
> (ibid.: 181)

With this passage – and like many a journalist after him – Burke distinguishes 'the chattering classes' from 'the silent majority'. Of course, you don't have to accept that his description is the only way to portray society. It could be that the noisy grasshoppers really do have something to say worth listening to. It could be that the big, apparently stupid, cattle are not following a 'natural wisdom' as if by instinct. They could be just what they appear.

Wollstonecraft's own objections to Burke's anti-rationalism are similar to the ones I have raised here. For example, she dismisses repeated claims to know what 'we' the English think as appeals to 'inbred feelings and secret lights' (1995a: 35). She has her own line in rhetoric too and, in opposition to Burke's portrait of an English society, imbued with the wisdom of tradition and steering a course through history with the help of its light, she paints a different picture – a picture of a corrupt society, riddled with cruel and irrational class divisions.

As many readers will know, Mary Wollstonecraft was a pioneering feminist. She is best remembered for her *A Vindication of the Rights of Woman* (1995b). There is a passage in her *Vindication of the Rights of Men* in which she castigates Burke for fostering a stereotype of women as fluffy, empty-headed house ornaments, and the British class system for encouraging them to conform to it. It must be one of the earliest examples of its kind, so it is worth quoting. She begins with a reference to the attitude the wives and daughters of slave owners in the colonies are reputed, by some, to take towards their slaves:

> Where is the dignity, the infallibility of sensibility, in the fair ladies, whom, if the voice of rumour is to be credited, the captive Negroes curse in all the agony of bodily pain, for the unheard of torments they invent. It is probable that some of them, after the sight of a

flagellation, compose their ruffled spirits and exercise their tender feelings by the perusal of the last imported novel.

(ibid.: 46)

These are women who *would* be convinced by Burke's arguments. (This was a time when the anti-slavery movement, like feminism, was getting into gear.) Wollstonecraft continues as follows:

> You may have convinced them that *littleness* and *weakness* are the very essence of beauty; and that the Supreme Being, in giving women beauty in the most supereminent degree, seemed to command them, by the powerful voice of nature, not to cultivate the moral virtues that might chance to excite respect, and interfere with the pleasing sensations they were created to inspire. Thus confining truth, fortitude, and humanity, within the rigid pale of manly morals, they might justly argue, that to be loved, woman's high end and great distinction! They should 'learn to lisp, to totter in their walk, and nick-name God's creatures'.

(ibid.: 47)

Did I hear somebody whisper *plus ça change, plus c'est la même chose*?

Modern 'isms'

By now, it should be apparent that liberalism, socialism and conservatism are not the only modern 'isms'. It is true enough that, in contemporary societies, people tend to categorise their political allegiances under one or the other of these three headings. It is also true – I suppose – that, within political theory, a great deal of discussion can be represented, albeit in rough and ready terms, as an ongoing argument between liberals, socialists and conservatives. But to represent the debate as only that is to miss a great deal. Most especially, it is to underplay the role of movements in ideas which are less obviously connected with particular ideological standpoints, but which are – nevertheless – essential to our understanding of political thought. These can cut across the conventional distinctions. For example, there is no special connection between utilitarianism and liberalism. As we look back through time, the fact that, within the utilitarian movement, Bentham was succeeded by J.S. Mill sometimes tends to obscure this; for Mill was one of the world's greatest utilitarians as well as one of its greatest liberals. But there is no special reason for portraying Bentham as a liberal, although he was certainly a utilitarian. Again, as we have seen, Robert Owen was a utilitarian, although he was certainly no liberal and he was certainly a socialist.

That said, I shall now endeavour to move this narrative from the early years of the nineteenth century to the present, which means that from now on I shall be dealing with the theoretical positions by which the parameters of present day discussion are set, not just within political philosophy but within politics generally. In other words, the issues with which I shall now go on to deal will become increasingly live as I progress.

As a result, things will start to get a little more tricky – tricky for me, that is – and I should just say why. Briefly, there are two dangers. One is partiality. There is no point in my pretending that it's possible to take a neutral position on every issue I discuss. Everyone knows you can't do that. (Burke is an example. There would be no point in my pretending to like him. I just don't.) However, I shall try to give every argument I consider a reasonable run for its money, and I shall also try to avoid polemic. The other danger is selectivity. Since the beginning of the nineteenth century, so many political philosophers have lived and written that, if I were to deal with each in the same way that I have so far dealt with Plato, Aristotle, Hobbes and the rest, this book would be much too long and nobody would want to read it. The three writers on whom I have chosen to concentrate are John Stuart Mill, Karl Marx and John Rawls. That is because I believe them to be the political philosophers whose work has done most to shape political thinking in modern times. I don't just mean that liberalism (as exemplified by Mill and Rawls) and socialism (as exemplified by Marx) have been the dominant political movements – although I do mean that. I also mean that their respective philosophical approaches have set the frameworks of thought within which others have tended to move. But doesn't this expose me to a charge of partiality? Doesn't the particular selection I have made show that I take a particular view of who is important and who is less so, and doesn't it thereby commit me to a particular view of the history of philosophy? Of course it does, but then – just as it is impossible to maintain a neutral stance on every issue – so everyone has to tell a story in their own way. All I can say is that I am sure that even those readers who would have told the story differently will not think my approach too eccentric.

11

---·◦⊜◦·---

John Stuart Mill: utilitarianism and liberalism

As a moral philosopher, John Stuart Mill was a utilitarian. More than that, he was the foremost utilitarian philosopher of his generation. In fact, you could say that he was born to it for his father, James Mill, brought him up to be a utilitarian in both theory and practice.[1] Mill's reputation has persisted, and his essay *Utilitarianism* (1991b) remains the classic statement of the 'classical' utilitarian position. As a political critic and campaigner Mill was a radical and a liberal. He was a prolific essayist, but his best-known political works are, no doubt, *Principles of Political Economy* (1999), *On Liberty* (1991a), *Considerations on Representative Government* (1991c) and *The Subjection of Women* (1991d). In these works, he takes a liberal approach to – respectively – economic questions (including the rights and wrongs of private ownership, and of communism); the liberty of the individual and the press; democracy; and feminism. In all cases, he seeks to defend that approach in utilitarian terms.

Two things should be clear from this. The first is that, in the earlier half of the nineteenth century, utilitarianism was much more than an esoteric philosophical thesis, its proponents confined to a small group of academic philosophers. Far from it; it was the creed of an active movement with a role to play in the real world. The second is that there is a close relationship between Mill's utilitarianism and his liberalism. It is for the latter reason that I have chosen to focus on that relationship in this chapter. As we shall see, reconciling utilitarianism with liberalism is not quite as easy as it might at first appear to be.

To start with then, I should say what I mean by 'utilitarianism' and 'liberalism'. Actually, readers will know by now that utilitarianism is the moral and political philosophy founded on the principle of utility or 'greatest happiness principle'. In the previous chapter, I suggested that one reason for its success in the earlier years of the nineteenth century was its simplicity and straightforwardness. With a single principle, utilitarianism promises to sweep away all manner of muddle and mystification.[2] At least, that it is how it looked to Bentham. But then, perhaps the simplicity is merely apparent. Mill certainly thought so. He also realised that Bentham's conception of human nature and its relation to human society is too simple to do justice to the way things are. Even so, Mill never abandoned utilitarianism. Rather than do that, he tried to develop a version of utilitarianism which could adequately match real-life complexities. As a result – and as we shall eventually see – some interesting stresses and strains show up in his arguments.

The statement that Mill was a 'liberal' needs a little more explanation, for 'liberal' is one of those words which tends to be used in a number of ways. For example, it is quite often used by those sympathetic to the political right, as a pejorative term for those who stand to the left of themselves. For those who use 'liberal' this way, Mill would certainly qualify as a liberal simply for his progressive views. However, if we are to understand what Mill's liberalism amounted to, we have to specify it more precisely than that. Again, 'liberalism' is sometimes used as a shorthand term for 'economic liberalism', the doctrine that the market works best when left to itself, or *laisser-faire*. Yet again, I have tended to use the expression 'liberal democracy', throughout this book, as a shorthand for the type of system which prevails, at present, throughout 'the West'. In fact, Mill did put a case for *laisser-faire* in his *Principles of Political Economy*, albeit a qualified one.[3] He was also a supporter of 'liberal democracy'. However, the liberalism for which Mill is most remembered is neither of these, or not exactly; so, before going any further, I should state more precisely what I take Mill's liberalism to be.

Mill's liberalism

What is liberalism?

What was it, then? I would say that Mill's political philosophy qualifies as 'liberal' because it passes three tests. First, it attaches a great deal of importance – if not supreme importance – to freedom.[4] In fact, this is something of an understatement where Mill is concerned, for his essay *On Liberty* (1982) remains the most influential, most frequently cited, text on the subject, even though it was first published as long ago as 1859.

In a way, you would think this enough. After all, what could 'liberalism' refer to, if not – purely and simply – any doctrine which values freedom? However, a doctrine which only matched this one criterion, and neither of the others, would not qualify as liberal in the sense of 'liberal' at issue. The reason is that valuing freedom can be rather like valuing niceness and goodness. Who could possibly be against it? Even Edmund Burke values freedom – or at least he says he does.[5] However, you could hardly describe Burke as a liberal (and nor is it a description in which he could have recognised himself). Liberalism – real liberalism – has to pay more than lip service to liberty. It needs teeth.

It is here that a second criterion comes into play. Mill holds that it is only where certain liberties are respected that a society can be described as truly free. In a famous passage, he puts it as follows:

> there is a sphere of action in which society, as distinguished from the individual, has, if any, only an indirect interest: comprehending all that portion of a person's life and conduct which affects only himself or, if it also affects others, only with their free, voluntary, and undeceived consent.
>
> (1982: 71)

Mill then goes on to specify the liberties which fall within the 'sphere'. These are 'first, the inward domain of consciousness, demanding liberty of conscience, in the most comprehensive sense, liberty of thought and feeling, absolute freedom of opinion and sentiment on all subjects, practical or speculative, scientific, moral, or theological'. This first liberty is also meant to include 'the liberty of expressing and publishing opinions'. 'Secondly', says Mill, 'the principle requires liberty of tastes and pursuits, of framing the plan of our life to suit our own character, of doing as we like, subject to such consequences as may follow' provided that we do no harm to others. And 'Thirdly, from this liberty of each individual follows the liberty, within the same limits, of combination among individuals; freedom to unite for any purpose not involving harm to others' (ibid.). Mill states his opinion that:

> No society in which these liberties are not, on the whole, respected is free, whatever may be its form of government; and none is completely free in which they do not exist absolute and unqualified
>
> (ibid.)

This idea, that certain liberties must remain protected if a society is to count as free, is absolutely crucial to those philosophical texts which lie at the core of the liberal tradition. We have encountered it once already in the form of Locke's argument that we have fundamental 'natural' rights; notably the rights to life and liberty. In the twentieth century, the same idea was re-expressed by Rawls, according to whom our 'basic liberties' include 'political liberty (the right to vote and to be eligible for public office) together with freedom of speech and assembly; liberty of conscience and freedom of thought; freedom of the person along with the right to hold (personal) property; and freedom from arbitrary arrest and seizure as defined by the concept of the rule of law' (Rawls 1972: 61). Like Locke, Rawls describe these liberties as *rights*. In this, Mill differs from the other two. He writes: 'It is proper to state that I forgo any advantage which could be derived to my argument from the idea of abstract right as a thing independent of utility. I regard utility as the ultimate appeal on all ethical questions' (1982: 69–70). This is just what you would expect from Mill.

Otherwise, each writer's list of fundamental freedoms is similar. For each the list crucially includes liberty of action, liberty of conscience and the liberty to have a say over who rules you and what they do. (As we saw, for Locke, the last of these means the freedom to withdraw your consent from the government. As befits a twentieth century writer, Rawls connects it more specifically with the 'right to take part in, and to determine the outcome of, the constitutional process' (1972: 221).) This similarity is, no doubt, a consequence of a third feature, characteristic of liberal philosophy, namely that the idea of a protected sphere is grounded in a more general conception of freedom construed as the liberty to live your own life in your own way (or to live 'autonomously' as one currently fashionable term has it). In Mill's case, this idea finds expression in his view that to be free is to be unprevented from acting as you would like. Consequently, the 'object' of *On Liberty* is to assert 'one very simple principle, as entitled to govern absolutely the dealings of society with the individual in the way of compulsion and control'. As he goes on to explain:

> That principle is that the sole end for which mankind are warranted, individually or collectively, in interfering with the liberty of action of any of their number is self-protection. That the only purpose for which power can be rightfully exercised over any member of a civilised community, against his will, is to prevent harm to others. His own good, either physical or moral, is not a sufficient warrant.
>
> (1982: 68)

Why be a liberal?

Most readers will agree with me, or at least I think they will, that liberalism as characterised – that is, the political/philosophical position which matches the three stated criteria – has become a prevailing orthodoxy by now. Arguably, it is *the* prevailing orthodoxy. It would be an exaggeration to describe it as 'what everybody believes', but it would certainly be difficult, these days, to find anyone who would disagree that we have certain fundamental (or 'human') rights, or with the claim that the individual should be sovereign over his or her own body and mind. Notice, too, that liberalism, so characterised, is compatible with many other belief systems. For example, you can be a liberal and take a conservative attitude to social change. Alternatively, you can be a liberal and a socialist. In either case, it will depend, not on your liberalism, but on what *else* you believe. You may believe that change is a great threat to people's fundamental freedoms, as it is to their autonomy. Or, you may believe that freedom and autonomy are best protected under socialism. (So whereas socialism is incompatible with *economic* liberalism, many forms of socialism are perfectly compatible with the *political* liberalism exemplified by Mill.)

It follows that answers to the question, 'why be a liberal?', can take different forms. They may be traditionalist, socialist, utilitarian, or they may take some other form. (As we shall see later, Rawls offers a contractualist answer.) In Mill's work, we should expect to find a utilitarian answer. Utilitarians hold that the principle of utility is fundamental to everything else, so – if Mill is right – his liberalism has to be derivable from his utilitarianism; that is, it has to follow from it as a logical consequence. Let us now see if it does.

Utilitarianism: the pursuit of happiness

'Classical' utilitarianism's two most basic features are these. First, there is an account of human nature, of what we are fundamentally like. This takes the form of the thesis that we are, all of us, motivated by the desire for happiness (and, of course, the corresponding desire to avoid unhappiness). Secondly, there is an ethical principle, the principle of utility. So far as classical utilitarians are concerned it is one of the principle's greatest strengths that it recognises the truth about human nature, and that it is, therefore, realistic. As Bentham put it, systems which attempt to question the principle of utility 'deal in sounds instead of sense, in caprice instead of reason, in darkness instead of light' (2000b: 87). Let us take each feature in turn, beginning with utilitarianism's account of human nature.

Valuing pleasure

To start with, then, there is clearly *something* right about the claim that we are, at root, seekers of happiness. For example, 'I want to be happy' is not a statement which requires further explanation, or not usually. In this, it differs from 'I want to be rich' (or free, powerful, or famous). I mean that, whereas it can make perfect sense to ask someone 'Why do you want to be rich/free/powerful/famous?' – and whereas the question can be especially pointed where there is a supposition that being any of these is not likely to make the person to whom it is addressed happy – there seems to be something not quite in order about 'Why do you want to be happy?' Somehow or other, the question seems to have been forestalled by the initial statement. On the other hand, the statement 'I want to be *un*happy' requires a great deal of explanation. In these post-Freudian days you would expect there to be, at the very least, a psychoanalytic account of how it can be possible for anyone to say such a thing. So far, all that seems obvious enough, but it is not so easy to go beyond the obvious here.

Bentham attempted to theorise the special role happiness appears to play in the explanation of action by equating happiness with pleasure, and pleasure with having pleasurable sensations. He made the latter equation because he thought of pleasure and pain as opposites. A pain is a sensation. That is quite obvious, so it follows that a pleasure must be too, or so

Bentham assumed. *The Principles of Morals and Legislation* contains a chapter in which Bentham outlines his 'felicific calculus'. As he sees it, there are six characteristics which determine 'the value of a pleasure or pain'. These are (what he calls) its intensity, its duration, its certainty or uncertainty, its propinquity or remoteness, its fecundity (i.e. 'the chance it has of being followed by sensations of the same kind: that is, pleasures, if it be a pleasure: pains, if it be a pain'), and its purity (i.e. 'the chance it has of not being followed by sensations of the opposite kind'). If Bentham is right, it follows that, when making a decision, you must consider – in turn – every alternative facing you. For each alternative, you must then estimate the pleasures and pains you are likely to experience as a result of taking it and assess them against the criteria Bentham lists. The alternative with the highest score – that is, with the greatest balance of pleasures over pains – is the one you should take. Legislators and others who formulate policy must carry out the same calculation for everyone likely to be affected by their decisions. (For all this, see Bentham 2000b: 115ff.)

There are spectacular drawbacks to Bentham's account of how to make a decision. Not the least of these is the impossibility of knowing exactly what you are supposed to do when you attach a 'value' to some feature of a sensation. Do you rank these on a scale of ten, with 'pluses' for pleasures and 'minuses' for pains? If so, how do you know what numbers to attach to what? For example, when does a sensation score, say, seven for intensity and when does it only score six? It's not as if pleasures and pains come with numbers attached, like the priced items in a supermarket. The very idea seems bizarre (although it is probably no more bizarre than many a present day exercise in 'cost–benefit analysis', a procedure of which Bentham's calculus is a precursor). Then again, it is just not true that pleasure is always, or even usually, a question of having pleasurable sensations. Imagine asking someone who, quite credibly, claims to derive pleasure from the study of philosophy how many pleasurable sensations he or she gets over a period of half an hour when reading the average philosophy book. Imagine asking that person whether the sensations in question are, say, tickly, throbbing or warm. You only have to imagine the possibility to see how ridiculous the question is. Nor is it so obvious that living a happy life and living a life of pleasure are necessarily identical. (It's easy to imagine someone looking back and saying, 'If only I hadn't spent so much time having fun'. You may recall that we have already, once, contrasted Bentham's account of happiness with an alternative, Aristotle's. Aristotle is not open to this particular objection.)[6]

But it is one thing to deride Bentham's manifestly inadequate theory of motivation, and quite another to come up with a satisfactory account of one's own. Take Mill's distinction between 'higher' and 'lower' pleasures. It is an implication of Bentham's theory that, for any two activities, provided that each yields equal pleasure – and provided that there is, for each, an equal balance of pleasure over pain – the two are equivalent in value. As

187

Mill paraphrases this, it was Bentham's view that '*quantity* of pleasure being equal, push-pin is as good as poetry' (Mill 1987a: 173–4, my emphasis). (It is usually thought that by 'pushpin' Bentham was referring to a child's game, but he could have been alluding to something more saucy.)[7] Against this, it is Mill's contention that 'It would be absurd that while, in estimating all other things, quality is considered as well as quantity, the estimation of pleasures should be supposed to depend on quantity alone' (Mill 1991b: 138–9). A little later, he adds that although 'It is indisputable that the being whose capacities of enjoyment are low, has the greatest chance of having them fully satisfied' whereas 'a highly endowed being will always feel that any happiness which he can look for, as the world is constituted, is imperfect', even so,

> It is better to be a human being dissatisfied than a pig satisfied; better to be Socrates dissatisfied than a fool satisfied. And if the fool, or the pig, is of a different opinion, it is because they only know their own side of the question. The other party to the comparison knows both sides.
>
> (1991b: 140)

As I have already pointed out, Mill took the view that Bentham's philosophy was over-simple, and here we have an example of that view at work. Even so, as a response to Bentham, this is inadequate, if only because it is inaccurate to describe Bentham as having sidelined quality of pleasure for the sake of quantity. Far from it. Both writers assess pleasure in terms of quality. It is just that each measures quality by a different standard. For Bentham, the quality of a pleasure is determined by such factors as its intensity and duration, whereas, for Mill, the 'higher' pleasures tend to be the pleasures of the high-minded intellectual – philosophy, poetry and public service.

The trouble is that, rather as Bentham provides no satisfactory criterion for assessing the 'value' of a pleasure, Mill isn't much help when it comes to distinguishing 'higher' from 'lower' pleasures. According to Mill, it is possible to apply a sort of behavioural test here. He thinks that a person who is equally capable of appreciating both types of pleasure will normally opt for the 'higher' when given a choice. '[Now] it is an unquestionable fact', he writes, 'that those who are equally acquainted with, and equally capable of appreciating and enjoying, both, do give a most marked preference to the manner of existence which employs their higher faculties' (ibid.: 139). But this is questionable. Certainly, if Mill means that a person capable of experiencing both types of pleasure will *invariably* choose the higher, then his claim is false. For example, when I cast my eye along the rack of CDs in my living room, my finger is just as likely to alight on *Great Rock and Roll Hits of the 'Seventies* as on a recording of Beethoven's work or John Adams'. Even so, I am quite sure that I am capable of appreciating and enjoying the latter. It seems reasonable to describe me as choosing the 'lower' pleasure here, even though I am capable of appreciating both types, in which case Mill is wrong.

But then, perhaps that is not quite what Mill means. All he says is that people capable of both types of pleasure 'give a most marked preference to the manner of existence which employs their higher faculties', which need only denote a tendency, and not an invariable recurrence. It could be that, when I listen to CDs I am normally quite tired. I opt for 'lower' pleasures on these occasions, even though I am someone who generally chooses the 'higher'. (That's why I bought the Beethoven CD in the first place.) If something is possible on one occasion, why can't it be possible throughout a life? I suggest that Mill is confusing two senses of 'preference' here. One is the sense in which a preference can be the result of a reasoned evaluation. (For example, a critic says 'I prefer this opera to that one because the score has great melodic quality and the narrative structure is strong.') The other is the more straightforward sense in which what I prefer is what I like to do. I suggest that, for any activity, it is perfectly possible to hold one sort of preference but not the other. If I am right, it is perfectly possible for someone to appreciate, say, Wordsworth's poetry (first sense of 'preference') while not liking it much (second sense). Given the choice between an evening reading Wordsworth and an evening in the bar, such a person will always choose the latter. Would Mill then have to take this as evidence that getting drunk is a 'higher' pleasure than reading Wordsworth? He certainly wouldn't want to.

Foundation and superstructure

What is going on here? I shan't pursue the foregoing line of argument any further because I am less interested in demonstrating the inadequacy of Mill's distinction than I am in simply pointing out that it is questionable. In philosophy, it quite often happens that the really interesting question is not 'Exactly what is wrong with such-and-such an argument?' but 'Why did the philosopher who thought of it want to come up with *that* argument in the first place?' Here, we have a case in point.

As I see it, the root cause of Mill's difficulty lies in his political philosophy's attempt to erect a liberal superstructure on a utilitarian foundation. Unfortunately, the foundation is too flimsy and ill-adapted for the purpose he intends it to serve. As a result, tensions and weaknesses have a habit of showing up in the superstructure, and in this case, there is a tension between liberalism's ambitions for the human individual, and utilitarianism's portrait of that same individual as a rationally-choosing seeker of happiness.

Here is how it arises. As we have seen, liberalism places a high value on individual freedom construed as personal autonomy. For Mill, the ideal person is the independent, self-determining chooser; that is, the person who is in charge of his or her own life, who really can act as 'sovereign' over his or her 'own body and mind' (1991a: 14). But in the real world – the world as it is – people are not always so autonomous. They are subject to interfering, paternalistic, legislation. Worse, they are subject to 'the tyranny of the majority'. This is the 'tyranny of the prevailing opinion and feeling'. It is 'the tendency of society to impose, by other means than civil penalties, its own ideas and practices as rules of conduct on those who dissent from them'. It seeks to 'fetter the development and, if possible, prevent the formation of any individuality not in harmony with its ways, and compel all characters to fashion themselves upon the model of its own' (ibid.: 9). It was a tyranny Mill particularly feared, and it is against the conformity it imposes that his autonomous individual is juxtaposed as an ideal. In short, his political liberalism idealises people as they *could be*. It does not take people as they *are*.

By contrast, the utilitarian account of motivation sets things up in a way which tends to take people as they are and not as they could (or should) be. It pulls in the reverse direction. This happens because the principle of utility is, in essence, a device for reconciling the diverse and conflicting wants of many individuals, *whatever those wants happen to be*. (That may not be utilitarianism's whole point, but it is certainly one of its main points; and – as I suggested in the previous chapter – it explains why utilitarianism can hold a special attraction for policy makers working in plural societies.) Consistently with this, Bentham's attitude to the desires and wants, the 'pleasures' of others is completely non-judgemental – hence the equation of 'pushpin' with 'poetry'. The only distinctions he will allow are distinctions, between pleasures, of intensity, duration, purity, and so on. Bentham *never* says 'You may want x, but it would be better if you wanted y'. But then, Bentham was no liberal. A society run on Benthamite lines could be a society of happy slaves; that is, a society in which the mass of the population is kept docile, and reconciled to its place with techniques for keeping people happy, with 'bread and circuses', as the Romans put it. (Why use force when a tabloid press – or a water supply laced with truckloads of Prozac – will do your work for you?)

In such a society, people would quite evidently not be the free, autonomous, individuals of Mill's liberal ideal, and, by contrast with Bentham, Mill does want to say 'You may want x, but it would be better if you wanted y'. As a result, there is a tension between his liberalism, which idealises people as they could be rather than taking them as they are, and his utilitarianism, which takes people as they are rather than as they could be. In fact, utilitarianism *has* to take people as they are, because – by definition – a world in which people were forced to do things they did not, in fact, want to do could not, at the same time, be a world in which the principle of utility was used to reconcile conflicting wants in order to produce the greatest happiness. Can these various positions be reconciled? For all I know, they can be. For the moment, though, I am simply pointing out that, if you want to be a liberal and a utilitarian, you can make life difficult for yourself, and that the weaknesses inherent in Mill's attempt to distinguish levels of pleasure is a symptom of the difficulty. Nothing more. (Of course, it would help Mill a great deal if it were true, as he claims, that people capable of experiencing both inevitably, or normally, opt for higher pleasures. If it were, the world of people as they should be would, *at the same time*, be the world of people as they are. Unfortunately for Mill, it isn't true.)

A look back and a glance forward

A look back

Before considering further symptoms of the same difficulty, let us pause for a moment and take stock. We have now moved all the way from the fourth century BC to the middle years of the nineteenth century AD, and as I write, not even 150 years have passed since *On Liberty*'s publication in 1859. It ought to be possible to look back along the road we have travelled, and detect a few recurring patterns. One is especially worth mentioning at this point, and that is the recurrence of two contrasting conceptions of the relation between state and individual.

According to one conception, the relationship is, so to speak, *instrumental*. Individuals are portrayed as coming to the state more or less 'fully formed'. If the state, or the political environment more generally, has played any role in the formation of their wants, needs, beliefs or talents, the fact is of no special significance. It is simply a device for helping them satisfy needs and wants more effectively. We first encountered this conception in Plato's argument that within a state, or community, everyone should specialise in exercising the special talents he or she happens to have. Plato argues that, within the state, there is division of labour, with the result that everyone benefits. Later, we encountered it again in the argument of Hobbes' *Leviathan* (Hobbes 1981). For Hobbes, instinctively competitive individuals require a strong state, with a strong sovereign, to keep them in check. In a word, the state's purpose is security. Yet another version of this conception is Bentham's, that the law and the state exist to reconcile conflicts of 'interest' between individuals in a way which satisfies the greatest happiness principle.

According to the other conception, the relationship is portrayed in more *organic* terms. Emphasis is placed on the way individuals' characteristics – wants, needs, values – can themselves result from particular types of social and political arrangement. You could say that, on this type of account, the state is represented as the soil from which the individual grows. For the designer of political institutions, the problem is, thus, to devise an environment within which the individual can develop to his or her full potential. We encountered one version of this type of account in the work of Aristotle, according to whom the full and appropriate exercise of virtue (or *aretē*) requires the (right sort of) *polis*. We encountered another in Rousseau's idea that humans are 'perfectible' creatures, who can only develop to their full potential in true communities governed in accordance with the general will. (Recall his contrast between the latter and the life of the 'savage' whose simple needs match a simple lifestyle; and between it and the ostentation and deceit characteristic of the 'despotism' he saw all around him.)

To which conception did Mill subscribe? The answer is *both*.[8] The former is presupposed by the principle he explicitly sets out to defend in *On Liberty*, the principle that 'the only purpose for which power can be rightfully exercised over any member of a civilised community, against his will, is to prevent harm to others' (1991a: 14). Later, when discussing 'the limits to the authority of society over the individual', he expands upon the principle as follows:

> As soon as any part of a person's conduct affects prejudicially the interests of others, society has jurisdiction over it, and the question whether the general welfare will or will not be promoted by interfering with it, becomes open to discussion. But there is no room for entertaining any such question when a person's conduct affects the interests of no persons besides himself, or needs not affect them unless they like (all the persons being of full age and the ordinary amount of understanding). In all such cases there should be perfect freedom, legal and social, to do the action and stand the consequences.
>
> (ibid.: 83–4)

Mill insists that each individual is by far the best judge of his or her own interests. '[But] neither one person, nor any number of persons', he writes, 'is warranted in saying to another human creature of ripe years, that he shall not do with his life what he chooses to do with it.' This is because 'he is the person most interested in his own well-being', so that 'with respect to his own feelings and circumstances, the most ordinary man or woman has means of knowledge immeasurably surpassing those that can be possessed by anyone else' (ibid.: 84–5). With this premise, you get a picture of the social world as composed, fundamentally, of discrete individuals, each pursuing his or her chosen trajectory, with the legitimate state acting as traffic cop. In other words, if each individual is the best judge of his or her own interest, it follows that the state's only job should be to prevent harm-producing collisions. It is a picture which inevitably holds a strong appeal for anyone who hates to be bullied or patronised, and who, in that sense, values individual freedom highly.

But then, Mill *also* believes that the state can act more positively, by creating the conditions within which humans can develop and fulfil their potential. It is with sentences such as the following that he gives expression to one of his most deeply held convictions:

> Human nature is not a machine to be built after a model, and set to do exactly the work prescribed for it, but a tree, which requires to grow and develop itself on all sides, according to the tendency of the inward forces which make it a living thing.
>
> (ibid.: 66)

Here, Mill is invoking the second of the two conceptions I distinguished above. The chapter of *On Liberty* in which the sentence occurs is entitled 'Of Individuality, as One of the Elements of Well-Being'. In it, Mill argues that it is only where people are left free from interference to pursue their chosen ends that there is any chance of their realising their potential. But is this true? Why suppose that people left free from interference to pursue the ends they *in fact* have (first conception) are more likely to flourish into the individuals they could *ideally become* (second conception)? It would certainly help Mill if this were the case, but why not suppose that all you will really get is a society based on 'bread and circuses'? We shall return to the question. Before that, let us consider one more example of a text in which both ideals have a part to play.

A glance forward

Mill opens *The Subjection of Women* (1991d) with the following paragraph:

> The object of this essay is to explain, as clearly as I am able, the grounds of an opinion which I have held from the very earliest period when I had formed any opinions at all on social or political matters, and which, instead of being weakened or modified, has been constantly growing stronger by the progress of reflection and the experience of life: That the principle which regulates the existing social relation between the two sexes – the legal subordination of one sex – is wrong in itself, and now one of the chief hindrances to human improvement: and that it ought to be replaced by a principle of perfect equality, admitting no power or privilege on the one side, nor disability on the other.
>
> (ibid.: 471)

It is beyond doubt that, even as recently as the mid-nineteenth century, the situation of women, relative to that of men, was very poor. (*The Subjection of Women* was published in 1869.) Mill was especially angered by the fact that, on marriage, a woman's property became her husband's. That was the law. He was equally angered by the fact that women were denied the vote, which rendered them unable to use the political system to change their situation. As Mill saw it, such factors combined to rob women – especially married women – of their independence. The system made slaves of them. Worse than that, it tormented the slaves by forcing them to live in close proximity to their masters.

> Every one of the subjects lives under the very eye, and almost, it may be said, in the hands, of one of the masters – in closer intimacy with him than with any of her fellow subjects; with no means of combining against him, no power of even locally overmastering him, and on the other hand, with the strongest motives for seeking his favour and avoiding to give him offence. In struggles for political emancipation, everybody knows how often its champions are bought off by bribes, or daunted by terrors. In the case of women, each individual of the subject class is in a chronic state of bribery and intimidation combined. In setting up the standard of resistance, a large number of the leaders, and still more of the followers, must make an almost complete sacrifice of the pleasures or the alleviations of their own individual lot. If ever any system of privilege and enforced subjection had its yoke tightly riveted on the necks of those who are kept down by it, this has.

> (ibid.: 482)

As this passage demonstrates, Mill's invective could be quite as powerful, and quite as militant, as you will find in many a subsequent feminist text. From our point of view, however, the point to note is the *form* Mill's arguments take. Very roughly, these fall into three categories.

First, there are arguments from justice. It is generally recognised that, between equals, there should be equality of treatment and opportunity, and since there is no reason for thinking that, in matters which concern legislation, women are not relevantly equal, their subordination is unjust. 'In no instance except this', says Mill, 'which comprehends half the human race, are the higher social functions closed against any one by a fatality of birth'. In this way, 'The social subordination of women thus stands out as an isolated fact in modern institutions; a solitary breach of what has become their fundamental law' (ibid.: 491).

Secondly, there are utilitarian arguments that the happiness of women as they are will be increased once their legal subordination is removed. In the case of the unhappily married women for whom the yoke of subjection is 'tightly riveted on the necks of those who are kept down by it [the system]' (ibid.: 482), this practically goes without saying. In addition there is the consideration that personal independence is itself 'an element of happiness' (576) and – for example – the consideration that doors will be opened to those women capable of participating in public office. After all, says Mill, 'There is nothing, after disease, indigence, and guilt, so fatal to the pleasurable enjoyment of life as the want of a worthy outlet for the active faculties' (578). (Arguments of this type are reinforced by the similarly utilitarian argument that everyone would be better off 'if women were free' (557ff).)

Thirdly, there is the argument that it is only when legal barriers are lifted that women will develop to their full potential. In a passage which echoes his claim, in *On Liberty*, that human nature is 'a tree, which requires to grow and develop itself on all sides, according to the tendency of the inward forces which make it a living thing' (1991a: 66) Mill writes:

> What is now called the nature of women is an eminently artificial thing – the result of forced repression in some directions, unnatural stimulation in others. It may be asserted without scruple, that no other class of dependants have had their character so entirely distorted from its natural proportions by their relation with their masters; for, if conquered and slave races have been, in some respects, more forcibly repressed, whatever in them has not been crushed down by an iron heel has generally been let alone, and if left with any liberty of development, it has developed itself according to its own laws; but in the case of women, a hothouse and stove cultivation has always been carried on of some of the capabilities of their nature, for the benefit and pleasure of their masters.
>
> (1991d: 495)

Looking on, men 'indolently believe that the tree grows of itself in the way they have made it grow' (ibid.: 496) but they are mistaken. With this passage Mill raises a spectre which has continued to haunt modern feminist theory, the downtrodden 'Stepford wife'[9] who has become so inwardly 'socialised' to her subordinate role that she is perfectly happy with it. In short, this is the specifically feminist variant of the 'happy slave' problem. As Mill puts it himself, most men 'desire to have, in the woman most nearly connected with them, not a forced slave but a willing one; not a slave merely, but a favourite. They have therefore put everything in practice to enslave their minds' (ibid.: 486).

What of the relationship between the three types of argument I have distinguished? Well, to start with, the relationship between the first – the argument from justice – and the other two could be problematic, but that is something we shall consider later. For the moment, it is the relationship between the second and third types of argument which is most to the point. This is because arguments of the second type take women (and sometimes people more generally) as they are, whereas arguments of the third type invoke an ideal of women as they could be – so a pattern we have noted in other parts of Mill's work recurs here too.

Is there a tension between these two forms of argument which is strong enough to threaten Mill's pro-feminist case? I would say not, at least, not in the sense that the two forms of argument are logically inconsistent with each other. There is no contradiction in maintaining that, if women's equality were achieved, those capable of developing more fully would do so, whereas the less capable would remain as they are. Nevertheless, perhaps there is something which hangs on the question of how likely it is that happily socialised women would remain content with their subordinate role. Mill considers the possibility that 'the rule of men over women differs from all these others in not being a rule of force: it is accepted voluntarily; women make no complaint, and are consenting parties to it' (ibid.: 484). However, he finds that he can't take it seriously. But what if he is wrong? As evidence for his scepticism Mill points out that 'a great number of women do not accept it', and that 'an increasing number of them have recorded protests against their present social condition: and recently many thousands of them, headed by the most eminent women known to the public, have petitioned Parliament for their admission to the Parliamentary Suffrage' (ibid.).[10] He then goes on to describe the rise of a women's movement which was, as he saw it, taking place across the world. But to this it is – I suppose – possible to object that even 'many thousands' of women is not a very large proportion of all the women there are and that, in any case, the 'most eminent women known to the public' are the strong, literary, radically politicised women of the sort Mill admired, and – as such – unrepresentative of women taken as a whole.

I shan't continue with this line of thought because I only want to suggest that it would make a difference to Mill's argument if it were true that most women would remain contentedly reconciled to their role, whatever their legal status. So, *The Subjection of Women* is another example of a work by Mill in which he argues that people left free from interference to pursue ends they in fact have are most likely to flourish into the individuals they could ideally become; but in which he can only be right if a further, factual, claim is true. In this case, it is the claim that, in reality, very few women are happy to assume a subordinate role. (In other words, the world in which women have been released from their chains might not – quite – turn out to be the world Mill would like to see.)

Although it was written by a man, *The Subjection of Women* is one of feminism's early texts. However, it was not the first. As Mill himself says, 'It is scarcely three generations since women, saving very rare exceptions, have begun to try their capacity in philosophy, science, or art' (ibid.: 545). We have already discussed Mary Wollstonecraft. Her *A Vindication of the Rights of Woman* (Wollstonecraft 1995b) was published in 1792, not quite eighty years before Mill's work, so his estimate seems to be about right. Also, many women readers – perhaps all women readers – will be reflecting, wryly, that my narrative had to come quite a long way before a woman philosopher, let alone a feminist text, appeared on the scene. To this, I can only respond with the comment that it has, indeed, been a long time, but that time will tell. As Mill says, 'It cannot be inferred to be impossible that a woman should be a Homer, or an Aristotle, or a Michael Angelo, or a Beethoven, because no woman has yet actually produced works comparable to theirs in any of those lines of excellence' (1991d: 528). If he were alive now, I like to think that he would consider his optimism to have been justified.

Utilitarianism: the greatest happiness principle

'Utility versus rights'

As I stated earlier, there are two fundamental components to classical utilitarianism. One is the theory of human nature according to which we are all motivated by the desire for happiness (and the corresponding desire to avoid unhappiness). We have now discussed this at some length, so let us now turn to the other. This is the principle of utility, or 'greatest happiness' principle itself.

In fact, the principle that 'the greatest good is the greatest happiness of the greatest number' is fraught with difficulties. Here, though, I shall concentrate on just one. It is a difficulty which arises from the fact that the principle is *consequentialist*, in other words that it enjoins you to consider the likely consequences of the various possibilities facing you when deciding what you should do. This it clearly does. In its simplest form, utilitarianism applies the greatest happiness principle at the level of every single act you perform. It states that, each time you act, you must assess the likely consequences of each alternative facing you, and choose the one which (in your view) is the most likely to increase happiness – or, at least, not to create unhappiness. Moreover, this very simple 'act' utilitarianism states that there is no other factor to consider. (For the most part, it will be sufficient to concentrate on simple 'act' utilitarianism here, although I shall mention a more complex variant later.) When applied at the political level, the principle states that, out of a range of policies, an administrator must always select the alternative which, on the best evidence available, is the most likely to increase the general happiness. According to the objection in question utilitarianism fails because – resting as it does on a consequentialist principle – it cannot account for some very basic features of morality. The latter are non-consequentialist in character. From the point of view of political philosophy, this is especially serious – or so the objection runs – as it means that utilitarianism cannot account for the existence of natural or (if you prefer the expression) human rights.

In a moment, I shall outline the objection in more detail, but let me first explain why I want to concentrate on that objection in particular. It is simply that a great deal of recent work in political philosophy takes the objection as its starting point. I am thinking especially of work which has been produced since 1972, when John Rawls' *A Theory of Justice* was published (Rawls 1972). Open any academic journal of philosophy published since then and you are almost certain to find at least one article on the subject of 'utility versus rights', in which the author either tries to defend some version of utilitarianism against the objection or else tries to press it home. Indeed, Rawls himself formulates his own theory as a response to the difficulty I am about to outline. In short, then, unless you understand why it is that utilitarianism is supposedly unable to account for the existence of rights, you will find it impossible to follow a great deal of contemporary argument.

So how does the objection run? The best way to introduce it is with an example. Suppose, then, that you and I are colleagues. We work together. One Friday, I find myself short of cash. I am unable to get to the bank before it shuts, so I ask you to lend me a sum of money – say, twenty pounds. You agree, but only on condition that I promise to repay you in one week's time. I accept, and – placing my hand on my heart – I say, 'I promise to pay you back twenty pounds this time next week'. You then hand me a twenty pound note.

So far so good, but now consider what happens next. As I am at home that evening I decide to re-read Bentham's *Principles of Morals and Legislation* (Bentham 2000b). This time, I find its argument powerful and utterly persuasive, so much so that I become a convert to Benthamite ('act') utilitarianism. In other words, I resolve that in future, whenever I am faced with a choice, I will take the alternative which, so far as I can see, will most increase the sum of happiness. Nothing else will count. From that moment on, quite a number of practical difficulties threaten to beset me. (For example, what if I have to choose between, on the one hand, making one or two people very happy indeed and, on the other, making a large number of people just a little bit more happy? What does the principle of utility tell me to do? It looks as though the injunction to increase the greatest happiness of the greatest number could turn out to be ambiguous. Or again, what of very long term consequences? Anything I do could have 'knock on' effects which continue well into the future – for twenty or thirty years or, maybe, even longer – and there is no way in which I can foresee these, or take them into account. These are standard difficulties with utilitarianism. Still, I put these to one side and concentrate on just the one in hand.)

Even so, things go relatively smoothly until Friday comes around and I am on my way to work, on foot, with a crisp new twenty pound note in my pocket, ready to give you. I have almost reached our workplace when I am approached by a desperate and needy-looking down-and-out. He tells me a long and heartrending story from which I glean that he is in urgent need of cash; in fact, that he is in need of precisely twenty pounds. (There is a place he has to get to, and that is the cost of the fare.) I then assess the alternatives facing me. On the one hand, I can see that the down-and-out is in a bad way, and that he could really use the money. On the other, I know that you are a miserly character. All you will do with the note is add it to the stock of twenty pound notes you already have, and which you keep in a jar on your shelf. (For you, the increase in 'marginal utility' created by the extra twenty pound note would be small.) What should I do? There is really no problem. As an act utilitarian all I can reasonably do is give the note to the tramp – so I give it to him. Now, as well as creating extra happiness for the down-and-out, I experience a little glow of my own. This comes from my knowledge of having done a good deed, and it lasts right up to the moment at which I meet you. What happens next is this: You say, 'Please could I have that twenty pounds back', to which I respond by telling you the whole story of how, last week, I became a convert to Benthamite utilitarianism, of how I was approached by a down-and-out, and all the rest of it.

How do you respond? Well, of course, what could happen is that you tell me the story of how you also re-read Bentham's book last week and of how – similarly – you have also become converted to act utilitarianism. You agree with me that, as a utilitarian, my only option was to give the money to the down-and-out. We smile, shake hands, and remain friends. However, as I think you will agree, that is not the most likely eventuality. It is far more likely that you would object and exclaim, e.g., 'But you *promised*!!' Moreover, I think most readers will agree that you would be quite entitled to do so.

The story may be used to illustrate a number of points. The first is that, when you make a promise to someone, you create an expectation on the other person's part. More than that, you create an *entitlement*. Thus, in the story, as a result of my having said, 'I promise . . .' you have a moral claim on my behaviour, in this case the claim that I should repay you on the appointed day. Secondly, as a result of the promise, you have a claim that I should act in such-and-such a way, even if I could make a greater contribution to the general good by breaking the promise. (How could it be a claim, unless this were so?) In the story as I told it, it is quite obvious that I would create more happiness by breaking the promise and giving the money to the down-and-out. Even so, thanks to the promise, you are entitled to repayment. Thirdly, the story illustrates that utilitarianism, thanks to its consequentialist structure, is completely unable to account for such facts. Of course, there are limits to the force carried by every claim. If the down-and-out had been on the point of starvation – or if I had told a story in which, by breaking a promise, I would prevent nuclear war – everyone would agree that the promise should be broken. But those are extreme cases. Notice, though, that it follows from act utilitarianism that a promise should be broken, even when there are very slight differences between the amounts of happiness which can be created by different actions. For example, suppose that by giving the money to the down-and-out I could create *just slightly* more happiness than I could if I repaid you. If act utilitarianism were correct, it would still follow that I should break the promise, which is not a conclusion which accords with the way promises are normally thought to bind their makers in normal, less than extreme, cases.

The claim a promisee has on the behaviour of a promiser is a claim of *right*; you have a right that I should pay you the money back. It follows, in line with the objection, that utilitarianism cannot account for the existence of at least one right, namely the right you have that promises made to you are kept. It is – I suppose – possible for a utilitarian to respond to this by insisting that the principle of utility is indeed the only rational basis for a moral system, and that all the story shows is that the practice of promising should be abandoned as irrational. Well, maybe so, but just imagine how much we would have to give up if we were to abandon promising. If act utilitarianism were generally embraced, no one would ever make a promise to anyone else (because nobody could be trusted to keep a promise). Promising, as a practice, would lose its point. We would have to jettison a large and significant feature of morality as we understand it. Given the choice between abandoning the practice and abandoning utilitarianism, most of us would – I think – agree to abandon the latter.[11]

The foregoing conclusions can be generalised to cover other rights. To see how, you only need to think up parallel stories in which, for good utilitarian reasons, morally reprehensible things are done. For example, to deter crime an example is made of some innocent people. They are punished horribly and with great publicity. If that is wrong, it is because the innocent have a right not to be 'punished' or, rather, victimised. The average standard of living is greatly enhanced (in itself a good thing) by the efforts of slaves, who are forced to work very hard for nothing. (But there is a right to liberty.) In search for a cure for cancer (good) lethal experiments are performed on humans, without their consent (but there is a right to life), . . . and so on. It follows – as the objection states – that utilitarianism cannot account for rights. More than that, some critics would say that the objection positively demonstrates the existence of human rights. Philosophers who advance this type of objection sometimes describe themselves as 'Kantians', after Immanuel Kant, who held that it is a defining feature of morality that, within it, individuals are treated as 'ends in themselves' and never only as means to the ends of others (see Kant 1948). On this view, the trouble with utilitarianism is that it sanctions the 'use' of one person by another for the latter's purposes.[12]

How might a utilitarian respond to this criticism? I will only mention one possible response here, mainly because it appears to be the response Mill himself would have made. According to this, the objection only applies to a very simple – even naive – version of utilitarianism. Against this, it is argued that it is more plausible and realistic to think of the principle of utility as applying not at the level of individual acts but at the level of moral rules, rules such as 'keep promises' and 'don't tell lies'. On this 'rule utilitarian' view, I ought to keep my promise because there is a moral rule stating that I should, and the rule exists because its existence contributes to the greatest happiness. This is what Mill says:

> It is a strange notion that the acknowledgement of a first principle is inconsistent with the admission of secondary ones. To inform a traveller respecting the place of his ultimate destination, is not to forbid the use of landmarks and direction-posts on the way. The

proposition that happiness is the end and aim of morality, does not mean that no road ought to be laid down to that goal, or that persons going thither should not be advised to take one direction rather than another. Men really ought to leave off talking a kind of nonsense on this subject, which they would neither talk nor listen to on other matters of practical concernment. Nobody argues that the art of navigation is not founded on astronomy, because sailors cannot wait to calculate the Nautical Alamanack. Being rational creatures, they go to sea with it ready calculated; and all rational creatures go out upon the sea of life with their minds made up on the common questions of right and wrong, as well as on many of the far more difficult questions of wise and foolish.

(1991b: 156–7)

How convincing is this? That is not a question I shall pursue here because to continue with it any further would be to deviate too far from this chapter's main theme. In any case, as the argument between act and rule utilitarians continues, so the amount of relevant literature grows. It is there for interested readers to consult.

Two illustrations: democracy and free speech

Democracy

This chapter's main theme is Mill's utilitarianism and the liberalism he attempts to found upon it. The objection to utilitarianism we have just been considering suggests that the former could have odd consequences for the latter and, moreover, that there has to be a serious tension between the two. The reason is that, whereas utilitarianism (apparently) cannot account for rights, liberalism, in the sense of 'liberalism' at issue, is partly defined by the claim the we do have certain fundamental rights – or, if not, at least that 'there is a sphere of action in which society, as distinguished from the individual, has, if any, only an indirect interest' (1982: 71). You would expect anomalies and tensions to show up in Mill's arguments, and so they do, quite frequently. I shall give just two examples here. The first is a proposal he makes in *Representative Government*, namely that some people should have more votes than others (1991c: 336ff). The other is the famous defence of 'the liberty of thought and discussion' which you can find in the second chapter of *On Liberty* (1991a: 20ff).

To take the former, then, in *Representative Government* Mill defends a political system which is, pretty much, the system now in place in the 'liberal democracies' of Europe, North America, and in certain other nations too. Unsurprisingly, the system Mill describes most resembles the British system of his, and our own time. Mill portrays it as the system best fitted for a plural society, that is a society composed of numerous and diverse interest groups. Each geographical constituency elects representatives who serve, for a period, in a general assembly. The assembly's job is to make laws and to keep a check on the power of a permanent executive (or civil service). I would say that, in our own time, this version of democracy has become the 'received view'. Mill's arguments or arguments very like them are, if you like, the arguments for democracy with which most us have been brought up. (For a contrast, think of Rousseau, whose arguments for democracy were discussed in Chapter 9.)

And yet, there are strange anomalies, one of which is Mill's proposal for a system of plural voting. '[But] though every one ought to have a voice', he writes, 'that every one should have an equal voice is a totally different proposition' (1991c: 334).

> If, with equal virtue, one [person] is superior to the other in knowledge and intelligence – or if, with equal intelligence, one excels the other in virtue – the opinion, the judgement, of the higher moral or intellectual is worth more than that of the inferior: and if the institutions of the country virtually assert that they are of the same value, they assert a thing which is not.
>
> (ibid.)

In other words, people who are wiser and more intelligent than others should have more votes than others. But who qualifies as more intelligent? Unfortunately, there is no 'really national education' and no 'trustworthy system of general examination', so Mill suggests that occupation can be used as a rough guide:

> An employer of labour is on the average more intelligent than a labourer; for he must labour with his head, and not solely with his hands. A foreman is generally more intelligent than an ordinary labourer, and a labourer in the skilled trades than in the unskilled. A banker, merchant, or manufacturer is likely to be more intelligent than a tradesman, because he has larger and more complicated interests to manage.
>
> (285)

A little later he adds:

> The liberal professions, when really and not nominally practised, imply, of course, a still higher degree of instruction; and wherever a sufficient examination, or any serious conditions of education, are required before entering on a profession, its members could be admitted at once to a plurality of votes. The same rule might be applied to graduates of universities; and even to those who bring satisfactory certificates of having passed through the course of study required by any school at which the higher branches of knowledge

are taught, under proper securities that the teaching is real, and not a mere pretence.

(285)

I think you will have got the point. Now, is this 'democratic' or isn't it? What do you, the reader, think? It seems to me quite likely that many readers, even some of those who are not thoroughly horrified by Mill's suggestion, will want to object that, far from being democratic, it is thoroughly elitist. If that is your response then, unlike Mill, you are thinking of democracy as more than a 'decision making procedure', a mechanism for choosing governments and policies. You think that, to qualify as democratic, an arrangement of political institutions, or a policy, must be in some way egalitarian, which makes it all the more likely that you will want to give each person just one vote, irrespective of intelligence or occupation. And, if that is what you think, you can, in fact, draw upon some strong arguments to support you. For a start, there is a recognised sense of 'democratic' as 'favouring or characterised by social equality; egalitarian' (*The New Oxford Dictionary of English*). Then there is the consideration that, as a definition, that one is fairly close to the original Greek. In Greece, *dēmokratia* meant rule by the *dēmos*, or the ordinary people, as opposed to rule by this or that elite – the aristocracy or the oligarchs. You can also draw on the support of some powerful recent work in political philosophy. For example, John Rawls himself includes 'political liberty (the right to vote and to be eligible for public office)' in his list of 'basic liberties'. Such liberties are 'required to be equal' by Rawls' theory of justice (Rawls 1972: 61). So there is a tension here. It is not a tension within Mill's argument so much as a tension between Mill's conclusion and one widely shared understanding of what it means to be democratic.

So, unlike Rawls, Mill thinks it possible to be a liberal, a democrat and – at the same time – an elitist. How come? The answer is that Mill's argument for democracy is consequentialist. In fact, it is utilitarian. On a first reading of *Representative Government*, it can be a little hard to appreciate the latter, because Mill seems to spend far less time talking about happiness than he does 'improvement'. One 'criterion of the goodness of a government' is, thus, said to be 'the degree in which it tends to increase the sum of good qualities in the governed, collectively and individually' (193); a great virtue of a 'representative constitution' is held to be that it is 'a means of bringing the general standard of intelligence and honesty, and the individual intellect and virtue of its wisest members, more directly to bear upon the government' (195); the possession of a vote gives you an influence on public affairs, albeit a small one, and this, in its turn, creates an interest in the world around you. Says Mill, it is 'from political discussion, and collective political action, that one whose daily occupations concentrate his interests in a small circle round himself, learns to feel for and with his fellow citizens, and becomes consciously a member of a great community', whereas 'political discussions fly over the heads of those who have no votes, and are not endeavouring to acquire them' (1991c: 328–9); one advantage of the system of proportional representation Mill advocates is held to be that it makes it easier for the person 'who has only talents and character' (i.e. who has no affiliation to a political party) 'to gain admission into the House of Commons' (264). That way, although 'the superior intellects and characters will necessarily be outnumbered' they will at least be heard (266); and so on. There is more in the same vein. Of course, here Mill is describing what he has elsewhere called 'utility in the largest sense' (1991a: 15). It is the utility sought by those capable of appreciating the 'higher' pleasures.

Still, the point now at issue so far as I am concerned is not the intelligibility or otherwise of that last conception. It is just as follows. If you think of a voting system as a sort of machine – that is, as a device with a particular function – it is highly unlikely that you will design a system in which everyone has one vote each. What you will do is 'weight'. You will try to make sure that each person's input into the system helps the machine to function in the way you want it to. In short, this is a *consequentialist* way of thinking which is almost guaranteed to yield a result to offend anyone who believes that each person has a right to just one vote because each has an equal *right* to vote. So, as I said, there is a conflict between consequentialism and rights here. (Note the similarity between Plato and Mill. Neither believes that democracy can be guaranteed to yield the best decisions. The difference is that whereas the former relies on philosopher rulers to solve the problem, the latter relies on plural voting.)

Mill thinks that one purpose of government is to 'improve' people morally and intellectually, so he tries to make sure that the wise and the good have more influence than others. There is something else that worries him too, and it is worth mentioning. One interesting feature of *Representative Government* is the glimpse it gives you into the class structure of nineteenth century Britain. As I said earlier, Mill thought his system the most suitable for a plural society, so he quite often refers to different social classes and groups. What, then, were the social groups whose existence he thought noteworthy? Well, then – just as now – there were ethnic and religious groups:

> Suppose the majority to be whites, the minority negroes, or *vice versa*: is it likely that the majority would allow equal justice to the minority? Suppose the majority Catholics, the minority Protestants, or the reverse; will there not be the same danger? Or let the majority be English, the minority Irish, or the contrary: is there not a great probability of similar evil?
>
> (249)

And then, of course, 'In all countries, there is a majority of poor, a minority who, in contradistinction, may be called rich. Between these two classes, on many questions, there is complete opposition of apparent interest' (ibid.). In fact, it is the following passage which reveals the class division by which Mill was most concerned:

> A modern community, not divided within itself by strong antipathies of race, language, or nationality, may be considered as in the main divisible into two sections, which, in spite of partial variations, correspond on the whole with two divergent directions of apparent interest. Let us call them (in brief general terms) labourers on the one hand, employers of labour on the other.
>
> (225)

As both these passages show, Mill was worried by the prospect of one class dominating another. Something he especially feared was 'tyranny of the majority'. One purpose of plural voting, proportional representation, and the rest of it, is to ensure a balance of power between classes. As the second passage shows, Mill was trying to come to terms with the existence of a working class. In an earlier chapter, I remarked that the events of the French Revolution 'traumatised Europe'. But, of course, the revolution wasn't all that happened (and, in any case, by the time Mill was writing over half a century had passed since 1789). Another phenomenon – new, surprising, and alarming to many – to which the Victorians had to adapt was industrialisation. Over a short period, huge new towns devoted to manufacturing, with their factories and their terraces of shoddy houses, had sprung into being. To some, it must have seemed that they came from nowhere. And with the towns there had come a numerous new class of industrial labourers. It was a theme which preoccupied many writers of the period.[13]

Free speech

What of the other example? We should cast a brief glance in the direction of Mill's defence of 'the liberty of thought and discussion' if only because it is so famous and so influential. The second chapter of On Liberty contains a helpful passage in which Mill sums up his argument, so rather than try to summarise it in my own words, let me just quote him. Mill claims to have 'recognised the necessity to the mental well-being of mankind' 'of freedom of opinion, and freedom of the expression of opinion, on four distinct grounds'. The 'grounds' are as follows:

> First, if any opinion is compelled to silence, that opinion may, for aught we can certainly know, be true. To deny this is to assume our own infallibility.
>
> Secondly, though the silenced opinion be an error, it may, and very commonly does, contain a portion of the truth; and since the general or prevailing opinion on any subject is rarely or never the

whole truth, it is only by the collision of adverse opinions that the remainder of the truth has any chance of being supplied.

Thirdly, even if the received opinion be not only true, but the whole truth; unless it is suffered to be, and actually is, vigorously and earnestly contested, it will, by most of those who receive it, be held in the manner of a prejudice, with little comprehension or feeling of its rational grounds. And not only this, but, fourthly, the meaning of the doctrine itself will be in danger of being lost or enfeebled, and deprived of its vital effect on the character and conduct; the dogma becoming a mere formal profession, inefficacious for good, but cumbering the ground and preventing the growth of any real and heartfelt conviction from reason or personal experience.

(1991a: 59)

Mill's argument has itself been a subject of much thought and discussion. There is a great deal I could say but, here, I shall confine myself to just two observations. The first is that Mill's argument is consequentialist throughout. As you can see, it states that where people are left free to think and discuss then, *as a consequence*, their chances of arriving at the truth are increased. With his four 'grounds' Mill draws our attention to the various ways in which this can happen. Thus, to 'assume infallibility' (first ground) is to pretend that you are in possession of the truth when you are not. It is also to deprive others of the chance of reaching the truth themselves; it is the 'collision' of opinions which takes place when ideas are discussed that most facilitates the search for truth (second ground); 'prejudice' and 'dogma' are to be condemned for the way they impede the search for truth (third and fourth grounds). (The argument is utilitarian but – as I am sure I don't really have to tell you by now – it is 'utility in the largest sense' which concerns Mill here. People capable of intelligently discussing ideas and opinions are, he thinks, people who employ their 'higher' faculties. It worries him that, as his fourth ground states, where a doctrine cannot be discussed it can be 'deprived of its vital effect on the character and conduct'.)

Now, thanks to its consequentialist structure, Mill's argument immediately faces us with the question of whether it is, in fact, true that the connections Mill describes actually hold. Does the liberty of thought and discussion really increase our chances of arriving at the truth? Well, I'll leave you to decide that for yourself. The important thing is to point out that it is possible to raise the question. For what it's worth, let me just add that, in my opinion, Mill's claim *is* true, but that it is only true for situations of a certain type. Thus: Imagine a group of intelligent, informed, people. They are meeting together because they are interested in a particular question. Perhaps they are physicists, intrigued by some aspect of the latest cosmological theory, or perhaps they are literary critics, trying to assess the merits of a recently published novel. Within this 'seminar group' each person is free to state his or her opinion while the others respectfully listen. Everyone is at liberty to be as critical of the others as he or she can, and so on. I believe that, where such conditions prevail, there is an increased chance of reaching truth. (The physicists will most probably refine their theoretical positions and increase their accuracy. As for the critics, even if you think that there is no such thing as 'truth' in literary criticism, you must still admit – I think – that each critic will have increased his or her 'comprehension' and 'feeling [for] the rational grounds' of the opinions discussed.) It is my belief that the more a situation resembles this 'seminar group' model, the more Mill's arguments apply; but the less it resembles the model, the less they do.[14]

Now, although Mill is defending 'the liberty of thought and discussion' and not 'free speech', his argument is more often than not taken to be a defence of the latter. None of this would matter so much otherwise. It is a measure of Mill's influence, I think, that even people who have never heard of him will tell you that the silencing of an opinion is an assumption of infallibility, or that the collision of ideas is a necessary precondition for the discovery of truth – just as Mill does – when seeking to defend an individual's right to publish something, or to speak publicly on some particular occasion. So, the question is: Can Mill's consequentialist argument for the liberty of thought and discussion be used to defend an individual's right to free speech? In answer, it follows from what I have just been saying that it can, but only for situations which resemble the 'seminar group' model.

For example, just suppose that a small neo-Nazi, ultra-racist, group wants to hold a rally in your local park next month. If they do, there will be speakers, skilled at rhetoric, who rave and rage against the modern corruption, the alien menace threatening to swamp our culture and our public services – and so on, and so forth. The crowd will be whipped into a fervour and their sense of solidarity will be reinforced. Some local residents will feel cowed and intimidated on that day. If the local authorities were to prevent the rally from taking place, would they be violating the speakers' 'right to free speech'? I don't know. However, I do think it is clear that Mill's argument could not be used to show that they would, for the situation I have just described is in no way an example of the sober pursuit of truth by people in a rational frame of mind. Finally on this point – and to generalise – similar considerations apply to many other cases. We are all familiar with the type of situation in which the tabloid press conducts a campaign against some well-known media personality, publishing embarrassing details of that person's private life, and potentially destroying his or her reputation and career; or in which, for reasons best known to himself, some cranky fascist publishes a book in which he argues, quite implausibly, that the Holocaust never took place, thereby causing great offence to Holocaust survivors and many others. Can the tabloids or the Nazi plead a right to free speech in defence of their activities? Well, if they can, it's hard to see how Mill's argument could help them.

In conclusion, recall that Mill's insistence that there is a 'sphere of action' over which the individual is sovereign is an essential constituent of his liberalism. Recall, too, that the 'sphere' is meant to encompass, amongst other things, 'absolute freedom of opinion on all subjects, practical or speculative, scientific, moral, or theological'. To this, Mill adds that 'the liberty of expressing and publishing opinions' is 'practically inseparable' from the former because it rests 'in great part on the same reasons' (1991a: 16–17). Against this, my argument suggests that such a conclusion cannot be derived from Mill's consequentialist argument for the liberty of thought and discussion.

Conclusion

In the middle years of the nineteenth century, political thought was largely shaped by the work of two great philosophers. John Stuart Mill was one. Throughout that century, the twentieth, and into our own, his spirit has continued to inform the way political philosophers construct the problems with which they are preoccupied and the approach they take to their solution. That is why it matters that there is a tension between his utilitarianism and his liberalism. It is a tension we have inherited. In our own time, the prevailing temper has tended to be secular and pragmatic – in that sense, it has been the temper of Mill's utilitarianism – and the prevailing political order has tended to be liberal. It is just as well to be aware that the two do not sit so easily together.

Mill's character, like his philosophy, was fraught with inner tensions. In his life, as in his writing, he tirelessly struggled to reconcile the utilitarianism he had inherited with a complex vision which the former was, in reality, too simple to support. This took its toll. It was the tension between the two which, no doubt, helps explain the terrible nervous breakdown, the 'mental crisis' he suffered in 1826, which he describes so movingly in his *Autobiography* (see Mill 1989: chapter 5). In his life, Mill also gave the lie to the stereotypical idea that a philosopher must be other-worldly, the disengaged resident of an ivory tower. Far from it; Mill took an active part in many movements for political reform and in public affairs generally. For a time, he served as Member of Parliament for Westminster. He spent his career working in the Examiner's Office of the East India Company. This eventually became the branch of the Foreign Office responsible for Britain's relations with India. In short, he was the equivalent of a senior civil servant.

When Mill was working there, the East India Company's offices were located in Leadenhall Street, in the City of London. Less than three miles away – only a few minutes' walk from the cabinet in which Bentham's remains are placed on display – there stands the British Museum, with its circular library and reading room (now museum pieces themselves). It was there, during the same period, that nineteenth century political philosophy's other towering genius – Karl Marx – spent his days laboriously forging his masterpiece.

12

Marx

Karl Marx has been described as 'the most influential thinker of the modern period' (Simon 1994: ix) and there are many who would agree with that. It isn't true, but that's only because there is no single philosopher who you could describe as *the* most influential thinker of the period. It is true, however, that Marx is one of a handful of philosophers whose vision, and whose arguments, have shaped modern political thought. It is also true that, unlike the others, his work inspired a movement of ideas which has continued to bear his name. We do not call liberalism 'Millism', even though J.S. Mill's writings were, and remain, the major inspiration for so much modern liberalism. Nor do we call conservatism 'Burkeism'. However, the usual epithet for Marxism is just that – '*Marx*ism'.

In some ways, this has been unfortunate for Marx's reputation. Commentators who describe Marx as the modern world's most influential political thinker tend to cite, as evidence, the fact that there were, until quite recently, plenty of 'Marxist regimes' in the world. Such regimes claimed Marx for their own. They cited Marx as the inspiration for policies which were, more often than not, as repressive as they were economically inefficient. (Doesn't everyone know that, in its official ideology, Stalin's Soviet Union was Marxist–Leninist?) However, it could be a mistake to blame Marx for every atrocity committed in his name. After all, John Locke's *Second Treatise* was a major inspiration for the 'founding fathers' who drafted the US constitution, but we do not normally describe the United States' government as a 'Locke-ist regime', nor do we lay the blame for its less attractive actions on Locke. In short, there could be guilt by association here.

It is certainly the case that, where Marx is concerned, the ascription of guilt by association is a tradition which began quite early. For example, you can find it in the report of the police agent, sent from Prussia to spy on Marx and his family while they were living in exile in London. (It would have been written sometime between 1850 and 1856, when the Marxes were living in a small two room apartment.)[1] 'When you enter Marx's room', reported the agent, 'smoke and tobacco fumes make your eyes water so much that for a moment you seem to be groping about in a

210

cavern', and 'Everything is dirty and covered with dust, so that to sit down becomes a thoroughly dangerous business. . . . Here is a chair with only three legs, on another the children are playing at cooking.' Moreover,

> In private life he is an extremely disorderly, cynical human being, and a bad host. He leads a real gypsy existence. Washing, grooming and changing his linen are things he does rarely, and he is often drunk. Though he is often idle for days on end, he will work day and night with tireless endurance when he has a great deal of work to do. He has no fixed times for going to sleep and waking up. He often stays up all night, and then lies down fully clothed on the sofa at midday and sleeps till evening, untroubled by the whole world coming and going through the room.
>
> (Briggs 1982: 39, 40)[2]

For some readers, the description will cast Marx in an attractive light, making him appear a little wild and larger than life. However, it is easy to see that, to the orderly-minded policeman, Marx's lifestyle must have epitomised the most shocking bohemianism. Also, I think we can take it that he was telling his superiors what they wanted to hear. (Can we really believe the policeman's claim to have known just how infrequently Marx changed his underwear?) The report's unspoken 'subtext' is 'What else could you expect? A man with such disreputable ideas could only have a disreputable lifestyle.' In reality, however, quality of lifestyle and quality of ideas need not go together, hand-in-hand, which means that it is impossible to make an inference from one to another. If Marx was badly behaved on occasions, it doesn't follow that his philosophy is flawed, nor can the same conclusion be drawn from the bad behaviour of self-styled 'Marxist' regimes.

In short, we must not prejudge the issue. It is important to get Marx right, and that is what I shall try to do in this chapter.

What did Marx understand by 'capitalism'?

The meaning of 'capitalism'

One thing everyone knows about Marx is that the greater part of his work is devoted to the critique of the economic system he called 'capitalism', so a good way to begin is by asking precisely what he meant by that. Actually, there is nothing mysterious about it. The system Marx attacks is precisely the system Locke defends in his chapter on property. Of course, things had moved on by the time Marx was writing. In Locke's time, the economy had been largely based on agriculture, whereas, by Marx's, manufacturing had come to play a far more prominent role. That apart, though, the economic system with which both writers are concerned is, in essence, a system which functions through the repeated exercise, by many individuals, of two distinct kinds of property right.

First, there is what Locke conceives to be the property each of us has in his or her own 'person'. As you will recall, Locke holds this right to be 'inalienable'. Marx does not believe in inalienable rights, of course, but there is a parallel within his system, namely the freedom each of us has to buy and sell. Under capitalism, each person is equally free to sell what he or she owns and to buy what he or she can. Even the worker who owns nothing else is free to hire his or her labour (or 'labour-power' as Marx would say) to an employer, for a period, in return for a wage. This is one feature which distinguishes capitalism from feudalism, the system which preceded it historically. Under feudalism, there are gradations of rank – 'feudal lords, vassals, guild-masters, journeymen, apprentices, serfs' (Marx and Engels 2000: 246) – and each status can be defined in terms of the distinct set of rights which goes with it. It is a feature which also distinguishes capitalism from communism, the system Marx believed would eventually come to pass. In a communist system, workers cease to be competing agents in a market for labour – each with a property in his or her own person, and nothing more – but the owners, each in common with the others, of the entire means of production and exchange.

The second type of property right is the right each person has over the items of property he or she owns. This includes the right to 'alienate' a property right in an item by transferring it to someone else. In a capitalist, or 'free market', system, this is normally done by sale, gift, bequest or, as in the case of labour-power, by loaning or hiring it out to someone else for a period. You can think of a pure 'capitalist' system at work as – in essence – the repeated exercise of these rights, over time, by a large number of individuals as they exchange property right for property right; again including property rights each person has in his or her own labour.

I should emphasise two points here. The first is that where a 'pure' capitalist system, thus defined, is at work, the function of the state must be confined to the protection of property. In other words, it must ensure that people observe the rules, and it must do no more than that. (If it did more – for example, if it began to 'redistribute' wealth from the rich to the poor – it would no longer be a pure capitalist system. It is arguable that there are no absolutely 'pure' capitalist systems in the world, although there are, no doubt, some which approximate to the ideal-type.) The second point is that there is nothing about capitalism, as I have characterised it so far, from which you can conclude that there is anything wrong with it.

In fact, by the time Marx was writing, quite a number of philosophers had argued that capitalism has great virtues. Locke was one. As you know, so far as Locke was concerned, the great virtue of the system is that it (supposedly) respects natural rights. More recently than Locke, Adam Smith had advanced a different, consequentialist, defence of capitalism. In *The Wealth of Nations* (Smith 1937), Smith argued that it is only where people are left free to trade, without interference, that the system is guaranteed to work for the greatest advantage of all, even though individuals act from pure self-interest when they trade. In 1776, when *The Wealth of Nations* was first published, it became an immediate bestseller, and the following passage is famous:

> Give me that which I want, and you shall have this which you want, is the meaning of every [such] offer; and it is in this manner that we obtain from one another the far greater part of those good offices which we stand in need of. It is not from the benevolence of the butcher, the brewer, or the baker that we expect our dinner, but from their regard to their own interest.
>
> (Smith 1937: 14)

Later in *The Wealth of Nations*, there is a very well-known passage in which Smith remarks that, within the context of a free market, although every individual 'intends only his own gain', he is *'led by an invisible hand* to promote an end which was no part of his intention' (423). Marx agreed with none of this. To see why not, we need to dig a little deeper.

Emergent features

In the chapter on Locke, I compared the operation of a capitalist, or 'free market' economy with a game of *Monopoly*. The comparison is apt here too. For a start, there is the fact that just as *Monopoly* is definable as a set of rules, so are the private property relationships which prevail under capitalism. In the case of the former, the rules state that each player must begin with an equal supply of *Monopoly* money, an equal number of counters, etc.; that players must take turns at throwing the dice, and so on. Moreover, just as property rules define *rights*, so do the rules of *Monopoly*. For example, in the case of the latter, there is a rule stating, in so many words, that each player only has a right to throw a dice when his or her turn comes round.

There is something else too. As a game of *Monopoly* progresses – with each player observing the rules – the situation of each, relative to the others, begins to change. They may have started out equal but, after time, some will have more (money, houses, hotels, title-deed cards) than others, and some will have been forced to quit the game completely. The situation of inequality which inevitably transpires as a game of *Monopoly* progresses is an example of what I shall call an 'emergent feature'. There are 'emergent features' to the capitalist 'game' as well, features which show up over time as individuals, bound by the rules of private property, trade one with another. It is in such features that we can begin to locate Marx's objections to capitalism. Inequality is just one, and Marx lays special emphasis on the following.

Bourgeoisie and proletariat

'The history of all hitherto existing societies is the history of class struggles', says Marx in *The Communist Manifesto* (Marx and Engels 2000: 245) and, a little later,

> Our epoch, the epoch of the bourgeoisie possesses, [however], this distinctive feature: it has simplified the class antagonisms. Society as a whole is more and more splitting up into two great hostile camps, into two great classes directly facing each other: Bourgeoisie and Proletariat.
>
> (ibid.)

For Marx, the bourgeoisie and the proletariat are distinguished in terms of what they own. The bourgeoisie own property in the form of capital; that is, in order to survive, they can use it to generate wealth for themselves. Capital can take a number of forms – money for lending at a profit, land for renting out – or it can take the form of buildings, machinery, etc., and so used to manufacture commodities for sale at a profit. By contrast, the proletariat own nothing but their own labour. If the proletarian is to survive, he or she must work for a (bourgeois) capitalist in return for a wage. Of course, Marx was not so naive that he thought that every single person must neatly fall into one or the other of these two categories. On the contrary, so far as Marx was concerned, the distinction between bourgeoisie and proletariat had a particular significance because it was the inevitable conflict of interest between the two which was driving history. As he says in the passage, they are 'two great hostile camps'. As he saw it, sooner or later there would be a revolution, with the proletariat seizing the property of the bourgeoisie, and instituting a new era (the 'dictatorship of the proletariat').

The division of labour

The phrase 'the division of labour' originated with Adam Smith, the first chapter of whose *The Wealth of Nations* is entitled 'Of the Division of Labour' (Smith 1937). In it, Smith compares the time it would take one man to make a pin all by himself, with the time it would take to make one in a factory, where the task is divided into a number of operations, each performed by a different worker. This is what happens in the factory:

> One man draws out the wire, another straights it, a third cuts it, a fourth points it, a fifth grinds it at the top for receiving the head; to make the head requires three distinct operations; to put it on is a peculiar business, to whiten the pins is another; it is even a trade by itself to put them into the paper; and the important business of making a pin is, in this manner, divided into about eighteen distinct

operations, which, in some manufactories, are all performed by distinct hands, though in others the same man will sometimes perform two or three of them.

(ibid.: 4)

According to Smith, the division of labour has a number of advantages; workers become more skilled through concentrating on a single task; the time it would take moving from one task to another is saved; and – most of all – it becomes possible to use machinery. (By the way, just in case you are puzzled by the passage, by 'pins' Smith means large flat-headed nails, and not the type of pins used in sewing.) Smith estimates that, in a typical factory, with the division of labour ten persons 'could, when they exerted themselves, make among them about twelve pounds of pins a day'. That's about 48,000 pins. 'Each person, therefore making a tenth part of forty eight thousand pins, might be considered as making four thousand eight hundred pins in a day.' Compare this with the fact that, 'by himself, and without the division of labour, a workman, could scarce, perhaps, with his utmost industry, make one pin a day, and certainly could not make twenty' (ibid.). In Smith's opinion the division of labour has brought about the greatest increase in the productive powers of labour ever, and his sole aim is to illustrate the point. Now compare the foregoing passage with the following lines from *The Communist Manifesto*:

> Owing to the extensive use of machinery and to division of labour, the work of the proletarians has lost all individual character, and, consequently, all charm for the workman. He becomes an appendage of the machine, and it is only the most simple, most monotonous, and most easily acquired knack, that is required of him.
>
> (Marx and Engels 2000: 251)[3]

Smith and Marx describe the same phenomenon, but from completely different perspectives.

Market forces

To say that 'market forces predominate' in a capitalist economy is to use a modern expression. It is not an expression Marx himself would have used. Nevertheless, it is quite clearly what he had in mind. As Marx sees it, competition is all pervading. Capitalists must compete with other capitalists if they are to remain in business as capitalists. Workers must compete with other workers if they are to survive. It is competition which inevitably gives rise to the other phenomena just listed – the increasing polarisation of bourgeoisie and proletariat, and the increasing division of labour.

From description to critique

But then what is wrong with all *that*? So far, I have described capitalism as a free market system based on the private ownership of property, and I have pointed out that its operation must inevitably result in the existence of two major classes, an increase in the division of labour, and the pre-dominance of market forces. This is a description which the most outright defender of capitalism can accept. Typically, defenders of capitalism will argue that an economic system within which market forces prevail is far more productive – and far more efficient at satisfying people's wants – than any other system. They will argue that the existence of two major classes – bourgeoisie and proletariat – is only to be expected, and that there is nothing at all objectionable about it, and that, likewise, the division of labour is only to be expected. It's just a price you pay for efficiency.

It follows that, if we are to move from 'value-neutral' description to critique – that is, if we are to understand what Marx thought was wrong with capitalism – we must look deeper still. You won't be surprised to learn that, in Marx's view, there were plenty of things wrong with capitalism. Amongst other things, he believed that one consequence of capitalism is 'alienation'. He also believed that, under capitalism, the worker produces 'surplus value' which the capitalist pockets. These are specifically Marxian objections to capitalism, and we shall consider them in the following section. Before that, let me just mention two familiar objections. Both are frequently raised by socialists and others although the first is not – I think – an objection Marx would have raised himself. The second is.

According to the first objection, the inequality which inevitably results from the operation of a free market, capitalist, system is, in itself, objectionable. Such inequality is 'unfair', or 'unjust', or so the objection runs. (I haven't attributed this objection to anyone in particular, but I am sure readers will recognise it as something one often hears said.) To this, defenders of capitalism are apt to reply that there is nothing especially objectionable about inequality itself. Perhaps they will add that complaints about inequality are sometimes nothing more than expressions of envy. They will argue that, where there are inequalities, this can sometimes mean that even the worst off people are better off than they would otherwise be, and that, in such cases, inequality is a good thing. Sometimes they will add that it is, in any case, impossible to formulate a coherent definition of 'social justice'. (Again, I haven't attributed such arguments to anyone in particular, although you will find all these points made in, for example, F.A. Hayek's *The Mirage of Social Justice* (1982). If you want my opinion, they are mistaken arguments, but that's another story.)[4]

Marx's response to the objection would have been different, but equally contemptuous. So far as he is concerned, it is not that objections along such lines get capitalism wrong (they don't) but that they concede far too much to the opposing case. By way of illustration, take his *Critique of the Gotha Programme* (2000h). The *Gotha Programme* was a joint manifesto drawn up by the leaders of Germany's main socialist parties at a meeting in the German town of Gotha, held in 1875. The *Critique* is composed from the angry notes Marx scribbled in the margin.[5] At one point, the programme states that 'the emancipation of labour' demands, amongst other things, 'a fair distribution of the proceeds of labour' (so this is a version of the objection under discussion). This prompts Marx to raise some rhetorical questions. 'What is "fair" distribution?', he asks, and 'Do not the bourgeois assert that present-day distribution is "fair"? And is it not, in fact, the only "fair distribution" on the basis of the present-day mode of production?' (2000h: 612). However he comments later that it is hardly surprising that the *Gotha Programme*'s authors should have made such a remark, because after all we are dealing with a communist society 'as it is when it has just emerged after prolonged birth-pangs from capitalist society' (2000h: 615). That is why 'equal right here is still in principle – bourgeois right' (ibid.: 614). As Marx goes on to explain,

> this equal right is still constantly stigmatised by a bourgeois limitation. The right of the producers is proportional to the labour they supply; the equality consists in the fact that measurement is made with an equal standard, labour.
>
> But one man is superior to another physically or mentally and so supplies more labour in the same time, or can labour for a longer time; and labour, to serve as a measure, must be defined by its duration or intensity, otherwise it ceases to be a standard of measurement. This equal right is an unequal right for unequal labour. It recognises no class differences, because everyone is only a worker like everyone else; but it tacitly recognises unequal individual endowment and thus productive capacity as natural privileges. It is, therefore, a right of inequality, in its content, like every right.
>
> (ibid.)

But if Marx is right, isn't it just inevitable – under *any* system – that treating people as equals according to one criterion of equality means treating them as unequals according to another (as when paying people equally for equal hours worked means ignoring the fact that some are stronger or more capable than others)? Marx thinks not. As he goes on to say:

> In a higher phase of communist society, after the enslaving subordination of the individual to the division of labour, and therewith also the antithesis between mental and physical labour, has vanished; after labour has become not only a means to life but life's prime want; after the productive forces have also increased with the all

217

round development of the individual, and all the springs of co-operative wealth flow more abundantly – only then can the narrow horizon of bourgeois right be crossed in its entirety and society inscribe on its banners: from each according to his ability, to each according to his needs!

(ibid.)

These are well-known passages, and they illustrate at least three features of Marx's approach to philosophy. The first is that he regarded one of the traditional problems of political philosophy as a non-problem. This is the problem of formulating a principle for the distribution of resources in a way which is just and fair. You can think of Locke's defence of property and the principle of utility as, each in their own way, attempts to solve this difficulty. (The same goes for John Rawls' second principle of justice, which is discussed in the following chapter.) For example, if the utilit-arians are right, then the fairest distribution is the one which most serves to produce the greatest happiness. However, this is only a problem where resources are scarce, even if they are only a little scarce. Why worry other-wise? Where there is plenty of air to go around, we do not seek a principle for the fair distribution of air. As Rawls was to say, later than Marx, questions of justice arise only where there is 'moderate scarcity' (Rawls 1972: 127ff). But so far as Marx was concerned, such scarcity is bourgeois scarcity. For him, the problem is not to formulate a principle of just distribution, but to overcome the conditions which make it necessary.

So, the second feature of Marx's philosophy illustrated by these pas-sages is that, like many a Victorian, he was an optimist when it came to the possibilities latent in new technology. In his view, scarcity arises under capitalism not because it is inevitable but because production is, in a sense, organised irrationally. Machines are our masters when they ought to be our slaves. As the passages show, Marx thinks that once communist society has reached 'a higher phase', 'productive forces' will increase and 'all the springs of co-operative wealth [will] flow more abundantly'. Thirdly, then, they illustrate my point that Marx did not accept at least one familiar objection to capitalism.

However, there is another such objection for which Marx would have had more time. According to this capitalism is detrimental to *freedom*, especially the freedom of the proletariat. The point can be argued in a number of ways. Marx himself would frequently point out that the situ-ations of the slave and the proletarian are materially equivalent. It is true that each differs from the other in legal status – the slave is owned as property whereas the proletarian is a free agent in the labour market – but for all the difference it makes to the proletarian's conditions of life, the two might as well be equivalent.[6] Again, it can be argued that because the proletarian works such long hours for little more than a subsistence wage – as Marx thought all proletarians must – there is very little he or she is free to do. (Marx would no doubt agree with this, although it is not the point he was especially concerned to make.) Moreover, it can be argued that the power relationship between capitalist and worker is 'coercive'. Marx would certainly agree. As he puts it, the worker's labour is 'not voluntary but compulsory, forced labour' (2000a: 88).

Within contemporary 'analytic' philosophy defenders of capitalism have tended to respond to such points by suggesting that they rest on a misinterpretation of the concepts of freedom and coercion. For example, a great deal has been made of Sir Isaiah Berlin's insistence, in his 'Two Concepts of Liberty', that a mere inability to do something does not necessarily count as a lack of freedom to do it. According to Berlin, 'If I say that I am unable to jump more than ten feet in the air . . . it would be eccentric to say that I am to that degree enslaved or coerced' (Berlin 1969: 122). Berlin may or may not be right to claim that it is a mistake to think of gravitational force as something essentially freedom restricting, but his implication is that the same (therefore) goes for a market force. As he goes on to say, 'It is argued, very plausibly, that if a man is too poor to afford something on which there is no legal ban' – for example, a loaf of bread – 'he is as little free to have it as he would be if it were forbidden him by law' but 'if my poverty were a kind of disease, which prevented me from buying bread . . . as lameness prevents me from running, this inability would not naturally be described as a lack of freedom' (ibid.). Clearly, if Berlin's suggestion is right, it is false that the proletarian's long working hours and low pay add up to a deprivation of liberty. Again, it has been argued – most notably by Robert Nozick – the simply being 'forced' (by circumstances) to choose from a range of highly unattractive alternatives is not equivalent to being coerced into choosing. If you have to choose between marrying someone unattractive and staying single you are not coerced (says Nozick) and, likewise, the labour of the proletarian faced with a choice between an unattractive job and starving is not (as Marx thought) coerced. Needless to say, other contemporary philosophers have contested such arguments.[7]

It is very important to get these arguments right, if only because capitalism is still with us in a big way. Getting the philosophical arguments right is part of what you have to do if you are to understand capitalism. Even so, I shan't pursue them further because they are not Marx's arguments, or not especially. As I have indicated, he would have gone along with some, though not others, but his central case against capitalism is different from these. In many ways, it runs more deeply.

Production

If we are to understand human nature, human history and a great deal else besides, it is first of all crucial to understand the role played by the activity of production, or so Marx thought. The following passage shows just how crucial he thought it was.

> The practical creation of an objective world, the working-over of inorganic nature, is the confirmation of man as a conscious species-being, that is, as a being that relates to the species as to himself and to himself as to the species. It is true that the animal, too, produces. It builds itself a nest, a dwelling, like the bee, the beaver, the ant, etc. But it only produces what it needs immediately for itself or its off-spring; it produces one-sidedly whereas man produces universally; it produces only under the pressure of immediate physical need, whereas man produces freely from physical need and only truly produces when he is thus free; it produces only itself whereas man reproduces the whole of nature. Its produce belongs immediately to its physical body whereas man can freely separate himself from his product. The animal only fashions things after the standards and needs of the species it belongs to, whereas man knows how to produce according to the measure of every species and knows everywhere how to apply its inherent standard to the object; thus man also fashions things according to the laws of beauty.
>
> (Marx 2000a: 90–1)

You will find the passage in one of Marx's earlier works, an essay entitled 'Alienated Labour'. It is one of the *Economic and Philosophical Manuscripts* of 1844, which represent the earliest draft of the project which was eventually to be developed by Marx and published as *Capital.* There are several characteristically Marxian theses at work within the passage[8] but, if we are to get to the heart of Marx's philosophy, it is the following three we need to grasp.

Producing animals

Clearly, it is Marx's view that the feature which distinguishes humans most sharply from other animals is the fact that we produce. We labour and, with our efforts, we transform nature. Equally clearly, there are echoes of Locke here. Like Locke, Marx thinks that if we are to survive we have to labour to make nature usable. But there is more to it than that. Marx thinks that production is so fundamental that it permeates and conditions every aspect of our being. (This is not true of animals. Even those who do produce work in limited and routine ways.) So, just as Aristotle defined 'man' as 'by nature a political animal' (Aristotle 1981: 1253a1) – meaning that we are creatures who 'by nature' inhabit a *polis* (a city-state) – you could say that Marx defines the human as a 'producing animal', the fact is so crucial to the understanding of the type of creatures we are.

To this, I think it is worth adding that Marx is, surely, right. At least, his contention that we are, fundamentally, producing animals is borne out by some fairly obvious biological facts with a good evolutionary explanation. Any zoologist will tell you that the physiological features which distinguish *homo sapiens* most sharply from other animals are bipedality (having two feet), a voluminous brain (relative to body size), and an opposable thumb. There is a relationship between these features: Each is explained by the fact that, as a species, we are adaptive creatures. There is no specific environmental niche to which we have become peculiarly fitted by evolution. On the contrary, we survive by adapting the way we live to a wide range of environmental conditions, and we can do this because we are intelligent and because we are tool users. It is the relatively large brain which explains our intelligence (relative to other species), but it is the bipedality which leaves our arms free to manipulate tools and the opposable thumb which enables us to grip them. It follows that Marx's definition is by no means arbitrary.

There is something else too. Humans differ from other animals in that, for humans, production is '[T]he practical creation of an objective world' (2000a: 90). As Marx goes on to say in the following paragraph, 'he [man] duplicates himself not only intellectually, in his mind, but also actively in reality and thus can look at his image in a world he has created' (ibid.: 91). This is undoubtedly true also. For every generation of humans the world is different, thanks to the way the previous generation has changed it. In this sense, we do produce a world in our own image, and this is not so in the case of any other animal. As Marx thinks, this yields a further reason for treating production as fundamental (the next on my list) for it means that it is production which supplies history with its dynamic.

Production and history

Roughly speaking, the argument runs as follows. First, humans are creatures to whom the activity of production is fundamental. To this it has to be added – just in case it isn't obvious – that we are creatures who, for the most part, produce by working together, not in isolation. (If each person, working in isolation, were able to produce enough to satisfy his or her own needs, history would have been very different.) Second, as we work, we constantly transform the world. As Marx puts it, 'man' duplicates himself 'actively in reality and thus can look at his image in a world he has created' (ibid.: 91). However, the fact that we transform the world by our efforts does not mean that we change it in ways we intend or like. There are such things as 'unintended consequences', and, as production is carried on over generations, patterns emerge which no one can have wanted or deliberately planned. As Marx puts it, 'In the social production of their life, men enter into definite relations that are indispensable and independent of their will' (2000d: 425). What are these relations? Well, as you would expect, the relations on which Marx focuses are what he calls 'relations of production'. According to Marx, the sum total of these relations 'constitutes the economic structure of society'.

The much-quoted passage in which these lines occur is such a clear representation of Marx's position that I may as well present it to you more fully. Marx describes it as 'The general result at which I arrived and which once won, served as a guiding thread for my studies', and he says:

> In the social production of their life, men enter into definite relations that are indispensable and independent of their will, relations of production which correspond to a definite stage of development of their material productive forces. The sum total of these relations of production constitutes the economic structure of society, the real foundation, on which rises a legal and political superstructure and to which correspond definite forms of social consciousness. The mode of production of material life conditions the social, political, and intellectual life process in general. It is not the consciousness of men that determines their being, but, on the contrary, their social being that determines their consciousness.
>
> (ibid.)

Note the distinction Marx draws between economic 'foundation' and ideological 'superstructure'. (It is one reason why the passage is so frequently quoted.) Whereas the former is said by Marx to consist of the 'sum total of [these] relations of production' and to constitute 'the economic structure of society', the latter is said to be 'legal and political' in its nature and to manifest itself in 'definite forms of social consciousness'. Moreover, it is in terms of relevant aspects of the foundation that aspects of the superstructure have to be *explained*. (In the passage, Marx uses the terms 'condition', correspond' and 'determine' – although he is certainly no simple-minded 'causal determinist'.)

This is one of those points on which critics of Marx have tended to focus. The question: Can the distinction between foundation (or 'base') and superstructure be coherently drawn? If it can't, then his 'materialistic' account of historical change fails – or so one type of objection runs. Naturally enough, defenders of Marx have been unimpressed by this type of charge, and for various reasons. It would be beyond the scope of this present book to enter into the controversy (which is fortunate for me, I think). Moreover, even if the foundation/superstructure distinction can be drawn coherently, there remains the question of *precisely how* the foundation is meant to 'condition' or 'determine' the superstructure. That is another question which, having 'flagged' its existence, I can leave you, the reader, to follow up.

The passage makes one thing very clear. It is Marx's view that the fundamental determinants of historical and social change are economic. It is the economic structure of society by which the superstructure is conditioned. And what of the relations of production (including property relations) which go to make up that? Well, as Marx says, these 'correspond to a definite stage of development of their material productive forces' (ibid.). The remark is clearly related to something Marx says elsewhere (though with a degree of simplification), namely that 'The hand-mill gives you society with the feudal lord; the steam-mill society with the industrial capitalist' (2000c: 219–20). So, wherever you may get after picking at details, Marx's central idea is quite apparent. It is just this: With economic 'advance' – that is, with the development of manufacturing, the expansion of markets, and so on – you get corresponding changes in the economic structure; that is, in the prevailing set of relations of production, including property relations. With the latter you get, in turn, corresponding superstructural changes.

As Marx saw it, capitalism was itself a part of the process, a manifest-ation of the dynamic at work at a particular point in its progression. (It is one of the features which made Marx's contribution to the critique of political economy so distinctive. Others had concentrated upon dynamic processes at work, but only within capitalism, not on the 'outside' forces which brought it into being. Adam Smith's 'invisible hand' thesis is a good example.) It was Marx's belief that, with developments in the economic foundation history had moved in a particular direction. 'In broad out-lines', he wrote, 'Asiatic, ancient, feudal, and modern bourgeois modes of production can be designated as progressive epochs in the economic for-mation of society' (2000d: 426). In his writings, however, he tended to concentrate on the transition from feudalism to capitalism. (See, for example, the account he gives in *The Communist Manifesto* (Marx and Engels 2000).) As for the future, in his predictions Marx tended to emphasise what (as he believed) was about to happen next. For example, in the *Preface to 'A Critique of Political Economy'*, after distinguishing foundation from superstructure (in the passage under discussion), Marx goes on to say this:

> At a certain stage of their development, the material productive forces of society come in contact with the existing relations of pro-duction, or – what is but a legal expression for the same thing – with the property relations within which they have been at work hitherto. From forms of development of the productive forces these relations turn into their fetters. Then begins an epoch of social revolution. With the change of the economic foundations the entire immense superstructure is more or less rapidly transformed.
>
> (2000d: 425)

That is one of Marx's many predictions of revolution. Afterwards – what? Well, if the proletariat is to 'wrest, by degrees, all capital from the bour-geoisie, to centralise all production in the hands of the state', and so on, it will inevitably have to make 'despotic inroads' on the prevailing property rights and conditions of production (Marx and Engels 2000: 261). Only a 'dictatorship of the proletariat' can follow the revolution. But eventually, when 'all production has been concentrated in the hands of associated individuals, the public power will lose its political character', and 'In place of the old bourgeois society, with its classes and class antagonisms, we shall have an association, in which the free development of each is a condition for the free development of all' (ibid.: 262).

Production and human flourishing

Yet a third characteristically Marxian thesis concerns (what you could call) the 'appropriateness' or otherwise of the relationships which hold between humans and various aspects of production. In the passage under discussion – that is, the passage from the *1844 Manuscripts* with which I opened this section on production (p. 220) – this manifests itself in Marx's remarks that 'man produces freely from physical need and only truly produces when he is thus free' and that man 'knows everywhere how to apply its inherent standard to the object' so that 'man also fashions things according to the laws of beauty' (2000a: 90–1). In the immediately preceding paragraph Marx uses the expression 'conscious vital activity'. According to him, it is this which 'differentiates man immediately from animal vital activity', and he adds: 'It is this and this alone that makes man a species-being.'

To readers unfamiliar with the terminology Marx employs here – i.e. most readers – his meaning will not be immediately transparent. (It is a terminology which derives from Hegel and from his 'Young Hegelian' followers, most notably Ludwig Feuerbach, by whom the young Marx was heavily influenced.) However, to anyone who reads Marx more extensively his meaning will, I think, become clear enough. For Marx, an appropriate relationship holds between a person and the thing he or she produces – the 'object' of production as he calls the latter – when, for example, that thing satisfies a genuine need or purpose (or as he sometimes puts it, when it has 'use value'). Such a relationship also holds when a thing is produced to satisfy aesthetic standards, fashioned 'according to the laws of beauty'. There can also be appropriate relationships between producers and the act of production itself. These hold when the production is a 'free' and a 'conscious vital activity'. (As Marx was to say in a later piece, 'Really free labour, the composing of music for example, is at the same time damned serious and demands the greatest effort' (2000f: 403).) Thirdly, a producer can be related to his or her fellow producers in appropriate or inappropriate ways. '[Thus] it is in the working over of the objective world that man first really affirms himself as a species-being' says Marx (2000a: 91).

I have been using the rather inadequate term 'appropriate' to try to capture Marx's view. I'm afraid it is the best I can think of. One reason for its inadequacy is that it fails to capture the fact that Marx is concerned with what you could call 'human flourishing'. I have already drawn one comparison between Marx and Aristotle in this chapter, namely that both fix upon a particular feature of human nature and treat it as fundamental. For Aristotle 'man' is 'by nature a political animal' (Aristotle 1981: I, 2, 59) – that is, a member of a *polis* – and for Marx 'man' is a 'producing animal'. Two further parallels are useful here. The first is that, for both philosophers, there is a particular environment in which – human nature being what it is – people 'do well' as humans, or flourish. For Aristotle, it is the *polis*. For Marx, it is the environment in which 'appropriate' relationships hold between producers and various aspects of production. The second is that, according to both, a life lived outside the 'best' environment is compromised and degraded. As Aristotle sees it, a man without a city is like an isolated piece in a game of draughts. As Marx sees it, the labour of the proletarian, under capitalism, is inevitably 'alienated labour'.

Alienated labour

What does Marx mean by 'alienation'?

You can't really summarise the meaning Marx attaches to 'alienation' in a brief definition or a simple formula. Far better to let him speak for himself, so let us take a fairly lengthy passage from his 1844 essay 'Alienated Labour', the passage in which he describes the worker's alienation in relation to the 'object' of production (i.e. the commodities the worker produces). 'We start with a contemporary fact of political economy', writes Marx, namely that 'The worker becomes poorer the richer is his production, the more it increases in power and scope. The worker becomes a commodity that is all the cheaper the more commodities he creates.' Then:

> What this fact expresses is merely this: the object that labour produces, its product, confronts it as an alien being, as a power independent of the producer. The product of labour is labour that has solidified itself into an object, made itself into a thing, the objectification of labour. The realisation of labour is its objectification. In political economy this realisation of labour appears as a loss of reality for the worker, objectification as a loss of the object or slavery to it, and appropriation as alienation, as externalisation.
>
> The realisation of labour appears as a loss of reality to an extent that the worker loses his reality by dying of starvation. Objectification appears as a loss of the object to such an extent that the worker is robbed not only of the objects necessary for his life but also of the objects of his work. Indeed, labour itself becomes an object he can only have in his power with the greatest of efforts and at irregular intervals. The appropriation of the object appears as alienation to

such an extent that the more objects the worker produces, the less he can possess and the more he falls under the domination of his product, capital.

(2000a: 86–7)

In the passage, Marx is describing how capitalism, in its normal operation, works to distort and degrade the relationship between the worker and the object the worker produces. Remember the 'emergent features' I listed earlier. One was the fact that, within a capitalist system, market forces predominate to the extent that competition becomes all pervasive. Capitalists compete amongst themselves to sell commodities, and – likewise – there is a labour market within which workers compete with each other. It is, quite clearly, Marx's belief that the latter can only culminate in the systematic impoverishment of the worker, as labour becomes increasingly casualised and wages decrease progressively towards subsistence level. As he says, 'The worker becomes a commodity that is all the cheaper', and 'labour itself becomes an object he can only have in his power with the greatest of efforts and at irregular intervals'. The process is exacerbated by the fact that competition between capitalists forces them more and more to introduce productive techniques which rely upon the division of labour (another of the emergent features I listed). As a result, the type of labour required becomes less skilled and more routine. Therefore it will command a lower price on the labour market.

Then again, there is the question of *what* it is that the worker produces. Where capitalism holds sway, the answer has to be *commodities*; that is, objects (or services) the capitalist can market. Does it matter what those commodities are – spark-plugs, triangles of processed cheese, cans of deodorant, parts for nuclear missiles, or whatever? No, it does not. Given the 'logic' of the system then, from the worker's point of view, all that matters is that he or she can successfully market his or her labour. (Of course, it also means that, for the capitalist, all that matters is that he can find a commodity to market.) This means that the desirable, or 'appropriate', relation between worker and object is broken. Rather than create objects directly for their 'use value', the worker creates commodities for the capitalist, for whom their prime value is realised as 'exchange value'. Moreover, given the power relationship between capitalist and worker (a further emergent property) this also means, as Marx says, that the 'object' of labour 'confronts' labour itself 'as an alien being, as a power independent of the producer'. In *The Essence of Christianity*, Ludwig Feuerbach had argued that the Christian idea of God is, in fact, a projection of our unrealised ideals. Unlike us, God is almighty, merciful and loving, and he inhabits a world in which – unlike our own – immortality can be achieved. It is a way of compensating for our inadequacies which inhibits practical attempts to deal with them here on earth (Feuerbach 1989). Marx expresses a similar idea, only in his case it is the commodity which does the work of God. 'It is just the same in religion', he writes, 'The more man puts into God, the less he retains in himself. The worker puts his life into the object, and this means that it no longer belongs to him, but to the object' (2000a: 87).

A page or so later, Marx turns from the object of production to alienation (or 'externalisation') in the act of production itself. He writes:

What does the externalisation of labour consist of then?

Firstly, that labour is exterior to the worker, that is, it does not belong to his essence. Therefore he does not confirm himself in his work, he denies himself, feels miserable instead of happy, deploys no free physical and intellectual energy, but mortifies his body and ruins his mind. Thus the worker only feels a stranger. He is at home when he is not working and when he works he is not at home. His labour is therefore not voluntary but compulsory, forced labour.

(ibid.: 88)

And so on. Here, too, the workings of capitalism are portrayed as distorting the relationship which ought to hold between the worker and work itself. (The worker 'does not confirm himself in his work, he denies himself'.) Also, there is a similar reference to religion:

As in religion the human imagination's own activity, the activity of man's head and his heart, reacts independently on the individual as an alien activity of gods or devils, so the activity of the worker is not his own spontaneous activity. It belongs to another and is the loss of himself.

(ibid.: 89)

As we have seen, Marx thinks that 'it is in the working over of the objective world that man first really affirms himself as a species being' (i.e. a being whose nature it is to produce) (ibid.: 91). A line or so later, he remarks that 'alienated labour degrades man's own free activity to a means, it turns the species life of man into a means for his physical existence'. And then, of course, there is the fact that an 'immediate consequence' of all this is 'the alienation of man from man' (ibid.).

Is it true?

Marx paints a powerful and compelling portrait of the plight of the worker under capitalism, but is he doing anything more than that? If Marx's alienation thesis is really just a portrait, drawn from a certain perspective, then we must treat it as no more authoritative than that. On the other hand, if we are to take it seriously as philosophy, we must ask: Is it really true that workers under capitalism suffer alienation, in Marx's sense of the term? (I won't be discussing other uses of the word 'alienation' here.)

If I were asked to make out a case against Marx, then I would concentrate on the fact that the concept of alienation has both structural and psychological elements. What I mean is this: First, in the passages I have been quoting, the alienation of the worker is quite clearly defined in terms of the relationships which hold between the worker and various features of the capitalist system itself: the relationship of the worker to the object of production; the relationship to the act of production; the relationship between bourgeois and proletarian from which these inevitably flow; and so on.

Secondly, though, Marx defines alienation in terms of the worker's state of mind. Sometimes he does so directly, for example when he states that the worker 'does not confirm himself in his work, he denies himself, feels miserable instead of happy' (2000a: 88). Sometimes he does so by implication, for example when he writes that 'The realisation of labour appears as a loss of reality to an extent that the worker loses his reality by dying of starvation' (ibid.: 86). (No one can feel good when starving to death.)

Clearly, this raises the question of what happens to the concept of alienation if we prise the structural and the psychological elements apart. For example, suppose that capitalism is working quite well. The system is based on private property, there are owners and workers, there is a free market in commodities and another in labour, and so on; but suppose that the workers are neither impoverished nor unhappy. Of course, this is the scenario envisaged by enthusiasts for capitalism who believe that Adam Smith's 'invisible hand' will, if left to itself, ensure that everyone's needs and wants are met. However, you don't have to be such an enthusiast to agree that there can be times when the workings of a free market do not result in the impoverishment and misery of the working class. For example, it can be argued – quite plausibly I am sure – that since the end of World War II the economic history of Western countries has, to a great extent, been the outcome of compromises struck between powerful working class movements and equally powerful governments. (It is because it has been 'bought off' in this way that Marx's predicted revolution has never happened, or so it can be argued.) As a result of such a process you get workers who – if not entirely happy – are at least not massively discontented either. Or, if not that, just suppose that capitalism is undergoing a periodic boom, with the result that the workers in certain industries can negotiate good wages and conditions for themselves.

In short, suppose that you have both capitalism and a happy, or at least a contented, workforce. Just to flesh it out, suppose – if you like – that you are a researcher in industrial psychology. You visit a factory and you ask a group of production line workers to complete a questionnaire. The work is routine and, in itself, boring. However, the workers tell you that they enjoy the factory atmosphere, they welcome the chance to meet their friends and exchange gossip (plus there is MTV, a drinks machine, good coffee, and so on). Does it follow from Marx's argument that these workers are no longer alienated?

So far as I can see, the question places him in something of a dilemma. On the one hand, if Marx were to reply that, being happy, they are not alienated, this would mean jettisoning the structural components of his account, for these workers could still be producing commodities with no 'use value', they would still be creating a world of commodities which 'confronts' them 'as a power independent of the producer', and so on. In fact, jettisoning these components would seem to mean jettisoning the very idea that capitalism generates alienation. That apart, there is something quite facile about the idea that simply making workers happy means ending alienation. 'Happy workers' could be happy because they are on drugs, and a Marxist could argue that such workers are prey to 'false consciousness', the inability to appreciate the true nature of their situation. On the other hand, if Marx were to reply that happy workers remain alienated nevertheless, this would invite the question *so what*? If workers are happy, it is difficult to see why it should matter that their relationship to their work, to the things they produce, and so on, is not as Marx thinks it should be. (Any Marxist taking this line would be exposed to the objection that he or she is simply expressing a condescending 'bourgeois' prejudice that work should be 'meaningful'.)

Having said that, let me now add that, so far as I can see, the foregoing objection to Marx is right, but only up to a point. It is true, I am sure, that the presence of both structural and psychological elements in his account of alienation creates difficulties for him, but I also feel that the objection fails to capture the spirit of Marx's argument, and that it misses its mark as a consequence. In that way, it is quite typical of many of the arguments which tend to be directed against Marx, not just to his account of alienation, but to other parts of his philosophy. Now, it is not my intention to make out an anti-Marxist case here. Rather, because this is meant to be an introduction to the subject, what I should try to do is set out the parameters; that is, to give you an idea of how such a case could be made and how it could be answered. So, with that in mind, let us now consider how a Marxist might try to answer the objection I have just raised.

Well, for a start, the Marxist could try to take the objection on its own terms; that is, he or she could try to show that there is, in fact, no real tension between the structural and psychological elements in Marx's account of alienation. Since I have no idea how such a counter-argument would go, I shan't consider this possibility. But there is something else the Marxist might do, and that is counter the objection with a charge which is quite frequently raised against Marx himself, the charge of psychological naivety. It is sometimes said that Marx's anticipation of a future communist society – 'an association, in which the free development of each is a condition for the free development of all' (Marx and Engels 2000: 262) – is psychologically naive, because people are insufficiently altruistic to satisfy the demands which life in such an association would place on them. However, it seems to me that the same charge could be made with equal justification (perhaps more) against my suggestion that people doing routine and boring work could, at the same time, be happy. Just how realistic is this supposition, really? Perhaps it's true that all of them could be happy for some of the time, even that some of them could be happy for all of the time, but the supposition that the majority of them could be happy for the greater part of the time could well be a fantasy. If this is right, my objection still stands but – because it lacks point except where an unrealistic supposition is made – it has no teeth.

That is the sort of consideration which applies to a great many objections to Marx's argument – or so it seems to me. You can pick away at the details, but fail to grasp the seriousness of the points lying at the heart of his moral vision. Of course, *no* philosopher writing now would attempt to frame a moral vision in the sort of neo-Hegelian terms used by Marx. However, in Marx's case we should not let the difficulties inherent in the latter blind us to the former.

Surplus value: exploitation

I have focused on Marx's thesis that, within a capitalist economy, the labour of the proletarian is alienated because it takes us right to the heart of his world view. The particular manuscript upon which I have been concentrating, 'Alienated Labour' (2000a: 85–94), is one of Marx's earlier works. However, alienation is a theme which recurs throughout his writings, and there are discussions of alienated labour in *Capital*, the first volume of which was published much later, in 1867 (2000g). It is also a theme which, once grasped, casts light upon certain otherwise puzzling aspects of Marx's philosophy. For example, Marx's writings contain no detailed or specific description of future communist society. Exactly what does he think it will be like? One thing a reading of his work does make clear, though, is that Marx is anticipating a time when alienation will have ended. Communist society will be 'the only society in which the original and free development of individuals ceases to be a mere phrase' (2000b: 207). The 'enslaving subordination of the individual to the division of labour, and therewith also the antithesis between mental and physical labour [will have] vanished' (2000h: 615).

However, there is more to Marx's philosophy than the alienation thesis – much more – and it would be remiss of me not to give some sort of account of certain other characteristically Marxian themes. Unfortunately, if I were to deal with them in the same detail as I have alienation, I would end up by writing a book on Marx – and that is very far from my intention. Instead, I shall offer a few observations on just two other Marxian theses, the 'theory of surplus value' as it is sometimes called, and in this chapter's concluding section, the idea that history develops in a certain direction.

Very briefly, then, the 'theory of surplus value' is founded on the premise that labour is a commodity. The labourer's wage is, thus, the price the capitalist is prepared to pay for labour. To put it another way, the wage represents the 'exchange value' of labour. From this it follows, or so Marx thinks, that the wages will tend to gravitate to subsistence; that is, the level required to maintain the proletariat in existence as a class, and nothing more. And, indeed, this would follow if, as is often the case, there is a free market in labour within which supply exceeds demand. The argument then goes on to point out that the worker creates 'surplus value', as demonstrated by the fact that the capitalist is able to make a profit from the sale of the commodities the worker produces. In short, the claim is that, under capitalism, the worker creates surplus value which goes, not to the worker, but to the capitalist. The worker is, thus, *exploited.*

Although the foregoing summary may be brief – and although it omits the technicalities Marx frequently introduces into his discussion – I do not believe that it represents an oversimplification of his view. So, notice first that – stated thus baldly – the surplus value thesis appears exposed to a fairly obvious objection. This states that that there are, in fact, only two values at work in Marx's scenario, and that both are exchange values. There is, first, the exchange value of the labour (or 'labour-power') the capitalist employs to manufacture commodities. Secondly, there is the exchange value of the commodities he sells, i.e. the price he gets for it. And – as the objection insists – *that is all there is to it.* All Marx has done is describe a fairly evident feature of the capitalist economy at work, but, or so it continues, he has failed to convince us that there is anything wrong with what goes on (apart from the fact that the worker is paid at subsistence level, that is). The surplus value argument suggests that the capitalist is, in a sense, stealing from the worker. So, either the surplus value argument is suggesting, quite simply, that the profit which goes to the capitalist should in fact go to the worker, or it is suggesting that there is some ghostly third value – a 'surplus value' – something which is not an exchange value, which is created by the worker, but which is expropriated by the capitalist. If the former, then we need a *further* explanation of why it is that making a profit should count as theft, or so the objection holds. (Why isn't Marx just expressing a prejudice?) If the latter, we need to know precisely what it is that the capitalist is supposed to steal.

Well, in part, Marx could answer this type of objection with his 'labour theory of value', according to which the value of a product is a function of the amount of labour which has gone into producing it. From this, it would follow that the value created by the worker is, indeed, a function of the worker's labour, his or her *own* labour. If this is right, then it clearly follows that the capitalist is stealing from the worker. However, I would not want to rest a defence of Marx upon a labour theory of value alone, if only because there are few contemporary thinkers, including Marxists, who would take this type of theory seriously. Moreover, there seems to be more to Marx's view than that. For example, in *Wage Labour and Capital*, he gives the following account of what happens when a capitalist, having paid a worker – in this case a weaver – from previously accumulated stock, proceeds to market the product:

> It was possible that he did not get even the amount of the wages by its sale. It is possible that he sells it very profitably in comparison with the weaver's wages. All that has nothing to do with the weaver. The capitalist buys the labour of the weaver with a part of his available wealth, of his capital, just as he has bought the raw material – the yarn – and the instrument of labour – the loom – with another part of his wealth. After he has made these purchases, and these purchases include the labour necessary for the production of linen, he produces only with the raw materials and instruments of labour belonging to him. For the latter include now, true enough, our good weaver as well, who has as little share in the product, or the price of the product as the loom has.
>
> (2000d: 275)

Marx concludes that 'Wages are, therefore, not the worker's share in the commodity produced by him'.

But, so what? Well, in this case, Marx goes on to connect the characteristic worker–capitalist relationship, as described, with alienation. He continues as follows:

> But the exercise of labour is the worker's own life-activity, the manifestation of his own life. And this life-activity he sells to another person in order to secure the necessary means of subsistence. Thus, his life-activity is for him only a means to enable him to exist. He works in order to live. He does not even reckon labour as part of his life, it is rather a sacrifice of his life. It is a commodity which he has made over to another.
>
> (ibid.: 275–6)

So, in this case, it is the worker's 'life-activity' of which he is being robbed by the capitalist. In the same essay, Marx writes that 'it is just this noble reproductive power that the worker surrenders to the capitalist in exchange for means of subsistence received' and that 'He has, therefore, lost it for himself' (ibid.: 282–3). As Marx sees it, capitalism (rather than the individual capitalist) has robbed the worker of his 'essence', his 'vital activity' by distorting the relationship between the worker and production – its products and the act of production itself. Clearly, whether you find Marx's argument convincing here will largely depend on how convinced you are by his alienation thesis.

In his later work, Marx sometimes analysed 'the labourer's working-day' into that part which is 'assigned to the reproduction of the value of his own labour-power' and that part during which the labourer produces surplus value. For example:

> It is obvious that if the labourer needed his whole day to produce his own means of subsistence (i.e. commodities equal to the value of his own means of subsistence), there could be no surplus value, and therefore no capitalist production and no wage labour. This can only exist when the productivity of social labour is sufficiently developed to make possible some sort of excess of the total working-day over the labour time required for the reproduction of the wage – i.e. surplus labour, whatever its magnitude.
>
> (2000i: 436)

But once again, *pace* the line of criticism under discussion, isn't it just a fact that workers must spend part of their day producing commodities for capitalists to sell, and if that is all there is to it, where is the objection to capitalism? Marx writes as if something is being *taken* from the worker, but what can it be? Is it just time? Well, it's certainly true that the time the worker spends producing commodities for the capitalist to sell is time which could otherwise be spent doing other things. However, this is not equivalent to the claim that the worker creates extra *value*.

To this, I will add just one more comment, namely that there seems to me to be a kind of inverse Lockean intuition at work in Marx's 'surplus value' argument. As we saw, Locke argued that a right of ownership can be derived, initially, from the fact that someone laboured on nature, making it useful and so removing it from the common stock. Says Locke, 'this labour being the unquestionable property of the labourer, no man but he can have a right to what that is once joined to' (Locke 1964b: II, 27).[9] Locke derives a right to private ownership from this argument. By contrast, Marx is insisting that the industrial labourers themselves should have a right of ownership in what they have produced. Is it possible to explain the surplus value thesis more specifically? That said, I am sure that there will be readers sympathetic to Marx's position who will have quite a few comments to make on what I have said here. I am equally sure that others, critical of Marx, will have quite a lot to say. Be that as it may, however, I shall now move on.

Conclusion: Marx and history

Two questions remain. First: Was Marx right about history? Second: Has history been right about Marx?

The former question itself resolves into two subquestions. The first concerns the mechanism which, Marx thinks, drives social change. As we have seen, it is Marx's stated view that changes in the ideological 'superstructure' are 'conditioned' or 'determined' by changes in the economic 'foundation'. The former is 'legal and political' in nature. The latter is 'the sum total of [these] relations of production' and it 'constitutes the economic structure of society'. Marx writes that, for example, 'The mode of production of material life conditions the social, political, and intellectual life process in general'. (For all this see 2000e: 425.) Some critics have questioned the coherence of this distinction. For example, John Plamenatz (1963) has argued that it is impossible to define 'foundation' and 'superstructure' independently. In rough summary his reason is that 'relations of production' must include property relations (such as the relation between the owner of private property and the worker) but that property relations are in fact legal relations. According to Marx, relations of production are foundational, whereas legal relations form part of the superstructure, so it follows that Marx has – so to speak – positioned property relations with a foot in both camps.

It is not my intention to enter into this particular controversy here, so I will just comment that I find Plamenatz's argument unpersuasive. Plamenatz would have a point if Marx had intended us to construe 'foundation determines superstructure' as a simple causal statement, like 'drinking coffee keeps you awake' or 'petrol makes the car go'. Following Hume,[10] many philosophers would agree that if something is to count as a genuine causal statement it must be possible to specify cause and effect independently (which is why, on this account, 'opium makes you sleep because it has a "dormative power"' is not a genuine causal statement). However, as I see it, the claim that the foundation determines, or conditions, the superstructure, need not be construed on such a simple causal model. For a comparison, take the claim – familiar within evolutionary theory – that features of the environment condition (or 'determine') biological features of an organism. For example, the length of the giraffe's neck is conditioned by the fact that the leaves it needs to eat grow at a certain height. (We can explain the former fact in terms of the latter.) This is true, but it doesn't follow that the leaves *make* the giraffe's neck grow.

The second subquestion relates to Marx's prediction of how things are likely to turn out. Certainly, there has, so far, been no revolution of the sort he predicted. But is there going to be? Well, no one could deny that, within capitalism, there are inequalities of wealth and power which could supply the dynamic. Could the tensions become so severe that revolution follows? Earlier I mentioned the argument that the revolution has never happened because governments have repeatedly 'bought off' the workers with a series of compromises.[11] That may be so, but I think it's worth remarking here that the argument gains a great deal of its plausibility by focusing on the relationships between governments and workers which hold within nation-states, or small groups of them such as the states which form the European Union. However, everyone knows that trade and corporate power now cross international boundaries. If you focus upon the relationship between the rich of the very rich nations and the poor of the 'third world' the argument starts to look less convincing. What of Marx's prediction that the state will eventually wither away, to be succeeded by future communist society? Who knows? It depends on what a future communist society is supposed to be like and upon how much our nature contains the potential for change.

But what if Marx is wrong on the last point? This brings me to the second of my two questions. With hindsight, what are we to make of Marx's contribution to political philosophy? These days, one sometimes hears it said that, because Marx's prediction of a revolution followed by the dawning of a new communist era has failed to come true (so far) it follows that his philosophy is an irrelevance, and that we might as well ignore it. In other words, Marx has been out of fashion for a while. On this, I can only comment – first – that Marx is not alone in having made predictions which failed to materialise. Another good example is John Stuart Mill. In *Representative Government*, Mill predicted that the system of plural voting he advocated – the system under which the (supposedly) more knowledgeable and intelligent have more votes than everyone else – would soon be widely adopted. '[T]he time will certainly arrive', he wrote, 'when the only choice will be between this and equal universal suffrage, whoever does not desire the last, cannot too soon begin to reconcile himself to the former' (Mill 1991c: 338). (Mill had previously argued that no rational person could desire 'equal universal suffrage'.) No such thing has happened and, with hindsight, Mill's prediction appears laughable. Does it follow that Mill's philosophy as a whole has become an irrelevance? Of course not. Mill's legacy lies in the critical apparatus he elaborated – his liberal picture of the political world – and the understanding which comes with it. Likewise, Marx's importance lies not in the success or otherwise of this or that prediction but in his critique of capitalism and the insights it yields.

So, how shall I summarise this account of Marx's philosophy? In the chapter with which I opened Part III (Chapter 10) I commented that as this narrative begins to approach our own times it will become increasingly difficult to take an impartial position. Marx is a case in point, for there are, at present, many Marxist philosophers and social scientists, and there are striking contrasts between the positions they take. The best I can do here is offer you my own opinion, for what it's worth.

It is this: It is important to distinguish the theoretical framework within which Marx tries to organise his insights, and those insights themselves. If the former is in some ways creaky and a little antiquated, this should not lead us to ignore the latter. To take the framework first, Marx's thesis that the human essence (as a productive being) must pass through several stages before it achieves full realisation in a de-alienated future society is, of course, a 'materialised' version of Hegel's view that 'mind' must, similarly, undergo many transformations before it achieves full realisation.

Marx began his intellectual life as a follower of Hegel and it is the need to draw a 'materialistic' parallel which, as much as anything else, fuels his more optimistic (and probably more unrealistic) predictions. Indeed something else one sometimes hears said is that 'you can't understand Marx unless you understand Hegel'.

Marx is frequently described as having 'stood Hegel on his head'. But this belittles Marx's achievement in certain ways, for it suggests that Marx was no more than a Hegelian, someone who followed in Hegel's footsteps but just gave his argument a new twist. There is more to Marx than that. For reasons I have already given, you might just as easily describe him as having turned Locke on his head, and you can certainly describe him as having turned the British 'political economists', Adam Smith and David Ricardo, on *their* heads. (Isn't his major work just that – a 'critique' of 'political economy'?) Indeed, Marx has left quite a few people standing upside down, and Lenin's observation that the three 'component parts' of Marxism are 'German philosophy, English political economy, and French socialism' (Lenin 1991: 23ff) is nearer the mark. This is a measure of Marx's breadth, although it also ignores another source of difficulty for – as I have argued – it is not so obvious that Marx's intuitions on the subject of 'surplus value' can be easily incorporated within the conceptual framework of conventional economic theory.

As for the insights, who could deny the following: (i) that the degree to which we have to produce in order to survive distinguishes us markedly from every other animal; (ii) that the manner in which we produce – consciously and in accordance with standards – also distinguishes us markedly from every other animal; (iii) that such facts run deep, and explain a great deal about the sorts of beings we essentially are; (iv) that our actions have unintended consequences and that, over time, these can manifest themselves in historical movements and social structures; (v) that there is such a thing as 'meaningful work'; (vi) that, in a rational world, machines would be our slaves and not – as they are at present – our masters; (vii) that there has to be a better alternative to the present order.

None of the foregoing is, specifically, a 'Marxian' thesis, but we owe it to Marx for having brought them to our attention and for having been one of the first philosophers to incorporate them within the context of a powerful philosophical theory. Moreover, if you want to question any of these claims then, as things stand at present, you would need very good reasons for doing so. It is that, more than anything else, which demonstrates the extent to which our times are still infused by Marx's spirit.

13

—◦☺◦—

Rawls: through reason to justice

When John Rawls' *A Theory of Justice* was first published, in 1972, Stuart Hampshire, writing in the *New York Review of Books*, described it as 'the most substantial and interesting contribution to moral philosophy since the war' (Hampshire 1972). Three years later, Robert Nozick felt able to remark that 'Political philosophers now must either work within Rawls' theory or explain why not' (Nozick 1974: 183). Almost thirty years after that, in his obituary of Rawls, Ben Rogers commented that 'the English-speaking world [has] lost its leading political philosopher' (Rogers 2002). These are no exaggerations. Because the times of Rawls have also been my own times, I think you can take my word for it. Throughout the period in question, Rawls' theory has set the background – or a sizeable section of it – against which every serious political philosopher must define his or her own work. It is just as the lines I have quoted suggest.

Things will eventually change. Of course they will. But, given the present situation, it is clearly essential to grasp the nature of Rawls' achievement. So, what did he do? I am sure that the enthusiasm with which *A Theory of Justice* was received can be explained, in part, by the fact that within political philosophy so little interesting work was being done in the period immediately prior to its publication. Since the end of World War II at the very least, political philosophy had been a deeply unfashionable subject. On the whole,[1] professional philosophers had tended to portray philosophy as 'linguistic analysis', the activity of untangling language with a view to showing how apparent problems arise from a misunderstanding of how it works. Moreover, they had tended to concentrate on problems of logic, language and philosophical psychology (which often lend themselves, quite readily, to the 'analytic' approach), so much so that one political philosopher, Peter Laslett, felt able to proclaim that 'For the moment anyway, political philosophy is dead' (Laslett 1956: vii).

A Theory of Justice changed all this. Rawls was well aware of the work being done by his contemporaries but, far from being merely descriptive and 'analytic', his own is constructive and imaginative. Moreover, it also illuminated many traditional questions in new and interesting ways, so – if nothing else – it gave political philosophers something to discuss and get their teeth into. However, to explain the significance of Rawls' contribution simply in terms of its novelty – the fact that there was nothing much else around at the time – would be to belittle it. Rawls' approach to political thought is profound, and it deserves to be taken very seriously indeed.

In the following section, then, I shall give a brief outline of what I take the basis of Rawls' approach to be, and I shall say why I think it should be taken so seriously. After that, I shall give a brief indication of where I think his theory's major strengths and weaknesses lie. Note that one thing I shall *not* try to do is subject Rawls' argument to a detailed analysis and critique of my own. There are several reasons why not. One is that it would take more than a single chapter to do his argument justice. I would need more space, and the task would not be helped by the fact that – as we shall see – Rawls has modified his position since *A Theory of Justice* was published. Another is that the critical literature on Rawls is already vast. There would be little point in my adding yet another brief critical essay to the mountain, especially when I can refer you to other texts. So, rather than present you with my own critique, my aim is simply to explain the importance of Rawls' enterprise and the general structure of his argument.

Rawls's guiding conception

The original position

Anyone reading Rawls' work will have to confront some difficult, technical and detailed passages. However, right at the heart of his philosophy there lies a very simple, straightforward and powerful idea. In part, Rawls' genius lies in the persistence with which he works that idea through, with which he constantly revises and reinforces it, draws out and takes seriously its logical implications, and so on. So, it is with that guiding conception that we must begin.

How shall I explain it? Well, here is one explanation (my own, not Rawls'). Imagine a group of people who – for whatever reason – find themselves having to co-operate with each other. It's not essential but, if you like, you can imagine them marooned on an island. They know that it will probably be some time – months or years – before a passing ship turns up to rescue them. In the meantime, they have to survive, and so – knowing this – they are holding a meeting. Its purpose is to determine 'ground rules'. These rules will govern the way they behave towards each other, the way tasks are to be allotted, the way food is to be distributed, how future decisions are to be made, and much else besides. Now suppose that they succeed in agreeing a set of rules. The first point to note is that the set of rules they agree can, quite naturally, be described in a number of ways. For example, it seems right to describe the rules as the community's 'constitution', for there can be no doubt that, whenever disagreements subsequently arise, people will refer back to the rules as a way of settling disputes. Also, there is a sense in which you could describe the rules as 'principles of justice', if only for the specific group of individuals in question.

Does it follow that the rules embody *the* principles of justice; that is, do they embody principles which you or I would recognise as principles of justice, even though we are not members of the group marooned on the island and were not present at the meeting? Of course not, the reason being that, for any group of real people, it is always possible that there will be circumstances which would bias the outcome of a meeting in some way. For example, suppose that there is a subgroup of intimidating bullies. This subgroup succeeds in getting the others to agree to rules which confer special privileges upon its members. Even so, it would be wrong to describe such rules as 'just' for it is a requirement of any conception of justice that it applies to individuals impartially. Or again, suppose that one person has a special talent which everyone knows will be in short supply. (For example, suppose this person is a doctor, skilled at curing diseases.) What if he or she uses the talent to extort concessions from the others? Again, the outcome could be a biased rule granting special privileges, and not something you or I could recognise as a principle of justice. But now – by contrast with the foregoing scenario – imagine a group of individuals placed in a situation from which anything which could arbitrarily bias their choice of principles has been eliminated. Would they then choose principles unmistakably recognisable as principles of justice? Rawls' answer is that they would.

As you will have gathered by now, the question Rawls sets out to solve is, to put it loosely, 'the question of justice'. 'Justice', says Rawls, 'is the first virtue of social institutions, as truth is of systems of thought'. It is the concept in terms of which we evaluate, at the most fundamental level, all social and political arrangements. 'A theory however elegant or economical must be rejected or revised if it is untrue', says Rawls, and 'likewise laws and institutions no matter how efficient and well-arranged must be reformed or abolished if they are unjust' (1972: 3). That is why he thinks the question important. In a way, it is the question Plato addresses in the *Republic*. However, whereas Plato thinks of justice as a virtue manifest in certain political relationships – the philosopher rulers are in charge, the ordinary people 'mind their own business' and so on – for Rawls the justice of an arrangement is a question of the degree to which it matches certain principles. The problem is to discover what those 'principles of justice' are. Further – and as you will also have gathered by now – Rawls thinks that the principles of justice are the principles which would be chosen by individuals in a situation from which everything which might bias their choice has been eliminated. It is this straightforward insight which lies at the heart of Rawls' philosophy, and which serves as its guiding thread.

Rawls labels the imaginary situation from which rational individuals are pictured as selecting principles of justice 'the original position', and he believes that the principles they would, in fact, select are his famous two principles of justice. Let us now consider these, each in its turn.

Rawls' two principles of justice

At one point in *A Theory of Justice*, Rawls formulates the first principle as follows:

First Principle
Each person is to have an equal right to the most extensive total system of equal basic liberties compatible with a similar system of liberty for all.

(1972: 302)[2]

Stated thus baldly, and out of its supporting context, the principle clearly stands in need of some explanation, so perhaps it would help if I were to put Rawls' point less formally, as follows. Roughly speaking, then, Rawls is stating that, in a just society, liberty is distributed equally between individuals, with each person getting as much liberty as he or she can (compatibly with everyone else's having an equally large amount). Notice too that Rawls' political orientation is evident from this first principle and the way he attaches so much importance to it. Like John Stuart Mill before him, Rawls is out to defend a version of liberalism. In fact, it would be more accurate to put the point more strongly for, just as Mill was the foremost liberal political philosopher of the nineteenth century, so Rawls will be remembered as that of the twentieth. You may recall that, in the chapter on Mill (Chapter 11), I specified three criteria a political philosophy must satisfy if it is to qualify as liberal. The first was that it must embody the belief that freedom (or liberty)[3] is hugely – if not supremely – important. In Rawls' philosophy this belief is expressed, not simply by the fact that liberty forms the subject of his first principle, but in his strict insistence that the first principle takes priority over the second. As Rawls puts it, 'a departure from the institutions of equal liberty required by the first principle cannot be justified by, or compensated for, by greater social and economic advantages' (1972: 61). Secondly, I stated that, to count as liberal, a political philosophy must embody the claim that it is only where a set of specified liberties is respected that a society can be described as truly free. In Mill's case, this takes the form of his insistence that there is a 'sphere of action' within which specific liberties are 'comprised' and which ought to be protected (Mill 1991a: 71). In a parallel manner, Rawls intends us to understand liberty, as distributed in accordance with his first principle, as the liberty embodied in a set of fundamental rights or 'basic liberties' – the right to vote, freedom of speech, liberty of conscience, and so on (see Rawls 1972: 61).[4] As the principle itself puts it, in the version quoted above, each person is to have an equal right 'to the most extensive total system of equal basic liberties'. Thirdly, I stated that, within a liberal political philosophy, the former belief is underpinned by a more general conception of freedom construed as the liberty to live your own life in your own way (or 'autonomously'). In Rawls' philosophy, this is embodied in his argument that his two principles would be chosen by rational individuals with an interest in fulfilling plans and purposes of their own.

What of Rawls' second principle of justice? In just the same section of *A Theory of Justice*, Rawls formulates it as follows:

Second Principle
Social and economic inequalities are to be arranged so that they are both:
a.) to the greatest benefit of the least advantaged, consistent with the just savings principle, and
b.) attached to offices and positions open to all under conditions of fair equality of opportunity.

(1972: 302)

The second principle is meant to govern the distribution of 'primary social goods' which 'to give them in broad categories, are rights and liberties, opportunities and powers, income and wealth' and – or so Rawls adds – 'a sense of one's own worth' (ibid.: 92). Rawls' formulation of the principle, as quoted, is, if anything, even more technical than that of his first principle, so here too it is worth my trying to put his point less formally. In this case, let me just stress the principle's essential feature, namely that Rawls is not against inequality *per se*. In his view, inequality is unjust but *only if* it works to the detriment of the worst off individuals. By contrast, where an inequality improves the situation of the worst off, by raising it to a level higher than it would otherwise be, inequality is acceptable. In the latter case, objections to inequality are nothing more than expressions of irrational envy (cf. 1972: 530ff). (I shan't dwell on the technicalities introduced by Rawls' reference to the 'just savings principle' or by his unexceptionable insistence that relative advantages must be 'attached to offices and positions open to all under conditions of fair equality of opportunity'.)

I could be wrong – I haven't carried out a systematic survey – but my guess is that the attitude to inequality to which Rawls' second principle gives expression is characteristic of a great deal of mainstream political opinion. There are many who would agree with Rawls that there is nothing wrong with inequality in itself, but that inequality is objectionable where the better off can be charged, in one way or another, with living at the expense of the worse off. If I am right that would hardly be surprising for, like every philosopher to have been discussed in this book, Rawls is a child of his time. I mean that rather as it is possible to think of Hobbes as the philosopher of the English civil war, for example, and Marx as the philosopher of nineteenth century industrialisation, so it is possible to think of Rawls' second principle as an expression of the 'post-war consensus' which prevailed throughout the West from the end of World War II until the early 1980s (roughly speaking). In the USA, the consensus was first given practical expression at the level of public policy by the 'Fair Deal' reforms instituted by President Harry S.Truman from 1945 onwards. As Truman put it in his 1949 State of the Union address, 'Every segment of our population and every individual has a right to expect from our Government a fair deal'. As he saw it, 'no unfair prejudice or artificial distinction should bar any citizen of the United States of America from an education, or from good health, or from a job that he is capable of performing' (Truman 1949). (In the UK, the equivalent measures were the sweeping reforms which introduced the British 'welfare state': the 1944 Education Act, the setting up of the National Health Service, and so on.)

Now, I say this knowing very well that Rawls rarely made his views on this or that issue of policy public. (The great exception is the horror he expressed at the nuclear attacks on Hiroshima and Nagasaki launched by the United States in 1945.)[5] However, there are fundamental features of his approach which render his sympathies perfectly evident. For example, there is Rawls' insistence, throughout his career, that society must be viewed as a 'system of co-operation', and that the purpose of any theory of justice must be to establish 'fair terms' on which co-operation can take place. (See, for example, Rawls 2001: 5ff.) In line with this, his second principle is quite clearly *redistributive*. In other words, Rawls believes that it is perfectly in order for a state to take from the relatively well off for the benefit of the relatively badly off, where fair co-operation requires that this should be done.

Just to summarise this account of Rawls' principles, then: Rawls is both a *liberal* (by the first principle) and, though not a strict egalitarian, a *redistributivist*. Critics and defenders of Rawls sometimes become exercised by questioning the logical relationship between the two principles. Are they consistent with each other? Are they really independent, or does the first collapse, logically, into the second – and so on. Such questions provide intriguing material for philosophers who enjoy detailed, intricate, argument (although I don't consider them in this chapter). However, lying behind them is the far more down-to-earth question of whether a prevailing political consensus is in fact coherent.

The original position

Contractualism and utilitarianism

By this point, you should have gained some idea of Rawls' general position, and the argument with which he defends it. However, to fully appreciate the power of that argument it is necessary, first of all, to take a closer look at his conception of an 'original position'. The following passage is taken from that part of *A Theory of Justice* with which he first introduces it:

> This original position is not, of course, thought of as an actual historical state of affairs, much less as a primitive condition of culture. It is understood as a purely hypothetical situation characterised so as to lead to a certain conception of justice. Among the essential features of this situation is that no one knows his place in society, his class position or social status, nor does any one know his fortune in the distribution of natural assets and abilities, his intelligence, strength, and the like. I shall even assume that the parties do not know their conceptions of the good or their special psychological propensities. The principles of justice are chosen behind a veil of ignorance. This ensures that no one is advantaged or disadvantaged in the choice of principles by the outcome of natural chance or the contingency of social circumstances. Since all are similarly situated and no one is able to design principles to favour his particular condition, the principles of justice are the result of a fair agreement or bargain.
>
> (1972: 12)

With its 'veil of ignorance' this is not a situation we are, any of us, likely to find ourselves in, although we can all go there imaginatively, with the help of a 'thought experiment'. (As Rawls says, it is a 'purely hypothetical' situation. In a later specification, he even denies the parties knowledge of their own race, ethnicity and sex (see Rawls 2001: 15).) But that is hardly the point. With his description of the original position, and whatever modifications he made to it over the course of his life, Rawls' purpose was always to mirror – on the one hand – those elements we must take to structure any conception of justice (impartiality and so on) and, on the other, certain deep, all pervasive features of the human condition itself. The latter consideration applies, similarly, to his description of the individuals he pictures choosing principles from within the original position. They are pictured as limited in altruism and as capable of forming 'rational plans of life' for themselves; that is, of formulating goals, making plans, and of trying to carry them through in a rational and systematic way. It is assumed that everyone stands to gain from co-operating with the others and that, when choosing principles, no one is in a position to coerce anyone else. Most importantly, it is supposed that the hypothetical individuals in this hypothetical situation are *rational.*

Secondly, and as the last feature listed indicates, note that this is an exercise in rational choice theory. Indeed, there is a parallel between the role played by the conception of an original position in Rawls' argument, and the role played by the conception of a state of nature in classical social contract theory. It is a parallel drawn explicitly by Rawls himself. Specifically, rather as Hobbes seeks to resolve the problem of political obligation with an account of why rational individuals, placed in a state of nature, would choose to institute an absolute sovereign, so Rawls seeks to resolve the question of justice with an account of what rational individuals would choose from a carefully specified original position. This 'contractualism' is another reason why Rawls' argument aroused so much interest and excitement when *A Theory of Justice* first appeared. Prior to 1971, social contract theory had appeared little more than a historical curiosity. Since then, it has turned out to be very much alive.[6]

Thirdly, before moving on we should take note of the relationship between Rawls' approach and utilitarianism. Earlier, in the chapter on Mill, I raised the (by now very familiar) objection to the latter that, being a consequentialist philosophy, utilitarianism cannot account for the existence of rights.[7] Of course, like everything in philosophy, the accuracy of the objection is itself open to question. However, the point to note here is that Rawls accepts it. Indeed, it is Rawls himself who was largely responsible for bringing it so forcefully to the attention of philosophers working in recent times, and one of his explicitly stated aims is to formulate a theory of justice which gives a better account of rights than utilitarianism can. That is one reason why he ascribes limited altruism and 'rational self-interest' to his hypothetical rational choosers. The latter are not rabidly competitive and egocentric – they are not like the individuals portrayed by Hobbes – but they will be concerned to defend their ability to work towards the fulfilment of the plans they have set themselves. This promises a better account of rights because a claim of right is, in a sense, a self-interested claim. No purely altruistic person would ever say: 'You can't do that. You must do this. I have such-and-such rights.'

The original position and the human condition

Earlier, I remarked that Rawls' contribution to political thought deserves to be taken extremely seriously, but precisely why it should depends upon precisely how we are meant to interpret the theoretical status of the original position. The hypothetical choosers of the original position are meant to be 'stand-ins' for ourselves, but it is important to see *exactly* how they function as stand-ins, and in *just what* respects they resemble us. Let me explain, as follows.

When *A Theory of Justice* was published, it appeared to many (including

me) that Rawls was advocating a certain, possibly questionable, univer-
salism. I mean that any reader of that work could easily be forgiven for
thinking that Rawls intended his principles to apply equally in all circumstances; that is to all cultures at all times.[8] In this case, or so it could be
argued, he would have to assume that there is a 'universal human nature',
and that his description of choosers in the original position reflects this.
Moreover, it could also be argued that, since his theory is an attempt to
link justice with rationality via the alternatives the choosers select, he must
assume that there is a single, universally applicable, standard of rationality; (that there is, if you like, such a thing as Rationality with a capital 'R').
If such assumptions are incorrect, then it could be that Rawls is exposed
to some damaging objections, or so it appeared.

For example, what if Marx and Engels were right to say that the history
of ideas proves only that 'intellectual production changes its character in
proportion as material production is changed', so that 'the ruling ideas of
each age have ever been the ideas of its ruling class'? (Marx and Engels
2000: 260). Or, if not precisely that, what if *something like* it is right?
Wouldn't the liberalism for which Rawls argues then be a merely 'local'
phenomenon, the expression of a particular culture at a particular stage of
its development? If so, couldn't it be argued that, by falsely portraying a
peculiarly 'Western' value system (liberalism) as founded upon universally
applicable principles, Rawls becomes guilty of a sort of cultural
imperialism?

Well, maybe. However, I shan't pursue that line of thought any further.
That is not only because I don't believe the charge can be made to stick,
but because Rawls has strenuously rejected universalistic interpretations
of his work on a number of occasions since the publication of *A Theory of
Justice*. In his later work, 'political liberalism' – the name he adopted for
his position in the later part of his career – is described as a set of principles which is peculiarly appropriate to individuals living through a particular historical period. In his *Introduction* to a later work, itself entitled
Political Liberalism (Rawls 1993), Rawls traces the origins of liberalism
to the religious divisions which split Europe during the sixteenth and
seventeenth centuries. 'The Reformation had enormous consequences', he
writes, and:

> During the wars of religion people were not in doubt about the
> nature of the highest good, or the basis of moral obligation in divine
> law. These things they thought they knew with the certainty of faith,
> as here their moral theology gave them complete guidance. The
> problem was rather: How is society even possible between those of
> different faiths? What can conceivably be the basis of religious toler-
> ation? For many there was none, for it meant the acquiescence in
> heresy about first things and the calamity of religious disunity. Even
> the earlier proponents of toleration saw the division of Christendom

as a disaster, though a disaster that had to be accepted in view of the alternative of unending religious civil war.

Thus, the historical origin of political liberalism (and of liberalism more generally) is the Reformation and its aftermath, with the long controversies over religious toleration in the sixteenth and seventeenth centuries.

(1993: xxiii–iv)

In short, liberalism is the philosophical expression of the compromise which had to be reached after the upheavals of the Reformation. As this shows, Rawls is no cultural relativist. His argument is meant to carry relevance for humanity considered as a whole. But, on the other hand, nor are his ambitions over-demandingly universalist. They only carry such relevance once humanity has reached a certain stage in its development. Thus: As children of the Reformation, we are constrained to share the planet with others, and those others will adhere to belief systems, to systems of value, and follow lifestyles which are very different from our own. Things may have been different once, but that is now an inescapable feature of the human condition. In his later work, then, Rawls came to think of his philosophy as an attempt to come to terms with the modern fact of pluralism, and to present 'the problem of political liberalism' in terms such as the following: 'How is it possible that there may exist over time a stable and just society of free and equal citizens profoundly divided by reasonable religious, philosophical, moral doctrines?' (1993: xxv).

The theme is pursued in Rawls' most recent work, *Justice as Fairness: A Restatement* (2001). (Sadly, it was also his last.) In that work, it is emphasised that the original position is a thought-experiment for individuals living in the 'here and now' to perform. Rawls writes:

the significance of the original position lies in the fact that it is a device of representation or, alternatively, a thought-experiment for the purpose of public- and self-clarification. We are to think of it as modelling two things.

First, it models what we regard – here and now – as fair conditions under which the representatives of citizens, viewed solely as free and equal persons, are to agree to the fair terms of co-operation whereby the basic structure is to be regulated.

Second, it models what we regard – here and now – as acceptable restrictions on the reasons on the basis of which the parties, situated in fair conditions, may properly put forward certain principles of political justice and reject others.

(2001: 17)

The terminology may be unfamiliar but I think Rawls' central point is clear enough.[9] He is asking us – you and me, his readers – what we would agree to given (i) the inescapable fact of pluralism and (ii) the moral

246

requirement to view others as free and equal persons. It is this which explains certain changes of emphasis in his later work, for example the emphasis he comes to place on 'overlapping consensus' and 'public reason'. (Consensus is something real individuals, living in the 'here and now' can – pragmatically – achieve. The value of 'public reason' arises from the requirement to treat others as free and equal. Says Rawls, 'If free and equal citizens are to co-operate politically on a basis of mutual respect, we must justify our use of our corporate and coercive political power . . . in the light of public reason' (2001: 91).)

Many critics have been disappointed by Rawls' shift of emphasis. They have tended to see it as a retreat from philosophy into pragmatism. Just for example, Chandran Kukathas and Philip Pettit have this to say:

> In making the latter move, Rawls comes to place much greater emphasis on the need to secure practical agreement among competing religious and moral views, and to see this rather than the pursuit of truth as the task of political philosophy. We have treated this as an unwelcome development in Rawls's thought. It suggests an aspiration for the political philosophy to end all political philosophies. Yet it also suggests despair as to the possibility of anything being accomplished in politics by philosophical inquiry.
>
> (Kukathas and Pettit 1990: 151)

But I am not so sure, and in Rawls' defence against this type of charge I would just say the following. Pluralism – the necessity to share the planet with others who adhere to different 'conceptions of the good' (Rawls' phrase) – really is an inescapable feature of the modern human condition. It may well have arisen with the Reformation, but in our own times – in the 'global village' we increasingly inhabit – the necessity has become all the more pressing. Look at it in that light, and you can see his philosophy as a serious, even desperate, attempt to come to grips with a pressing contemporary problem. It's real-life stuff. Rawls' constant re-emphases and revisions of his basic idea appear as workings and reworkings in a struggle to get it exactly right. Of course, Rawls' project could eventually turn out to have been a failure; that his problem is insoluble at a philosophical level because there are no rationally determinable ethical principles upon which there can be general agreement. If so, things could be so much the worse for us, because it would mean that the only way to deal with a pluralistic reality is pragmatic; that our only hope can be to establish a *modus vivendi* with our neighbours through whatever *ad hoc* methods happen to be available. However, as things stand, we have every reason for taking it very seriously indeed.

How to think critically about Rawls

What of the argument's weaknesses? As I said earlier, I shan't try to develop a sustained critique of Rawls' argument – not here. What follows should be treated as nothing more than a rough guide, a few suggestions as to where weak spots could turn out to lie. Here, it can be useful to bear in mind the parallels between Rawls' argument (in its earlier and its later versions) and the argument of Hobbes' *Leviathan*. Both are exercises in rational choice theory. Each is self-consciously constructed as theorem, and is meant to take the form of a deductive argument from premise to conclusion. In the chapter on Hobbes, the critique of *Leviathan* followed its argument through, step by step, from the former to the latter.[10] It follows that one way to think about Rawls is to try to conduct a parallel critique – so here goes.

The premise: the original position

At one point, in the course of the discussion of Hobbes, we noted the distinction between *logical validity* and *truth*. Just to remind you, take the argument that 'All men are mortal' (first premise); that 'Socrates is a man' (second premise); and that – therefore – 'Socrates is mortal' (conclusion). The argument is logically valid – i.e. the conclusion follows logically from the premises – but we can only be confident that the conclusion is true if we already know that the premises are true.[11] As I remarked in the earlier chapter, if 'Socrates' is, in fact, your pet name for your desktop computer, then one of the premises, the second, will be false, in which case this would be an example of a logically valid argument which yields a false conclusion.

It follows that, when assessing an argument which claims to establish a true conclusion by logically valid steps, a good way to start is with the question, 'Are the premises true?' In Hobbes' case, this meant questioning the truth of his account of human nature, and the plausibility of the account of life in the state of nature he tries to derive from it. In Rawls' it means raising questions about the original position. For one thing, it means asking whether his account of that situation reflects features of human nature, such as the (supposed) facts of our limited altruism and our ability to form 'rational plans of life' for ourselves. In the case of Rawls' later work it means asking whether the 'fact of pluralism' (as I called it a moment ago) really is as serious and inescapable as Rawls thinks (and as I have also suggested it is). I have said enough on these points, and so I shall leave it to you to decide.

However, the original position is a hypothetical construct which is also meant to represent, not just features of human nature, but features of the concept of justice itself. Ordinarily, we think of justice in such a way that there are certain requirements which have to be met by any philosophically worked-out conception of justice, or so Rawls thinks. For example, it almost goes without saying that justice must be impartial. In his account of the original position, Rawls meets this requirement by placing his rational choosers behind a veil of ignorance, just so they cannot select principles which arbitrarily favour themselves. Again, Rawls specifies that, in the original position, each person stands to gain from co-operating with the others and he assumes that, unless this were so, questions of justice would not arise. Like the former, this is an assumption which can seem so obviously correct that it is almost superfluous to state it.

However, the latter could be wrong or – if not that – it could represent just *one* way to think about justice; and the assumption has certainly been questioned by some of Rawls' critics, most notably Robert Nozick in *Anarchy, State, and Utopia* (Nozick 1974). Specifically, it is more likely to appeal to you if, when thinking about justice, you tend to picture a group of individuals sharing a geographical space and selecting principles on the basis of which they can co-operate. And that, of course, is precisely what Rawls does. For example, it is noticeable that, in describing 'the objective circumstances which make human co-operation both possible and necessary' (and which therefore give rise to questions of justice) Rawls supposes – among other things – that 'many individuals coexist together *at the same time* on *a definite geographical territory*' (1972: 126) (my emphasis). By contrast, you are likely to find Rawls' approach less than persuasive if you are inclined to think of a just distribution as the outcome of free transactions between individuals, each of whom is the bearer of fundamental rights, and each of whom carefully respects the fundamental rights of the others. To put it another way, you will find Rawls the more persuasive the more you are susceptible to *patterned* accounts of just distribution. You will be less convinced if you tend to think of justice in a *historical* way as the transfer of entitlements from one individual to another over time.

In this context, the distinction between patterned and historical accounts of justice is significant because, while each has much to recommend it, each yields conclusions which conflict logically with those yielded by the other. So, you can't have both. For example, the former can entail the compulsory expropriation of wealth from the better off to ensure that a preferred pattern of distribution is satisfied, something the latter must treat as anathema. Moreover, as Nozick emphasises, there is absolutely no guarantee that, as individuals exercise their rights over time, a given pattern of distribution will result. *Any* outcome is possible. (Like the principle of utility, Rawls' second principle embodies a patterned view. Nozick's 'entitlement' thesis is 'historical', like Locke's argument for property. Otherwise, and as you may recall, I have outlined the distinction between historical and patterned accounts of justice once already, in the context of a discussion of Locke. So, if what I have just said isn't clear, I suggest you turn back to Chapter 8, where it is explained at more length.[12]

So, out of the two, which approach to our understanding of the conception of justice is the more correct? Well, as it happens, on the point in question my own sympathies tend to lie more with Rawls although, for the present, I shall offer no arguments in his favour. As I said, I am not out to offer a critique of my own here, only to suggest guidelines for such a critique. Here, then, is a question for Rawls, as it is for anyone seeking either to defend or attack his account of justice: How accurately – really – does his description of the original position mirror requirements which, on independent grounds, we would expect any philosophically worked-out conception of justice to meet? That said, let us move on.

The first principle: reason, liberty, liberalism

If we are to proceed systematically, the second question we should raise is this: Does the conclusion follow logically from the premises? In other words, is it valid? In Hobbes' case, this meant asking whether humans, as he supposes them to be, really would choose to escape from the state of nature in the way he describes, and establish an absolute sovereign to rule over them. (Recall that we are using Hobbes' contractualist theorem as a template here.) In the case of Rawls, it means – for a start – asking whether rational individuals, selecting principles of justice from the original position, really would choose his two principles of justice. Let us take each principle in turn, starting, in this section, with the first.

As we saw, the first principle of justice distributes *liberty*. In the formulation I quoted, it states that 'Each person is to have an equal right to the most extensive total system of equal basic liberties compatible with a similar system of liberty for all' (1972: 60). Would Rawls' rational choosers select this principle? In answer, it seems to me that they would, at least to the extent liberty can be thought of as a kind of undifferentiated 'stuff', something which can be easily divided and shared, rather as if it were cake. In fact, examples which involve the division of cake readily lend themselves to the illustration of the reasoning behind Rawls' first principle.

Thus: Imagine a large cake and a group of people, each of whom is quite hungry and could, himself or herself, easily polish off quite a large portion of the cake. However, the cake is to be divided, and nobody gets any cake until a principle of division is proposed which everyone agrees to. Everyone is rational and no one is in a position to coerce anyone else. If these people were altruists of complete selflessness, everyone would say 'After you' to everyone else, and no one would get any cake. If they were utilitarians, they would carry out a complicated survey, designed to establish exactly how much happiness each person derives from a given quantity (say, a gram) of cake. (Some people will be hungrier than others. Some will enjoy cake more than others, and the cake will be divided

250

unevenly with a view to bringing about the greatest happiness of the greatest number.) But the individuals we are asked by Rawls to picture are neither. They are Rawlsian rational egoists, and each is self-interestedly concerned to defend his or her interests against the others. What principle of division would they choose, then? So far as I can see, the only possibility is a principle of equal division according to which each person gets the largest slice of cake he or she can have, consistently with everyone else's having an equally large slice; i.e. 'Each person is to have an equal right to the most extensive slice of cake compatible with a similarly big slice of cake for all.' Delete the phrases 'most extensive slice of cake' and 'similarly big slice of cake' from the foregoing sentence, substitute – respectively – 'most extensive total system of basic liberties' and 'similar system of liberty', and there you have Rawls' first principle of justice.

But to what extent is it really possible to think of liberty in this way; that is, as something which can be divided into portions and distributed? Actually, the idea is not so silly, especially if you construe liberty on the model of 'negative liberty' as articulated by, for example, Sir Isaiah Berlin. According to Berlin, 'political liberty' in this 'negative' sense is 'simply the area within which a man can act unobstructed by others', so that, 'If I am prevented by others from doing what I could otherwise do, I am to that degree unfree' (Berlin 1969: 122). (You may recall that we discussed Berlin's distinction between 'positive' and 'negative' conceptions of liberty earlier, in the chapter on Rousseau.)[13] Clearly, to think of liberty that way is to think of the degree of a person's liberty as the amount of space he or she has available to move around in, and of course space is something which can be divided into shares, like cake.

However, perhaps such considerations only apply in a limited set of cases. What if there is more to liberty than negative liberty, so much so that it cannot always be construed on a 'cake model'? The question is apposite because Rawls does believe that, in a genuinely free society, the government, or state, must do more than respect the 'spaces' within which individuals are free to move so far as it possibly can. As we have seen, his contractualist premises are meant to supply a foundation, not just for liberty, but for liberalism – and that's different.

Let me try to explain the difficulty which, as I see it, faces Rawls' argument here. First, notice that for every single one of us there is an enormous number of actions which we are negatively free to perform, there being no obstacle sufficient to prevent our performing them. For example, think of a city thousands of miles from where you live and which you have no need or desire to visit. There is a street in that city along which you would be negatively free to drive if you were to go there, and the same goes for many other streets in many other cities, none of which you have any desire to visit. You are negatively free to drive along those streets too. But, so what? By hypothesis, you have no desire to go there, so why should it matter to you? Likewise, there is, for each of us, a huge number of actions we are negatively unfree to perform. Suppose that there is another street in the same city across which the authorities have placed a barrier, making it impossible to drive along it from one end to the other. You lack the freedom to drive along the street. But, again, so what? It is clear enough, I think, that it only matters to us that we should be negatively free to perform certain actions when those actions are ones we want, or need, to perform (or, at least, when they are actions we think we may at some point want to perform).

Secondly, then, note that a society in which people are, on the whole, negatively free to do what they want is not necessarily equivalent to a liberal society. It all depends on what people want to do. Imagine a very traditional, hierarchically structured, society. There is a hereditary aristocracy in whom political authority and decision making power is invested. There is an all embracing system of religious belief, to which nearly everyone subscribes, and in terms of which the authority structure is rationalised and justified. Most people are peasants whose way of life has been unchanged for generations, and which will remain unchanged for the foreseeable future. Women and men have clearly circumscribed domestic roles. There is a pastoral priesthood, whose job it is to interpret the religion, and to help people as they travel the pre-ordained course of life. To the extent that people accept the traditional view of things, this will be a society in which people are, on the whole, negatively free to do the things they want to do. However, it is hardly liberal society – and certainly not a liberal society as conceived by Rawls – for, in it, people are not free to exercise the 'basic liberties' which, as he sees it, are necessary conditions for the existence of a liberal political order. Indeed, as we have already supposed, political authority is invested in a hereditary aristocracy, so there is no democracy and, consequently, no freedom to vote. Because the expression of opinion is controlled by the governing class, including the priesthood, it is easy to imagine that there is no free press in this country, no freedom of speech and expression. And, thanks to the dominant religion, there is no liberty of conscience. Heretics are burnt, or so we may imagine. But, so far as the subjects of the regime are concerned, none of this matters for – with the exception of a few 'extremists' perhaps – nobody wants to exercise such liberal freedoms.

That said, here is how the difficulty facing Rawls' argument arises: Quite early in *A Theory of Justice*, Rawls categorises liberty as a 'primary good', the latter being a thing that 'every rational man is presumed to want' (1972: 62). This seems right. At least it seems right to the extent that, in the normal run of things as least,[14] there appears to be something illogical about claiming to want to do some action x, while at the same time claiming not to want to be free to do x. (What sense would you make of someone who said, for example, 'I want to go to the cinema tonight but I do not want to be free to go to the cinema tonight'?) In line with this, Rawls adds that primary goods, like liberty, 'normally have a use whatever a person's rational plan of life' (ibid.). Much later, he distinguishes between liberty and its 'worth', 'the worth of liberty to persons and groups' being 'proportional to their capacity to advance their ends' (ibid.: 204).

Now, as all this suggests, the basic thinking behind Rawls' argument for his first principle runs along something like the following lines. In the original position, situated as they are behind a 'veil of ignorance', the hypothetical rational choosers have no idea what plans, purposes, wants, desires, etc. they will turn out to have once the veil is raised and they find themselves back in 'normal' society. However, they do know that they will have *some* plans and purposes. As Rawls puts it, everyone knows that he or she will have a 'rational plan of life', for it is definitive of our humanity that we are creatures who form such plans. (It is, if you like, an aspect of 'human nature'.)[15] Therefore, knowing this, the choosers also know that they will want the liberty to carry out their plans. To put it another way: Knowing that they will want to do something, it follows that they will want the freedom to do it, whatever it turns out to be. That is why they choose a principle which distributes *liberty*. Further constraints, imposed within the original position, determine that it distributes liberty equally.

Fair enough, but the trouble is that, by itself, this argument only establishes that the choosers will select a principle which distributes *negative* liberty – that is, the freedom from obstructions to do whatever it is they want to do – and not the full panoply of 'basic' liberal freedoms for which Rawls wants to argue. Suppose that, after the principle has been selected, the veil of ignorance is raised, and the choosers find themselves inhabiting the traditional, hierarchically structured, society I described a moment ago. It follows from the argument that they would have no reason for complaint, provided that they never found themselves wanting to step beyond the constraints imposed by that society.

Here, then, is a further question for Rawls: How can it be shown that, from the original position, rational choosers will select a principle which distributes, not just liberty, but liberty as embodied in the 'total system of basic liberties' characteristic of a liberal society? If he wants to defend liberal values, that is what he has to show; to which point, let me just add the following. First, it would be ridiculous if I were to suggest that either Rawls or his critics were unaware of the difficulty I have just outlined. Indeed, a great deal of Rawls' work is devoted to answering the question I have just raised. Once again, let me stress that I am not out to conduct an original critique of Rawls' argument. I just want to indicate points within it where difficulties lie. Here is one such point. Secondly, then, so far as I can see, the 'earlier' Rawls tackles the question in a very different manner from the way the 'later' Rawls tackles it; but it's not so obvious that either attempt is successful.[16] However, that said, I will leave you to read Rawls for yourself, and to make up your own mind on the point.

Thirdly, and lastly, picky arguments over precisely what Rawls' hypothesised agents would select from within the original position can, no doubt, be a source of fun for philosophers who enjoy that sort of thing. However, behind those arguments there lies a really serious problem, for human rights – the rights for which liberals argue – fall into two categories. On the one hand there are rights of access to material resources and institutional arrangements which are essential conditions for the living of any sort of decent life. These include rights to food, shelter, and to equal treatment before the law (which is a condition for predictability and stability). On the other, there are what you could call 'developmental' rights – the rights to free speech, to play a part in political decision making, and so on. It is certainly arguable that the latter are less basic; that they are more particularly associated with a certain world view. (In the traditional society I described, the former are respected, but not the latter.) For a liberal, the challenge is to demonstrate that justice requires the recognition of both categories of right as equally fundamental. Rawls' work is the most serious attempt to have been made, within recent years, to meet that challenge at the philosophical level.

The second principle: reason, risk, and fairness

What of the second principle, 'the difference principle' as it has become known? As we saw, this relates to social and economic inequalities and, in the version I quoted earlier, its first clause states that such inequalities are to be arranged so that they are 'to the greatest benefit of the least advantaged'. Why should the rational choosers, selecting principles from behind a veil of ignorance, opt for this one? After all, there are other possibilities. One is a principle of strict equality; that is, a principle which distributes opportunity, power, income, wealth – the sorts of 'goods' of which those who express concern over social and economic inequality tend to be thinking – in precisely equal amounts.[17] Another is the 'principle of average utility', a version of the principle of utility according to which resources should be distributed in a manner which makes the average person as well off as possible. Why not select one of these alternatives?

Well, on Rawls' account, the choice of the former would be irrational, because it is conceivable that, where strict equality applies, everyone would be worse off than even the most badly off person where goods are distributed in accordance with the difference principle. Likewise, where the average person is as well off as possible, it could turn out that the worst off person is very badly off indeed. To put it another way, suppose you had to choose between being the worst off person in a society where everyone is strictly equal, one where the principle of average utility applies, and one in which goods are distributed in accordance with his second principle. Obviously – or so Rawls thinks – it depends on which worst off person, out of these possibilities, is the most badly off, not upon the presence or absence of inequalities themselves. As he sees it, the rational thing to do is select the principle which renders the worst off person better off than he or she would be under any other arrangement, i.e. the difference principle.

I think it should be clear that Rawls is making two suppositions here. The first is that the way in which co-operation is organised can make a difference to the total quantity of goods available. (Remember that he thinks of society as 'a system of co-operation' and that one of his stated purposes is to establish 'fair terms' under which co-operation can take place.) As he sees it, it is a mistake to suppose that there is a pot of some fixed size, from which everyone may draw an allotted share. (If there were such a pot, then, as he thinks, strict equality would obviously have to apply.) On the contrary, it could be that, by arranging things in a certain way, people will co-operate in a manner which serves to increase the total available. (Just for example in certain circumstances it could be that, by easing the tax burden on the relatively well off, you give them an incentive to invest in new equipment, take new initiatives, and so on, thereby generating new wealth and new opportunities for employment. In such cases, even the worst off people are better off than they would otherwise be, so this would be a case in which inequalities work to the greatest benefit of the least advantaged.) Secondly, Rawls is clearly assuming that the rational policy for each individual situated in the original position to adopt is a policy of 'least risk'. Reasoning from behind the veil of ignorance, each has to assume that – once the veil is lifted – he or she could turn out to be a member of the least advantaged group. It is a risk from which it follows, according to Rawls, that the most rational choice is a principle which ameliorates the situation of the worst off as much as possible.

But is 'least risk' always the most rational policy to adopt? The question is worth raising because quite a few of Rawls' critics have focused their attention upon this aspect of his argument, and – as this illustrates – there could be a further source of weakness in his theory here.

To start with, then, it is certainly true that most people would think it rational to take out an insurance policy against fire and theft when buying a house or a car. In fact the probability that your house will catch fire and burn down is extremely low. Even so, they prepare for the worst in just the same way that Rawls' choosers prepare for the worst when they select his second principle. But perhaps that is one sort of case. Contrast it with the case of someone who chooses not to buy a lottery ticket on the same principle. Now, as I write, the price of a UK lottery ticket is one pound, which means that, for most UK citizens, the purchase of a lottery ticket would make no significant inroad into the weekly budget. Compared with this, the gain for a winner can be huge. It can run into millions of pounds. This means that, for a prospective ticket-purchaser (i) the worst thing that can happen is that he or she loses one pound and (ii) the best thing that can happen is that he or she wins several million pounds. To this, it is relevant to add (iii) that the probability that the worst will happen here is extremely high. I was once told, and I have no reason to disbelieve it, that in the UK your chances of winning the lottery are appreciably lower than your chances of being killed in a domestic accident involving a refrigerator, i.e. vanishingly small. Given all this, what would you think of someone who, when contemplating the purchase of a lottery ticket, decided against doing so on the grounds[18] that there is a risk that the worst could happen? Would you think that person rational? I think not.

I am sure most readers will agree with me that, as the example illustrates, 'least risk' is not always the most rational policy to pursue. And there are plenty of everyday examples with which the same point might have been illustrated. What would you say about someone who always carried a heavy overcoat, even on the sunniest day; or someone who never took a foreign holiday for fear that the plane might crash; or who never ate at a restaurant for fear of food poisoning? (Sudden rainstorms, plane crashes, outbreaks of food poisoning can all happen, although the probabilities of their happening are normally slight.) If you are inclined to think of such behaviour as irrational, as I am, it follows that it is quite often irrational *not* to risk the worst. I surmise that, for each of us, what counts as a rational choice is often a function of the relationship between (i) the seriousness of the harm or damage which would result were the worst to happen, (ii) the degree of benefit which would result were the best to happen, and (iii) the probability that the worst will happen. My guess is that there is variation between individuals in the judgements they make as to how much risk it is rational to take, and that such variation also exists across cultures.

Still, be that as it may, my main point is that it can be far from rational not to take risks. Now, if this is right, the implications for Rawls' argument would appear to be considerable. As we have seen, Rawls' philosophy is, in essence, an attempt to derive principles of justice from an account of rational choice. So, for a start, if there can be no single, universally applicable, standard of rationality – and the argument just outlined suggests that there can't be – then it must follow that a rational choice argument cannot be used to derive principles of justice to which every rational person must agree, or so you would think. Again, if it is sometimes rational to take risks, it follows that it could be rational to select some principle other than the difference principle from within the original position. The obvious candidate here is the 'principle of average utility'. As you will recall, this states that the best arrangement is that under which the average person (as opposed to the worst off) is better off than he or she would be under any other system. Rawls initially rejects this on the grounds that, under it, the average person's advantaged position can be bought at a cost to the position of the worst off person. (For example, this could happen where a small force of slaves is forced to work very hard for the benefit of everyone else.) But now consider two situations. In the first – where things are arranged in accordance with

Rawls' second principle – the worst off person is better off than he or she would be under any other arrangement. In the second – where things are arranged in accordance with the principle of average utility – 90 per cent of people are far better off than anyone in the first situation, although 10 per cent are much worse off than anyone in the first situation. Which is it rational to prefer? Well, once *risk* enters the picture, a rational chooser might well reason that, since there is a high probability (9:1) that he or she will be a member of the well off 90 per cent, it's worth taking a chance on it. If this is right, it follows that rational choosers would not necessarily select the difference principle, in which case it also follows – finally – that Rawls has no argument against utilitarianism here. If so, these are considerations which go right to the basis of his system.

Now, I say '*if* this is right' and '*if* so' advisedly, because it would be ridiculous if I were to pretend to be the first person ever to think up the foregoing line of criticism against Rawls or to claim to have the last word. In fact there is much to be said on the other side, in defence of Rawls. Indeed Rawls tried to meet this type of objection himself in his last book, *Justice as Fairness: A Restatement.*[19] Of course, this raises the further question of whether Rawls' defence is successful. As you would expect, a lively discussion is still going on. However, rather than continue with the question, let me now turn to another possible objection to Rawls' argument, one which raises a more fundamental difficulty.

Consider the following example: You are in need of money to keep you going for the next few months, so you go to the employment agency, looking for a job. There are two available. Call these Job A and Job B. The two jobs are practically similar. (In both, the work is the same. We can suppose that both are routine office jobs, for example, or that each involves working at a till in a supermarket. The two workplaces are next door to each other, and so on.) The only difference is that the pay for Job A is lower than the pay for Job B. (The figures don't really matter, but, if it helps, suppose that Job A pays 100.00 pounds per week and Job B 125.00 pounds per week.) Now ask: Which, out of the two jobs, is it rational to take? In this case, the answer is obvious. You take Job B. How could you choose otherwise, when (i) your sole purpose in seeking a job is to earn money and (ii) the only salient variable is the difference in pay. Notice too the similarity between the situation from which you choose a job, in this example, and the original position from which, according to Rawls, his choosers select his second principle. In the latter it is assumed, likewise, (i) that their motive is to maximise the degree to which certain 'primary goods' ('rights and liberties, opportunities and powers, income and wealth', and so on) are available to them (see 1972: 92) and (ii) that the only relevant variables, distinguishing the situations between which they choose, are the degree to which such goods are available and the manner in which they are distributed.

But now contrast the foregoing with the following example. There are two adjacent countries, Country A and Country B. Country A used to be a colony of a major Western power, but – after a long struggle – it has recently gained independence. Country A now faces enormous problems. For example, the economy has long been geared to producing cash crops for the colonialists, but it must now become stronger and more independent. Still, there is a popular leader and a strong ethos of equality. Because it is generally considered by the public that all are comrades – that everyone is a brother or a sister to the others and that all are in it together – the leader is able to mobilise the population in the effort to reconstruct. Consistently with all this, everyone's income is roughly equal. Let us suppose, then, that in Country A everyone is paid 5,000 currency units per year, whatever his or her particular skill and responsibilities may be. (As in the former example, the figures don't really matter.) By contrast, in Country B – where the currency is the same – there are huge inequalities. The senior executives of its major corporations are paid in zillions of currency units, sometimes even more. Middle management are paid far less than this, and the workers – who are quite poor – even less. However – and here is the point – even the worst off people in Country B are better off than anyone in Country A. Suppose, then, that in Country B the worst off people are paid 5,500 currency units per year.

Now suppose that you are living in Country A and that you have a choice. Either you remain in that country – where everyone is poor but all are equal – or you take a short walk across the border to Country B, where there are great inequalities but where even the poorest person is better off than anyone in Country A. If you do, you will be one of the poorest, but you will still earn more than you would if you stay where you are. The question is: What is the rational thing to do? And, so far as I can see, Rawls' second principle yields a single, straightforward answer here, namely that, if you are rational, you will move to Country B. (Recall that, according to Rawls, the rational thing to do is select the situation in which the worst off person is better off than he or she would be in any other situation.)[20] However, it is extremely hard to believe that things are really that simple, for, in this example, there is more to the story than a set of income differences. This equality of wealth which prevails in Country A is part of a package. It is inseparable from the prevalent ethic of comradeship and, no doubt, from other features of that country's way of life. In reality, making a choice means taking the whole set of features into consideration and evaluating. Likewise, in Country B, there will, no doubt, be other features which go hand-in-hand with inequalities of income and an industrialised economy. (All this is in addition to the improbable assumption that the real value of a 'currency unit' will be the same in both countries.) Of course, I am not saying that it would be more rational to remain in Country A after all, only that there is no single answer here because different people will evaluate these situations differently.

Out of the two examples just discussed, the latter bears less resemblance to a case of choice from the original position. On the other hand, unlike the former it is, at least, a choice between distributions which are putatively 'just'. So, there are, no doubt, lessons to be drawn here for the way Rawls sets things up; that is, for the way he attempts to derive a conception of justice from an account of rational choice. However, at present I have no precise idea of what those lessons might be. In any case, I have said enough. Let me simply remind you that, as with the first principle, there is a serious, down-to-earth question which gives point to all the philosophical intricacy, the question of how closely, if at all, 'welfarist', 'redistributivist' policies accurately reflect social justice. Let me then commend the subject to you. There is more to say about Rawls – plenty more – and reading him can be difficult. However, I hope I have said enough to persuade you that – whatever you may think of the position for which he argues – it is worth the effort.

Conclusion

The situation in which philosophy is dominated by the work of a single figure – so much so that even those who disagree with the position that person takes must define their own in relation to it – is a recurring one. When Aristotle first came to the Academy, intellectual life in Greece would have been dominated by the thought of Plato. Throughout the Dark Ages and into the medieval period, European thought was dominated by the ideas of Aristotle himself. With *Leviathan*'s social contract argument, Hobbes set the conceptual agenda followed by political philosophers for the next century or so. Marx and his contemporaries started out as 'young Hegelians', and there are many other instances. If it is true that, at present, political philosophers writing in English must define their positions in relation to Rawls' arguments – that, as Nozick thought, 'Political philosophers now must either work within Rawls' theory or explain why not' (Nozick 1974: 183) – then, on the basis of past experience, we can be confident that things will eventually change. Let us now consider some alternatives.

14

---◦◦◦---

After Rawls

For the past three decades or so, Rawls may well have been the dominant figure within political philosophy, but that doesn't mean that everyone has agreed with him. Philosophy isn't like that. In the earlier part of this chapter, I shall offer a brief account of two major alternatives to Rawls' philosophy. Each has been developed since the 1970s, and each demonstrates Rawls' dominance, not by agreement with him, but by having been introduced into the debate by a text which self-consciously set out to place itself in opposition to his argument. Thus, in his libertarian text, *Anarchy, State, and Utopia* (1974), Robert Nozick sets out to defend an 'entitlement' account of justice, one which is meant to be an alternative to Rawls' 'redistributivist' account. Likewise, in *Liberalism and the Limits of Justice* (1982) – which is admittedly only one of communitarianism's defining texts – Michael Sandel defends his own position through a critique of Rawls' philosophy. These texts come 'after Rawls', if only in the sense that each represents a reaction to *A Theory of Justice*. (Otherwise, it is difficult to describe anything much as having come after Rawls at present. As I write, only six months have passed since his death and only about eighteen since the publication of his last book (Rawls 2001).) In the following chapter, I shall offer a few observations on future prospects.

Libertarianism and communitarianism

So, briefly, what is 'libertarianism' and what is 'communitarianism'? To start with the former, libertarianism is a defence of the minimal or 'nightwatchman' state; that is, the state which limits its functions to the enforcement of contracts and to protection against force, theft and fraud. Libertarians are staunch supporters of the free market, and they stand opposed to any form of state 'interference', including the redistribution of wealth for (what the state judges to be) the public good. Libertarians are hostile to socialism as, indeed, they are to any form of welfare state. (So, you could say that rather as Rawls is the philosopher of the 'post-war consensus' in favour of redistributivism, so Nozick's work is a defence of the pro-*laisser-faire* reaction which succeeded it and held sway throughout the 1980s.)[1] As the name 'libertarianism' indicates, libertarians believe that where there is a free market and a minimal state human freedom is respected, and that freedom is compromised and restricted by the arrangements to which they are opposed. (Libertarians tend to describe the latter as 'coercive'.) In the USA, there was an active libertarian movement before Nozick appeared on the scene, but Nozick's book is by far the most philosophically sophisticated treatment of the subject.

Similarly, there is a communitarian movement, practical, committed to change, and based mainly in the USA. Roughly speaking, its guiding principle is that the way forward for America lies in a return to the communal values. As one communitarian website states, 'Communitarians believe with America's Founding Fathers that it is possible to build the good society based upon the core values of the American people as defined by the Declaration of Independence, the Constitution, and the Bill of Rights.' These core American values are said to include 'the belief that the society should provide its citizens with equality of opportunity, material well being, and the opportunity for individual self-fulfilment, and that it should operate on the principles of fairness, justice and compassion'.[2] However, the relationship between this and the philosophical communitarianism with which we are concerned here – and which should interest you if you have read this far, whether you are American or not – appears to be rather more oblique than that between the practical libertarian movement and Nozick's work. Broadly speaking, *philosophical* communitarianism is the thesis that liberalism misportrays the relationship between individual and community in certain crucial respects; that the latter's representation of those relationships is rather 'thin'. (Clearly, there is not much resemblance between the communitarianism of contemporary philosophy and the communitarianism of Robert Owen's time.)

That is a 'broad-brush' portrait of course. It tells you nothing about the precise arguments with which libertarians and communitarians seek to support their positions. I could now go on to summarise these, taking each position in turn. I could then go on to conduct a critical analysis, taking libertarianism and communitarianism in turn. However, I shan't do that. Instead, I shall take a number of the questions which have tended to recur throughout this history and give a brief account of how liberals, libertarians, communitarians and others now tend to approach them. That way – and bearing in mind, of course, that the neat tripartite division suggested by this procedure is something of an oversimplification – I will be better able to achieve my aim, which is to give you an idea of the present state of the debate.

Questions

What is a person?

I should put this question more specifically, as follows: What features of the person are most relevant to the understanding of the political aspects of our nature? You will see what I mean if you recall that for the 'classical' utilitarians – Bentham and Mill – a person is essentially a locus of experiences, a seeker of pleasures and a shunner of pains. On this view, a world of many persons is, in a sense, an 'atomised' world, a world in which each individual, in pursuit of his or her own 'interests', is set on a trajectory which is more than likely to cross those of the others. One of the classical utilitarians, Mill, was also a classical liberal, and so this view of the person is – in that sense at least – a liberal view as well. Rawls' view is, in a way, similar to this although, as you would expect, it is more subtle and nuanced. For Rawls, it is an important feature of persons that each person is capable of forming his or her own conception of the good and following a 'rational plan of life' in pursuit of that conception. Rawls' persons are not Bentham's simply conceived atoms, busily zapping about, but – similarly to Bentham – Rawls believes that individuals in pursuit of their rational plans will inevitably cross.

For libertarians too, the disparity between individuals of their aspirations and plans is an inescapable fact of life, something we have to take as given. However, so far as libertarians are concerned, the most important defining feature of the 'moral person' is not that, but the fact that we are bearers of rights. Thus, Nozick opens *Anarchy, State, and Utopia* with the assertion that 'Individuals have rights, and there are things no person or group may do to them (without violating their rights)' (1974: ix). In effect, libertarians take seriously one implication of the anti-utilitarian, anti-consequentialist, argument I outlined in the chapter on Mill. Consequentialism (more straightforward versions of it at least) has the implication that it is morally permissible for one person to use another as a means to an end where that end is a good end. This implication is morally counter-intuitive, at least it can seem that way if you tell the right story: a story of innocent people being 'punished' to deter criminals, for example, or a story in which the majority's happiness is greatly improved thanks to the efforts of a minority group of badly treated slaves. Libertarianism's guiding thought – or one of them – is that the counterintuitiveness of this implication demonstrates that people have rights which others are bound to respect. As Nozick puts it, a person's rights act as 'side-constraints' on the behaviour of others.

For communitarians, things are more complex. Writing against a 'deontological ethic' (i.e. Rawls' ethic) which 'insists that we view ourselves as independent selves, independent in the sense that our identity is never tied to our aims and attachments' (1982: 179) Sandel has this to say:

[But] we cannot regard ourselves as independent in this way without great cost to those loyalties and convictions whose moral force consists partly in the fact that living by them is inseparable from understanding ourselves as the particular persons we are – as members of this family or community or nation or people, as bearers of this history, as sons and daughters of that revolution, as citizens of this republic. Allegiances such as these are more than values I happen to have or aims I 'espouse at any given time'. They go beyond the obligations I voluntarily incur and the 'natural duties' I owe to human beings as such. They allow that to some I owe more than justice requires or even permits, not by reason of agreements I have made but instead in virtue of those more or less enduring attachments and commitments which taken together partly define the person I am.

(ibid.)

In short, the person you are – the precise nature of your identity – is very much a question of your specific cultural and historical situation. It is 'more or less enduring attachments and commitments' which 'partly define' that person. This is a thesis concerning personal identity. So, the question for Rawlsians to ask, and for Sandel to answer, is precisely why it should be relevant to the question of justice. Still, as I said, I am trying to give you a picture of the present state of the debate, not to take sides, so let us move on.

Rights: Do we have rights? If so, how do we know we have them, and what rights do we have?

In political philosophy it is customary to distinguish moral rights from positive rights. Our possession of the former – which are sometimes called 'natural' rights and sometimes 'human' rights – is (if they exist at all) independent of the existence of any legal system. By contrast, our 'positive' rights are simply the rights we are specified as having by the prevailing legal system. It is a distinction which has been discussed at a number of points throughout this narrative. You will recall that the classical utilitarians denied the existence of natural rights and that Bentham described the very idea as 'nonsense upon stilts' (Bentham 2000c: 405). Similarly, in the first chapter of *On Liberty*, John Stuart Mill wrote, 'It is proper to state that I forgo any advantage which could be derived to my argument from the idea of abstract right as a thing independent of utility' (Mill 1991a: 15). On this account, the only rights we have are positive, legal, rights. So, for utilitarians, the question is, what rights ought we to have by law, and their answer – obviously – has to be that we should have the rights derivable from the principle of utility. In other words, the best legal system is the one which most serves to promote the greatest happiness of the greatest number. This creates a difficulty for utilitarians such as Mill, who are also liberals, for it means they have to show how the rights (or 'liberties') characteristic of the liberal view – free speech, the right to live your life in your own way, and so on – can be derived from that principle.

Rawlsian liberals construe rights differently, as do libertarians. For both, we can be said to have moral rights independent of our positive rights and, for both, the former set a standard against which we can measure the legal system which defines the latter. According to Rawls' argument, the moral rights we have are defined by the terms of the agreement which would be reached by rational choosers, negotiating from the original position. Like Mill, he has to derive a characteristically liberal set of rights from his basic philosophical position. By contrast, libertarians tend to argue that, because we have rights which others must respect, there is a general right not to be coerced by others into surrendering any of our rights, most especially our rights to any items of property we may own. Otherwise, libertarians tend to be fairly unspecific as to what rights we actually have. That is probably because what libertarians do is construct rights in general on the model of property rights. The consequence is an account of justice which models itself on the pattern of Locke's defence of property. Indeed, *Anarchy, State, and Utopia* (Nozick 1974) is a self-conscious reworking of Locke's argument.

As for communitarians, we have seen that Sandel is opposed to the idea of a 'deontological ethic'. On his account we have 'allegiances' – 'loyalties and convictions whose moral force consists partly in the fact that living by them is inseparable from understanding ourselves as the particular persons we are' (1982: 179). If this is right, it follows that there can be no *general* answer to the question of what rights (or what duties) we have. On the contrary, arguments over obligation, duty, etc. must be conducted between individuals whose commitments and sense of identity flow from their relationship to a specific community. This is a characteristically communitarian view. For example, it is quite similar to Alasdair MacIntyre's view that, in ethics, meaningful discussion can only take place within a cultural context, a 'tradition'. Liberals will find this abandonment of the idea that there can be general principles disturbing. In their turn, communitarians, or some of them, will want to accuse liberals of a sort of cultural imperialism. Either way, it will be clear that serious issues hang on this type of dispute.

Individual, community, and state: What is the relationship between them?

For communitarians, as the name implies, all is community. The relationship between individual and community is, so to speak, symbiotic. The individual is partly defined by that relationship; as are the loyalties and allegiances he or she has towards it. Communitarians are apt to criticise liberals for treating that relationship as 'instrumental'. When applied to the classical utilitarians – certainly when applied to Bentham – the description is fair enough. The pleasure-seeking, pain-shunning, social 'atoms' of classical utilitarian theory can only treat the community – and the state likewise – as devices for helping them achieve their ends more easily. In the case of Rawls, however, we should be more circumspect. He is perfectly happy with the idea that citizens 'may have, and often do have at any given time, affections, devotions, and loyalties that they believe they would not, indeed could and should not, stand apart from and evaluate objectively' (2001: 22), and that they may 'regard it as simply unthinkable to view themselves apart from certain religious, philosophical, and moral convictions, and from certain enduring attachments and loyalties' (ibid.). So far as he is concerned 'community' and 'political society' are two different things. 'Political liberalism does not view political society as an association', he writes. 'Quite the contrary, it insists on the distinction between a political society and an association' (2001: 94). His principles of justice are meant to apply only in the case of the former. (Of course, the problem is to determine the dividing line.) As for libertarians, so far as they are concerned, there is really no such thing as 'community'. As Nozick puts it, 'there is no *social entity* with a good that undergoes some sacrifice for its own good. There are only individual people, different individual people, with their own individual lives' (1974: 94). And, as for the state, where a state does more than maintain an environment within which market relations can operate, libertarians can only think of the state as 'coercive'.

Conclusion: political philosophy now

I could continue. In fact I could continue for much longer. But I have said enough. Even so, having reached this point, I realise that – despite every disclaimer I have made – I am still open to the charge of having over-simplified things. For one thing, I may well have given the impression that philosophers working at present can be divided neatly into categories, as liberals (utilitarian or contractualist), libertarians, and communitarians. But, in fact, the borders dividing the positions real-life philosophers take are far more fluid than that.[3] Then again, if the account I have just been giving is true, readers will be wondering what has happened to certain other issues which – or so you would think – political philosophers argue about. Do philosophers no longer discuss feminism, Marxism, socialism, or conservatism? The answer is that of course they do. It's just that there are many 'isms', and that these fall into distinct categories. Moreover, categories can intersect and cut across each other in various ways. Those with which I have just been dealing – contractualism, communitarianism, and so on – set the terms for debate at a very general level. (As we have seen, they ask questions like 'Just what is a person?' and 'Are there general principles to which those who differ over the justice of a particular arrangement can appeal?') As things stand at present, more specific disputes tend to be conducted in terms set at that higher level of generality.

Moreover, there is a lot more going on than that. Anyone acquainted with the subject will be aware of two developments. One is an increasing awareness, within English-speaking philosophy, of work produced from outside the mainstream. This present book is intended as an introduction to that very mainstream, so I have not dealt with such developments directly (or only to the extent that English-speaking communitarianism claims to incorporate many post-Hegelian theses, developed and reworked in France and Germany). Another development is an increasing tendency to focus upon specific, relatively practical, issues. Open any recent edition of a journal such as *Philosophy and Public Affairs*, or *The Journal of Applied Philosophy*, or check out their websites, and this will immediately become apparent to you. For example, I have, just now, picked a recent edition of the latter journal, at random, from my bookshelf. (It is volume 19, number 2, 2002.) Looking through the index, I see that there are articles on the rights and wrongs of 'criminalising' certain forms of behaviour; the attitude we should take to the dead (e.g. to the victims of the Holocaust); the permissibility of 'entrapment' by journalists; the moral issues surrounding the 'outing' of gay people; love and privacy; land communitarianism (a 'green' issue); and nationalism. Far from being 'dead', as Laslett feared nearly fifty years ago (Laslett 1956: vii), political philosophy is plainly alive and kicking.

Postscript

—◦◯◦—

What happens next?

The themes I have pursued throughout this book dictate that, really, there are two rather more specific questions at issue here. The first is: What social and political changes can we anticipate in the world at large? The second is: What future developments are we likely to see in political philosophy, the subject?

To answer the former, there is no need to engage in self-indulgent futurology. Unless we are stupid enough to bomb ourselves back to the Stone Age, or even to annihilate ourselves completely, there can be no doubt that, in the foreseeable future, we will see an acceleration in 'globalisation'; the latter being an umbrella term for a number of processes. Here, it would be out of place to attempt a precise definition of the term – in any case, there is a considerable literature on the subject already – but the broad outlines are clear enough. The concentration of wealth and, as a consequence, economic power into the hands of enormous multinational corporations means that we will inevitably witness a decline in the real significance of the nation-state, even its demise. (It is already the case that the sales of many corporations, measured in US dollars, are equivalent to the Gross Domestic Products of some sizeable nations.)[1] At the level of international relations, the ability of powerful nations to move armies across the globe, to places where they can cause enormous havoc, makes the need to develop a viable system of international law all the more pressing. The existence of enormous discrepancies in wealth between the richest nations and the poorest – discrepancies for which the former are often responsible and which can, in any case, be alleviated by them – raise questions of how the former ought to behave towards the latter, questions of 'global justice'. Similar questions are also raised by the depletion of the earth's resources to an extent which affects us all. Communications technology is now so highly developed that information and images can be transmitted instantaneously, and with ease, from any point on the globe to any other. This will, no doubt, have many consequences. Certainly, at the level of culture, there is a threat that the cultures and practices of minority groups will be swamped by those of the more numerous and affluent. I could continue with this list, but the picture is familiar enough.

Instead, what of the second question I raised? We can be fairly sure that future developments in political philosophy will reflect these changes in one way or another. However, I can't predict with any precision what form those developments will take. If I could, I would have written the next major work of political philosophy myself. But I haven't done that. One thing of which I am fairly sure, though, is that, for all its merits, Rawls' philosophy is in a way quite ill-equipped to deal with such changes. As we saw, its fundamental structure – the way it is set up – best lends itself to the understanding of situations in which a group of individuals, located in a given geographical area at a given time, behave towards each other. Issues which relate to the behaviour of one generation to another over time are more awkward for it, as are issues related to the behaviour of one discrete group to another, located elsewhere. Rawls himself was aware of this difficulty from the beginning. In *A Theory of Justice*, this shows up in his attempt to formulate a just savings principle to regulate such obligations as the duty to conserve resources for future generations (see for example Rawls 1972: 284ff). It is a feature of his theory on which Nozick developed his critique, and to which the latter's own 'entitlement' account of justice is an alternative. And it is a weakness which arguably vitiates the thesis of the *Law of Peoples* (Rawls 1999b), one of Rawls' last books. In it, Rawls attempts to formulate principles of international law while at the same time preserving the separateness of groups, of 'peoples'. On this I will only remark that it could turn out to have been a project which was destined to fail from the outset. Certainly, Rawls has already been scathingly denounced by one authoritative critic, Peter Singer, for never having given serious attention to 'the issue of how the rich nations and their citizens are to respond to the needs of the more than one billion desperately poor people', the urgency of which issue, as Singer sees it, 'overrides the longer-term goal of changing the culture of societies that are not effectively regulated by a public conception of justice' (Singer 2002: 180). So, if the influence of Rawls' philosophy is approaching its sell-by date, here we have an explanation why.

That said, let me sum things up as follows: As I see it, the history of political philosophy is a history of hope expressed in sentences of blood. The blood is only to be expected. After all, Max Weber's definition of the state gets it about right. According to Weber, a state is a human community that claims the monopoly of the legitimate use of physical force within a given territory.[2] Weber's definition places force, and the threat of force, centre stage, and it is undeniable that coercive institutions – the military, the police, the judiciary, the prison system, and suchlike – are necessary conditions for the existence of any state. So, the definition is to that extent accurate, and even though the nation-state is, in many ways, due to be superseded, the necessity for threats and force will remain. There will be a tendency for the structures which replace it – international and multinational institutions of various forms – to become equally bloodstained, if only from time to time. But, as Weber's definition also emphasises, states claim legitimacy. Accordingly, one of political philosophy's central concerns has always been to set terms under which the exercise of force can be viewed as acceptable. It is here that the hope comes in. Why else would anyone try?

Given the parameters set by hope and blood it follows, logically, that we are facing one out of only three possible futures. If hope wins out, we shall eventually see all the people sharing all the world and living life in peace. It's up to us I guess. Alternatively, we could be facing the future George Orwell foresaw, a future symbolised by a jackboot stamping on a human face forever. The third possibility – and, I suppose, the most likely – is that there will be a continuing series of uneasy compromises between the other two. But, whatever happens, there will be philosophers to help us interpret, understand, and deal with it.

Suggestions for further reading

Chapter 1: Socrates

This brief account of Socrates' life and times is only meant to serve as a prelude to the discussion of Plato's *Republic* which follows. For a fuller treatment of Socrates, I recommend Janet Coleman's *A History of Political Thought from Ancient Greece to Early Christianity*, especially Chapter 2 (Coleman 2000). One of the leading experts on Socrates is Gregory Vlastos. See his *The Philosophy of Socrates* (1971) and his more recent *Socrates, Ironist and Moral Philosopher* (1991). One of the most readable accounts of the events leading up to Socrates' execution is I.F. Stone's wonderful *The Trial of Socrates* (Stone 1988). A very good general account of Greek history and culture is Antony Andrewes' *Greek Society*. Chapter 4, 'Outlines of Political History', is especially relevant here (Andrewes 1971). For a more 'in depth' account of Athenian democracy, I recommend R.K Sinclair's *Democracy and Participation in Athens* (Sinclair 1991).

Chapter 2: Plato, *The Republic*

In this chapter I have concentrated on *The Republic* but, of course, Plato was the author of more than just that one work. A very good introduction to Plato's work as a whole is David J. Melling's *Understanding Plato* (Melling 1987). There is a full discussion in the third chapter of Janet Coleman's *A History of Political Thought from Ancient Greece to Early Christianity* (Coleman 2000). For an interesting collection of essays, I recommend Richard Kraut, ed., *The Cambridge Companion to Plato* (Kraut 1992). Plato returned to the subject of the 'ideal' constitution in his last dialogue, *The Laws* (Plato 1970). There, he describes a state which is, if anything, bleaker and more authoritarian than the state of *The Republic*. The case against Plato, that he is a precursor of 'totalitarianism' is – famously and eloquently – made by Karl Popper in Volume 1 of his *The Open Society and its Enemies* (Popper 1945). My argument that democracy

270

allows people a chance to prove their ideas without our having to accept their arguments fully or having to place ourselves irrevocably under their control, is similar to – though not, I think, equivalent to – Popper's argument that democracy enables us to get rid of bad leaders before they do too much damage.

Chapter 3: Aristotle

There are plenty of good introductions to Aristotle's philosophy as a whole, but not so many which concentrate upon his political philosophy. One notable exception to this rule is Chapter 4 of Janet Coleman's *Political Thought from Ancient Greece to Early Christianity* (Coleman 2000). The chapter is long and scholarly (longer than many books). R.G. Mulgan's *Aristotle's Political Theory: An Introduction for Students of Political Theory* (Mulgan 1987) is also well worth consulting. A very good, short and readable introduction to Aristotle's philosophy is Jonathan Barnes' *Aristotle* (Barnes 1982). Two lengthier, and much recommended, introductions are J.L. Ackrill's *Aristotle the Philosopher* (1981) and Sir David Ross' *Aristotle* (1964). As for contemporary, neo-Aristotelian 'virtue ethics', a foundational, powerfully argued text is Alasdair MacIntyre's *After Virtue: A Study in Moral Theory* (1981). On the latter subject, a good collection of articles by philosophers writing at present is Roger Crisp and Michael Slote, eds, *Virtue Ethics* (1997). One very interesting, and prominent, neo-Aristotelian philosopher writing at present is Martha Nussbaum (see especially her articles, Nussbaum 1988 and 2000).

Chapter 4: What happened next?

There is a dearth of accessible commentaries on the political thought of Cicero, as there is on the political thought of Saint Augustine. However, two notable exceptions to this rule are Neal Wood's *Cicero's Social and Political Thought* (Wood 1988) and Herbert A. Deane's *The Political and Social Ideas of Saint Augustine* (Deane 1990). Janet Coleman's *A History of Political Thought from Ancient Greece to Early Christianity* contains extended, and rewarding, discussions of both philosophers (Coleman 2000, Chapters 5 and 6). The authoritative study of the 'Great Chain of Being' idea remains Arthur O. Lovejoy's. *The Great Chain of Being: A Study of the History of an Idea* (Lovejoy 1936 and 1964).

Chapter 5: Hobbes goes to Paris

For the most part, my references are to the Anscombe and Geach translation of Descartes' *Philosophical Writings* (Descartes 1954a and 1954b). However, there are plenty of other good, affordable and easily available translations of Descartes' *Discourse on Method* and *Meditations*. Three good critical commentaries on Descartes' philosophy are Anthony Kenny's *Descartes* (Kenny 1968), Bernard Williams' *Descartes: The Project of Pure Enquiry* (Williams 1978), and John Cottingham's *Descartes* (Cottingham 1986). There is a discussion of the Cartesian method in Chapter 2 of Cottingham's book. For an 'in depth' intellectual biography of Descartes, see Stephen Gaukroger's impressive *Descartes: An Intellectual Biography* (Gaukroger 1995). This contains a lengthy chapter on Descartes' method (Chapter 4). For 'background reading' on British history throughout the period covered by Part II – the English civil war, its aftermath, and so on – you could do no better than consult Simon Schama's *A History of Britain: The British Wars, 1603–1776* (2001) (or get the video). As for Hobbes, see suggested reading for Chapter 6 (below).

Chapter 6: Hobbes: raising the great Leviathan

Two good, brief, accounts of Hobbes' thought are D.D. Raphael's *Hobbes: Morals and Politics* (1977) and Richard Tuck's *Hobbes* (1989). The literature on Hobbes contains a number of 'classic' studies, in each of which the author articulates a particular interpretation of Hobbes' work. For example, in his *The Political Philosophy of Hobbes* (1957) Howard Warrender discusses Hobbes' theory of obligation and concludes that he is far more traditional in his approach than is generally supposed. Leo Strauss' *The Political Philosophy of Hobbes* (1963) discusses Hobbes' relationship to seventeenth century science, and argues that its influence on his political thought has been overplayed. (It should be obvious that I agree with neither Warrender nor Strauss.) C.B. MacPherson's *The Political Theory of Possessive Individualism* (1964) traces the origins of modern justifications of 'possessive market society' back to Hobbes' work, and D.P. Gauthier's *The Logic of Leviathan* (1969) concentrates on the 'rational choice' structure of Hobbes' argument. I particularly enjoyed J.W.N. Watkins' illuminating *Hobbes's System of Ideas* (1973). Two particularly useful collections of essays are Maurice Cranston and Richard Peters, eds, *Hobbes and Rousseau* (1972) and Christopher W. Morris, ed., *The Social Contract Theorists* (1999). The civil war was by no means the first political upheaval to have rocked England, but it was one of the first to have taken place when people were, generally speaking, literate. The quantity of political literature dating from that period is immense. If you are interested in this, I suggest A.S.P. Woodhouse's edited collection, *Puritanism and Liberty* (1974). For a discussion of literature which was specifically aimed at Hobbes you could do no better than consult John Bowle's *Hobbes and his Critics* (1951). For the historical background, Chapter 3 of Simon Schama's *A History of Britain, 1603–1776* (2001) is good.

Chapters 7 and 8: Locke

There are plenty of good books on Locke, but not so many on his political thought. Two notable exceptions are A.J. Simmons' *The Lockean Theory of Rights* (1992) and *Locke on Government* by D.A. Lloyd-Thomas (1995). This is the best book with which to begin if you are thinking of following up this chapter with further reading. Another exception, of a completely different kind, is C.B. Macpherson's classic *The Political Theory of Possessive Individualism* (1964). See especially Chapter 5. Macpherson argues that it is possible to resolve certain difficulties in Locke's text, once certain assumptions about the nature of social and economic reality are taken into account, assumptions which would have come naturally to anyone living in the seventeenth century. Macpherson's argument caused a certain amount of controversy when his book was first published. One good critique of that argument is Alan Ryan's article, 'Locke and the Dictatorship of the Bourgeoisie' (1968). See also the first chapter of Ryan's *Property and Political Theory* (1984). For a relatively recent discussion of Locke's account of consent see P. Russell's 'Locke on Express and Tacit Consent' (1986). See also Hannah Pitkin's influential article, 'Obligation and Consent' (1965–6). Pitkin relates the difficulties inherent in Locke's argument to the nature of his social contract as an exercise in rational choice theory. Peter Singer's *Democracy and Disobedience* (1973) remains one of the most clearly written, and interesting, introductions to the philosophical problems raised by the idea of democracy. The revival of enthusiasm for *laisser-faire* 'free market' economic policies which began in the late 1970s and continued throughout the 1980s was accompanied by a revival of interest in Locke's argument for property. The second part of Robert Nozick's *Anarchy, State, and Utopia* (1974) is meant to be a modern reworking of that argument. (Nozick is discussed in more detail in Chapter 14 of this book.) Two good, clear, introductions to the philosophy of property are Lawrence Becker's *Property Rights* (1977) and James Tully's *A Discourse on Property* (1980). For an illuminating comparison of Locke and Marx see G.A. Cohen's 'Marx and Locke on Land and Labour' (1985). Locke was more than just a political philosopher. He was one of the leading philosophers of his time, and his *magnum opus* is *An Essay Concerning Human Understanding* (1964a). It is a classic treatment of some traditional philosophical problems of knowledge, meaning and the nature of the mind. If you are interested in Locke's life and times,

I strongly recommend Maurice Cranston's wonderful *John Locke: A Biography* (1985).

Chapter 9: Rousseau

There are many books on Rousseau written, or translated into, English. However, out of these, only a few focus specifically on his political thought. Moreover, most books on Rousseau take an interpretive approach; that is, they tend to concentrate on such topics as Rousseau's intentions, the place of his main arguments within the context of his central vision, and the relationship between his various works. Very few take the analytical, directly critical, approach I have taken in this chapter. One notable exception – i.e. a directly critical work which focuses on Rousseau's politics – is Chapter 10 of the first volume of John Plamenatz's *Man and Society* (1963). It is quite a long time since Plamenatz's book was published, but it is still cited by most authorities on Rousseau. The essays on Rousseau in Cranston and Peters' collection *Hobbes and Rousseau* (1972) are also worth consulting, as is J.B. Noone's more recently published *Rousseau's 'Social Contract': A Conceptual Analysis* (1981). Other – less critical but more interpretive – studies of Rousseau's political thought are Alfred Cobban's *Rousseau and the Modern State* (1964), John Charvet's *The Social Problem in the Philosophy of Jean-Jacques Rousseau* (1974) and Judith Shklar's *Men and Citizens* (1985). John W. Chapman's *Rousseau: Totalitarian or Liberal?* (1968) addresses one of the questions on which I have concentrated here. More general studies include Ernst Cassirer's classic, *The Question of Jean-Jacques Rousseau* (1967), N.J.H. Dent's *Rousseau* (1988) and Robert Wokler's *Rousseau* (1995), which is a good, short, introduction to his philosophy. Sally Scholz's *On Rousseau* (2001) is a lively and entertaining study. As for Rousseau's own work, one text that I have not discussed in this chapter, but which students of political thought should find interesting, is *The Government of Poland* (1985). It is a draft proposal for a constitution Rousseau produced at the request of a Polish delegation. Written in 1771, but published posthumously, it should give you some idea of the way he conceived the relationship between the ideal state of *The Social Contract* and practical reality. To anyone not considering embarking on a major study, I would strongly recommend John Hope Mason's collection *The Indispensable Rousseau* (1979). This contains extracts from *Émile*, *La Nouvelle Heloise*, the other *Discourses*, and much else besides. Rousseau led an interesting life. He was an itinerant music teacher as well as a writer, and his autobiography, *The Confessions* (1954) is well worth reading. As for some of the other topics covered in this chapter, Joan McDonald's *Rousseau and the French Revolution, 1762–1791* (1965) is a study of the relationship between Rousseau's ideas and the French Revolution. Hannah Arendt's *The Origins of Totalitarianism*

(1973) is the definitive study of the topic and I found Leonard Schapiro's *Totalitarianism* (1972) a useful discussion of the subject. This includes a treatment of the question of definition. Two articles critical of Berlin's distinction between negative and positive freedom are Charles Taylor's 'What's wrong with Negative Liberty?' (1979a) and my own 'Models of Liberty: Berlin's "Two Concepts"' (1991).

Chapter 10: After the flood

There are many collections of Bentham's work, but I think Ross Harrison's *Selected Writings on Utilitarianism: Bentham* (2000) is good. Not only does it contain the full text of *The Principles of Morals and Legislation*, it also contains *Anarchical Fallacies*, and some other material which would otherwise be hard to come by. One of the best studies of Bentham's thought is John Stuart Mill's essay 'Bentham' (1987a). Two relatively recent studies, well worth consulting, are Ross Harrison's *Bentham* (1983) and John Dinwiddy's book also called *Bentham* (1989). Turning to Hegel, if you don't feel like ploughing your way through his entire body of work, a useful collection is Stephen Houlgate's *The Hegel Reader* (1998). There are plenty of books on Hegel, but I found Peter Singer's *Hegel: A Very Short Introduction* (1983) very helpful and illuminating. I also greatly enjoyed Dudley Knowles' *Hegel and the Philosophy of Right* (2002). As the title indicates, this concentrates on Hegel's *Philosophy of Right*. One much recommended study of Hegel's social thought is Charles Taylor's *Hegel and Modern Society* (1979b) and a recent study is Alan Patten's *Hegel's Idea of Freedom* (1999). Karl Popper's withering attack on Hegel in *The Open Society and its Enemies* (1945) is well worth reading, even though most commentators seem to agree that his argument misses the mark. (Hegel is yet another philosopher to have been accused of advocating 'totalitarianism'.) For an antidote to the tired platitude that 'analytic' philosophers take no interest in 'continental' work, see the chapters on Hegel in Rawls' *Lectures on the History of Moral Philosophy* (2000). So far as I know, there is no full length treatment of Edmund Burke's thought. However, for a contemporary equivalent, you could do worse than consult Roger Scruton's *The Meaning of Conservatism* (1980). For a more critical account of conservative thought see Ted Honderich's *Conservatism* (1990). Finally, V. Sapiro's *A Vindication of Political Virtue: The Political Theory of Mary Wollstonecraft* (1992) is described by Susan Khin Zaw, in the *Routledge Encyclopedia of Philosophy*, as 'the first book-length study of Wollstonecraft's philosophy' and 'generally reliable'.

Chapter 11: John Stuart Mill: utilitarianism and liberalism

On ethics and political philosophy respectively, Mill's two best known and most significant works are *Utilitarianism* (1991b) and *On Liberty* (1991a). There are so many editions available that it seems ridiculous to single one out. John Gray, ed., *John Stuart Mill: On Liberty and Other Essays* (1991) is useful mainly because it contains *The Subjection of Women* in addition to more readily available material. Geraint Williams, ed., *John Stuart Mill on Politics and Society* (1976) contains a good selection of Mill's essays. If you want a fuller picture of Mill's social and political ideas, it is well worth reading through. Finally, I would recommend Mill's *Autobiography* (1989) to anyone, whether or not they are interested in political ideas. In my opinion, it is one of the great classics of English literature. In particular, there is a moving description of Mill's 'mental crisis', all done without the help of Freudian terminology. Two very useful introductory commentaries on Mill's thought are Roger Crisp's *Mill on Utilitarianism* (1997) and Jonathan Riley's *Mill on Liberty* (1998). Most commentaries concentrate on *On Liberty*. Some influential, in depth studies, each of which takes a particular interpretation, are Maurice Cowling's *Mill and Liberalism* (1963) and Gertrude Himmelfarb's *On Liberty and Liberalism: The Case of John Stuart Mill* (1974). (Cowling argues that Mill was an elitist and Himmelfarb holds him responsible for everything that happened in the 1960s – bad in her opinion.) C.L. Ten's *Mill on Liberty* (1980) is clear and straightforward and John Gray's *Mill on Liberty: A Defence* (1983) is a defence of Mill against some common criticisms. On Mill's treatment of specific issues mentioned in this chapter I recommend Julia Annas' article 'Mill and the Subjection of Women' (1977) and Dennis Thompson's *John Stuart Mill and Representative Government* (1976). Part One of my own *Free Speech* (1998) is an extended treatment of Mill's argument for the liberty of thought and discussion. On utilitarianism and consequentialism more generally, I suggest Geoffrey Scarre's *Utilitarianism* (1996) and, for a recent in depth treatment of the issues, Brad Hooker's *Ideal Code, Real World: A Rule-Consequentialist Theory of Morality* (2000). Samuel Scheffler, ed., *Consequentialism and its Critics* (1988) is a useful collection of articles, and I think everyone will enjoy reading John Harris' much collected article, 'The Survival Lottery' (1975).

Chapter 12: Marx

If you are new to Marx's thought, and would like to learn more, then the one thing I would advise you *not* to do is start by reading *Capital*. The book is incredibly long (there are three volumes) and the earlier chapters are extremely technical and difficult. Moreover, they will give you no real idea of Marx's general philosophical position. (Their subject is the circulation of money.) Many commentators recommend beginning with *The Communist Manifesto*, and that's not a bad suggestion. In it, Marx and Engels give a clear overview of their position and – after all – it was written by them specifically for people with little or no previous knowledge of Marxism. There are many editions. In the UK, the most easily available is – most probably – the Penguin edition (1967). Rather than that I would, personally, suggest getting hold of a collection of Marx's writings and reading through it. After all, Marx was – amongst other things – a political activist and pamphleteer. His ideas are articulated in many places, though not always in full in any one. Reading a collection through will give you a better impression than reading any one work. There are many collections available, but, in my opinion, by far the best is David McLellan's *Karl Marx: Selected Writings* (2000). There are several good biographies of Marx. For example, Francis Wheen recently published *Karl Marx* (1999) which is a readable, and no doubt accurate, account of Marx's life. However, for my money Isaiah Berlin's *Karl Marx* (1978) remains by far the best. Berlin tells a good story but, unlike the others, he also has a master's grasp of political ideas. In his narrative he moves back and forth between biography and philosophical exposition in the most extraordinary way. There are *numerous* commentaries on, and interpretations of, Marx's work. (You could say that there are almost as many Marxes as there are commentators.) In McLellan's, *Selected Writings* runs to many pages. I will just mention a few here. One is Peter Singer's *Marx: A Very Short Introduction* (1980). Singer writes with sensitivity and enviable clarity. For an accessible and thoroughly up to date discussion I recommend Jonathan Wolff's *Why Read Marx Today?* (2002). David McLellan is a scholar who has written prolifically on Marx, and who tends to stress the continuity between the 'early' and the 'later' Marx. See especially his *The Thought of Karl Marx* (1971). In relatively recent years, one of the most significant and scholarly contributions to the study of Marx has been G.A. Cohen's *Karl Marx's Theory of History: A Defence* (1978). Peter Singer describes this as a brilliant argument for 'a more old-fashioned interpretation of Marxism as a scientific theory of history' (Singer 1980: 105). Singer has a point, but I think his description underestimates Cohen's work. At the time of its publication, a number of philosophers – with clear anti-Marxist sympathies – had advanced some fairly persuasive criticisms of Marx's work. See for example H.B. Acton's *The Illusion of the Epoch: Marxism-Leninism as a Philosophical Creed* (1955) and Plamenatz's treatment of Marx in his *Man and Society* (1963: Vol. 2). (I refer to this in my discussion; see Chapter 12, pp. 234ff.) Despite this, most Marx scholars were content to ignore such criticisms, and to concentrate instead on questions of interpretation, on the precise relationship of Marx's work to Hegel's and so on. One great virtue of Cohen's book lies in the way it confronts the right's arguments directly and faces them down. See also his *History, Labour, and Freedom* (1994). There are some good collections of articles by philosophers, of various persuasions, on Marx's ideas. See for example the three volume collection edited by John Mepham and David Hillel-Ruben, *Issues in Marxist Philosophy* (1979). See also Cohen, Nagel and Scanlon, eds, *Marx, Justice, and History* (1980).

Chapter 13: Rawls: through reason to justice

Rawls published *A Theory of Justice* in 1972 and his next book, *Political Liberalism*, in 1993. That's a gap of twenty-one years. How come he published no other books during that period? The answer is that he was publishing an enormous amount, but that this was appearing not in the form of books but in the form of articles published in academic journals. Indeed, for most of his life that seems to have been Rawls' preferred method of publication. In fact, the argument of *A Theory of Justice* was first framed in an article, 'Justice as Fairness' (1958), and he had developed it in several more before the book was published. You could hardly say that it surprised an unsuspecting world by appearing unannounced. *Political Liberalism*, the book, was also prefigured by an article, 'Justice as Fairness, Political not Metaphysical' (1985). Rawls' articles have now been gathered together and published as Samuel Freeman, ed., *John Rawls: Collected Papers* (Rawls 1999a). Commentaries on Rawls, by other people, can be divided into commentaries on the early and the later Rawls. Brian Barry's *The Liberal Theory of Justice* (1973) is one of the best, and most incisive, to fall into the former category. I would also place Chandran Kukathas and Phillip Pettit's *Rawls: A Theory of Justice and its Critics* (1990) in that category, although it does contain one chapter on Rawls' later work. Part Two of Nozick's *Anarchy, State, and Utopia* (1974) and Michael Sandel's *Liberalism and the Limits of Justice* (1982) also count as critiques of the early Rawls, although both also count as definitive texts of, respectively, libertarianism and communitarianism. Norman Daniels' collection, *Reading Rawls: Critical Studies of A Theory of Justice* (1975), is one of the most valuable contributions to the critique of Rawls' earlier work. Critical studies of Rawls' later philosophy are thinner on the ground, but see Victoria Davion and Clark Wolf, eds, *The Idea of Political Liberalism: Essays on Rawls* (1999). I think we can anticipate that much more work on the later Rawls will appear in the next few years.

Chapter 14: After Rawls

Turning away from Rawls to other developments, two authoritative critiques of Nozick are Jonathan Wolff's *Robert Nozick: Property, Justice, and the Minimal State* (1991) and G.A. Cohen's *Self-Ownership, Freedom and Equality* (1995). See also my own *Anti-Libertarianism: Markets, Philosophy and Myth* (1994). Communitarians other than Sandel include Charles Taylor and (I would say) Alasdair MacIntyre (even though I know he has rejected the label). See Taylor's *Sources of the Self: The Making of Modern Identity* (1989). For a good collection of MacIntyre's writings, with a clear and informative introduction, see Kelvin Knight, ed., *The MacIntyre Reader* (1998). A useful collection of readings is Shlomo Avineri and Avner de-Shalit's *Communitarianism and Individualism* (1992). Finally, two excellent surveys of contemporary political philosophy are Will Kymlicka's *Contemporary Political Philosophy: An Introduction* (1990) and Stephen Mulhall and Adam Swift's *Liberals and Communitarians* (1992).

Postscript: What happens next?

There are, by now, quite a few books on globalisation. I found Manfred B. Steger's *Globalization: A Very Short Introduction* (2003) extremely useful, as I did David Held and Anthony McGrew's *Globalization: Anti-Globalization* (2002). However, out of the numerous studies of the subject, there are few written by philosophers. A notable exception is Charles Jones' pioneering study, *Global Justice: Defending Cosmopolitanism* (2000). Another is Peter Singer's *One World: The Ethics of Globalisation* (2002). Finally, *Global Justice*, edited by Thomas Pogge (2001), contains some interesting essays.

Notes

——o☙o——

Introduction

1. The only difference between historiography and other branches of the subject is, of course, that in the former the texts themselves are a primary source.
2. At this point quite a few readers will be wanting to object that there are no women on this list. For the same reason, others will be heaving a sigh of resignation. The truth is women philosophers did not begin to acquire an independent voice until quite recently; that is, not until the late eighteenth century, a time from which the origins of modern feminism can also be dated. (See below, for example Chapter 10, p. 179ff. and Chapter 11, p. 193ff.) Any women political philosophers there may have been writing before that are excluded by my 'influence' criterion. If they existed, they have remained obscure however brilliant they may have been.

Chapter 1: Socrates

1. The source of Socrates' income isn't known. He must have derived support from somewhere. As Rodney Pickering tells me, it is most probable that, like many Greek citizens, he owned a smallholding which he could leave to be looked after by a couple of slaves while he remained in the city.
2. On the one occasion Socrates did leave Athens, it was to perform military service. He fought against the Persians, as an infantryman, at the Battle of Salamis in 480 BC.
3. I say 'his' advisedly. To qualify as a citizen you had to be male. However, see what I have to say below on the subject of just how democratic Athens was (p. 11).

Chapter 2: Plato, *The Republic*

1. Of course, it is one thing to point out that Plato could contemplate the possibility of there being female philosopher rulers, but quite another to credit him with having been an early feminist. He was certainly no such thing. On this point see especially Susan Moller Okin's *Women in Western Political Thought* (Okin 1979).
2. Throughout this chapter I quote from Desmond Lee's translation of *The Republic* (Plato 1987). However, the page references are to a much earlier edition, the Stephanus of 1578. It is customary for translations of *The Republic* – including Lee's – to carry page references to Stephanus in the margin. The advantage of doing things this way is that you will be able to find the passages I am referring to, whatever the translation you may be using.
3. The purpose of these sessions is to breed good leaders, not a 'master race'. It does not follow that Plato was a racist, as Hitler was a racist.
4. Most recently, this has been forcibly argued by Alasdair MacIntyre in his *After Virtue* (see MacIntyre 1981: Chapter 10, especially p. 123ff.).
5. In Sparta, the *helots* were governed by a military caste, the *Spartiates*. You could think

of Plato's ideal state as Sparta with an extra layer of rational governors imposed at the apex of the pyramid. That seems quite a good suggestion to me. I owe it to Rodney Pickering.

6. A word of caution here: I absolutely do *not* mean to suggest that Socrates' account of the progress of the soul after death, as given here, represents Plato's most considered, 'official' view of the nature of the forms. You can find this in a different dialogue, the *Timaeus*.

7. I ignore the well-known problem of scepticism over the existence of an 'external world'. The problem is interesting, but it is not especially relevant to the point I am making here.

8. I say 'invites us to think' of a line advisedly, because – in his original manuscript – Plato did not actually produce a diagram. However, it is customary for his modern translators to do so, which is very helpful. See, for example, the Lee translation, Plato (1987), p. 250. As you will see from my description, I am thinking of the line as vertical.

Chapter 3: Aristotle

1. Aristotle was absent from Athens for twelve years, during which he was married twice, first to Hippias' niece, Pyrthias, by whom he had a daughter. Sadly Pyrthias died. After that, Aristotle became the lover of Herpyllis, the mother of his beloved son Nicomachus. (It is not known if he married her.) When Aterneus was captured by the Persians in 341 BC they tortured Herpyllis to death. Fortunately for us (but for Aristotle, who knows?) Aristotle had embarked upon his travels by then. He travelled extensively throughout Greece – especially maritime Greece – until he was recruited to Philip of Macedon's court in 343 BC. I haven't written a 'potted' biography for every philosopher I discuss in this book, but the events of Aristotle's life seem to me so extraordinary that I have thought it worth recording them, if only in this note.

2. Some say that the *Nicomachean Ethics* was dedicated to Nicomachus by Aristotle himself; others that the book was so called because it was Nicomachus who put it together by organising Aristotle's notes after his death.

3. I say this because in most of his dialogues Plato is concerned to elucidate the nature of a virtue – courage or justice for example – or, if not quite a virtue, a value, such as knowledge.

4. Except for my opening quotation I have used the Sinclair translation of Aristotle's *Politics*, revised and re-presented by Trevor J. Saunders (Aristotle 1981). However, when referring to specific passages it is customary to use the method devised by I. Bekker in his edition of 1831 (*Aristotelis Opera*, Berlin, 1831). Bekker refers to the Greek text by page, column and line, so that, for example, *Politics* 1294b21 refers to *Politics*, page 1294, column b, line 21. I am using this system myself, not because I expect readers to possess the original Greek text – or even because I expect them to understand ancient Greek – but because every reasonable translation of the *Politics* uses the same system. That should make passages easy to find, whatever the edition you have.

5. References to *The History of Animals* use the Bekker system. See above, note 4.

6. Aristotle records that the octopus has a second mouth, that the snake has no penis, and that, during copulation, the female fly inserts a tube into the male fly, 'this being the reverse of the operation observed in other creatures'. He adds that 'This phenomenon may be witnessed if anyone will pull asunder flies that are copulating' (1910: V, 8). He is also notorious for having stated that the bison 'defends itself against an assailant by kicking and projecting its excrement to a distance of eight yards; this device it can easily adopt over and over again, and the excrement is so pungent that the hair of hunting dogs is burnt off by it' (ibid.: IX, 45). None of these claims is right, but we shouldn't let such mistakes detract from Aristotle's achievement.

7. Which is not to deny that Aristotle took a 'patriarchal' view of things. He did. On this see Susan Moller Okin (1979), Chapter four.

8. See especially E.O. Wilson (1975), Chapter 26.
9. The best-known version of this 'objection from integrity' is Bernard Williams'. See Williams (1973), p. 97ff.
10. References to the *Nicomachean Ethics* follow the Bekker system. See note 4 above.
11. I put this cautiously because there is a passage in *The Physics* in which Aristotle discusses whether it could be that, in nature, things come to be 'organized spontaneously in a fitting way'. However it would be an exaggeration to describe Aristotle's view as a theory of evolution. In any case, he goes on to insist that 'it is impossible that this should be the true view'.

Chapter 4: What happened next?

1. To take one very evident example. In Cicero's *Republic*, there is a passage in which he argues that a state which leaves the process of choosing leaders to chance 'will be overturned as quickly as a ship in which a man chosen by lot from among the passengers has taken over the helm' (Cicero 1998a: 24). This clearly echoes Plato's famous argument that democracy resembles a ship in which '[T]he crew are all quarrelling with each other about how to navigate the ship, each thinking that he ought to be at the helm' (*Republic*: 488a–9a). Actually, whereas Plato is attacking democracy, Cicero is defending it – but only because he thinks people will 'naturally' choose the best rulers.

Chapter 5: Hobbes goes to Paris

1. Apparently, Mersenne was the 'only effective channel of communication' with Descartes at this time. Descartes was 'virtually in hiding in The Netherlands'. Hobbes and Descartes eventually met, but not until 1648. My source for this is Tuck (1989), p. 5.
2. In *Le Monde*, Descartes argues for a heliocentric universe; that is, he states it as his view that the sun, not the earth, is at the centre of the universe. It is said that he withheld publication for fear of offending the Catholic authorities. After all, Descartes had been raised as a Jesuit. It is probably not the case that he would have suffered the severe treatment meted out to his contemporary, Galileo, by the Catholic authorities in Florence. Galileo had also argued that the universe is heliocentric.
3. You will have realised, of course, that all this is grossly unfair to Aristotle, who was a virtuoso of the empirical method. (See Chapter 3.)
4. Hobbes had met Galileo, in Florence, in 1636.
5. The most famous of these are Benedict de Spinoza (1632–77) and Gottfried Wilhelm Leibniz (1646–1716).
6. See Schama (2001), p. 13.

Chapter 6: Hobbes: raising the great Leviathan

1. At one point in his *Second Treatise of Civil Government* Locke tetchily responds to the suggestion that there may have been no social contract with the remark that 'if we may not suppose Men ever to have been in the State of Nature, because we hear not much of them in such a State, we may as well suppose the Armies of Salmanasser, or Xerxes were never children, because we hear little of them, till they were Men, and imbodied in Armies' (Locke 1964b: II, 101). In other words, there must have been a social contract, and Locke is not going to be swayed by mere lack of evidence.
2. The expression 'no-state situation' is Robert Nozick's.
3. Although social contract theory is a form of rational choice theory, the converse does not apply. Not all rational choice theory is social contract theory. For example, when economists seek to derive general economic laws from a consideration of what rational people would do in market situations – mainly when they buy and sell – they

are conducting an exercise in rational choice theory. However, it would be wrong to describe this as social contract theory.

4. John Rawls gives the following example of a prisoner's dilemma. '[Thus] imagine two prisoners who are brought before the attorney general and interrogated separately. They both know that if neither confesses they will receive a short sentence for a lesser offence and spend a year in prison; but that if one confesses and turns state's evidence, he will be released, the other receiving a particularly heavy term of ten years; if both confess each gets five years. In this situation, assuming mutually disinterested motivation, the most reasonable course of action for them – that neither should confess – is unstable. . . . To protect himself, if not to try to further his own interests, each has a sufficient motive to confess, whatever the other does. Rational decisions from the point of view of each lead to a situation where both prisoners are worse off' (Rawls 1972: 269n).

5. Howard Warrender gives a rather different explanation for this law of nature's two part structure. It is Warrender's thesis that Hobbes is writing well within the natural law tradition according to which the sovereign is morally bound to promulgate laws which fall within the remit of the natural law. (This is contrary to the received view of Hobbes.) According to Warrender one part of Hobbes' formulation states an obligation we have under natural law, the obligation to 'endeavour peace'. The second part states that we are only bound to act on the obligation when there is 'hope of obtaining it'. According to Warrender, it is Hobbes' view that, in the state of nature, the latter 'validating condition' is absent. For this, see Warrender 1957. See also Taylor 1938. I am unconvinced, but it would be beyond the scope of this chapter to argue the point.

6. On this definition of 'natural person' a robot would be a natural person. Still, I'm not sure that complication would have occurred to Hobbes.

7. Here, I have decided to stick to 'economic man' rather than use the phrase 'economic person'.

8. In Hobbes' scenario, the sovereign himself is not a party to the contract, which suggests that he can do whatever he likes. However, see also note 10 below.

9. This is argued by Robert Nozick in *Anarchy, State, and Utopia*. See Nozick 1974: Part One.

10. Hobbes' sovereign is not Hitler or Stalin, and Hobbes insists that justice requires equity. For him, it is a requirement 'from him, or them that have the Soveraign Power, that Justice be equally administred' (1981: 385). 'The Inequality of Subjects', he writes, 'has no more place in the presence of the Soveraign; that is to say, in a Court of Justice, than the Inequality between Kings, and their Subjects, in the presence of the King of Kings' (ibid.). Like the requirement for absolute sovereigns, this belief in equality before the law is presented as a logical outcome of Hobbes' argument. Exactly how this squares with other parts of Hobbes' argument is not a question I shall consider here.

11. Both Pufendorf and Grotius believed in a divinely instituted natural law. Grotius is best known as the author of one of the earliest treatises on international law, *Prolegomena to the Law of War and Peace* (Grotius 1957).

Chapter 7: Locke and the modern order

1. The most notable example of a contemporary philosopher who takes a Lockean position on property is Robert Nozick, whose *Anarchy, State, and Utopia* (Nozick 1974) is meant to be a modern reworking of Locke's argument.

2. Locke wrote two *Treatises of Civil Government*, the First and Second. In each, the paragraphs are numbered. As is customary, my references to these works are by treatise and paragraph. So, for example, (II, 4) refers to the *Second Treatise*, paragraph 4. Incidentally, I decided to use the version of Locke's *Treatise* contained in David Wootton's edition of Locke's *Political Writings* (Locke 1993), rather than Peter Laslett's edition of the *Second Treatise* (Locke 1964b). The latter is attractive (to me at least)

because it preserves Locke's seventeenth century grammar and spelling. However, in the end I decided that using the former would make for greater clarity.

3. Incidentally, it is an idea with a long history. You can trace its origins at least as far back as Cicero, and you can find its influence in the modern practice of drawing up charters of human rights. (Hobbes' notoriety amongst his contemporaries is, no doubt, explained in part by the way he undermined it.)

4. In legal contexts, 'the civil law' is sometimes contrasted with 'the criminal law'. Perhaps I should emphasise that I am not using 'civil law' in that sense here. The contrast between 'civil' and 'natural' law is a different one.

5. Note that this move is not open to moral relativists, according to whom what is right or wrong 'for' members of one culture need not be so 'for' members of another.

6. Although Locke did not believe in the natural superiority of men over women. In this, he was – perhaps – unusual for his time. (See, for example, his remarks on 'paternal' and 'parental' authority (II, 52, 53).)

7. This difficulty is discussed by Macpherson, who makes the interesting suggestion that there is an ambiguity in Locke's description of the state of nature. On the one hand, Locke thinks of society 'as composed of equal undifferentiated beings'. On the other, he thinks of society 'as composed of two classes differentiated by their level of rationality', the 'industrious and rational' property owners and the labouring classes. Macpherson suggests that Locke 'would not have been conscious' of the contradiction between them thanks to the 'social assumptions' he would have made (see Macpherson 1964: especially p. 238ff.). The suggestion that people could form 'mutual protection agencies' is made by Nozick (1974: especially Chapter 2).

8. One (John Plamenatz) has described it as an 'odd expedient' to which a desperate Locke can only have resorted in order to save his argument (Plamenatz 1963: I, 225). More recently, another (David Lloyd Thomas) has confessed himself unable to propose a reading of Locke which is consistent with everything Locke says on the subject of tacit consent (Lloyd Thomas 1995: 38).

9. In his *Democracy and Disobedience*, Peter Singer makes the suggestion that participation in an electoral procedure can normally be taken to indicate consent to its outcome. Singer writes, 'it is reasonable to assume that someone does consent if he votes, voluntarily and without indicating that he does not consent' (Singer 1973: 51). I disagree. It seems to me that in representative democracies voters normally think of the electoral system as something which is simply there to be taken advantage of, like the transport system or the health service.

10. In this, I follow Plamenatz, though roughly (see Plamenatz 1968: p. 5ff.). Of course, there is a parallel definition which applies to cases in which P's *not* doing x is contingent upon Q's consent. For reasons of clarity I have not included the relevant parenthesised subclauses. I think I am safe in assuming that readers are bright enough to work out the parallels for themselves.

11. Here, I am deeply indebted to one of Routledge's anonymous readers. An earlier version of this contained a much more confusing definition of tacit consent. The reader in question made a number of very helpful suggestions and, although I haven't followed any one of them precisely, I do hope he/she approves of what I have come up with.

12. See Sartre (1969), p. 55ff.

13. I would not like to give the impression that the revolution was entirely bloodless. Irish readers will be especially aware that the revolution in question was followed by some very bloody events, including the Battle of the Boyne (1690).

Chapter 8: Locke: the argument for property

1. At meetings of the French National Assembly, the more radical members tended to occupy seats towards the left of the debating chamber, the less radical members to occupy seats towards the right.

2. Actually, I suppose the point is arguable, but that's certainly how it seems to me at the moment.
3. See above, Chapter 6, p. 78ff.
4. This bizarre cross-cultural comparison speaks volumes about seventeenth century Europe's perceptions of life in the New World. Presumably a stereotypical English day-labourer of the period would have lived in a solid dwelling, had a coat to keep him warm in winter, big boots, a regular daily routine, and a good slice of cheese or bacon for breakfast. By contrast, the stereotypical Native American would have been more thinly clad and led a nomadic, less structured life. The idea that there is a common standard of comparison in terms of which the life of the former can be judged 'better' than that of the latter is, so far as I can see, crazy.

Chapter 9: Rousseau

1. During his lifetime, Rousseau's most popular works were *Émile*, a treatise on education, and *Julie ou La Nouvelle Héloise*, a romantic novel (1974 and 1997).
2. See especially Schapiro (1972).
3. This ought to go without saying, but it doesn't because it is sometimes claimed that the two words differ in meaning. For example, fairly recently I attended a meeting at which Ronald Dworkin made just that claim. However, I think the truth is as follows: Because English is a hybrid of a Germanic language (Saxon) and French, it quite often happens that, in English, you get two words for the same thing (or pretty much the same thing). Here we have a case in point for 'freedom' is clearly related to the German *freiheit*, whereas 'liberty' is related to the French *liberté*. The fact that, for some centuries after the Norman Conquest, England was governed by a French speaking ruling class may go some way towards explaining Dworkin's claimed 'intuition' that 'liberty' is more legalistic in its connotation. Even so, the two words are now identical in meaning, even though their etymology is different.
4. For my own opinion of Berlin's essay, see Haworth (1991).
5. See above, Chapter 3, pp. 44–5.
6. For details, see the earlier chapters of Rousseau's *Confessions* (1954) [1781].
7. In real life, the resulting increase would be infinitesimal, but – for the sake of argument – please can we ignore that.
8. Here, my argument echoes arguments advanced by Brian Barry and Jonathan Wolff (see Barry 1965: 190ff. and Wolff 1996: 87ff.).

Chapter 10: After the flood

1. If you want to see what Bentham now looks like, you can visit the website of University College's Bentham project at www.ucl.ac.uk/Bentham-Project/Faqs/auto_icon.htm. The site also gives more information about the auto-icon.
2. Like any good social contract theorist, Rousseau goes on to compare his method with that 'used every day by our physicists to explain the formation of the earth' (1984: 78).
3. I say 'self-styled' because the word 'postmodernism' suggests that it is a progressive new development, and not just a sideshow. We mustn't take the postmodernists' own valuation of their activities for granted.
4. Compare Burke's description with the passage from Simon Schama's *Citizens* (1989) I quoted in the final section of the previous chapter. Unlike Burke, Schama repeatedly refers to evidence, to statistics and eyewitness accounts, for example.

NOTES

Chapter 11: John Stuart Mill: utilitarianism and liberalism

1. Mill received an intensive 'hothouse' education from his father. For details of this, and other remarkable episodes in Mill's life, see his *Autobiography* (1989).
2. I discussed the attractions utilitarianism must have held for Bentham and his contemporaries in the previous chapter. See above, Chapter 10, p. 165ff.
3. See Mill's *Principles of Political Economy* (1999), especially Book Five.
4. I am using 'freedom' and 'liberty' interchangeably. For the reasons why, see above, Chapter 9, note 3.
5. Burke boasts, 'I flatter myself that I love a manly, moral, regulated liberty' (Burke 1986: 89).
6. An alternative is to think of happiness as the concept in terms of which one *evaluates* the course of a life. If this is right, then 'happiness' does not refer to a state of mind, such as a sensation, at all. (There is a discussion of this 'Aristotelian' view, and its merits relative to utilitarianism, in Chapter three; see above, p. 49ff.)
7. *Chambers Twentieth Century Dictionary* defines 'pushpin' as 'a children's game in which pins are pushed one across another'. However, I prefer to go by the Penguin *Dictionary of Historical Slang* (1972) according to which 'pushpin' is an eighteenth century euphemism for sex, as in 'She would never tell/Who play'd at pushpin with her'. I prefer it because it renders Bentham's remark even more dismissive, and less prissy too.
8. These are very broad categories, and a lot depends on how you interpret them. In some versions they could well be logically consistent with each other. It is not a question I discuss.
9. *The Stepford Wives* (1975), Dir. Bryan Forbes – starring Katharine Ross, Paula Prentiss, Peter Masterson, Nanette Newman and Tina Louise.
10. This is a reference to a petition for a Women's Suffrage Bill. It was organised in 1865 by a group known as 'The Ladies of Langham Place'. Mill's close companion, Helen Taylor, was closely allied to the group, and Mill was to be the Member who presented it to Parliament.
11. Such considerations have been used, by some writers, as the basis for an argument that act utilitarianism is paradoxically self-defeating. See, for example, Mackie (1977), p. 133ff. and Parfit (1984), p. 24ff.
12. Both John Rawls and Robert Nozick claim to be Kantians.
13. Two notable examples are Dickens' *Hard Times* (1969) and Engels' *The Condition of the English Working Class* (1999).
14. I argue this at length in *Free Speech* (1998).

Chapter 12: Marx

1. Readers familiar with London may be interested to know that the address was 64 Dean Street, W1. There is now a blue plaque on the house.
2. The source from which I am quoting is Briggs (1982), although Isaiah Berlin tells the same story (see Berlin 1978: 142–3). Berlin cites its original source as Nicolaievsky and Maenchen-Helfen (1976).
3. A word of warning: Sometimes Marx, or Marx and Engels use the phrase 'the division of labour' to mean 'specialisation' and nothing more, and not the extreme subdivision of a task into simple components in order to boost productivity. A case in point is the distinction Marx and Engels draw between 'mental' and 'material' production in *The German Ideology* (see Marx 2000b: 184).
4. For my opinion, see my *Anti-Libertarianism: Markets, Philosophy, and Myth* (1994).
5. For details of these events see Berlin 1978: 195–7.
6. For example, in *The Communist Manifesto* they write, 'Not only are they slaves of the bourgeois class, and of the bourgeois state; they are daily and hourly enslaved by the machine, by the overlooker, and, above all, by the individual bourgeois manufacturer himself' (2000: 251).

7. Thanks to Wittgenstein and others, philosophy in the twentieth century took a 'linguistic turn'. Philosophers became far more aware of the way philosophical problems can originate with confusions about meaning, and were consequently far more interested in the analysis of language and meaning. For anti-Marxists and Marxists alike, this has meant trying to specify the meanings of key political terms more accurately. For Nozick's 'marriage-market' example, see his *Anarchy, State, and Utopia* (1974: 262). For my 'analytic' philosopher's critique of such arguments see my articles in *Economy and Society* (1990, 1991, 1992).

8. I don't pay any special attention to Marx's notion that man is a 'species being' here.

9. I don't mean that Marx is consciously echoing Locke, though he may have been. It's just that the parallel strikes me as clear.

10. For Plamenatz's criticisms of Marx on the foundation/superstructure distinction see Plamenatz 1963: 279. For G.A. Cohen's rejoinder see Cohen 1978: 166ff. For a completely different account of the distinction (written by a prominent left-wing historian) see Thompson 1978.

11. This is argued by Popper, for example.

Chapter 13: Rawls: through reason to justice

1. I say 'on the whole' because there were exceptions to this general rule. Popper's *The Open Society and its Enemies* (1945) is one. Also, Isaiah Berlin was producing a great deal of work during this period. My view of events – which is the conventional view – would be questioned by some writers. See for example Gray (1995), Chapter 1, 'Against the New Liberalism', p. 1ff. All I can say is that the conventional view is the one which squares with my own experience of this period.

2. Throughout his life, Rawls repeatedly reformulated the two principles. I could have quoted any one of a number of passages, each of which reads differently. For present purposes, it probably doesn't matter especially, so long as you get the general idea.

3. I am using the words interchangeably.

4. For a comparison of Mill and Rawls on basic rights, see above, Chapter 11, p. 184ff.

5. See Rawls' 'Fifty Years since Hiroshima' (1995). Rawls states his opinion that 'both Hiroshima and the fire-bombing of Japanese cities were great evils that the duties of statesmanship require political leaders to avoid' (ibid.: 570).

6. The recent work of quite a few prominent contractualist philosophers, with alternative theories to that of Rawls, is testimony to this. Two other contemporary exercises in contractualism are Scanlon (1982) and Barry (1995).

7. See above, Chapter 11, p. 197ff.

8. See, for example, Sandel (1982) and Walzer (1983).

9. By the 'basic structure' of society, Rawls means 'the way in the major social institutions distribute fundamental rights and duties and determine the division of advantages from social cooperation'. By 'major institutions' he means 'the political constitution and the principal economic and social arrangements' (1972: 7).

10. See above, Chapter 6, p. 81ff.

11. I put it in this slightly awkward way because it is, in fact, possible to derive a true conclusion from false premises. However, in such cases, whatever it is that makes the conclusion true has nothing to do with the fact that it follows from the premises. By contrast, and as I say, where the premises are true 'you can be confident' of the truth of the conclusion.

12. See above, Chapter 8, p. 119ff.

13. See above, Chapter 9, p. 142ff.

14. I say 'in the normal run of things' because there are exceptional cases. For example, when passing the sirens, Ulysses had himself bound to the mast because he absolutely did *not* want to be free to do what he most wanted to do.

15. Imagine a creature incapable of forming plans and purposes and there is good reason

for doubting that you have really imagined a person at all. That's why there is, e.g., a philosophical problem about whether someone in a terminal coma is really a person.

16. Take free speech as an example, and let me describe two difficulties. The first shows up in the argument of *A Theory of Justice*. The second shows up in Rawls' later work. First, in *A Theory of Justice*, then, Rawls' derivation of the basic liberties is largely *instrumental* in character. In an argument for 'liberty of conscience' – an argument which, as he thinks, 'can be generalised to other freedoms' (1972: 206) – Rawls claims that people 'will not want to take chances with their liberty by permitting the dominant religious or moral doctrine to persecute or to suppress others if it wishes' because they will regard some of their religious or moral convictions as too serious to gamble with (1972: 207ff.). The difficulty arises because this is a defensive argument. It states that rational choosers will agree to equal liberty of conscience because they have something to protect. In fact, it works quite well for the freedom to practise your own religion, if only in the privacy of your own home. But then religion is, in that sense, a 'private' affair, and, as it seems to me, the argument does not promise to work so well for free speech which, as previously noted, has a public dimension to it.

   Turning to Rawls' later work, as noted earlier, this places far more emphasis on such values as 'public reason' and 'public justification'. Roughly speaking, the idea is that rational individuals who regard each other as free and equal will attempt to publicly justify the positions they advocate. With such an emphasis, it's possible that Rawls can answer the difficulty I have just outlined, but it appears to give rise to a different difficulty. In his later work, Rawls takes great pains to insist that the principles of 'political liberalism' only apply to what he calls the 'basic structure' of society, which is said to consist of 'the main political and social institutions and the way they fit together as one scheme of co-operation' (2001: 4). The latter are said to be distinct from institutions such as the family, or organisations formed for a particular purpose (such as clubs). Here the difficulty is that Rawls needs to demarcate two realms: a realm to which public reason appropriately applies, and a 'private' realm of 'comprehensive' religious, moral and philosophical belief. But it is not so obvious that a clear dividing line can be drawn, and – if it can – it is not so obvious what falls to which side of it.

17. I ignore the question of precisely how you measure this.

18. Of course, you might have other reasons for not buying a ticket.

19. See Rawls 2001: 87ff. and 106ff.

20. Would it help Rawls if I were to write the 'primary good' of self-respect into this scenario? All I can say here is that somehow I doubt it.

Chapter 14: After Rawls

1. You could say that, rather as Rawls' theory of justice is the political philosophy of the post-war 'welfarist' consensus, so Nozick's work is a philosophically sophisticated defence of 'Reaganomics' – or, if you're British, the economic philosophy of 'Thatcherism'.

2. See, for example, the website of the Institute for Communitarian policy studies: www.gwu.edu/~icps/about.html.

3. See for example Richard Rorty 1989, especially Chapters 3 and 4. I don't think that Rorty's work fits too neatly into these categories.

Postscript: What happens next?

1. See, for example, the table at Steger (2003), p. 49. This shows that, for example, General Motors' sales are equivalent to the GDP of Denmark, those of Exxon Mobil to South Africa's GDP, and Hitachi's to Chile's.

2. See Weber (1947), p. 156.

Bibliography

——◦◌◦——

Ackrill, J.L. (1981): *Aristotle the Philosopher*, Oxford: Clarendon Press.

Acton, H.B. (1955): *The Illusion of the Epoch: Marxism-Leninism as a Philosophical Creed*, London: Routledge & Kegan Paul.

Andrewes, Antony (1971): *Greek Society*, London: Penguin.

Annas, Julia (1977): 'Mill and the Subjection of Women', *Philosophy*, Vol. 52, pp. 179–94.

Anscombe, G.E.M. (1997) [1958]: 'Modern Moral Philosophy', *Philosophy*, Vol. 33, pp. 1–19, reprinted in Crisp and Slote (1997), *Virtue Ethics*.

Arendt, Hannah (1973) [1958]: *The Origins of Totalitarianism*, New York: Harcourt.

Aristotle (1910) [*circa* 335 BC]: *Historia Animalium*, ed. Sir David Ross, trans. D'Arcy Wentworth Thomson, Oxford: Oxford University Press.

Aristotle (1976): *Ethics*, trans. J.A.K. Thomson, revised with notes and appendices by Hugh Tredennick, London: Penguin.

Aristotle (1981) [*circa* 350BC]: *The Politics*, trans. T.A. Sinclair, revised and represented by Trevor J. Saunders, London: Penguin.

Aristotle (1997): *The Complete Works of Aristotle: The Revised Oxford Translation* (two volumes), ed. Jonathan Barnes, Princeton: Princeton University Press.

Ashcraft, Richard (1986): *Revolutionary Politics and Locke's Two Treatises*, New Jersey: Princeton.

Aubrey, John (1982): *Brief Lives*, ed. Richard Barber, Suffolk: Boydell Press.

Augustine (1963) [413–427]: *City of God*, trans. J.W.C. Wand, Oxford: Oxford University Press.

Avineri, Shlomo and de-Shalit, Avner, eds (1992): *Communitarianism and Individualism*, Oxford: Oxford University Press.

Barnes, Jonathan (1982): *Aristotle*: Oxford & New York, Oxford University Press.

Barnes, J. and Schofield, M. eds (1977): *Articles on Aristotle: Volume 2, Ethics and Politics*, London: Duckworth.

Barry, Brian (1965): *Political Argument*, London: Routledge & Kegan Paul.

Barry, Brian (1973): *The Liberal Theory of Justice*, Oxford: Clarendon Press.

Barry, Brian (1995): *Justice as Impartiality*, Oxford: Clarendon Press.

Baumrin, Bernard, ed. (1969): *Hobbes's Leviathan: Interpretation and Criticism*, Belmont, California: Wadsworth.

Becker, Lawrence C. (1977): *Property Rights*, Boston, London, Melbourne, Henley: Routledge & Kegan Paul.

Bentham, Jeremy (1987) [1789]: Selections from *An Introduction to the Principles of Morals and Legislation*, in Ryan, Alan, ed., *John Stuart Mill and Jeremy Bentham: Utilitarianism and Other Essays*, London: Penguin.

Bentham, Jeremy (2000a) [1776]: *A Fragment on Government*, in *Selected Writings on Utilitarianism: Bentham*, introduction by Ross Harrison, Hertfordshire: Wordsworth Editions.

Bentham, Jeremy (2000b) [1789]: *The Principles of Morals and Legislation*, in *Selected Writings on Utilitarianism: Bentham*, introduction by Ross Harrison, Hertfordshire: Wordsworth Editions.

Bentham, Jeremy (2000c) [1843]: *Anarchical Fallacies: An Examination of the Declaration of the Rights of Man and the Citizen Decreed by the Constituent Assembly in France* in *Selected Writings on Utilitarianism: Bentham*, introduction by Ross Harrison, Hertfordshire: Wordsworth Editions.

Berlin, Isaiah (1969) [1958]: 'Two Concepts of Liberty', in Hardy, Henry, ed., *Four Essays on Liberty*, Oxford and New York: Oxford University Press.

Berlin, Isaiah (1978) [1939]: *Karl Marx*, Glasgow: HarperCollins.

Berlin, Isaiah (1990): 'Joseph de Maistre and the Origins of Fascism', in Hardy, Henry, ed., *The Crooked Timber of Humanity*, Oxford: Oxford University Press.

Berlin, Isaiah (2002) [1952]: 'Rousseau', in Hardy, Henry, ed. *Freedom and its Betrayal*, London: Chatto & Windus.

Bowle, John (1951): *Hobbes and his Critics*, London: Frank Cass.

Briggs, Asa (1982): *Marx in London: An Illustrated Guide*, London: BBC.

Burke, Edmund (1986) [1790]: *Reflections on the Revolution in France*, London: Penguin.

Cassirer, Ernst (1967) [1932]: *The Question of Jean-Jacques Rousseau*, trans. Peter Gay, Bloomington & London: Indiana University Press.

Chapman, John W. (1968): *Rousseau, Totalitarian or Liberal?*, New York: AMS.

Charvet, John (1974): *The Social Problem in the Philosophy of Rousseau*, Cambridge: Cambridge University Press.

Churchill, Winston, S. (1956): *A History of the English Speaking Peoples*, Vol. 2, London: Cassell.

Cicero, Marcus Tullius (1998a) [AD 52]: *The Republic*, in *Cicero: The Republic & The Laws*, trans. Niall Rudd, Oxford: Oxford University Press.

Cicero, Marcus Tullius (1998b) [AD 51]: *The Laws*, in *Cicero: The Republic & The Laws*, trans. Niall Rudd, Oxford: Oxford University Press.

Cobban, Alfred (1964): *Rousseau and the Modern State*, second edition, London: George Allen & Unwin.

Cohen, G.A. (1978): *Karl Marx's Theory of History: A Defence*, Oxford: Clarendon Press.

Cohen, G.A. (1985): 'Marx and Locke on Land and Labour', *Proceedings of the British Academy*, 71

Cohen, G.A., ed. (1994): *History, Labour, and Freedom*, Oxford: Oxford University Press.

Cohen, G.A. (1995): *Self-Ownership, Freedom and Equality*, Cambridge: Cambridge University Press.

Cohen, Marshall, Nagel, Thomas and Scanlon, Thomas, eds (1980): *Marx, Justice, and History*, Princeton: Princeton University Press.

Coleman, Janet (2000): *A History of Political Thought from Ancient Greece to Early Christianity*, Oxford: Blackwell.

Cottingham, John (1986): *Descartes*, Oxford: Blackwell.

Cowling, Maurice (1963): *Mill and Liberalism*, Cambridge: Cambridge University Press.

Cranston, Maurice (1985) [1957]: *John Locke: A Biography*, Oxford: Oxford University Press.

Cranston, Maurice and Peters, Richard S., eds (1972): *Hobbes and Rousseau: A Collection of Critical Essays*, New York: Anchor Books.

Crisp, Roger (1997): *Mill on Utilitarianism*, London: Routledge.

Crisp, Roger and Slote, Michael, eds (1997): *Virtue Ethics*, Oxford: Oxford University Press.

Daniels, Norman, ed. (1975): *Reading Rawls: Critical Studies of A Theory of Justice*, Oxford: Clarendon Press.

Darwin, F. (1888): *The Life and Letters of Charles Darwin*, London.

Davion, Victoria and Wolf, Clark, eds (1999): *The Idea of Political Liberalism: Essays on Rawls*, Lanham, Maryland: Rowman & Littlefield.

Deane, Herbert A. (1990): *The Political and Social Ideas of Saint Augustine*, New York: Columbia University Press.

Dent, N.J.H. (1988): *Rousseau*, Oxford & New York: Basil Blackwell.

Descartes, René (1931) [1628]: *Rules for the Direction of the Mind*, in *The Philosophical Works of Descartes*, trans. Elizabeth S. Haldane and G.R.T. Ross, Cambridge: Cambridge University Press.

Descartes, René (1954a) [1637]: *Discourse on the Method*, in *Descartes: Philosophical Writings*, trans. E. Anscombe and P.T. Geach, London: Nelson.

Descartes René (1954b) [1637]: *Meditations on First Philosophy*, in *Descartes: Philosophical Writings*, trans. E. Anscombe and P.T. Geach, London: Nelson.

Dickens, Charles (1969) [1854]: *Hard Times*, London: Penguin.

Dinwiddy, John (1989): *Bentham*, Oxford: Oxford University Press.

Engels, Friedrich (1999) [1845]: *The Condition of the English Working Class*, Oxford: Oxford University Press.

Etzioni, A. (1995) *The Spirit of Community: Rights, Responsibilities and the Communitarian Agenda*, London: Fontana Press.

Euclid (1989) [*circa* 300 BC]: 'Elements', in Heath, Thomas L., ed., *The Thirteen Books of Euclid's Elements*, New York: Dover Publications.

Feuerbach, Ludwig (1989) [1853]: *The Essence of Christianity*, trans. George Eliot, Amherst: Prometheus Books (note: the German edition was published in 1841).

Filmer, Sir Robert (1949) [1680]: *Patriarcha, or the Natural Power of the Kings of England Asserted*, in Laslett, Peter, ed. (1949) *Patriarcha and Other Political Works of Sir Robert Filmer*, Oxford: Blackwell.

Gaukroger, Stephen (1995): *Descartes: An Intellectual Biography*, Oxford: Clarendon Press.

Gauthier, David P. (1969): *The Logic of Leviathan: The Moral and Political Theory of Thomas Hobbes*, Oxford: Oxford University Press.

Gray, John (1983): *Mill on Liberty: A Defence*, London: Routledge & Kegan Paul.

Gray, John, ed. (1991): *John Stuart Mill: On Liberty and Other Essays*, Oxford, Oxford University Press.

Gray, John (1995): *Enlightenment's Wake: Politics and Culture at the Close of the Modern Age*, London: Routledge.

Grotius, Hugo (1957) [1625]: *Prolegomena to the Law of War and Peace*, New York: Liberal Arts Press.

Hampshire, Stuart (1972): 'A New Philosophy of the Just Society: A Special Supplement', *New York Review of Books*, February 24.

Hare, R.M. (1952): *The Language of Morals*, Oxford: Clarendon Press.

Hare, R.M. (1963): *Freedom and Reason*, Oxford: Clarendon Press.

Harris, John (1975): 'The Survival Lottery', *Philosophy*, Vol. 50, pp. 81–7, also in Singer, Peter, ed., *Applied Ethics*, Oxford: Oxford University Press.

Harrison, J.F.C. (1969): *Robert Owen and the Owenites in Britain and America*, London: Routledge & Kegan Paul.

291

Harrison, Ross (1983): *Bentham*, London: Routledge.

Harrison, Ross, ed. (2000): *Selected Writings on Utilitarianism: Bentham*, Hertfordshire: Wordsworth Editions.

Haworth, Alan (1990): 'What's so Special about Coercion?', *Economy and Society*, Vol. 19, No. 3, pp. 245–59.

Haworth, Alan (1991): 'Models of Liberty: Berlin's "Two Concepts"', *Economy and Society*, Vol. 20, No. 3, pp. 245–59.

Haworth, Alan (1992): 'Coercion Revisited, or How to Demolish a Statue', *Economy and Society*, Vol. 21, No. 1, pp. 75–90.

Haworth, Alan (1994): *Anti-Libertarianism: Markets, Philosophy and Myth*, London: Routledge.

Haworth, Alan (1998): *Free Speech*, London: Routledge.

Hayek, F.A. (1982) [1976]: *The Mirage of Social Justice*, republished as Hayek, F.A., *Law, Legislation, and Liberty*, Vol. 2, London: Routledge.

Hegel, G.W.F. (1956) [1837]: *Lectures on the Philosophy of History*, trans. J. Sibree, New York: Dover.

Hegel, G.W.F. (1967) [1821]: *Philosophy of Right*, trans. T.M. Knox, Oxford: Clarendon Press.

Hegel, G.W.F. (1977) [1807]: *Phenomenology of Spirit*, trans. A.V. Miller, Oxford: Oxford University Press.

Held, David and McGrew, Anthony (2002): *Globalization: Anti-Globalization*, Oxford: Blackwell, Polity Press.

Himmelfarb, Gertrude (1974): *On Liberty and Liberalism: The Case of John Stuart Mill*, New York: Alfred A. Knopf.

Hobbes, Thomas (1969) [1668]: *Behemoth, or The Long Parliament*, London: Frank Cass.

Hobbes, Thomas (1981) [1651]: *Leviathan*, London: Penguin.

Honderich, Ted (1990): *Conservatism*, London: Hamish Hamilton.

Hooker, Brad (2000): *Ideal Code, Real World: A Rule-Consequentialist Theory of Morality*, Oxford: Clarendon Press.

Houlgate, Stephen, ed. (1998): *The Hegel Reader*, Oxford: Blackwell.

Hume, David (1953) [1752]: 'Of the Original Contract', in Hendel, Charles W., ed., *David Hume's Political Essays*, Indianapolis: Bobbs-Merrill.

Hume, David (1969) [1739/40]: *A Treatise of Human Nature*, ed. Ernest C. Mossner, London: Penguin.

Isocrates (1954–6) [390 BC]: *Helen*, in Norlin, George, trans., *Isocrates*, Vol. 1, Cambridge, Mass.: Loeb Classical Library.

Jones, Charles (2000): *Global Justice: Defending Cosmopolitanism*, Oxford: Oxford University Press.

Kant, Immanuel (1948) [1785]: *Groundwork of the Metaphysic of Morals*, trans. H.J. Paton, *The Moral Law*, London: Hutchinson.

Kenny, Anthony (1968): *Descartes*, New York: Random House.

Kitto, H.D.F. (1951): *The Greeks*, London: Penguin.

Knight, Kelvin, ed. (1998): *The MacIntyre Reader*, Cambridge: Polity Press.

Knowles, Dudley (2002): *Hegel and the Philosophy of Right*, London: Routledge.

Kraut, Richard, ed. (1992): *The Cambridge Companion to Plato*, Cambridge: Cambridge University Press.

Kukathas, Chandran and Pettit, Phillip (1990): *Rawls: A Theory of Justice and its Critics*, Cambridge: Polity Press.

Kymlicka, Will (1990): *Contemporary Political Philosophy: An Introduction*, Oxford: Oxford University Press.

Laslett, Peter, ed. (1956): *Philosophy, Politics, and Society: First Series*, Oxford: Basil Blackwell.

Lee, Christopher (1998): *This Sceptred Isle*, London: Penguin.

Lenin, V.I. (1991) [1913]: 'The Three Sources and Three Component Parts of Marxism', in *Marx, Engels, Selected Works* (revised edition), London: Lawrence & Wishart, New York: International Publishers.

Lloyd Thomas, David (1995): *Locke on Government*, London & New York: Routledge.

Locke, John (1964a) [1690]: *An Essay Concerning Human Understanding*, edited and abridged by A.D. Woozley, Glasgow: Collins.

Locke, John (1964b) [1690]: *Two Treatises of Government*, student edition, ed. Peter Laslett, Cambridge: Cambridge University Press.

Locke, John (1993) [1690]: *Two Treatises of Civil Government*, in Locke, *Political Writings*, ed. David Wootton, London: Penguin.

Lovejoy, Arthur O. (1936 & 1964): *The Great Chain of Being: A Study of the History of an Idea*, Harvard & London: Harvard University Press.

McDonald, Joan (1965): *Rousseau and the French Revolution, 1762–1791*, London: Athlone Press.

Machiavelli, Niccolo (1961) [1532]: *The Prince*, trans. George Bull, London: Penguin.

MacIntyre, Alasdair (1981): *After Virtue: A Study in Moral Theory*, London: Duckworth.

MacIntyre, Alasdair (1990): *Three Rival Versions of Moral Enquiry*, Notre Dame, Indiana: University of Notre Dame Press.

Mackie, J.L. (1977): *Ethics: Inventing Right and Wrong*, London: Penguin.

McLellan, David (1971): *The Thought of Karl Marx*, London & New York: Harper & Row.

McLellan, David, ed. (2000): *Karl Marx: Selected Writings*, Oxford: Oxford University Press.

Macpherson, C.B. (1964) [1962]: *The Political Theory of Possessive Individualism*, Oxford: Oxford University Press.

Marx, Karl (2000a) [1844]: *Economic and Philosophical Manuscripts of 1844*, in McLellan, David, ed., *Karl Marx, Selected Writings*, second edition, Oxford: Oxford University Press, pp. 83–121.

Marx, Karl (2000b) [1846]: *The German Ideology*, in McLellan, David, ed., *Karl Marx, Selected Writings*, second edition, Oxford: Oxford University Press, pp. 175–208.

Marx, Karl (2000c) [1847]: *The Poverty of Philosophy*, in McLellan, David, ed., *Karl Marx, Selected Writings*, second edition, Oxford: Oxford University Press, pp. 212–33.

Marx, Karl (2000d) [1849]: *Wage Labour and Capital*, in McLellan, David, ed., *Karl Marx, Selected Writings*, second edition, Oxford: Oxford University Press, pp. 273–94.

Marx, Karl (2000e) [1859]: *Preface to 'A Critique of Political Economy'*, in McLellan, David, ed., *Karl Marx, Selected Writings*, second edition, Oxford: Oxford University Press, pp. 424–7.

Marx, Karl (2000f) [1857]: *Grundrisse*, in McLellan, David, ed., *Karl Marx, Selected Writings*, second edition, Oxford: Oxford University Press, pp. 379–405.

Marx, Karl (2000g) [1867]: *Capital*, selected passages in McLellan, David, ed., *Karl Marx, Selected Writings*, second edition, Oxford: Oxford University Press, pp. 452–545.

Marx, Karl (2000h) [1875]: *Critique of the Gotha Programme*, in McLellan, David, ed., *Karl Marx, Selected Writings*, second edition, Oxford: Oxford University Press, pp. 610–16.

Marx, Karl (2000i) [1857–67]: *Theories of Surplus Value*, in McLellan, David, ed., *Karl Marx, Selected Writings*, second edition, Oxford: Oxford University Press, pp. 429–50.

Marx, Karl and Engels, Friedrich (1967) [1888]: *The Communist Manifesto*, London: Penguin.

Marx, Karl and Engels, Friedrich (2000) [1888]: *The Communist Manifesto*, in McLellan,

David, ed., *Karl Marx, Selected Writings*, second edition, Oxford: Oxford University Press, pp. 245–71.

Mason, John Hope (1979): *The Indispensable Rousseau*, London, Melbourne, New York: Quartet Books.

Melling, David J. (1987): *Understanding Plato*, Oxford: Oxford University Press.

Mepham, John and Hillel-Ruben, David, eds (1979): *Issues in Marxist Philosophy*, three volumes, Brighton: Harvester Press.

Mill, James (1955) [1820]: *An Essay on Government*, Indianapolis: Bobbs-Merrill.

Mill, John Stuart (1987) [1838]: *Bentham*, in Ryan, Alan, ed., *John Stuart Mill and Jeremy Bentham: Utilitarianism and Other Essays*, London: Penguin.

Mill, John Stuart (1989) [1873]: *Autobiography*, London: Penguin.

Mill, John Stuart (1991a) [1859]: *On Liberty*, in Gray, John, ed., *John Stuart Mill: On Liberty and Other Essays*, Oxford: Oxford University Press. Also available as Mill, John Stuart (1982) [1859]: *On Liberty*: London: Penguin.

Mill, John Stuart (1991b) [1861]: *Utilitarianism*, in Gray, John, ed., *John Stuart Mill: On Liberty and Other Essays*, Oxford: Oxford University Press. This is also available in many other editions.

Mill, John Stuart (1991c) [1861]: *Considerations on Representative Government*, in Gray, John, ed., *John Stuart Mill: On Liberty and Other Essays*, Oxford: Oxford University Press.

Mill, John Stuart (1991d) [1869]: *The Subjection of Women*, in Gray, John, ed., *John Stuart Mill: On Liberty and Other Essays*, Oxford: Oxford University Press.

Mill, John Stuart (1999) [1848]: *Principles of Political Economy*, in Riley, Jonathan, ed., *Mill, John Stuart, Principles of Political Economy and Chapters on Socialism*, Oxford: Oxford University Press.

Morris, Christopher W., ed. (1999): *The Social Contract Theorists: Critical Essays on Hobbes, Locke, and Rousseau*, Lanham, Maryland: Rowman & Littlefield.

Mulgan, R.G. (1987): *Aristotle's Political Theory: An Introduction for Students of Political Theory*, Oxford: Clarendon Press.

Mulhall, Stephen and Swift, Adam (1992): *Liberals and Communitarians*, second edition, Oxford: Blackwell.

Murdoch, Iris (1967): 'The Sovereignty of Good Over Other Concepts' (the Leslie Stephen Lecture), Cambridge: Cambridge University Press, reprinted in Crisp and Slote (1997), *Virtue Ethics*.

Nicolaievsky, B. and Maenchen-Helfen, O. (1976): *Karl Marx: Man and Fighter*, London: Penguin.

Nietzsche, Friedrich (1990) [1886]: *Beyond Good and Evil*, trans. R.J. Hollingdale, London: Penguin.

Nietzsche, Friedrich (1995) [1873]: 'On Truth and Falsity in their Extra-Moral Sense', in Grimm, Reinhold and Molina y Vedia, Caroline, eds, *Friedrich Nietzsche: Philosophical Writings*, New York: Continuum Publishing Co.

Noone, J.B. (1981): *Rousseau's 'Social Contract': A Conceptual Analysis*, Georgia: University of Georgia Press.

Nozick, Robert (1974) *Anarchy, State, and Utopia*, Oxford: Basil Blackwell.

Nussbaum, Martha (1988): 'Nature, Function, and Capability: Aristotle on Political Distribution', in *Oxford Studies in Ancient Philosophy*, Oxford: Oxford University Press.

Nussbaum, Martha (2000): 'Aristotle, Politics, and Human Capabilities: A Response to Antony, Arneson, Charlesworth, and Mulgan', in *Ethics*, Vol. 22, No. 1, pp. 145–84.

Oakeshott, Michael (1991) [1962]: *Rationalism in Politics*, Indianapolis: Liberty Fund.

Okin, Susan Moller (1979): *Women in Western Political Thought*, New Jersey: Princeton University Press.

Orwell, George (1954) [1949]: *Nineteen Eighty-Four*, London: Penguin.

Owen, Robert (1970a) [1821]: *Report to the County of Lanark*, in Gatrell, V.A.C., ed., *Robert Owen, Report to the County of Lanark and a New View of Society*, London: Pelican.

Owen, Robert (1970b) [1813–14]: *A New View of Society*, in Gatrell, V.A.C., ed., *Robert Owen, Report to the County of Lanark and a New View of Society*, London: Pelican.

Paine, Thomas (1985) [1791–2]: *Rights of Man*, London: Penguin (note: Part One was first published in 1791, and Part Two in 1792).

Parfit, Derek (1984): *Reasons and Persons*, Oxford: Oxford University Press.

Partridge, Eric (1972) [1937]: *A Dictionary of Historical Slang*, abridged by Jacqueline Simpson, London: Penguin.

Patten, Alan (1999): *Hegel's Idea of Freedom*, Oxford: Oxford University Press.

Pitkin, Hannah (1965 & 66): 'Obligation and Consent' *in American Political Science Review*, Vol. LIX No. 4, and Vol. LX No. 1, also in Laslett, Peter, Runciman, W.C. and Skinner, Quentin, eds (1972): *Philosophy, Politics and Society, Fourth Series*, Oxford: Blackwell.

Plamenatz, John (1963): *Man and Society* (two volumes), London: Longman.

Plamenatz, John (1968): *Consent, Freedom and Political Obligation*, Second edition, Oxford: Oxford University Press.

Plato (1954a) [*circa* 399 BC]: *The Apology*, in Plato (1954), *The Last Days of Socrates*, trans. Hugh Tredennick, London: Penguin.

Plato (1954b) [*circa* 380 BC]: *The Phaedo*, in Plato (1954), *The Last Days of Socrates*, trans. Hugh Tredennick, London: Penguin.

Plato (1970) [*circa* 350–40 BC]: *The Laws*, trans. Trevor J. Saunders, London: Penguin.

Plato (1987) [*circa* 375 BC]: *The Republic*, trans. Desmond Lee, London: Penguin.

Pogge, Thomas W., ed. (2001): *Global Justice*, Oxford: Blackwell.

Popper, Karl (1945): *The Open Society and its Enemies*, two volumes, London: Routledge.

Raphael, D.D. (1977): *Hobbes: Morals and Politics*, London: George Allen & Unwin.

Rawls, John (1958): 'Justice as Fairness', *Philosophical Review*, Vol. 67, No. 2, pp. 164–94, also in Rawls (1999): *Collected Papers*.

Rawls, John (1972): *A Theory of Justice*, Oxford: Clarendon Press.

Rawls, John (1985): 'Justice as Fairness: Political not Metaphysical', *Philosophy and Public Affairs*, Vol. 14, No. 3, pp. 223–51, also in Rawls (1999): *Collected Papers*.

Rawls, John (1993): *Political Liberalism*, New York: Columbia University Press.

Rawls, John (1995): 'Fifty Years since Hiroshima', in Rawls, *Collected Papers* (1999a), pp. 565–72.

Rawls, John (1999a): *Collected Papers*, Cambridge, Mass. & London: Harvard University Press.

Rawls John (1999b): *The Law of Peoples*, Harvard: Harvard University Press.

Rawls, John (2000): *Lectures on the History of Moral Philosophy*, Cambridge, Mass. & London: Harvard University Press.

Rawls, John (2001): *Justice as Fairness: A Restatement*, Harvard: Belknap Press.

Riley, Jonathan (1998): *Mill on Liberty*, London: Routledge.

Rogers, Ben (2002): Obituary of John Rawls, *The Guardian*, Wednesday, 27 November, p. 24.

Rorty, Richard (1989): *Contingency, Irony, and Solidarity*, Cambridge: Cambridge University Press.

Ross, Sir David (1964): *Aristotle*, fifth edition, London: Methuen.

Rothbard, Murray (1973): *For a New Liberty*, London: Macmillan.
Rousseau, Jean-Jacques (1954) [1781]: *The Confessions*, trans. J.M. Cohen, London: Penguin.
Rousseau, Jean-Jacques (1968) [1762]: *The Social Contract*, London: Penguin.
Rousseau, Jean-Jacques (1968) [1761]: *Julie or The New Heloise*, Pennsylvania: Pennsylvania State University Press.
Rousseau, Jean-Jacques (1974) [1762]: *Émile*, trans. Barbara Foxley, London: Dent.
Rousseau, Jean-Jacques (1984) [1755]: *A Discourse on Inequality*, trans. Maurice Cranston, London: Penguin.
Rousseau, Jean-Jacques (1985): *The Government of Poland*, trans. Wilmoore Kendall, Indianapolis: Hackett Publishing.
Russell, Bertrand (1991) [1946]: *History of Western Philosophy*, London: Routledge.
Russell, P. (1986): 'Locke on Express and Tacit Consent', in *Political Theory*, May.
Ryan, Alan (1968): 'Locke and the Dictatorship of the Bourgeoisie', in Martin, C.B. and Armstrong, D.M., eds, *Locke and Berkeley: A Collection of Critical Essays*, London & Melbourne: Macmillan.
Ryan, Alan (1984): *Property and Political Theory*, Oxford: Blackwell.
Sandel, Michael J. (1982): *Liberalism and the Limits of Justice*, Cambridge: Cambridge University Press.
Sapiro, V. (1992): *A Vindication of Political Virtue: The Political Theory of Mary Wollstonecraft*, Chicago: University of Chicago Press.
Sartre, Jean-Paul (1969) [1943]: *Being and Nothingness*, London: Routledge.
Scanlon, Thomas (1982): 'Contractualism and Utilitarianism', in Sen, Amartya and Williams, Bernard, eds, *Utilitarianism and Beyond*, Cambridge: Cambridge University Press.
Scarre, Geoffrey (1996): *Utilitarianism*, London: Routledge.
Schama, Simon (1989): *Citizens: A Chronicle of the French Revolution*, London: Penguin.
Schama, Simon (2001): *A History of Britain: The British Wars, 1603–1776*, London: BBC Worldwide.
Schapiro, Leonard (1972): *Totalitarianism*, London: Macmillan.
Scheffler, Samuel, ed. (1988): *Consequentialism and its Critics*, Oxford: Oxford University Press.
Scholz, Sally (2001): *On Rousseau*, Belmont, CA: Wadsworth.
Scruton, Roger (1980): *The Meaning of Conservatism*, London: Penguin.
Shklar, Judith N. (1985) [1969]: *Men and Citizens: A Study of Rousseau's Social Theory*, Cambridge: Cambridge University Press.
Simmons, A. John (1979): *Moral Principles and Political Obligations*, New Jersey: Princeton University Press.
Simmons, A. John (1992): *The Lockean Theory of Rights*, Princeton: Princeton University Press.
Simon, Lawrence H., ed. (1994): *Karl Marx: Selected Writings*, Indianapolis: Hackett.
Sinclair, R.K. (1991): *Democracy and Participation in Athens*, Cambridge: Cambridge University Press.
Singer, Peter (1973): *Democracy and Disobedience*, Oxford: Clarendon Press.
Singer, Peter (1980): *Marx: A Very Short Introduction*, Oxford: Oxford University Press.
Singer, Peter (1983): *Hegel: A Very Short Introduction*, Oxford: Oxford University Press.
Singer, Peter (2002): *One World: The Ethics of Globalisation*, Yale: Yale University Press; Australia & New Zealand: Text Publishing.
Smith, Adam (1937) [1776]: *An Inquiry into the Nature and Causes of The Wealth of Nations*, ed. Edwin Cannan, New York: Modern Library.

Steger, Manfred B. (2003): *Globalization: A Very Short Introduction*, Oxford: Oxford University Press.

Stone, I.F. (1988): *The Trial of Socrates*, London: Jonathan Cape.

Strauss, Leo (1963) [1936]: *The Political Philosophy of Hobbes: Its Basis and Genesis*, trans. Elsa M. Sinclair, Chicago & London: University of Chicago Press.

Talmon, J.L. (1952): *The Origins of Totalitarian Democracy*, London: Secker & Warburg.

Taylor, A.E. (1938): 'The Ethical Doctrine of Hobbes', *Philosophy*, Vol. XIII (October), pp. 406–24: also reprinted in Baumrin (1969).

Taylor, Charles (1979a): 'What's Wrong with Negative Liberty?' in Ryan, Alan, ed., *The Idea of Freedom*, Oxford: Oxford University Press.

Taylor, Charles (1979b): *Hegel and Modern Society*, Cambridge: Cambridge University Press.

Taylor, Charles (1989): *Sources of the Self: The Making of Modern Identity*, Cambridge, Mass.: Harvard University Press.

Taylor, C.C.W. (2000): 'Eudaimonia', in *Concise Routledge Encyclopedia of Philosophy*, London: Routledge, p. 260.

Ten, C.L. (1980): *Mill On Liberty*, Oxford: Clarendon Press.

Thompson, Dennis F. (1976): *John Stuart Mill and Representative Government*, Princeton: Princeton University Press.

Thompson, E.P. (1978): 'The Poverty of Theory', in Thompson, E.P, *The Poverty of Theory and Other Essays*, London: Merlin Press.

Thucydides (1954) [*circa* 410 BC]: *History of the Peloponnesian War*, trans. Rex Warner, London: Penguin.

Truman, Harry S. (1949): Annual Message to the Congress on the State of the Union: www. Presidency.ucsb.edu.

Tuck, Richard (1989): *Hobbes*, Oxford: Oxford University Press.

Tully, James (1980): *A Discourse on Property*, Cambridge: Cambridge University Press.

Vlastos, Gregory (1971): *The Philosophy of Socrates*, South Bend: University of Notre Dame Press.

Vlastos, Gregory (1991): *Socrates, Ironist and Moral Philosopher*, Ithaca: Cornell University Press.

Walzer, Michael (1983): *Spheres of Justice*, Oxford: Basil Blackwell.

Warrender, Howard (1957): *The Political Philosophy of Hobbes*, Oxford: Clarendon Press.

Watkins, J.W.N. (1973) [1965]: *Hobbes' System of Ideas*, London: Hutchinson.

Weber, Max (1947): *Theory of Social and Economic Organisation*, New York: Free Press.

Wheen, Francis (1999): *Karl Marx*, London: Fourth Estate.

Williams, Bernard (1973): 'A Critique of Utilitarianism', in Smart, J.J.C. and Williams, Bernard, *Utilitarianism: For and Against*, Cambridge: Cambridge University Press.

Williams, Bernard (1978): *Descartes: The Project of Pure Enquiry*, London: Penguin.

Williams, Geraint L., ed. (1976): *John Stuart Mill on Politics and Society*, Glasgow: Fontana.

Wilson, Edward O. (1975): *Sociobiology: The New Synthesis*, Cambridge, MA: Harvard, Belknap Press.

Wittgenstein, Ludwig (1953): *Philosophical Investigations*, Oxford: Basil Blackwell.

Wokler, Robert (1995): *Rousseau*, Oxford: Oxford University Press.

Wolf, Susan (1982): 'Moral Saints', *Journal of Philosophy*, Vol. 79, pp. 419–39: also in Crisp and Slote (1997), pp. 79–98.

Wolff, Jonathan (1991): *Robert Nozick: Property, Justice, and the Minimal State*, Cambridge: Polity Press.

Wolff, Jonathan (1996): *An Introduction to Political Philosophy*, Oxford: Oxford University Press.

Wolff, Jonathan (2002): *Why Read Marx Today?*, Oxford: Oxford University Press.

Wolff, Robert Paul (1998) [1970]: *In Defense of Anarchism*, California: University of California Press.

Wollstonecraft, Mary (1995a) [1790]: *A Vindication of the Rights of Men*, in Tomaselli, Sylvana, ed., *Mary Wollstonecraft: A Vindication of the Rights of Men and A Vindication of the Rights of Woman*, Cambridge: Cambridge University Press.

Wollstonecraft, Mary (1995b) [1792]: *A Vindication of the Rights of Woman*, in Tomaselli, Sylvana, ed., *Mary Wollstonecraft: A Vindication of the Rights of Men and A Vindication of the Rights of Woman*, Cambridge: Cambridge University Press.

Wood, Neal (1988): *Cicero's Social and Political Thought*, Berkeley & Los Angeles: University of California Press.

Woodhouse, A.S.P., ed. (1974) [1938]: *Puritanism and Liberty*, London: J.M. Dent & Sons.

Wordsworth, William (1932) [1805]: *The Poetical Works of Wordworth*, ed. Thomas Hutchinson, London: Oxford University Press.

Index

—◦◯◦—